CHRISTIAN WORSHIP
IN EAST AND WEST

A Study Guide to Liturgical History

Herman A.J. Wegman

CHRISTIAN WORSHIP IN EAST AND WEST

A Study Guide to Liturgical History

Translated by Gordon W. Lathrop

PUEBLO PUBLISHING COMPANY

New York

Design: Frank Kacmarcik

Originally published in Dutch as *Geschiedenis van de Christelijke Eredienst in het Westen en in het Oosten* © 1976 Gooi en Sticht bv, Hilversum.

English translation © 1985 Pueblo Publishing Company, Inc. 1860 Broadway, New York, NY 10023. All rights reserved.

Printed in the United States of America.

ISBN: 0-916134-71-7

Contents

Preface

In the fifteen years that I have been teaching liturgy, my principal
interest has changed more than once. At first the history of the
Roman rite was central for me and I attempted to convey its value.
This interest coincided with the renewal of the liturgy prescribed by
the Constitution on the Sacred Liturgy of the Second Vatican Council
and thereafter worked out in practice. Then came a period in which
the pastoral aspect of worship and the place of liturgy within the
whole of pastoral ministry had my primary attention; for that I found
good support in a knowledge of history. It was the time of my work
in the Pastoral Institute of Amsterdam. Then came a period, which
is still continuing, in which my attention was focused principally on
the eastern and western rites and on the development of piety and
of faith; of liturgy and the history of dogma. Along these lines I was
and am highly stimulated by the collaboration of my colleagues in
the Theological Faculty of the University of Utrecht.

So I have had various principal interests. But two clear lines of
continuity are also demonstrable: I have always tried to divide my
attention as well as possible among the different periods of liturgical
history (with the concurrent admission that the seventeenth, eighteenth, and nineteenth centuries have engaged me the least), and I
have sought what is characteristic of those periods. Moreover, I have
always laid emphasis upon the patient analysis of orders of service
(of rubrics and texts). Even before I was fully aware of what I was
doing, I was occupied with what is called "close reading." This
approach has become a sort of second nature over the course of
the years.

In order to keep on pursuing my principal interest in teaching and
research while yet working within the limits of a more and more
confining academic program, I have, in the past years, put together a
set of "lecture notes" for students in which I sketched the outline
of the history of worship and listed the most important sources. The

point of departure in preparing these notes was that the students should be able to acquire sufficient basic information by reading them and that the teacher should have kept open a number of possibilities to elaborate and explore so that he would not have to lecture simply by reading aloud the notes the student already had. These notes have been constantly shaved down and here and there have been somewhat supplemented (they are still incomplete). In the actual practice of teaching, they have proved to be useful by allowing me greater freedom in teaching.

It appeared necessary to duplicate a greater number of copies than was anticipated: many requests came from "outside." When this continued it seemed that the time had come to publish the notes as a book. This book now lies before you. One must not forget the prehistory of this book: it is a study book, an informative book about the history of worship, a guidebook for the interested. It is not a novel, and here and there it will have very dull pages. I leave it to the reader to skip these. I only hope that they are not the most important pages.

The structure of each chapter is the same throughout the book. First of all, some historical and cultural data are given in order, however briefly, to characterize the period. Then follows a description of the developing liturgy: the sources, general characteristics, and finally a detailed description of the aspects of worship. The sequence of these aspects is also the same in every chapter. One can read the book chapter by chapter: each chapter describes a period. One can also read a given category in each of the chapters (e.g., the rite of baptism) in order to trace its development. One could say that the book can be read horizontally (by period) or vertically (by category). An exception to this structure is found in the liturgy surrounding marriage, which is described only in the final forms of its evolution (chapters 4 and 5). The liturgy of death and funerals is dealt with in the second chapter, in the discussion of the development of the calendar of the saints.

It would be best if the reader, having read these notes, went directly to the original texts themselves; this is the best way to learn how to understand the liturgy. How could one speak about eucharistic prayers if one had never read such a prayer?

I am quite aware that colleagues will discover in this book lacunae, inaccuracies, and even mistakes. Sometimes they will say to themselves: "I would have structured that differently, written that differently." But, happily, I also know that this book can never replace teaching.

I have many thanks to give to many people. One of these I already expressly named at my inauguration in Utrecht: J. A. M. Prein. A second I want to name here: C. A. Bouman, professor of liturgy in Nijmegen. He was never my teacher, but he has given me much.

H.A.J.W.

Preface to the English Edition

The writing of a manual is a precarious affair: I know this now that the Dutch and German editions of my book have appeared. In this new edition in English, I have been able to make grateful use of the comments and criticisms of the reviewers in order to correct inaccuracies and mistakes. Nonetheless, I remain convinced of the value of the work and I dare to maintain ideas I have formulated here about the evolution of Christian worship (thus, for example, the difference between anamnetic proclamation of the history of salvation and the cultic representation of the same as a difference between the worship of the first and that of the second period of liturgical history). I have also kept the book functional: a guidebook, a signboard into the history of worship in the east and the west. This has meant that a selection had to be made from the rich material, and a selection remains, of course, subjective, leaving certain matters undiscussed. The goal has been, however, to enhance to some extent the readability of the book and especially to let this historical guidebook attempt to cast light upon the current shape of Christian worship, a goal that is evident from the structure of the chapters.

The publication of such a book as this is also a precarious undertaking for me for yet another reason. Actually, I ought to have made room in the book for music and poetry, archeology and iconography; personally I would have especially enjoyed doing this for iconography. What is more, in my own further research I have been much more expressly engaged with a facet of the history of worship that could not be discussed in this book, i.e., the reception of the (high) churchly liturgy by the people, or in other words, the history of popular religiosity. This research is still far from being ready for publication. Moreover, good work in this field could only be carried out by an intercontinental working team of interdisciplinary composition. Perhaps this is a utopian dream.

Meanwhile, this modest introduction to the book stands. Welcome to its pages and through them to the study of the history of the liturgy.

In the preparation of this English edition I have been greatly helped by the creative care that the translator, Gordon Lathrop, has devoted to my book. For that care I am thankful to him and to the publisher. We have been able to make some necessary improvements as well as certain needed additions to the bibliographies, and so we may hope that the work is now more reliable and thus more fit for achieving the goal for which it was written.

H.A.J.W.
August 1984

Introduction

1. Worship and liturgy are sometimes described as the outward form of a religion, the "expression" of inner religious feeling. This description is partly right: faith and the experience of faith call for expression, for visibility and audibility in words and signs. Faith is outwardly witnessed in certain concrete ritual actions in a rite. But in our western practice faith has been so interiorized, so spiritualized that the external expression has become less important. Human thought grew accustomed to the division between body and soul, between external and internal, and, in the hierarchy of values, the body and the external stood lower by definition. This meant that the external form, the rite, was seen as inferior: it would have been thought ideal if the external was not even necessary.

Let there be no doubt about it: the following pages are written from the conviction that there must be a connection between faith and its expression in language and sign, and that the human person is a spirited bodiliness who expresses that spirit in bodily words and deeds. In ritual, what is interior to the community becomes visible, audible, and palpable. For the believing person, "Out of the abundance of the heart the mouth speaks." And the ways of our God are the same. The Word has become a human being, body and soul, a person. God dwells with people through the words and signs of the incarnate Son. Worship is a dialogue between God and people: God gives, people receive and respond. But this dialogue is not just spiritual, withdrawn from bodily reality. It embraces the whole person, spirit and body. Therefore, the study of Christian rituals is of great importance: in the expressions of faith one discovers the faith of the church.

2. Liturgical scholarship investigates, by means of the historical method, the origin, the history, and the evolution of worship. This means research into sources, cultural ambience, and theology. But above all, it means analysis of orders of service, of external forms, and of texts, which must be studied keeping their growth and change in mind. One then often encounters the theological background of a

liturgical practice as well as the piety and the experience of faith that is hidden in the text. Such an investigation of worship can be of significance for the development of dogma and theology: one discovers how dogma was experienced, how theology influenced church life and vice versa.

I have chosen in this history to describe the basic structure of the orders of service (*ordo, akolouthía*) in each period. It is good to note that this is only one of the many methods of research. One could also proceed otherwise by, for example, historically investigating the smallest units, the constitutive elements, of a liturgy (prayer, song, reading, symbols), and thereafter looking at the great subdivisions in liturgy (such as the church year, the sacraments). I prefer the investigation of worship by historical periods because in this way the evolution of celebration in the church becomes clearer and one can show that a difference exists between essential rites and incidental rites, between what is structural and what is decorative. This distinction is all important if one is to be able to weigh differences in ecclesial traditions and describe the actual shape of a rite.

3. Worship in both the west and the east demonstrates certain constants in its development; one can speak of "the laws of liturgical evolution" formulated by A. Baumstark in his *Comparative Liturgy* (pp. 15–30).

First, there is a development from pluriformity to uniformity; i.e., strictly local worship disappears before worship that obtains more generally; local forms join together in recognizable families. Around the centers of Antioch, Alexandria, and Rome, for example, liturgical families arise out of many local usages. The imperial cities (Rome, Constantinople) were centers of power, even in regard to worship, because of the presence of the emperor, the patriarch, the pope.

Second, there is a development from freedom and improvisation to the use of transmitted texts. This happened not at the command of a synod or a council but simply because after a certain time improvisation was no longer possible. Moreover, a greater guarantee of orthodoxy was sought.

Third, the development in east and west goes from simplicity, transparency, and directness to exuberance, excess, and opaqueness. The structurally central is surrounded by incidentals; short prayers become long; one prayer is replaced by three or more prayers; central rites are embellished; old prayers are fitted to the theological insights of the current time.

Fourth, the old must often give way to the new; on the other hand, the oldest celebrations (such as the paschal feast) frequently retain ancient elements that had long ago disappeared from common use. The intercessions or prayers of the faithful, for example, disappeared from the Roman rite but were preserved in the liturgy of Good Friday.

Finally, the older a text is, the less it is directly "biblical," that is, it may breathe a biblical spirit but it does not actually incorporate the literal text. On the other hand, it is also noteworthy that more recent texts are more expressly doctrinaire and theologically laden.

In the evolution of worship, these laws will be confirmable at several points, and it is my hope that this present guidebook will demonstrate that and will serve as a useful help in the study of liturgy.

Bibliography

1. REFERENCE WORKS

Dictionary of Liturgy and Worship. J. G. Davies, ed. (London & New York, 1972).

Dictionnaire d'archélogie chrétienne et de liturgie. F. Cabrol & H. Leclerq, eds. (Paris, 1907–1953).

Encyclopedia Judaica (Jerusalem & New York, 1971).

Lexicon der christlichen Ikonographie. E. Kirschbaum, ed. (Freiburg, 1968–1976).

Lexicon für Theologie und Kirche. J. Höfer & K. Rahner, eds. (Freiburg, 1957–1967; 3 suppl. vols., 1967–1968).

Liturgisch Woordenboek. L. Brinkhoff et al., eds. (Roermond, 1958–1968; supplement, 1970).

The Oxford Dictionary of the Christian Church, 2nd ed. F. L. Cross, ed. (London, 1974).

Reallexicon für Antike und Christentum. T. Klauser, ed. (Stuttgart, 1950ff.).

Die Religion in Geschichte und Gegenwart, 3rd. ed. (Tübingen, 1957–1962).

2. HANDBOOKS: A SELECTION

Baumstark, A. *Comparative Liturgy,* rev. by B. Botte (London, 1958).

———. *Von geschichtlichem Werden der Liturgie* (Freiburg, 1923).

Cattaneo, E. *Il Culto Cristiano in Occidente: Note Storiche,* 3rd rev. ed. (Rome, 1978).

Dalmais, I. *Introduction to the Liturgy* (Baltimore, 1961).

Dix, G. *The Shape of the Liturgy,* rev. ed. (New York, 1981).

Fendt, L. *Einführung in die Liturgiewissenschaft* (Berlin, 1958).

Handbuch der Ostkirchenkunde (Düsseldorf, 1971).

Jones, C., G. Wainwright & E. Yarnold, eds. *The Study of Liturgy* (London & New York, 1978).

Jungmann, J. A. *The Early Liturgy to the Time of Gregory the Great* (Notre Dame, 1959).

————. *Public Worship: A Survey* (Collegeville, 1958).

Klauser, T. *A Short History of the Western Liturgy* (London, 1969).

Leiturgia, Handbuch des evangelischen Gottesdienstes, 5 vols. (Kassel, 1954–1970).

Martimort, A. G. *The Church at Prayer: Introduction to the Liturgy* (New York, 1968).

Nagel, W. *Geschichte des christlichen Gottesdienstes* (Berlin, 1962).

Paquier, R. *Traité de liturgique* (Neuchatel, 1959).

Raes, A. *Introductio in liturgiam orientalem,* 2nd ed. (Rome, 1963).

Reed, L. D. *The Lutheran Liturgy,* rev. ed. (Philadelphia, 1959).

Schmemann, A. *Introduction to Liturgical Theology* (London & Portland, Me., 1966).

Schmidt, H. *Introductio in liturgiam occidentalem* (Rome, 1960).

Vagaggini, C. *Theological Dimensions of the Liturgy* (Collegeville, 1976).

Verheul, A. *Introduction to the Liturgy: Towards a Theology of Worship* (Collegeville, 1968).

Vogel, C. *Introduction aux sources de l'histoire du culte chrétien au moyen-âge* (Spoleto, 1973).

3. PRINCIPAL JOURNALS

Besides journals of historical (especially *Revue d'Histoire ecclésiastique*) and theological focus, the following are of interest:

Archiv für Liturgiewissenschaft, Regensburg (until 1941 *Jahrbuch für Liturgiewissenschaft*).

Concilium, New York.

Ephemerides Liturgicae, Rome.

Irenikon, Chevetogne.

Jahrbuch für Liturgik und Hymnologie, Kassel.

La Maison-Dieu, Paris.

Liturgisches Jahrbuch, Münster.

Liturgy, Washington, D.C.

Le Muséon, Louvain.

Notitiae, Rome.

Orientalia Christiania Periodica, Rome.

Parole de l'Orient, Kaslik.

Questions Liturgiques, Louvain (until 1970 *Questions liturgiques et paroissiales*).

Revue Bénédictine, Maredsous.

Rivista Liturgica, Turin.

Studia Liturgica, Rotterdam.

Tijdschrift voor Liturgie, Affligem.

Vigiliae Christianae, Amsterdam.

Worship, Collegeville (until 1951 *Orate Fratres*).

Chapter One

The First Signs:
The Period before the Peace of the Church in 312 A.D.

I. HISTORICAL OUTLINE

Literature

B. Bagatti, *The Church from the Circumcision* (Jerusalem, 1971).

H. Chadwick, *The Early Church,* Pelican History of the Church, vol. 1 (London, 1967).

H. Conzelmann, *History of Primitive Christianity* (Nashville, 1973).

H. Jedin & J. Dolan, eds., *From the Apostolic Community to Constantine.* Handbook of Church History, vol. 1 (New York, 1965).

R. Kottje & B. Moeller, eds., *Oekumenische Kirchengeschichte,* vol. 1 (Mainz, 1970).

F. van der Meer & C. Mohrmann, *Atlas of the Early Christian World* (London & New York, 1959).

A. GENERAL HISTORICAL SETTING

Christianity originated and grew within the boundaries of the Roman empire, which, in the century before Christ, had undergone a great expansion: in the north to Scotland; in the west to the Atlantic Ocean (Portugal); in the south to the Sahara (i.e., the northern strip of the African continent); and in the east to Persia (to the Euphrates and Edessa).

Rome was the center of the *Imperium* and it has been estimated that the city had close to one million inhabitants in the year 300 A.D. Later it had to share the honor of principal city with Constantinople in the eastern Roman empire. The central position of Rome must primarily be regarded as political and administrative; the cultural centers lay elsewhere in the empire, particularly in the near east (Alexandria, for example).

The organization of the Roman empire must not be compared with that of the modern state. The empire was divided into great provinces (e.g., Gaul, Italy, Asia) over which a governor was appointed who acted more or less independently. Within the provinces all kinds of political subdivisions were possible (free cities or separate small regions). Communication between the parts of the immense empire was made possible by an extensive and ingeniously constructed system of roads and by a well-organized fleet, which, at the same time, was of great importance for trade. There were no imperial police but there was certainly a ubiquitous army, which was especially charged with guarding the borders. Political activity in the years of the beginnings of Christianity was directed toward the preservation of tradition, toward a stability and tranquility centered around the powerful emperor, and toward sound fiscal management (based on colonialism and a slave economy). The humanities and arts were of less account; civilization proceeded in a declining course in these closing centuries of the empire.

Civil law, on the other hand, was strong and well-defined. Prosperity stood at a moderate level, but with most possessions in the hands of a few. Internal unity was something that the authorities in the great empire had never known how to establish: the empire remained a collection of states under one administrative government.

As long as the tranquility was not disturbed by tumultuous new religions and sects, the state was tolerant; within certain limits every religion could develop freely and even recruit members, the Christian religion not excepted. The persecution of Christians in the first centuries must not be exaggerated, therefore, as was the case in later traditional tales. Christianity was able to develop rather freely, all the more so because initially it was in some sense connected with the Jewish religion, which in those days was spread widely throughout the empire, with synagogues in practically every city, above all in the east. Therefore, it is not surprising that Christian communities could be found in all parts of the empire, even in remote parts of the west.

The facts about the first Christian congregations are very scarce and hardly sufficient to form an image. From textual sources, it is demonstrable that in the second century there were congregations in Rome (the letter of Clement; Justin Martyr), in Lyons and Vienne, in Trier, in Cologne, and in North Africa (Carthage). Archeological discoveries probably indicate still more places, such as St. Denis, Arles, Nîmes, Narbonne, Ostia, and Puteoli. It is striking that these are frequently garrison towns: Christianity began in the cities and was carried along with the soldiers. We know nothing of Christianity in the countryside, which is not remarkable, for the countryside did not play such an important role in the Roman empire save for the estates of the patricians.

The cradle of Christianity lay around the eastern basin of the Mediterranean Sea: in Syria, Asia, Galatia, Cappadocia, Thrace, and Egypt. In these provinces in the second century, the map already shows many churches. They are expressly named in a variety of textual sources. As a rule, the principal episcopal cities and liturgical centers of later centuries go back to the first and second centuries (see F. van der Meer & C. Mohrmann, *Atlas of the Early Christian World*, maps 5 & 7).

What is certain is that the Christians—who as a rule were not revolutionaries and did not array themselves against the state, but lived in the expectation of a coming kingdom—nonetheless in the eyes of non-Christians did occupy a conspicuous place among the motley collection of religions of the time. Their faith—"Jesus is the Messiah, raised from the dead"—brought them into difficulties with some members of local Jewish communities, who then called on the local authorities to stop them. What is more, the Christians were secretive in all their doings and were, in a certain sense, intolerant, for the claims they made were not small. They met in private homes for rites about which non-Christians had the strangest ideas: they venerated a donkey's head or the genitals of their priests; they offered up the blood of children murdered for this purpose; their meals were orgies—so argued the Roman orator Cecilius about 180 A.D. Their social organization was strange (*caritas*) and their conception of marriage irritating. These presumptions were sufficient to awaken suspicion against the group which came to be called the "Christians" (Acts 11:26).

These suspicions led easily to local or regional hostilities. The governors or local officials in the empire, who were assigned to do everything possible to maintain peace and order, acted against the troublemakers. Christians were asked to take part in the emperor cult, not so much to provoke them as to force them to be loyal to the emperor, especially in their social behavior. Those Christians who resisted were persecuted and died as witnesses (martyrs). The Christians had no fixed legal position within the state. They were actually outlaws and were dependent upon the pleasure of local leaders, against which situation the lawyer Tertullian reacted with a sharp pen. A description of these times is given in Gregory Dix, *The Shape of the Liturgy* ("The Pre-Nicene Background of the Liturgy," pp. 141–152).

Radically abbreviated, these are the facts about the persecutions:

until the middle of the second century there was no general law against Christians. There were indeed incidents of punitive persecution. About the year 100 the emperor Trajan wrote to his governor Pliny in Asia Minor that imprisoned Christians must renounce their faith, but on the other hand, they must not be imprisoned on the basis of anonymous accusations; such an accusation is "unworthy of our time" (*nec nostri saeculi est*), he remarked (C. Kirch, *Enchiridion Fontium Historiae Ecclesiasticae Antiquae*, no. 31; cf. J. Stevenson, *A New Eusebius*, no. 15). Under the emperor Nero (54–68 A.D.) an "immense multitude" (*multitudo ingens*) died (Tacitus, *Annals* 15:44; cf. Kirch, op. cit., no. 34; Stevenson, op. cit., no. 3), among whom were probably Peter and Paul (1 Clement 5). There are indications that under Domitian (81–96 A.D.) the emperor cult was required. Under Trajan (98–117 A.D.), Simeon, the bishop of Jerusalem, and Ignatius of Antioch were killed. In the third century, periods of relative quiet alternated with fierce persecutions. Under Decius (249–251 A.D.), the old Roman traditions and especially the old religion were given new stimulus, and the increasing number of Christians fell victim, in one way or another, to this growth. According to Origen, while the number of Christians had increased, their quality had not. Christians were required to sacrifice to the gods and many did, whether in writing (*libellatici*) or in fact, all of which gave Cyprian and other bishops great problems (who was apostate and who was not?). Under Valerian (253–260 A.D.), measures were taken principally against the clergy (e.g., Cyprian) and for the confiscation of church property, which it appears earlier congregations had been able to acquire. Diocletian (284–305 A.D.) fought against Christianity on account of its subversive behavior. He attempted to destroy both churches and liturgical books, he forbade assemblies, and he arrested the clergy. Of course, he did not succeed in his plan.

Reports of the martyrdoms are to be found in the so-called *acta · martyrum* (a kind of court report of the trial, for example, of Justin or Cyprian: questions, answers, sentence); in the *passiones* (eyewitness accounts, for example, of Polycarp, the martyrs of Lyon and Vienne, or Perpetua and Felicity in North Africa; these "passions" were read in the liturgy); and in the *legenda* (precipitate of a richly imaginative popular faith; for knowledge of the ordinary life in a local church these legends are of great importance) (see further: J. Moreau, *Les persecutions du christianisme dans l'empire romain*, Paris, 1956).

By way of Jerusalem, Antioch, and Asia Minor, Christianity spread rather quickly in the empire, at the outset in Jewish congregations and soon thereafter also among the Gentiles. But the facts are scarce

4

in regard to actual congregational life. Perhaps initially gatherings took place in private houses, but soon larger spaces were acquired for use. There are excavations of these early sites but the findings are difficult to interpret.

B. CHRISTIAN AND JEW

The Christian communities of the first years were closely linked with the Jewish communities in Jerusalem, Palestine, Asia, and elsewhere, and that was true in spite of growing differences (one thinks of the letters of Paul). Even when Christianity went its own way, the Jewish influence was indelibly present. Into the fourth century, great influence must have continued to be exercised in the church by Christians from among the Jews (and, through them, also by Judaism itself). It was these Jewish Christians who adhered to the law and to the Jewish dating of festivals (especially the paschal feast), who appealed above all to the authority of James, "the brother of the Lord," and whose theology had its own characteristic accents. Much material in liturgical history becomes clearer if one considers the influence of this group. Concurrently, one may speak of a growing antagonism between the Gentile Christians, who wanted to be free of Jewish bonds, and the Jewish Christians. By the spread of congregations throughout the whole empire and the massive increase of Gentile Christians, the influence of the Jewish Christians constantly grew smaller.

In Jerusalem, Jewish Christians were probably in the majority, leading their own life in their own synagogues (cf. the *Gospel of the Hebrews*) until the second Jewish War (135 A.D.), in which conflict they remained neutral. After that war, Gentiles migrated to Jerusalem and among them were Gentile Christians, who obtained their own bishop and thereby contributed to the growing alienation from the Jewish-Christian congregations. The Jewish Christians ended up in the sectarian corner: the roots of later Arian theology may perhaps be found there. Jewish-Christian congregations are known to have existed in Palestine (Bethlehem, Hebron, Nazareth, etc.), in Syria and the Trans-Jordan (Pella among other places), and in Egypt. One cannot demonstrate separate congregations of Jewish Christians in Rome, but their influence was certainly present, as is demonstrated in the Easter controversy and in funerary inscriptions. No data are available for the west outside of Rome. It can be assumed that the Jewish elements in Christian worship came into the Christian church by way of Jewish Christians.

5

It is interesting to note that Hans Lietzmann, *Mass and Lord's Supper* (Leiden, 1953ff.), defends the thesis that the eucharist, which in keeping with Jewish tradition had been a table fellowship with the breaking of bread, was made by Paul into a meal in memory of the death of the Lord. This thesis has been rightly rejected, but it might still be discussed in light of the differences between Jewish-Christian and Gentile-Christian congregations.

II. CULTURAL DATA

Literature

M. Simon, *La civilisation de l'antiquité et de christianisme* (Paris, 1972).

F. van der Meer & C. Mohrmann, *Atlas of the Early Christian World* (London & New York, 1959).

F. van der Meer, *Atlas of Western Civilization*, 2nd rev. ed. (London & New York, 1960).

F. van der Meer, *Christus oudste gewaad* (Utrecht, 1949).

J. Waszink, et al., *Het oudste christendom en de antieke cultuur*, 2 vols. (Haarlem, 1951).

A. THE GREEKS

"What do we owe to the Greeks? Primarily that we are ourselves, that we are human beings worthy of the name, for all humanism goes back to the Greeks. The Greek of the fifth century is not awed by the universe. He has nothing to do with magic and has no fear of the stars. He submits calmly to Destiny, piously fulfills the traditional rites, but nonetheless weaves beautiful legends around his gods. He orders the sum of his experience around a single point, man. Order, the typical work of the intellect, was the true passion of the Greek. For his oriental neighbors the universe was a plaything of implacable gods. For the Greek, however, it was a *cosmos*, a perfectly ordered, measurable entity, that could be explored and expressed in mathematical terms. Such expression was made possible by the concept of Ideas—realities solely intuitable and perceptible in the abstract— upon which depended all complex, concrete, ordered and significant things. 'The creation of Ideas,' says Valery, 'is the outstanding European achievement'; it is the first definitive attempt to give order to our universe. Plato, who brought the concept to fruition, was not only a thinker, but a great artist, infinitely sensitive to the symbolic significance of the smallest details. . . .

"[T]he positive side remains a glorious achievement. The concept

6

of humanity, dignity, freedom, and law; the heroic life; a narrow but genuine patriotism; and the cult of reason joined to an insatiable thirst for knowledge and beauty" (*Atlas of Western Civilization*, pp. 11, 16).

This heritage of Greek humanism continued to be preserved in Hellenism. To this humanism, Stoicism also contributed clearly, albeit marking it with a somewhat more elitist character.

B. ROME

Rome, the center of the *Imperium*, took little notice of the culture of Greek thought and of Hellenism. Rome was pragmatic, appealed to its descent from simple Etruscan farmers, and did not understand the creative power of Hellenistic civilization because it was itself not creative. Rome was a conqueror with plebeian ambitions. It sought its safety in the material; it was set on exploitation and the advantages of exploitation; it had cultivated but few spiritual insights.

Nevertheless, bound up with the *pax romana* were indeed several characteristics very salutary for western civilization. The Roman was no artist, but did possess a substantial character. Roman culture was certainly affected by that of Greece. And the Roman was brilliant in governance, in making laws, in precise, terse, yet stately linguistic formulations, and in the preservation of values in the face of the barbarian peoples.

In contrast with the intellectual centers of Greek culture (Athens, Rhodes, Pergamum, Antioch, Alexandria), education in imperial Rome was poor (cf. J. Carcopino, *Daily Life in Ancient Rome*, New Haven, 1960). Elementary education signified very little; to be a teacher was no recommendation; the slave-pedagogue could assert little authority in teaching the children because of his position; popular education was a failure; aristocrats received instruction in grammar and rhetoric but even this was a rather trivial affair. Eventually all this led to disastrous consequences for Roman culture. A hollowing out of intellectual life over the centuries both introduced and completed the fall of the empire in the west: there was insufficient internal resistance against the invasions of other cultures. This process would be made clear only later (fifth century), but the causes were here. What the role of the church was at this time cannot be determined; little data are available. We do not know to what extent instruction took place within the congregations. Certainly a marked growth of Christian doctrine is evident (cf. J. N. D. Kelly, *Early Christian Doctrines*, 5th ed., London, 1978).

C. ISRAEL

Israel stood at the cradle of the Christian congregations. "The inheritance from the synagogue" (Baumstark) was great both in quantity and quality. It is asserted correctly that without Israel, Christianity in the content of its faith and in its worship could not be understood. Naturally, influence from Hellenistic civilization and thereby also from eastern religions and mysteries was also felt, but these remain nonetheless in the shadow of the Jewish influence. We have discussed already the "Jewish Christians," whose influence was so great in the first centuries of the Christian era. This meant that Jewish doctrine, Jewish practices, and Jewish worship were known widely in the Christian congregations. But what is meant by the term "Jewish Christian"? J. Daniélou, in *The Theology of Jewish Christianity* (London & Chicago, 1964), indicates several groups to whom this term can be applied.

First, the term may indicate those who recognized Christ only as a Messiah, not as the Son of God. They were in fact heterodox ("a separate class, halfway between Jews and Christians"): they were the Ebionites, as well as syncretistic groups in which Gnostic ideas played a large role (Simon Magus).

Second, the name "Jewish Christian" may be applied to the Christian congregations in Jerusalem and elsewhere in Palestine. They were Christians and, at the same time, observant Jews. After the fall of Jerusalem, their initially great influence was quickly diminished. These congregations then joined themselves to the Ebionites or to the Gentile Christians.

Finally, one may understand "Jewish Christian" to mean "a type of Christian thought expressing itself in forms borrowed from Judaism" (J. Daniélou, op. cit., p. 9). Those forms were the forms of late Judaism, i.e., Judaism as it was in the time of the first Christian congregations, determined by such groups as the Pharisees, the Essenes, and the Zealots, and in its images and content, by apocalypticism. It must however be noted that the opinion of Daniélou is not universally accepted (cf. R. Murray, *Symbols of Church and Kingdom*, Cambridge, 1975).

It has come to be apparent that for the development of Christian theology, Jewish-Christian thought was of great importance, as was gnosticism or movements of gnostic tendency. To understand the development of worship, it is necessary to be acquainted with Jewish observance and orthopraxis, for it was this practice that was followed by the Jewish-Christian congregations of Jerusalem and

Palestine. The influence of Jewish worship on Christian worship almost certainly came via these congregations in Palestine, which then, after the fall of Jerusalem, went into exile, perhaps to the east. It is possible that in the East Syrian rite, indications of continued Jewish influence are still to be found.

We cannot, however, just restrict ourselves to the second group named above. Liturgical uses derived from what we have called "late Judaism" were equally significant for all of Christian worship. The most recent overview is given by R. Boon, *De Joodse wortels van de christelijke eredienst* (Amsterdam, 1970).

In both cases, however, caution must be exercised: "But since the Jewish liturgy of that era is known to us only from sources which are several centuries later and which require critical analysis, we must avoid hasty conclusions" (B. Botte in A. G. Martimort, ed., *The Church at Prayer*, vol. 1, *Introduction to the Liturgy*, New York, 1968, p. 39). Questions remain: cf. M. Simon, "Problèmes du judéo-christianisme," in *Aspects du judéo-christianisme* (Paris, 1965, pp. 1–17).

D. EASTERN RELIGIONS

We ought also to mention the influence of the eastern religions that caught on in the empire. This influence has certainly been sometimes overemphasized but it cannot be entirely denied (cf. M. J. Vermaseren, ed., *Die Orientalischen Religionen im Römerreich*, Leiden, 1981).

E. GNOSTICISM

Gnosticism probably originated in the milieu of Hellenistic Judaism and taught that a divine spark is present in the human person. Because of that spark, the person is capable of being redeemed from the evil world and from death, capable of again becoming aware of his or her origin, his or her heavenly identity, capable of renewing his or her spiritual reality and relation to God. This *gnosis* also had a profound influence in Christian circles. Christian *gnosis* was christocentric and based on the intuitive experience of the Lord (cf. "knowing" in the fourth gospel). Marcion and Mani (216–277) must be mentioned here: they stand at the beginning of a gnostic church (cf. G. Quispel, *Gnosis als Weltreligion*, Zürich, 1972; K. Rudolph, *Die Gnosis, Wesen und Geschichte einer spätantiken Religion*, Göttingen, 1978; *Studies in Gnosticism and Hellenistic Religion*, presented to G. Quispel, Leiden, 1981). Representative texts are "A Valentinian Exposition" (xi, 40, on baptism; xi, 42, on baptism; xi, 43–44, on the eucharist) in J. Robinson, ed., *The Nag Hammadi Library in English* (New York, 1977, pp. 441–442).

We have briefly summarized here what is generally recognized. Christianity and Christian worship arose in the midst of an already existing culture (Hellenistic, Roman), from an already existing religion (Jewish), and encountered the influence of all the religious tendencies present in the immense empire. If we add to this some consideration of the defense of Christian teaching that was shaped in the philosophical thought patterns of the time, we will have a picture that, in rough lines, is close enough to being complete.

III. THE LITURGY:
ORDERS OF SERVICE AND TEXTS

Literature

In regard to the literature lists, here and in the following chapters I will give a selection of books determined by this principle: that one will be able to find in the cited books a good list of sources and a good description of the outline of development in one of the aspects of worship. I always try to cite at least one monograph where expanded bibliographic references may be found to avoid the danger of being too selective.

O. Barlea, *Die Weihe der Bischöfe, Presbyter und Diakone in vornicenischer Zeit* (Munich, 1969).

A. Baumstark, *Comparative Liturgy*, rev. by B. Botte (London, 1958).

————, *Nocturna laus* (Münster, 1957).

R. Cantalamessa, *La Pasqua della nostra Salvezza* (Turin, n.d.).

W. D. Davies, *Paul and Rabbinic Judaism* (London, 1970).

C. Dugmore, *The Influence of the Synagogue upon the Divine Office* (Westminster, 1964, repr. of 1944 ed.).

I. Elbogen, *Der Jüdische Gottesdienst in seiner geschichtlichen Entwicklung* (Hildesheim, 1964, repr.).

R. Fenneberg, *Christliche Passafeier und Abendmahl* (Munich, 1971).

B. Fischer, *Die Psalmenfrömmigkeit der Märtyrerkirche* (Freiburg, 1949).

A. Hänggi & I. Pahl, *Prex Eucharistica* (Freiburg, 1968).

W. Huber, *Passa und Ostern* (Berlin, 1969).

J. A. Jungmann, *Christian Prayer through the Centuries* (New York, 1978).

————, *Des lois de la célébration liturgique* (Paris, 1956).

10

————, *The Early Liturgy* (Notre Dame, 1960).

————, *The Mass of the Roman Rite* (New York, 1951–1955).

H. Karp, *Die Busse; Quellen zur Entstehung des altkirchlichen Busswesens* (Zürich, 1969).

J. Lemaire, *Les ministères aux origines de l'Eglise* (Paris, 1971).

W. Oesterley, *The Jewish Background of the Christian Liturgy* (Gloucester, 1965, repr. of 1925 ed.).

W. Rordorf, *Sabbat und Sonntag in der alten Kirche* (Zürich, 1970).

————, *Sunday* (London, 1968).

E. Whitaker, *Documents of the Baptismal Liturgy* (London, 1960).

A. THE NEW TESTAMENT

The data from the New Testament are at once scanty and rich. No order of service, no clear overview of worship in the first congregations, no service book is to be found there. In a variety of ways, however, the New Testament does give information about the first Christians, about their life of faith and its expression. They came together; they prayed corporately. The holding of meals and the breaking of bread is mentioned. Here and there hymn fragments are to be found. And according to some scholars, there are even direct liturgical sources, as, for example, 1 Peter, which is supposed to be a sort of baptismal catechesis. One can indeed more or less recover the origins of later liturgical forms in the New Testament, but never completely. We give here several examples (cf. J. Nielen, *Gebet und Gottesdienst im Neuen Testament,* Freiburg, 1937; H. Chirat, *L'assemblée chrétienne à l'âge apostolique,* Paris, 1949): Acts 2:41–47 (cf. also 4:32–35; 5:12–16) describes the practice of the Christian life in Jerusalem: there was a kind of catechesis; the people lived together (possibly in groups); bread was broken in private homes (perhaps the eucharist is intended here); Christians daily attended the temple for prayer (probably during morning and evening sacrifice). The center of all of this was the praise of God, an inheritance from Jewish worship (*berakah*). The use of *psalmoi, hymnoi,* and *odai* (Eph 5:19; Col 3:16) is known: *psalms,* which were read in a particular way, i.e., interpreted of Christ and his people (cf. J. Daniélou, *Etudes d'exégèse judéo-chrétienne,* Paris, 1966; P. Salmon, *Les 'tituli psalmorum' des manuscrits latins,* Paris, 1959); *hymns* and *songs* (e.g., 1 Pt 1:3–5; Phil 2:6–11; 1 Tm 3:15–16, and several examples in Revelation). It is probable that the congregation kept up the Jewish times of prayer.

One can also find examples of prayer in the New Testament. For both structure and content, Acts 4:24–30 is a good example of a memorial prayer: the community addresses itself to God, Sovereign and Creator, who in everlasting goodness remembers humanity, in the past and in the present. A hymnic memorial is found in the songs of Zechariah, Mary, and Simeon, which have been included in the gospel of Luke. The Lord's prayer was handed on in the Christian tradition as the key to every prayer, and one finds there the same structure as in these other prayers: praise and supplication.

The data are scarce concerning the celebration of the first day of the week, Sunday, with its focus on the resurrection of Christ. Probably it quickly became the custom to hold the meal on that day (cf. Acts 10:40–41; 20:7; Rv 1:10; 2:7, 17; 3:20; 22:14–17; and the stories concerning the appearances of the risen Lord). According to the tradition of Paul (1 Cor 11:20), the meal was concerned also with a remembrance of the last meal Jesus held before his death.

The celebration of Easter in the Christian congregation has its roots in the New Testament, but the precise development of this feast remains in darkness. Perhaps one may point to 1 Corinthians 5:7 and 1 Peter.

The New Testament informs us extensively about the significance of Christian initiation (understood as a water bath and baptism with the Holy Spirit). Baptism was practiced universally, but how it took place is variously described. A single, normative order of service does not exist (Acts 8:26–40). For the significance of baptism, cf. Romans 6:1ff.; Galatians 3:26–38; Colossians 2:11–12; 1 Corinthians 6:11; 10:1ff.; Ephesians 4:4–5; 1 Timothy 6:12–13; Titus 3:3–7; Hebrews 6: 1–6; and several passages in the gospel of John.

B. SOURCES

The number of direct sources for worship in this period is limited. Indirect information about the development of the liturgy is more copious. Here a short summary list is presented. For further detailed information, consult J. Quasten, *Patrology* (Utrecht & Westminster, Md., 1950, vol. 1; B. Altaner, *Patrology*, New York, 1960, cf. 8th German ed., 1978; J. Quasten, *Monumenta eucharistica et liturgica vetustissima*, Bonn, 1935–1937).

CREED
The development of a formula for the confession of faith is closely bound up with the practice of baptism in the first centuries (cf. J. Kelly, *Early Christian Creeds*, London, 1950).

DIDACHE

Text and translation: K. Lake, ed., *The Apostolic Fathers*, vol. 1 (Cambridge & London, 1912), pp. 303–333; J. Audet, ed., *La Didaché, Instructions des Apôtres* (Paris, 1958); W. Rordorf, ed., *Sources chrétiennes* 248.

"The Teaching of the Twelve Apostles," the *Didache*, written about 100 A.D., contains information regarding baptism, an *agape*-eucharist, Sunday, the fast on Wednesday and Friday, offices in the congregation, and several examples of prayer, such as that in chapter 10 (Lake, óp. cit., pp. 322–325):

10:1. Μετὰ δὲ τὸ ἐμπλησθῆναι οὕτως εὐχαριστήσατε·

2. Εὐχαριστοῦμέν σοι, πάτερ ἅγιε, ὑπὲρ τοῦ ἁγίου ὀνόματός σου, οὗ κατεσκήνωσας ἐν ταῖς καρδίαις ἡμῶν, καὶ ὑπὲρ τῆς γνώσεως καὶ πίστεως καὶ ἀθανασίας, ἧς ἐγνώρισας ἡμῖν διὰ Ἰησοῦ τοῦ παιδός σου· σοὶ ἡ δόξα εἰς τοὺς αἰῶνας.

3. σύ, δέσποτα παντοκράτορ, ἔκτισας τὰ πάντα ἕνεκεν τοῦ ὀνόματός σου, τροφήν τε καὶ ποτὸν ἔδωκας τοῖς ἀνθρώποις εἰς ἀπόλαυσιν, ἵνα σοι εὐχαριστήσωσιν, ἡμῖν δὲ ἐχαρίσω πνευματικὴν τροφὴν καὶ ποτὸν καὶ ζωὴν αἰώνιον διὰ τοῦ παιδός σου.

4. πρὸ πάντων εὐχαριστοῦμέν σοι, ὅτι δυνατὸς εἶ· σοὶ ἡ δόξα εἰς τοὺς αἰῶνας.

5. μνήσθητι, κύριε, τῆς ἐκκλησίας σου, τοῦ ῥύσασθαι αὐτὴν ἀπὸ παντὸς πονηροῦ καὶ τελειῶσαι αὐτὴν ἐν τῇ ἀγάπῃ σου, καὶ σύναξον αὐτὴν ἀπὸ τῶν τεσσάρων ἀνέμων, τὴν ἁγιασθεῖσαν, εἰς τὴν σὴν βασιλείαν, ἣν ἡτοίμασας αὐτῇ· ὅτι σοῦ ἐστιν ἡ δύναμις καὶ ἡ δόξα εἰς τοὺς αἰῶνας.

10:1. But after you are satisfied with food, thus give thanks:

2. "We give thanks to thee, O Holy Father, for thy Holy Name which thou didst make to tabernacle in our hearts, and for the knowledge and faith and immortality which thou didst make known to us through Jesus thy child. To thee be glory for ever."

3. "Thou, Lord Almighty, didst create all things for thy Name's sake, and didst give food and drink to men for their enjoyment, that they might give thanks to thee, but us hast thou blessed with spiritual food and drink and eternal light through thy child."

4. "Above all we give thanks to thee for that thou art mighty. To thee be glory for ever."

5. "Remember, Lord, thy Church, to deliver it from all evil and to make it perfect in thy love, and gather it together in its holiness from the four winds to thy kingdom which thou hast prepared for it. For thine is the power and the glory for ever."

13

6. ἐλθέτω χάρις καὶ παρελθέτω
ὁ κόσμος οὗτος. Ὡσαννὰ τῷ θεῷ
Δαυείδ. εἴ τις ἅγιός ἐστιν, ἐρχέσθω·
εἴ τις οὐκ ἔστι, μετανοείτω· μαρὰν
ἀθά· ἀμήν.

7. τοῖς δὲ προφήταις
ἐπιτρέπετε εὐχαριστεῖν ὅσα
θέλουσιν.

6. "Let grace come and let
this world pass away. Hosannah
to the God of David. If any man
be holy, let him come! If any
man be not, let him repent: Mar-
anatha. Amen."

7. But suffer the prophets to
hold Eucharist as they will.

CLEMENT OF ROME

Text and translation: K. Lake, *The Apostolic Fathers*, vol. 1, pp. 1–121; *Sources chrétiennes* 167.

Besides information about the forms of ministry in the congregation and the veneration of Peter and Paul in Rome, 1 Clement also
gives an example of a supplicatory prayer that makes use of at least
eight Jewish constructions. It is cited here as a model for the late
tradition of prayer (Lake, op. cit., pp. 110–117):

59:3. . . . ἐλπίζειν ἐπὶ τό
ἀρχέγονον πάσης κτίσεως ὄνομά
σου, ἀνοίξας τοὺς ὀφθαλμοὺς τῆς
καρδίας ἡμῶν εἰς τὸ γινώσκειν σε
τὸν μόνον ὕψιστον ἐν ὑψίστοις,
ἅγιον ἐν ἁγίοις ἀναπαυόμενον. τὸν
ταπεινοῦντα ὕβριν ὑπερηφάνων,
τὸν διαλύοντα λογισμοὺς ἐθνῶν,
τὸν ποιοῦντα ταπεινοὺς εἰς ὕψος
καὶ τοὺς ὑψηλοὺς ταπεινοῦντα, τὸν
πλουτίζοντα καὶ πτωχίζοντα, τὸν
ἀποκτείνοντα καὶ ζῆν ποιοῦντα,
μόνον εὑρέτην πνευμάτων καὶ θεὸν
πάσης σαρκός· τὸν ἐπιβλέποντα ἐν
τοῖς ἀβύσσοις, τὸν ἐπόπτην
ἀνθρωπίνων ἔργων, τὸν τῶν
κινδυνευόντων βοηθόν, τὸν τῶν
ἀπηλπισμένων σωτῆρα, τὸν παντὸς
πνεύματος κτίστην καὶ ἐπίσκοπον·
τὸν πληθύνοντα ἔθνη ἐπὶ γῆς καὶ
ἐκ πάντων ἐκλεξάμενον τοὺς
ἀγαπῶντάς σε διὰ Ἰησοῦ Χριστοῦ

59:3. . . . to hope on thy name,
the source of all creation, open
the eyes of our heart to know
thee, that thou alone art the
highest in the highest and re-
mainest holy among the holy.
Thou dost humble the pride of
the haughty, thou dost destroy
the imaginings of nations, thou
dost raise up the humble and
abase the lofty, thou makest rich
and makest poor, thou dost slay
and make alive, thou alone art
the finder of spirits and art God
of all flesh, thou dost look on
the abysses, thou seest into the
works of man, thou art the
helper of those in danger, the
saviour of those in despair, the
creator and watcher over every
spirit; thou dost multiply nations
upon earth and hast chosen out

τοῦ ἠγαπημένου παιδός σου, δι' οὗ
ἡμᾶς ἐπαίδευσας, ἡγίασας,
ἐτίμησας·

4. ἀξιοῦμέν σε, δέσποτα, βοηθὸν
γενέσθαι καὶ ἀντιλήπτορα ἡνῶν.
τοὺς ἐν θμίψει ἡμῶν σῶσον, τοὺς
ταπεινοὺς ἐλέησον, τοὺς
πεπτωκότας ἔγειρον, τοῖς δεομένοις
ἐπιφάνηθι, τοὺς ἀσθενεῖς ἴασαι,
τοὺς πλανωμένους τοῦ λαοῦ σου
ἐπίστρεψον· χόρτασον τοὺς
πεινῶντας, λύτρωσαι τοὺς δεσμίους
ἡμῶν, ἐξανάστησον τοὺς
ἀσθενοῦντας, παρακάλεσον τοὺς
ὀλιγοψυχοῦντας· γνώτωσάν σε
ἅπαντα τὰ ἔθνη, ὅτι σὺ εἶ ὁ θεὸς
μόνος καὶ Ἰησοῦς Χριστὸς ὁ παῖς
σου καὶ ἡμεῖς λαός σου καὶ
πρόβατα τῆς νομῆς σου.

60:1. Σὺ γὰρ τὴν ἀέναον τοῦ
κόσμου σύστασιν διὰ τῶν
ἐνεργουμένων ἐφανεροποίησας· σύ,
κύριε, τὴν οἰκουμένην ἔκτισας, ὁ
πιστὸς ἐν πάσαις ταῖς γενεαῖς,
δίκαιος ἐν τοῖς κρίμασιν,
θαυμαστὸς ἐν ἰσχύϊ καὶ
μεγαλοπρεπείᾳ, ὁ σοφὸς ἐν τῷ
κτίζειν καὶ συνετὸς ἐν τῷ τὰ
γενόμενα ἑδράσαι, ὁ ἀγαθὸς ἐν τοῖς
ὁρωμένοις καὶ χρηστὸς ἐν τοῖς
πεποιθόσιν ἐπὶ σέ, ἐλεῆμον καὶ
οἰκτίρμον, ἄφες ἡμῖν τὰς ἀνομίας
ἡμῶν καὶ τὰς ἀδικίας καὶ τὰ
παραπτώματα καὶ πλημμελείας.

2. μὴ λογίσῃ πᾶσαν ἁμαρτίαν
δούλων σου καὶ παιδισκῶν, ἀλλὰ
καθάρισον ἡμᾶς τὸν καθαρισμὸν
τῆς σῆς ἀληθείας, καὶ κατεύθυνον
τὰ διαβήματα ἡμῶν ἐν ὁσιότητι

from them all those that love
thee through Jesus Christ thy beloved child, and through him
hast thou taught us, made us
holy, and brought us to honour.
4. We beseech thee, Master,
to be our "help and succour."
Save those of us who are in af-
fliction, have mercy on the
lowly, raise the fallen, show thy-
self to those in need, heal the
sick, turn again the wanderers of
thy people, feed the hungry,
ransom our prisoners, raise up
the weak, comfort the faint-
hearted; let all "nations know
thee, that thou art God alone,"
and that Jesus Christ is thy child,
and that "we are thy people and
the sheep of thy pasture."

60:1. For thou through thy oper-
ations didst make manifest the
eternal fabric of the world; thou,
Lord, didst create the earth.
Thou that art faithful in all generations, righteous in judgment,
wonderful in strength and majesty, wise in thy creation, and
prudent in establishing thy
works, good in the things which
are seen, and gracious among
those that trust in thee, O "merciful and compassionate," forgive
us our iniquities and unright-
eousness, and transgressions, and
shortcomings.
2. Reckon not every sin of
thy servants and handmaids, but
cleanse us with the cleansing of
thy truth, and "guide our steps
to walk in holiness of heart, to

15

καρδίας πορεύεσθαι καὶ ποιεῖν τὰ
καλὰ καὶ εὐάρεστα ἐνώπιόν σου
καὶ ἐνώπιον τῶν ἀρχόντων ἡμῶν.
3. ναί, δέσποτα, ἐπίφανον τὸ
πρόσωπόν σου ἐφ' ἡμᾶς εἰς ἀγαθὰ
ἐν εἰρήνῃ, εἰς τὸ σκεπασθῆναι ἡμᾶς
τῇ χειρί σου τῇ κραταιᾷ καὶ
ῥυσθῆναι ἀπὸ πάσης ἁμαρτίας τῷ
βραχίονί σου τῷ ὑψηλῷ, καὶ ῥῦσαι
ἡμᾶς ἀπὸ τῶν μισούντων ἡμᾶς
ἀδίκως.
4. δὸς ὁμόνοιαν καὶ εἰρήνην
ἡμῖν τε καὶ πᾶσιν τοῖς κατοικοῦσιν
τὴν γῆν, καθὼς ἔδωκας τοῖς
πατράσιν ἡμῶν, ἐπικαλουμένων σε
αὐτῶν ὁσίως ἐν πίστει καὶ
ἀληθείᾳ, ὑπηκόους γινομένους τῷ
παντοκράτορι καὶ ἐνδόξῳ ὀνόματί
σου, τοῖς τε ἄρχουσιν καὶ
ἡγουμένοις ἡμῶν ἐπὶ τῆς γῆς.

61:1. Σύ, δέσποτα, ἔδωκας τὴν
ἐξουσίαν τῆς βασιλείας αὐτοῖς διὰ
τοῦ μεγαλοπρεποῦς καὶ
ἀνεκδιηγήτου κράτους σου, εἰς τὸ
γινώσκοντας ἡμᾶς τὴν ὑπὸ σοῦ
αὐτοῖς δεδομένην δόξαν καὶ τιμὴν
ὑποτάσσεσθαι αὐτοῖς, μηδὲν
ἐναντιουμένους τῷ θελήματί σου·
οἷς δός, κύριε, ὑγίειαν, εἰρήνην,
ὁμόνοιαν, εὐστάθειαν, εἰς τὸ διέπειν
αὐτοὺς τὴν ὑπὸ σοῦ δεδομένην
αὐτοῖς ἡγεμονίαν ἀπροσκόπως.

2. σὺ γάρ, δέσποτα ἐπουράνιε,
βασιλεῦ τῶν αἰώνων, δίδως τοῖς
υἱοῖς τῶν ἀνθρώπων δόξαν καὶ
τιμὴν καὶ ἐξουσίαν τῶν ἐπὶ τῆς γῆς
ὑπαρχόντων· σύ, κύριε, διεύθυνον
τὴν βουλὴν αὐτῶν κατὰ τὸ καλὸν
καὶ εὐάρεστον ἐνώπιόν σου, ὅπως
διέποντες ἐν εἰρήνῃ καὶ πραΰτητι
εὐσεβῶς τὴν ὑπὸ σοῦ αὐτοῖς

do the things which are good
and pleasing before thee" and
before our ruler.
3. Yea, Lord, "make thy face
to shine upon us" in peace "for
our good" that we may be sheltered by thy mighty hand, and
delivered from all sin by "thy
uplifted arm," and deliver us
from them that hate us wrong-
fully.
4. Give concord and peace to
us and to all that dwell on the
earth, as thou didst give to our
fathers who called on thee in
holiness with faith and truth,
and grant that we may be obedient to thy almighty and glorious
name, and to our rulers and governors upon the earth.

61:1. Thou, Master, hast given
the power of sovereignty to them
through thy excellent and inexpressible might, that we may
know the glory and honour
given to them by thee, and be
subject to them, in nothing resisting thy will. And to them,
Lord, grant health, peace, concord, firmness that they may administer the government which
thou hast given them without
offence.
2. For thou, heavenly Master,
king of eternity, hast given to
the sons of men glory and honour and power over the things
which are on the earth; do thou,
O Lord, direct their counsels according to that which is "good
and pleasing" before thee, that
they may administer with piety

16

δεδομένην ἐξουσίαν ἵλεώ σου
τυγχάνωσιν.

3. ὁ μόνος δυνατὸς ποιῆσαι
ταῦτα καὶ περισσότερα ἀγαθὰ
μεθ᾽ ἡμῶν, σοὶ ἐξομολογούμεθα διὰ
τοῦ ἀρχιερέως καὶ προστάτου τῶν
ψυχῶν ἡμῶν Ἰησοῦ Χριστοῦ, δι᾽
οὗ σοι ἡ δόξα καὶ ἡ μεγαλωσύνη
καὶ νῦν καὶ εἰς γενεὰν γενεῶν καὶ
εἰς τοὺς αἰῶνας τῶν αἰώνων. ἀμήν.

in peace and gentleness the
power given to them by thee,
and may find mercy in thine
eyes.

3. O thou who alone art able
to do these things and far better
things for us, we praise thee
through Jesus Christ, the high
priest and guardian of our souls,
through whom be glory and
majesty to thee, both now and
for all generations and for ever
and ever. Amen.

IGNATIUS OF ANTIOCH (PSEUDO-IGNATIUS?)
Text and translation: K. Lake, ed., *The Apostolic Fathers,* vol. 1, pp. 165–277;
Sources chrétiennes 10, pp. 66–181.

Bishop and martyr under the emperor Trajan (98–117 A.D.). Epistles to churches of Asia Minor, to Polycarp of Smyrna, and to the
congregation of Rome. According to R. Joly, *Le dossier d'Ignace d'Antioche* (Brussels, 1979), the epistles may have been written in Smyrna
about 165 A.D. In the texts of these letters, one encounters a writer
of profound faith who is obsessed with the imitation of the Lord and
anxious about the unity of the congregations. Of importance is his
vision of the church, the eucharist, ministerial office in the church
(especially that of the bishop), and martyrdom. For Ignatius on the
eucharist, see his letters *Eph.* 20:2; *Rom.* 7:3; *Philad.* 4:1; *Smyrn.* 7:1;
8:1–2; cf. also *Eph.* 5:2; 13:1; *Rom.* 4:1. For baptism *Ig. Polyc.* 6:2;
cf. *Rom.* 7:2; *Eph.* 18:2; for Sunday observance, *Magn.* 9:1; for marriage *Ig. Polyc.* 5:2; for the image of the assembly around the bishop
as a choir see *Eph.* 4:1–2; cf. *Eph.* 5:1; 19:2; *Rom.* 2:2.

POLYCARP OF SMYRNA
Text and translation: K. Lake, ed., *The Apostolic Fathers,* vol. 2, pp. 307–345;
Sources chrétiennes 10, pp. 242ff.

This bishop of Asia Minor is listed here especially because of the
report of his martyrdom (156 A.D.) contained in a letter from his
congregation. This report is of significance because of its vision of
martyrdom as imitation of the *pascha* (suffering and death) of Christ,
its acquaintance with the veneration of the martyrs on their day of
death (*natale*) and because of the prayer of Polycarp at his death
(Lake, op. cit., pp. 330–333):

17

14:1b. Κύριε ὁ θεὸς ὁ
παντοκράτωρ, ὁ τοῦ ἀγαπητοῦ καὶ
εὐλογητοῦ παιδός σου Ἰησοῦ
Χριστοῦ πατήρ, δι᾽ οὗ τὴν περὶ σοῦ
ἐπίγνωσιν εἰλήφαμεν, ὁ θεὸς
ἀγγέλων καὶ δυνάμεων καὶ πάσης
τῆς κτίσεως παντός τε τοῦ γένους
τῶν δικαίων, οἳ ζῶσιν ἐνώπιόν σου·

2. εὐλογῶ σε, ὅτι ἠξίωσάς με
τῆς ἡμέρας καὶ ὥρας ταύτης, τοῦ
λαβεῖν με μέρος ἐν ἀριθμῷ τῶν
μαρτύρων ἐν τῷ ποτηρίῳ τοῦ
Χριστοῦ σου εἰς ἀνάστασιν ζωῆς
αἰωνίου ψυχῆς τε καὶ σώματος ἐν
ἀφθαρσίᾳ πνεύματος ἁγίου· ἐν οἷς
προσδεχθείην ἐνώπιόν σου σήμερον
ἐν θυσίᾳ πίονι καὶ προσδεκτῇ,
καθὼς προητοίμασας καὶ
προεφανέρωσας καὶ ἐπλήρωσας, ὁ
ἀψευδὴς καὶ ἀληθινός θεός.

3. διὰ τοῦτο καὶ περὶ πάντων
σὲ αἰνῶ, σὲ εὐλογῶ, σὲ δοξάζω διὰ
τοῦ αἰωνίου καὶ ἐπουρανίου
ἀρχιερέως Ἰησοῦ Χριστοῦ,
ἀγαπητοῦ σου παιδός, δι᾽ οὗ σοὶ
σὺν αὐτῷ καὶ πνεύματι ἁγίῳ δόξα
καὶ νῦν καὶ εἰς τοὺς μέλλοντας
αἰῶνας. ἀμήν.

14:1b. "O Lord God Almighty,
Father of thy beloved and
blessed Child, Jesus Christ,
through Whom we have received
full knowledge of thee, the God
of Angels and powers, and of
all creation, and of the whole
family of the righteous, who live
before thee!"

2. "I bless thee, that Thou
has granted me this day and
hour, that I may share, among
the number of the martyrs, in
the cup of thy Christ, for the
Resurrection to everlasting life,
both of soul and body in the
immortality of the Holy Spirit.
"And may I, today, be
received among them before
Thee, as a rich and acceptable
sacrifice, as Thou, the God who
lies not and is truth, hast prepared beforehand, and shown
forth, and fulfilled."

3. "For this reason I also
praise Thee for all things, I bless
Thee, I glorify Thee through the
everlasting and heavenly high
Priest, Jesus Christ, thy beloved
Child, through whom be glory to
Thee with him and the Holy
Spirit, both now and for the ages
that are to come. Amen."

THE SHEPHERD OF HERMAS

Text and translation: K. Lake, ed., *The Apostolic Fathers*, vol. 2, pp. 1–305;
Sources chrétiennes 53.

A book containing revelations to Hermas of Rome (100–150 A.D.);
apocalyptic in character.

A Jewish-Christian background stands behind this writer's work.
The book is of great significance for the practice of penance and
reconciliation in the early church.

ODES OF SOLOMON

Text and translation: J. H. Charlesworth, *The Odes of Solomon* (Oxford, 1973); R. Harris & A. Mingana, *The Odes and Psalms of Solomon,* 2 vols. (Manchester, 1916, 1920); W. Bauer, *Die Oden Salomos, Kleine Texte* 64 (Berlin, 1933).

Forty-two hymns discovered in a Syriac manuscript (1905), but doubtless of very early origin (2nd century?) and perhaps of Jewish-Christian provenance. These remarkable, lyric compositions are significant, among other things, for their vision of the death and resurrection of Christ (odes 28 and 42), for their possible rich baptismal allusions (e.g., water references in odes 6, 11, 30, 35, 39 and passim, together with references to the garment, 11:11; 15:8; 21:3; 25:8; to the garland-crown, 1:1–2; 5:12; 9:8–11; 17:1; 20:7f.; and to the seal, 4:7; 8:13), and for this description of the ancient posture for prayer (ode 27, Charlesworth, op. cit., p. 106):

1. I extended my hands
   And hallowed my Lord,
2. For the expansion of my hands
   Is His sign.
3. And my extension
   Is the upright cross.
   Hallelujah.

THE INSCRIPTION OF ABERCIUS

Text: C. Kirch, *Enchiridion,* no. 154. *Translation:* J. Quasten, *Patrology,* vol. 1, p. 172.

From the year 216 A.D.(?), found in Phrygia.

THE INSCRIPTION OF PECTORIUS

Text: C. Kirch, *Enchiridion,* no. 236. *Translation:* J. Quasten, *Patrology,* vol. 1, p. 174.

360 A.D.; found near Autun (France).

PASSIONS AND ACTS OF THE MARTYRS

Text and translation: H. Musurillo, *The Acts of the Christian Martyrs* (Oxford, 1972).

Especially the *Martyrdom of Polycarp* (see pp. 17–18) and that of Perpetua and Felicity and their companions.

JUSTIN

Text: E. J. Goodspeed, ed., *Die ältesten Apologeten* (Göttingen, 1914).
Translation: C. C. Richardson, ed., *Early Christian Fathers,* vol. 1 of *Library of Christian Classics* (Philadelphia, 1953).

This cosmopolitan philosopher, who was born in Palestine but finally settled in Rome, defended the Christians in two apologies in about the year 150 A.D.

First Apology 65–67 gives very important information about the order of service for baptism and eucharist and about the meaning of the eucharist. The order of service for the eucharist is complete and was apparently determinative for the celebration in later centuries.

MELITO OF SARDIS

Text and translation: Stuart George Hall, *Melito of Sardis. On Pascha* (Oxford, 1979); *Sources chrétiennes* 123.

This bishop's homily is of great importance for a knowledge of the celebration of Easter.

APOCRYPHAL AND HERETICAL WRITINGS

Translations: E. Hennecke, W. Schneemelcher, & R. McL. Wilson, *New Testament Apocrypha,* 2 vols. (London, 1963, 1965); M. R. James, *The Apocryphal New Testament* (Oxford, 1924, repr. 1955). Cf. C. Vogel, "Anaphores eucharistiques preconstantiniennes," *Augustinianum* 20, 1980, pp. 401–410.

Several of these books contain rich data concerning the celebration of baptism, *sphragis* (sealing by anointing), and eucharist.

THE WRITERS OF THE THIRD CENTURY

In the third century in both the east and the west, writers are more numerous than in the second century. In the east, one thinks of Origen, Clement of Alexandria and the early Antiochene school. Of more importance for liturgical history, however, is:

THE DIDASCALIA

Text: F. Funk, *Didascalia et Constitutiones Apostolorum* (Paderborn, 1905, repr. Turin, 1962). See further J. Quasten, *Patrology,* vol. 2, pp. 147–152; cf. also R. H. Connally, ed., *Didascalia Apostolorum* (Oxford, 1929, repr. 1969).

A book of church order from Syria in the early third century, the compiler of which is unknown but most likely of Jewish-Christian origin. The author makes use of the *Didache,* and his work is, in turn, used by the compiler of the later *Apostolic Constitutions,* books I–IV.

The *Didascalia* is of importance for its precise descriptions of the weekly liturgy and the celebration of Easter and the Sunday eucharist, and for its information about church architecture.

The writings of at least three third-century authors in the west are of great importance for the history of the liturgy:

TERTULLIAN
See E. Dekkers, *Tertullianus en de geschiedenis van de liturgie* (Turnhout, 1946).

CYPRIAN
See V. Saxer, *Vie liturgique et quotidienne à Carthago vers le milieu du III siècle* (Rome, 1969).

HIPPOLYTUS
Text and translation: B. Botte, *La Tradition Apostolique de saint Hippolyte* (Münster, 1963, 1972). English translation, with introduction to the complicated textual history: G. J. Cuming, *Hippolytus: A Text for Students,* Grove Liturgical Study, no. 8 (Bramcote, 1976). See also Gregory Dix & Henry Chadwick, eds., *The Apostolic Tradition of St. Hippolytus of Rome* (London, 1968).

Hippolytus lived in Rome in the first half(?) of the third century. He was a rigorist in such matters as penance and marriage and, therefore, separated himself from bishop Callistus of Rome. Reconciled with the congregation of Rome about 235 A.D., Hippolytus is thought to have died as a martyr. He wrote the important liturgical document, the *Apostolic Tradition,* which contained detailed data about the celebration of baptism, the eucharist, ordinations, the *agape* meal, daily prayer, and a variety of blessings.

C. SUMMARIES OF THE LITURGICAL DATA

1. THE JEWISH BACKGROUND
Of fundamental significance for Christian worship is the genre of prayer called *berakah*. *Berakoth* are acts of praiseful remembrance and thanksgiving in which God is named and God's deeds are remembered and confessed, especially the deeds of creation and covenant. For the Christian, this meant preeminently God's deed in Jesus Christ, the risen Messiah and Son of God, and God's grace and continued faithfulness are besought for the congregation or the individual. A *berakah* is a prayer of anamnesis, in which past and present are interwoven in a kind of associative thinking and in which trust for the future is confessed because of God, whose name occurs

21

yet again at the end of the prayer (doxology). In the Christian tradition, this doxology is trinitarian, to the Father through the Son in the Holy Spirit, or to the Father and the Son and the Holy Spirit. This genre of prayer is found in the psalms, in the Jewish table prayers, in the morning and evening prayers of the synagogue, and in the whole Christian tradition (e.g., the songs of Zechariah and of Mary, which have become a part of Christian morning and evening prayer). For information regarding the *berakah*, see Joseph Heinemann, *Prayer in the Talmud* (Berlin & New York, 1977) and M. Kadushin, *Worship and Ethics* (New York, 1964). The latter asserts that the *berakah* is the result of "phenomenal experience," the experience of God's presence in the human person and in the surrounding world, and of "meditative experience," the consideration of God's salvation in history. The transition from *berakah* to Christian thanksgiving was, however, not a simple one; see R. Ledogar, *Acknowledgement* (Rome, 1968); James M. Robinson, "Die Hodajot-Formel in Gebet und Hymnus des Frühchristentums," in *Apophoreta* (Haenchen Festschrift, BZNW 30, 1964, pp. 194–235); and Thomas Talley, "From Berakah to Eucharistia: A Reopening Question," (*Worship* 50:2, 1976, pp. 115–137).

In the Jewish liturgy of the synagogue, the *Shema* (Dt 6:4–9; 11:13–21; Nm 15:37–41), spoken every morning and evening, is surrounded by a set of *berakoth*. In the morning, for example, it is preceded by two *berakoth*—*Yotzer* (cf. Is 45:7), the blessing for the light, and *Ahavah*, the blessing for the Torah—and followed by the blessing for the deliverance from Egypt (*Ge'ullah*). Fragments of these blessings may have been absorbed into the Christian tradition, for example in the old lauds (cf. A. Verheul, "De dienst van het woord in synagoge en christendom," in *Corona Gratiarum*, E. Dekkers Festschrift, Brugge, 1975, pp. 3–49).

Also of importance is the *tephillah* ("the prayer"), also called the *amidah* ("standing prayers") or *shemoneh-esreh* ("the eighteen"), the series of *berakoth*, eighteen in number (seven on the Sabbath), that forms a central part of synagogue liturgy. These prayers are said silently while standing, with the leader speaking aloud and all responding with the *Amen*. The *tephillah* has also been retained in the Christian tradition—in the letter of Clement, in the *Didache*, and in the genre of intercessions or prayers of the faithful (cf. C. Bouman, *Communis oratio*, Utrecht, 1959). The third of these *berakoth* is the *kedushah* (cf. Is 6:3); the relationship between *kedushah* and the Sanctus in the Christian tradition of the eucharist is contested.

Of similar importance is the significance of imagery in Jewish and Christian tradition. Humanity catches a glimpse of the glory of God and mirrors it in a human manner, always indirect, veiled, for one cannot truly gaze upon the glory of God. For the Christian, this mirroring has grown more intense as a result of the resurrection of Jesus, the complete image of the Father. In this mirroring, the believer looks toward the moment when the glory of God may be seen directly, with unveiled face. So also the liturgy in the temple, the synagogue, or the congregation is a reflection of the glory of the heavenly worship and a gazing forward to the fulfillment of time. Here are also to be found the roots of Christian typology. In the iconography of the early church, images always have multiple meanings; they evoke a deeper reality.

Finally, indirect Jewish influence can also be traced in the manner of reading from the scriptures, in the use of psalms, and in the responsorial manner of their singing (leader and people in turn; prayer and response).

2. DAILY PRAYER

Judaism knew three hours of prayer: morning prayer (*tephillat sharar*), afternoon prayer (*tephillat minhah*), which is probably an anticipated evening prayer, and evening prayer (*tephillat ha'erev*), which was introduced later when the evening sacrifice of the Temple and its corresponding prayer hour were transferred to the afternoon. Morning and evening prayer are known in the gospels (Mk 1:35; 6:46; cf. Lk 10:27) and appear to have been accorded great value by Christians in the later traditions. Lauds (morning) and vespers (evening) became a universal custom: communal prayers of praise and thanksgiving together with intercessions. Private prayers at specified hours also occurred: at the third, sixth, and ninth hours (roughly 9 A.M., noon, and 3 P.M.), before retiring, and during the night. The frequency with which this unwritten rule was kept was determined by the zeal with which a person practiced the faith. But churchly writers nonetheless had to insist upon these prayers; apparently people did not accept the practice all that easily (cf. M. Cassien & B. Botte, eds., *La prière des heures*, Paris, 1968, pp. 17–84).

The best information is given to us by Tertullian (*De orat.* 25), who speaks of required morning and evening prayers and of prayers during the day, and by Cyprian (*De or. dom.* 29, 34, 35, 36) and in the *Apostolic Tradition* of Hippolytus (35, 41). This last source speaks of prayers during the day and night, but does not mention evening prayer. It does mention the so-called *lucernarium* (*Apost. Trad.* 25), the blessing for the light in the evening (albeit not every evening) when the lamp was brought in. This practice goes back to the light ceremony in the Jewish family at the beginning of the sabbath and is a practice preserved in the later tradition of the church in the procession with the paschal candle and the singing of the paschal proclamation or *laus cerei* at the Easter vigil. The daily morning service, recommended to the faithful, included the reading of and reflection on scripture. The data thus indicate a daily practice that was, however, primarily private. Developed forms of communal prayer are found only later, after the peace of the church.

Very old prayers, hymnic texts, still exist that go back to this time: or example, the well-known Greek evening hymn, stemming perhaps from the second century, for the welcoming of the light while darkness is falling:

Φῶς ἱλαρὸν ἁγίας δόξης,	Joyous light of glory of the im-
ἀθανάτου πατρὸς οὐρανίου, ἁγίου,	mortal Father; heavenly, holy,
μάκαρος, Ἰησοῦ Χριστὲ, ἐλθόντες	blessed Jesus Christ. We have
ἐπὶ τὴν ἡλίου δύσιν, ἰδόντες φῶς	come to the setting of the sun,
ἑσπερινὸν, ὑμνοῦμεν Πατέρα καὶ	and we look to the evening light.
Υἱον και Ἅγιον Πνεῦμα Θεόν.	We sing to God, the Father, Son,
Ἄξιόν σε ἐν πᾶσι καίροις ὑμνεῖσθαι	and Holy Spirit: You are worthy
φωναῖς ὁσίαις, Ὑιὲ Θεοῦ, ζωὴν ὁ	of being praised with pure voices
διδούς διὸ ὁ κόσμος σε δοξάζει.	forever. O Son of God, O giver
	of life: The universe proclaims
	your glory.

Text: J. Julian, *A Dictionary of Hymnology*, 2nd. ed. (London, 1907, repr. New York, 1957). *Translation: Lutheran Book of Worship* (Minneapolis & Philadelphia, 1978).

A further example is found in the hymn *Doxa en hupsistois*, well-known in the west from its later place in the eucharistic liturgy, but perhaps going back to the second or third century. The oldest Latin text (Bangor Antiphonal, 690 A.D.) is translated in J. Jungmann, *The Mass of the Roman Rite*, 1-vol. ed., pp. 232–233. One should note the difference from the later mass text.

"Glory to God in the highest, and on earth peace to men of good will. We praise thee; we bless thee; we adore thee; we glorify thee; we magnify thee. We give thee thanks because of thy great mercy,

24

Lord, heavenly king, God the Father, almighty Lord, only-begotten Son, Jesus Christ, Holy Spirit of God. And we all say Amen. Lord, Son of God the Father, lamb of God, who takest away the sin of the world, have mercy on us. Receive our prayer; who sittest at the right hand of God the Father, have mercy on us. For thou alone art holy. Thou alone Lord, Thou alone glorious with the Holy Spirit in the glory of God the Father. Amen."

At this time, then, the structure of a liturgy of prayer is already present *in nuce* and is developed and expanded later in east and west. It begins with antiphonal versicles, continues with the singing of a psalm (and/or a hymn) and then with intercessions for God's congregation and for the world, and perhaps concludes with the Lord's prayer and (as in the *Didache*) its final doxology. There is evidence (*Apost. Trad.* 41) for the reading of scripture in the morning, although it was not every day and was not required of everyone. Although the eucharist was the center of the community's concern (on Sundays there was an assembly for the breaking of the bread), it was understood that during the week there were prayers at certain hours. Praise was not limited to the eucharist alone, but could also resound in the Christians' thanksgiving, their morning and evening "sacrifice" (Ps 63, 141). Knowledge of this Christian tradition of prayer has become available to us more fully through the immeasurable riches of the later written sources and their treasure of prayer and hymn texts.

3. FESTIVALS AND CELEBRATIONS THROUGHOUT THE YEAR

The celebration of the sabbath, which began on Friday evening with the *Kiddush*, the blessing for the arrival of the day, and with the blessing for the light, consisted of prayer, reading, and meditation, and was filled with a strong expectation of the coming of the Day of the Lord. Christians also kept the day in this way. Paul himself came to the synagogue on the sabbath. On the other hand, there had very quickly developed, perhaps among Gentile Christians, a critical stance in regard to the sabbath, as well as a reevaluation of Jewish observances in general, a sign of the growing tension between Jews and Christians. The Christians began to interpret the eschatological hope differently: the Messiah has come, is risen from the death he suffered at the hands of Jewish leaders and the Romans, and shall come to bring all to share in his life with God (see P. Grelot, "Du sabbat juif au dimanche chrétien," *La Maison-Dieu* 123, 1975, pp.

79–107; cf. Heb 3:1–4:13). For the Christians, then, the sabbath soon became a thing of the past because it was Jewish (Col 2:16ff.) and belonged to the old dispensation. There was even opposition to sabbath-keeping as being non-Christian: *"sabbatizontes"* are those who keep the sabbath (*Ign. Mag.* 9:1–3, and the *Epistle of Barnabas*). Christians must be free of the Jewish law and free to go the new way. It must nonetheless be understood that among Jewish Christians, the keeping of the sabbath continued for some time, but even they came to lay aside the custom eventually.

Sunday

Whatever may be the facts about the sabbath-keeping, there is incontrovertible evidence of the celebration of the first day of the week among the earliest Christians. This day, also called Sunday and regarded as an ordinary workday in the economy and society of the time, was for Christians the day of the remembrance of the risen Lord (Rv 1:10; 1 Cor 16:1; Acts 20:7–12). A direct or indirect mention of Sunday is found in many early writings: *Didache* 14:1; *Ign. Mag.* 9:1; Tertullian; Justin; Hippolytus; *Didascalia* (cf. W. Rordorf, *Sunday*, London, 1968). On Sundays in Bithynia, in Asia Minor, during the early second century, the Christians assembled in the early morning, presumably for a prayer service, and in the evening again for a shared meal, according to the governor Pliny (*Epp.* 10:96). In the year 112 A.D., in a letter to the emperor Trajan he states: "They [the lapsed Christians who had been taken as prisoners and who provided Pliny with his information] assured me that their fault or their error amounted only to this, that they regularly on a fixed day (*stato die*) came together before light to sing antiphonally a song to Christ as to a god (*carmen . . . Christo quasi deo*) and to bind themselves by an oath (*sacramento*). . . . After this was done they departed and assembled once again to hold a meal, an ordinary innocent meal . . . ." (text in C. Kirch, *Enchiridion*, no. 28; cf. translation in J. Stevenson, *A New Eusebius*, pp. 13–14; cf. also W. Rordorf, op. cit., pp. 107, 202ff., 251ff.).

Perhaps the meal of the Lord (*kuriakon deipnon*) influenced the origin of Sunday (*kuriakē hēmera*). The community gathered for the meal on the day on which, according to the testimony of the disciples, the Lord had held a meal with his followers after his resurrection. The term *kuriakon*, indicating that which pertains to the *Risen One*, was transferred from the meal to the day on which the meal was celebrated, and later evoked a theology of the Day of

26

the Lord: the fulfillment of the Day of Yahweh is realized in the resurrection of the Son, the Risen One, the *kurios*, Christ.

How was Sunday celebrated? It was an ordinary workday and so times for celebration had to be chosen outside the pattern of labor: very early in the morning and in the evening. Perhaps at first a service of prayer was held in the morning and the meal or the eucharist took place in the evening. This evening meal, however, soon came to be forbidden by governmental authorities (or so it appears; see Pliny's letter referred to above) because such horrible rumors had circulated concerning it or because "clubs" were generally forbidden. The meal was then shifted to the morning—certainly evidence that Christians held the celebration of the meal of the Lord to be the heart of Sunday. The Sunday morning celebration of the eucharist was the general tradition in Rome in the year 150 A.D., according to the description of Justin (*Apol.* 1:65–67), and that was very likely the case elsewhere. In later centuries, this image of Sunday was more accentuated but not essentially changed, even when Sunday became an official day of rest. Thus the heart of Christian celebration from ancient times has been Sunday in its week-by-week return. The foundations for this practice were laid in this ancient period and reach back to apostolic times: the disciples' experience of the Risen One still resonates in our celebration of Sunday.

It seems imprecise to call Sunday the "weekly Easter" because Easter, the annual feast, has a differently nuanced character and significance, as shall be explained below.

During the week, special attention was given to Wednesday and Friday. References to this are found already in *Didache* 8 and in the *Shepherd of Hermas, Sim.* 5:1:1, and in several places in Tertullian. These days, called station days (see C. Mohrmann, "Statio," *Vigiliae Christianae* 7, 1953, pp. 221–245), were days for fasting (already known among the Jews but observed on Tuesday and Thursday) which, in relationship to Sunday, were evenly distributed in the week. One fasted until the ninth hour (about 3 P.M., i.e., until about dinnertime) and broke this fast, according to Tertullian, by communing from the bread that remained from the Sunday (or daily?) eucharist and that had been taken home (*De orat.* 19; cf. also *Apost. Trad.* 37). It remains unclear whether eucharist was indeed celebrated on station days. The tradition of North Africa, however, is not to be assumed as general practice in all the churches. Further, it is not known whether at this time Saturday already had received its special character as an introduction to Sunday, as soon would become the case in the east.

The Paschal Feast

In this period, the data available to us about the celebration of Easter are difficult to interpret. The New Testament certainly contains material concerning a Christian interpretation of the Jewish *pascha* (1 Cor 5:6–8; 1 Pt 1:19; Jn 1:29, 36; 19:36; Rv 5:6, 9, 12; 12:11), but the New Testament says nothing about the actual celebration of the paschal feast.

We do find material about this celebration in Tertullian (*De bapt.* 19), in *Didascalia* 5:19–20, in the paschal homily of Melito of Sardis, in the paschal homily of Pseudo-Hippolytus (*Sources chrétiennes* 27), in Origen, and in Hippolytus (*Apost. Trad.*). But we are best informed by Eusebius in his church history (*Hist. Eccl.* V, 23–24), where he gives a report of the Easter controversy in the second century, a controversy about the date and the significance of the paschal feast in the churches. We give here this important text *in extenso*:

"23. At that time no small controversy arose because all the dioceses of Asia thought it right, as though by more ancient tradition, to observe for the feast of the Saviour's passover the fourteenth day of the moon, on which the Jews had been commanded to kill the lamb. Thus it was necessary to finish the fast on that day, whatever day of the week it might be. Yet it was not the custom to celebrate in this manner in the churches throughout the rest of the world, for from apostolic tradition they kept the custom which still exists that it is not right to finish the fast on any day save that of the resurrection of our Saviour. Many meetings and conferences with bishops were held on this point, and all unanimously formulated in their letters the doctrine of the church for those in every country that the mystery of the Lord's resurrection from the dead could be celebrated on no day save Sunday, and that on that day alone we should celebrate the end of the paschal fast. There is still extant a writing of those who were convened in Palestine, over whom presided Theophilus, bishop of the diocese of Caesarea, and Narcissus, bishop of Jerusalem; and there is similarly another from those in Rome on the same controversy, which gives Victor as bishop; and there is one of the bishops of Pontus over whom Palmas presided as the oldest; and of the dioceses of Gaul, of which Irenaeus was bishop; and yet others of those in Osrhoene and the cities there; and particularly of Bacchyllus, the bishop of the church of Corinth; and of very many more who expressed one and the same opinion and judgement, and gave the same vote.

"24. These issued the single definition which was given above; but the bishops in Asia were led by Polycrates in persisting that it was necessary to keep the custom which had been handed down to them of old. Polycrates himself in a document which he addressed to Victor and to the church of Rome, expounds the tradition which had come to him as follows. 'Therefore we keep the day undeviatingly, neither adding nor taking away, for in Asia great luminaries sleep, and they will rise on the day of the coming of the Lord, when he shall come with glory from heaven and seek out all the saints. Such were Philip of the twelve apostles, and two of his daughters who grew old as virgins, who sleep in Hierapolis, and another daughter of his, who lived in the Holy Spirit, rests at Ephesus. Moreover, there is also John, who lay on the Lord's breast, who was a priest wearing the breastplate, and a martyr, and teacher. He sleeps at Ephesus. And there is also Polycarp at Smyrna, both bishop and martyr, and Thraseas, both bishop and martyr, from Eumenaea, who sleeps in Smyrna. And why should I speak of Sagaris, bishop and martyr, who sleeps at Laodicaea, and Papirius, too, the blessed, and Melito the eunuch, who lived entirely in the Holy Spirit, who lies in Sardis, waiting for the visitation from heaven when he will rise from the dead? All these kept the fourteenth day of the passover according to the gospel, never swerving, but following according to the rule of the faith. And I also, Polycrates, the least of you all, live according to the tradition of my kinsmen, and some of them have I followed. For seven of my family were bishops and I am the eighth, and my kinsmen even kept the day when the people put away the leaven. Therefore, brethren, I who have lived sixty-five years in the Lord and conversed with brethren from every country, and have studied all holy Scripture, am not afraid of threats, for they have said who were greater than I, "It is better to obey God rather than men." '

"He continues about the bishops who when he wrote were with him and shared his opinion, and says thus: 'And I could mention the bishops who are present whom you required me to summon, and I did so. If I should write their names they would be many multitudes; and they knowing my feeble humanity, agreed with the letter, knowing that not in vain is my head grey, but that I have ever lived in Christ Jesus.'

"Upon this Victor, who presided at Rome, immediately tried to cut off from the common unity the dioceses of all Asia, together with the adjacent churches, on the ground of heterodoxy, and he indited letters announcing that all the Christians there were absolutely excommunicated. But by no means all were pleased by this, so they issued counter-requests to him to consider the cause of peace and unity and love towards his neighbours. Their words are extant, sharply rebuking Victor. Among them too Irenaeus, writing in the name of the Christians whose leader he was in Gaul, though he recommends that the mystery of the Lord's resurrection be observed only on the Lord's day, yet nevertheless exhorts Victor suitably and at length not to excommunicate whole churches of God for following a tradition of ancient custom, and continues as follows: 'For the controversy is not only about the day, but also about the actual character of the fast; for some think that they ought to fast one day, others two, others even more, some count their day as forty hours, day and night. And such variation of observance did not begin in our own time, but much earlier, in the days of our predecessors who, it would appear, disregarding strictness maintained a practice which is simple and yet allows for personal preference, establishing it for the future, and none the less all these lived in peace, and we also live in peace with one another and the disagreement in the fast confirms our agreement in the faith.'

"He adds to this a narrative which I may suitably quote, running as follows: 'Among these too were the presbyters before Soter, who presided over the church of which you are now the leader, I mean Anicetus and Pius and Telesphorus and Xystus. They did not themselves observe it, nor did they enjoin it on those who followed them, and though they did not keep it they were none the less at peace with those from the dioceses in which it was observed when they came to them, although to observe it was more objectionable to those who did not do so. And no one was ever rejected for this reason, but the presbyters before you who did not observe it sent the Eucharist to those from other dioceses who did; and when the blessed Polycarp was staying in Rome in the time of Anicetus, though they disagreed a little about some other things as well, they immediately made peace, having no wish for strife between them on this matter. For neither was Anicetus able to persuade Polycarp not to observe it, inasmuch as he had always done so in company with John the disciple of our Lord and the other apostles with whom he had associated; nor did Polycarp persuade Anicetus to observe it, for he said that he ought to keep the custom of those who were presbyters before him. And under these circumstances they communicated with each other, and in the church Anicetus yielded the celebration of the Eucharist to Polycarp, obviously out of respect, and they parted from each other in peace, for the peace of the whole church was kept both by those who observed and by those who did not.'

"And Irenaeus, who deserved his name, making an eirenicon in this way, gave exhortations of this kind for the peace of the church and served as its ambassador, for in letters he discussed the various views on the issue which had been raised, not only with Victor but also with many other rulers of churches."

Translation: K. Lake, ed. & trans., *Eusebius, Ecclesiastical History*, vol. 1 (Cambridge & London, 1926), pp. 503–513.

Thus already in the second century there was a struggle among the Christian communities that threatened to lead to schism. It concerned the date and the significance of the observance of Easter, of *pascha*/passover. Should Easter be celebrated on 14/15 Nisan as was the custom with the Jewish *pascha*? The Christians who followed this practice are called *quartodecimans*, "fourteeners," and they were found primarily in Asia Minor. Or should the Christian *pascha* be coupled with Sunday, the day of the resurrection? Should the passover be celebrated at all? It was, after all, according to some Christian conceptions, the feast at which the Jews had killed Jesus.

The interpretation of the data made available to us in Eusebius is not an easy task. Modern authors hold differing opinions. A good survey of the question is found in Cantalamessa's introduction to his collection of the ancient texts relevant to the paschal observance: *Ostern in der alten Kirche (Traditio Christiana IV*, Bern, 1981).

Some scholars (Holl, Huber) are of the opinion that in Asia Minor Easter was celebrated annually, but that in other communities (such as in Rome and Palestine) the feast was unknown. Only after 135 A.D. would it have been slowly introduced in those places. According to this view, the origin of Easter in Asia Minor is to be connected with the development of Christian theology, with a growing reflection upon the particular character of Christian proclamation in relationship to Judaism and Old Testament texts. The idea arose that the history of God's salvation in Jesus was already hidden in the salvation history of the Old Testament. For that reason Christians could celebrate the passover, but a passover now filled with a new significance. Indeed, they could read and understand Exodus 12 even better than it had been understood before Christ's death: the paschal lamb that is slain is Christ himself (1 Cor 5:7).

Other scholars (Mohrmann, Lohse, Cantalamessa) are of the opinion that the Christian paschal festival, which was most likely of apostolic origin, was celebrated in all the primitive congregations, but that differing accents had developed. The most noticeable difference between the two traditions would have been that while the Christians of Asia Minor celebrated *pascha* with the Jews on 14/15 Nisan, the other congregations observed it on the first following Sunday. In both traditions, central emphasis would have fallen on the Christian reading of the account of the paschal lamb in Exodus 12, but the Roman-Palestinian tradition would have connected this reading with the celebration of the resurrection of Jesus. In that tradition it would have seemed right that the unique reality of the resurrection, this new thing that had not been prefigured in the Old Testament, should be commemorated in the framework of Sunday.

In any case, it should be clear that the earliest Christian *pascha* was focused upon the memorial of Jesus' suffering, death, and resurrection—it was a "christological" feast. His "passover" was the core of this memorial day that annually recurred and that, together with the weekly celebration of Sunday, formed the beginning of the so-called church year. The Greek *pascha*, a translation of the Hebrew *pesach* ("passover"), was even understood in relationship to *paschein* ("to suffer"). The Greek *pascha* and the Latin *passio* largely determined the significance of the feast, but they did that as they were conjoined with the notion of victory: passing through suffering and death, the Lord has conquered and has restored life itself.

It is possible that the chronology of the passion account in the fourth gospel influenced the developing Christian celebration. Some congregations observed *pascha* just as it is described in that Gospel— on 14 Nisan. According to John, at the moment the paschal lambs were being slaughtered Jesus died on the cross (John 19:31–37), and therefore Christians fasted that day and spent the night listening to the scripture and (after the ending of the Jewish paschal meal) breaking the bread (eucharist). The Roman-Palestinian tradition went yet a step further and held to the schema of the days as found in the gospels. On Friday the Lord died; on Sunday, the first day after the great sabbath, he was raised. These Christians then drew Sunday into their paschal observance.

The Roman-Palestinian tradition was finally to win out, to be continued into the succeeding periods in liturgical history and to become the basis for further development. The quartodeciman tradition disappeared, partly through the decisions of the Council of

Nicea. By then that tradition seemed too much marked by judaizing to be acceptable to Christians.

Besides these two paschal traditions, we must also mention another interpretation of the Christian *pascha* that came later, to be sure, but was no less influential, an interpretation rooted in the Alexandrian tradition and going back to Origen. Origen saw Easter not so much as *pascha* but as *diabasis* (*transitus*, passage). Easter was the festival of the faithful who through Christ make the passage from sin to virtue, from death to life. Christian life was a spiritual exodus out of the slavery to sin, to Satan, and to Satan's dark power. Easter was dying and rising with Christ: the baptismal theology of Paul (Romans 6) came to stand at the center of interest. The historical dimension of the exodus was obscured and spiritualized. In the succeeding period of liturgical history, Origen would come to have a great influence on the Cappadocians in the east and Ambrose of Milan in the west. The attention would be gradually shifted from Exodus 12 to Exodus 13–14, and *pascha* would be observed as the passage through the sea, an emphasis in the commemoration of the feast that was also known in Jewish circles (cf. Philo of Alexandria).

The actual celebration of the paschal feast would have proceeded as follows. There was strict fasting before the vigil for one or two days, forty hours, or even a week. Then the community came together in the night to listen to the scripture. Certainly Exodus 12 was read and commented upon (the homily of Melito of Sardis shows this). Perhaps there was also reading from Genesis 22 (Isaac), Isaiah 53 (the Suffering Servant) and a harmonized passion history taken from the four gospels. Toward morning the vigil was concluded with the celebration of the meal of the Lord (participation in the meal was the actual breaking of the fast), and this signified the transition to the celebration of the joyful fifty days, the *pentecost*. The eucharist was "the earnest of our resurrection" (cf. *Didascalia* 21, ed. Vööbus, pp. 199–200). The *pentecost* itself was resurrection time: prayers were said standing and memorial was made of the giving of the Spirit, of the ascension, of the *parousia*, but none of this yet specifically connected to the fortieth and fiftieth days. The fifty days of Easter were as *one* day (a *laetissimum spatium*, says Tertullian in *De bapt.* 19).

Was Christian initiation (baptism and anointing) celebrated in the paschal night? In this period we do not yet see *pascha* conceived of as *the* baptismal night, although that will certainly be the case in the following period. Baptizing did take place in the paschal vigil (cf.

Tertullian, *De bapt.* 19; Hippolytus, *Apost. Trad.* 21) but that was not the exclusive practice. Perhaps Easter as baptismal night did originate and grow under the influence of the vision of Origen, but initially the theology of Paul (Romans 6) played no especially great role (cf. A. Benoit, *Le baptême chrétien au second siècle,* Paris, 1953).

4. THE SACRAMENTS

Baptism and Confirmation (Bathing and Anointing)
The meaning of Christian initiation is integral to the New Testament, but the first full description of a baptismal rite comes only after the *Didache* (in which the baptismal formula is reported, 7:1, and baptism in running water is emphasized, 7:2) and after the brief account in Justin's *Apology* 61. The rite itself is finally found in the *Apostolic Tradition* of Hippolytus, chapters 15 to 21. We do not know to what extent this ritual was followed either in Rome or elsewhere, but the description itself is complete. According to the *Apostolic Tradition,* baptism extends over a period of time. The description begins by listing who may and who may not be baptized, that is to say, which professions are excluded from entry into the Christian community. One should recall that Christianity found itself in a social situation in which the behavior of Christians was watched rigorously. (One might also recall, however, the struggle between Hippolytus and Callistus over who might be readmitted to the community, in which Hippolytus took the rigorist position.) There follows a description of the reception into the so-called catechumenate, i.e., a time of instruction by catechists lasting several years: the catechumens were introduced to the elements of Christian doctrine and ethics (both of which were significantly different from the social norms of the day). During this catechumenate, prayer services were held for the catechumens wherein they received a laying on of hands. After the time of instruction and an examination of the candidate's advancement in knowledge and life in the Christian faith, there followed a stage later called the time of the *electi* (or *competentes*), that is, those who had been found worthy to be baptized. This stage came before the actual baptismal celebration during the paschal vigil (and later it coincided with the six-week fast). It was a time of common prayer, of inquiry into the worthiness of the candidates, of laying on of hands and exorcisms (the later "scrutinies"); that is, it was a time of combat with evil in company with the whole congregation and a time of inquiry into the degree of the candidate's conversion. This period was closed with the actual celebration of baptism, which included

the renunciation of Satan (in concrete terms, the renunciation of one's pagan past), the confession of faith during the baptism in the pool, the laying on of hands and anointing of head and body, the kiss of peace, and the celebration of the eucharist with the congregation. A prayer of thanksgiving was made over the water of baptism (as also over the oil of anointing); specimens of such prayers from a later period are still extant. This all occurred preferably during the paschal vigil, but not exclusively so.

What is clear is that for Hippolytus, baptism was no one-shot affair, but a way of conversion that was ritually expressed and supported. The personal decision of the candidate was important, even determinative of many of the components of the ritual; happily, ritual and faith within a community went hand in hand.

The gift of the Holy Spirit (only much later called "confirmation" in the western tradition) came to ritual expression in the laying on of the bishop's hands, anointing, and the signing of a cross (called *sphragis*) on the forehead. But baptism in water and anointing with the Holy Spirit were still clearly part of a single celebration, belonging indissolubly together. Here we should also point out the double anointing after baptism by presbyter and bishop, a typically Roman practice. We can summarize by simply quoting the full text of Hippolytus:

"And when those who are to receive baptism are chosen, let their life be examined: have they lived good lives when they were catechumens? Have they honoured the widows? Have they visited the sick? Have they done every kind of good work? And when those who brought them bear witness to each; 'He has' let them hear the gospel.

"From the time that they were set apart, let hands be laid on them daily while they are exorcized. And when the day of their baptism approaches, the bishop shall exorcize each one of them, in order that he may know whether he is pure. And if anyone is not good or not pure, let him be put aside, because he has not heard the word with faith, for it is impossible that the Alien should hide himself for ever.

"Those who are to be baptized should be instructed to bathe and wash themselves on the Thursday. And if a woman is in her period, let her be put aside, and receive baptism another day. Those who are to receive baptism shall fast on the Friday. On the Saturday those who are to receive baptism shall be gathered in one place at the bishop's decision. They shall all be told to pray and kneel. And he shall lay his hand on them and exorcize all alien spirits, that they may flee out of them and never return into them. And when he has finished exorcizing them, he shall breathe on their faces; and when he has signed their foreheads, ears, and noses, he shall raise them up.

"And they shall spend the whole night in vigil; they shall be read to and instructed. Those who are to be baptized shall not bring with them any other thing, except what each brings for the eucharist. For it is suitable that he who has been made worthy should offer an offering then.

"At the time when the cock crows, first let prayer be made over the water. Let the water be flowing in the font or poured over it. Let it be thus unless there is some necessity; if the necessity is permanent and urgent, use what water you can find. They shall take off their clothes. Baptize the little ones first. All those who can speak for themselves shall do so. As for those who cannot speak for themselves, their parents or someone from their family shall speak for them. Then baptize the men, and lastly the women, who shall have loosened all their hair, and laid down the gold and silver ornaments which they have on them. Let no-one take any alien object down into the water.

"And at the time fixed for baptizing, the bishop shall give thanks over the oil, which he puts in a vessel: one calls it 'oil of thanksgiving.' And he shall also take other oil and exorcize it: one calls it 'oil of exorcism.' And a deacon takes the oil of exorcism and stands on the priest's left; and another deacon takes the oil of thanksgiving and stands on the priest's right. And when the priest takes each one of those who are to receive baptism, he shall bid him renounce, saying:

'I renounce you, Satan, and all your service and all your works.'

"And when each one has renounced all this, he shall anoint him with the oil of exorcism, saying to him:

'Let every spirit depart far from you.'

"And in this way he shall hand him over naked to the bishop or the priest who stands by the water to baptize. In the same way a deacon shall descend with him into the water and say, helping him to say:

'I believe in one God, the Father almighty. . . .'

"And he who receives shall say according to all this:

'I believe in this way.'

36

"And the giver, having his hand placed on his head, shall baptize him once.

"And then he shall say:

'Do you believe in Christ Jesus, the Son of God, who was born from the holy Spirit from the Virgin Mary, and was crucified under Pontius Pilate, and died, and rose again on the third day alive from the dead, and ascended into heaven, and sits at the right hand of the Father, and will come to judge the living and the dead?'

"And when he has said, 'I believe,' he shall be baptized again.

"And he shall say again:

'Do you believe in the holy Spirit and the holy Church and the resurrection of the flesh?'

"Then he who is being baptized shall say, 'I believe,' and thus he shall be baptized a third time.

"And then, when he has come up, he shall be anointed from the oil of thanksgiving by the presbyter, who says:

'I anoint you with holy oil in the name of Jesus Christ.'

"And so each of them shall wipe themselves and put on their clothes, and then they shall enter into the church.

"And the bishop shall lay his hands on them and invoke, saying:

'Lord God, you have made them worthy to receive remission of sins through the laver of regeneration of the holy Spirit; send upon them your grace, that they may serve you according to your will; for to you is glory, to Father and Son with the holy Spirit in the holy Church, both now and to the ages of ages. Amen.'

"Then, pouring the oil of thanksgiving from his hand and placing it on his head, he shall say:

'I anoint you with holy oil in God the Father almighty and Christ Jesus and the holy Spirit.'

"And having signed him on the forehead, he shall give him a kiss and say:

'The Lord be with you.'

"And he who has been signed shall say:

'And with your spirit.'

"So let him do with each one. And then they shall pray together with all the people: they do not pray with the faithful until they have carried out all these things. And when they have prayed, they shall give the kiss of peace.

"And then the offering shall be presented by the deacons to the bishop. . . ."

Apostolic Tradition 20–21. *Translation:* G. Cuming, *Hippolytus: A Text for Students* (Bramcote, 1976).

Material concerning the practice and components of baptism is also to be found in Tertullian: see especially his tractate *De baptismo* (text and translation: E. Evans, *Tertullian's Homily on Baptism*, London, 1964), and, further, *De corona* III:5–7; *De carnis resurrectione* 8; and *Apol.* 23:16. The basic parts of the liturgy and perhaps even its order are essentially the same in Tertullian's writings as in the *Apostolic Tradition*, as appears in this text:

. . . sed et caro abluitur ut anima emaculetur, caro unguitur ut anima consecretur, caro signatur ut et anima muniatur, caro manus impositione adumbratur ut et anima spiritu illuminetur, caro corpore et sanguine Christi vescitur ut et anima de deo saginetur.

The flesh is washed that the soul may be made spotless: the flesh is anointed that the soul may be consecrated: the flesh is signed that the soul too may be protected: the flesh is overshadowed by the imposition of the hand that the soul also may be illumined by the Spirit: the flesh is fed on the body and blood of Christ so that the soul as well may be made full of God.

De carn. res. 8:3; text from E. Evans, *Tertullian's Treatise on the Resurrection* (London, 1960); translation altered from E. C. Whittaker, *Documents of the Baptismal Liturgy*, 2nd. ed. (London, 1970), p. 10.

Thus, by this time in at least two centers in the west, a complete baptismal ritual possessing several components had developed. A bath in running water (by pouring or immersion), laying on of hands, and anointing and signing with a cross are all mentioned. It is likely that all of these components were also known to the Jews and perhaps became the common property of the Christian congregations by way of the first Jewish Christians. To what extent the pagan environment influenced the rites cannot be said with certainty. It is not likely, however, that it did so at this period since the Christian churches sought consciously to remain aloof from pagan practices. The practice of giving milk and honey to the newly baptized most

38

likely should not be seen as having been due to the pagan environment. Later the customs of the neighboring religions would indeed leave their mark.

From the east we also have data that are of later date than the description of Hippolytus, but that must at least be placed in the third century. There is, for example, *Didascalia* III:12(16) (text in Funk, op. cit., p. 208; translation in Whitaker, op. cit., pp. 12–13), and the apocryphal *Acts of Thomas* (cf. Whitaker, op. cit., pp. 13–19). The remarkable fact here is that baptism begins with the anointing and laying on of hands with prayer (a reference to the anointing of kings and priests in Israel) and only then proceeds to the immersion in water and the baptismal formula. The renunciation of Satan (and, for that matter, the confession of faith) is not mentioned in these sources. This ancient Syrian practice (baptism in this order: anointing, washing, meal) may remain discernible in later practice (in Cappadocia and Alexandria, for example) and, in any case, requires further study (cf. G. Winkler, "The Original Meaning and Implications of the Prebaptismal Anointing," *Worship* 52:1, 1978, pp. 24–45). The following is an account of the baptism of Gundaphorus in the *Acts of Thomas*, given here in translation from the Syriac text:

"And they begged of him that they might receive the sign, and said to him: 'Our souls are turned to God to receive the sign for we have heard that all the sheep of that God whom thou preachest are known to him by the sign.' Judas saith to them: 'I too rejoice, and I ask of you to partake of the Eucharist and of the blessing of this Messiah whom I preach.' And the king gave the orders that the bath should be closed for seven days, and that no man should bathe in it. And when the seven days were done, on the eighth day they three entered into the bath by night that Judas might baptize them. And many lamps were lighted in the bath. And when they had entered into the bathhouse, Judas went in before them. And our Lord appeared unto them, and said to them: 'Peace be with you, my brethren.' And they heard the voice only, but the form they did not see, whose it was, for till now they had not been baptized. And Judas went up and stood upon the edge of the cistern, and poured oil upon their hands, and said:

'Come, holy name of the Messiah;
come, power of grace, which art from on high;
come, perfect mercy;

come, exalted gift;
come, sharer of the blessing;
come, revealer of hidden mysteries;
come, mother of the seven houses, whose rest was in the eighth house;
come, messenger of reconciliation, and communicate with the minds of these youths;
come, Spirit of holiness, and purify their reins and their hearts.'

"And he baptized them in the Name of the Father and of the Son and of the Spirit of holiness. And when they had come up out of the water, a youth appeared to them, and he was holding a lighted taper; and the light of the lamps became pale through its light. And when they had gone forth, he became invisible to them; and the Apostle said: 'We were not even able to bear Thy light, because it is too great for our vision.' And when it dawned and was morning, he broke the Eucharist."

Translation: W. Wright in E. C. Whitaker, op. cit., pp. 13–14.

The meaning of baptism is multifaceted. Baptism is above all *huiothesia;* the baptized is made a child of God in him who is the Son of God's good pleasure and in whose name he or she is baptized. It follows then that the model of Christian baptism is the baptism of Jesus in the Jordan. In this baptism, Jesus began his life's journey. He fulfilled this baptism in the death through which he has become the Son of glory. So also is the follower of the Lord baptized. Furthermore, baptism is the celebration of the Holy Spirit, the sealing of the Spirit, the full gift of grace in the Spirit, especially as noted in Syrian sources. One is baptized in water and with fire and so reborn to new humanity. By the Spirit the baptized are gathered into the assembly, the people of priests and kings, the congregation, the church of the Lord, in order to go the way of the Lord together. Baptism is thus dynamic: the baptized person is started on the way of following the Lord. Such a way connotes conversion and the forgiveness of sin. The baptized, in the company of the church, journeys toward the kingdom of the Father.

Eucharist
The literature on the eucharist in the New Testament is extensive. We mention here one of the most recent studies in this field: R. Fenneberg, *Christliche Passafeier und Abendmahl* (Munich, 1971). The

40

first mention of the eucharist in the New Testament is in 1 Cor 11: 17–36, where Paul relies on an early tradition. The synoptic evangelists report in their own manner the story of the institution in the context of the passion of the Lord. By comparing these data (perhaps adding to it also the meal references in Acts and the material in John that can be interpreted as referring to the eucharist), one must come to the conclusion that in the apostolic congregation, a development had already taken place in the rite and especially in the understanding of the meal of the Lord. A meal is spoken of, with the accent on rites during or framing the meal, specifically the blessing over bread, with the bread-breaking, and over a cup, both as practiced in the Jewish tradition. There is a remembrance of what Jesus did during his last meal and there is a clear concern that a connection be made between the meal in the church and the death of the Lord (recall such words as "betrayed," "broken," "poured out") and also between the meal and the risen Lord who presided at meals with his disciples. All these data cannot be analyzed here (see the literature listed at the beginning of this section), but what must be noted is that the New Testament is not clear about how the eucharist was actually celebrated. Was it always in the context of a meal? When did it take place and where? Here one can only guess.

After the completion of the New Testament, some information can be found about the celebration and meaning of the eucharist (e.g., *Ign. Eph.* 13; *Magn.* 6; *Smyrn.* 8 or the inscription of Abercius), but a complete description of the actual celebration of eucharist is given only by Justin in his *1 Apology* 65 and 67. This detailed description is of immense importance, for it makes it possible to trace the evolution of the rite of the eucharist and to determine with precision where the roots of the later celebration lie.

Justin's description is as follows: in the Sunday assembly "the memoirs of the apostles" (*ta apomnēmoneumata*) and "the prophets" (the Old Testament surely is intended) are read aloud for as long as time allows. Thus, there is reading from the New Testament (*in statu nascendi*) and from the Old Testament, but there is still not a precisely ordered liturgy of the word as would later be the case. After the reader finishes, the president (*proestōs*) preaches on the texts that have been read; after his homily all stand and pray, i.e., the assembly stands (as in the case of the so-called "standing prayers" in the synagogue) and prays the intercessions, an example of which is to be found in the letter of Clement (see pp. 14–17). The intercessions are concluded with the kiss of peace (called by Tertullian *signaculum orationis* in *De orat.* 18). After this service of readings, the service of the table follows: bread and wine and water are brought (from which it is apparent that the celebration is no longer a full meal) and over them the president speaks a prayer of thanksgiving (recognizable as the later eucharistic prayer, the anaphora, but without a model text—the prayer was itself improvised, albeit within a given genre). After the prayer, the gifts are distributed (and taken away to those absent) by the deacons. Justin appends this note to his description of the Sunday eucharist: "And the wealthy who so desire give what they wish, as each chooses; and what is collected is deposited with the president. He helps orphans and widows, and those who through sickness or any other cause are in need, and those in prison, and strangers sojourning among us; in a word he takes care of all those who are in need" (translation in R. C. D. Jasper & G. J. Cuming, *Prayers of the Eucharist*, 2nd ed., New York, 1980, p. 20).

The data in Tertullian (see E. Dekkers, op. cit., pp. 49–66) and Cyprian (V. Saxer, op. cit., pp. 189–264) fundamentally agree with this description, as do those in Hippolytus (*Apost. Trad.* 21). Tertullian and Cyprian mention the Lord's Prayer as taking place at the time of intercessions and the kiss of peace. It appears that communion of the bread was received in the hand and that one could take the gifts home so as to receive communion on other days. Furthermore, the gifts were brought to those who were sick.

In a few decades, a fixed ritual for the celebration of the eucharist had come into being. The important difference between this ritual and the institution accounts in the New Testament is that the meal has been changed into a ritualized meal and a ceremonial taking of food; one can no longer speak of it as an ordinary meal. The reasons for this change are now unclear, but it is not unlikely that the social situation settled the matter: the meals of Christians were too suspicious to the authorities. Furthermore, the number of believers grew, making a common meal more difficult. What remained was the blessing over the gifts of bread and cup and the eating of these foods of the blessing, actions that were also of central significance in the Jewish meal (cf. the *birkat ha-mazon*) and were already emphasized in the accounts of the institution. The shape of the eucharist came to be changed. In the eucharistic celebration, all that remained from the original practice were the ritual and meaning of the blessing at the meal, the blessings found at the beginning and end of the meal itself, and the *berakoth* (but now in characteristic Christian form: the thanksgiving). The designation "eucharist" emerges as an essential name for the whole ritual: apparently the key to the action of Jesus was presumed to be found in his blessing of the bread and wine during his last meal.

The first basic element of the resulting celebration of the eucharist is the reading of "the scriptures," i.e., reading aloud and preaching on the text so read. Great value was given to the "memoirs" of the apostles as the basis for the existence of the church, because in this way the words and actions of the Lord himself could be encountered. There is still much uncertainty about the manner in which the service of the scriptures took its place in the order for the eucharist. It may have been due to direct influence of the Jewish liturgy of the synagogue. Due to the paucity of evidence, a genuine proof for that influence cannot be provided. It was almost inevitable, however, that there should be read in the weekly assemblies the "memoirs of the apostles," those writings that were collated after the death of the apostles. These works were regarded as bearing apostolic witness and authority and were preserved as precious pearls in the communities. Where could better support be found for the authenticity both of the message and of the church of the Lord? It was just as obvious that the Old Testament also received an important place as "witness beforehand" (*testimonia*), since the preaching of the apostles, like that of Jesus himself, had its roots in the law and the prophets, and unveiled the deepest dimensions of those scriptures. One finds here the basis of the later liturgy of the word in the eucharist and in other celebrations of the assembly.

The second basic element is the service of the table and therein especially the anamnetic prayer that we call the "eucharistic prayer." This prayer goes back indirectly to the Jewish *berakah* and has an almost identical structure: the naming and blessing of God, the thankful remembrance of creation and covenant, and the supplication of God's faithfulness. In Christian use, thanksgiving for the eschatological deed of God comes to dominate the prayer. It follows that the remembrance of God's deed is focused on the Son, the Messiah Jesus, whose prayer and action during his last meal were handed on in the gospels (the institution account) and were related to his suffering, death, resurrection, and sending of the Spirit. On the basis of this remembrance, this anamnesis, the assembly prays over the gifts that the Holy Spirit will enable the people to participate worthily in the sacred mysteries and that he will unify the whole church of God.

The origin of the eucharistic prayer has not yet been fully clarified, but the rough outline of its early history can certainly be sketched.

In the text from *Didache* 10 given above, an anamnetic prayer of three strophes is found that is comparable to the Jewish table prayers. In later texts, such as the anaphora of Addai and Mari or that from an early Egyptian papyrus, the same three-strophe structure is discovered. It is possible that in the earliest celebration of the eucharist, the structure of the Jewish table prayers served as the model while the content of the prayers was determined by Christian faith. This would mean that the oldest eucharistic prayers had the form of table blessings of three strophes, still without the institution narrative and without the thereto connected formal anamnesis and epiclesis, such as would be found in the later tradition (described in chapter 2). (For further study see L. Ligier, "The Origins of the Eucharistic Prayer," *Studia Liturgica* 9, 1973, pp. 161–185; H. Wegman, "Généalogie hypothétique de la prière eucharistique," *Questions Liturgiques* 61, 1980, pp. 263–278).

In regard to the peculiar content of these Christian table prayers two facets may be mentioned especially. The first is memorial, anamnesis (as characteristic of the whole prayer), the remembrance of Jesus, through whom God gives spiritual food and drink to the congregation, signs of eternal life (cf. *Didache* 10). The second is the notion of "sacrifice," a central idea of later Christian eucharistic prayers. This notion was certainly present in these early prayers, but not yet so precisely determined as in the following period. The sacrifice here encompasses the offering of praise and thanksgiving by the assembly to the Lord in fulfillment of the prophecy of Malachi (1:11) and on the grounds of the memorial of Jesus' dying and rising. Such "sacrifice" is the spiritual cultus of the new congregation of the Lord (cf. Rom 12:1). (See further: H. Cazelles, "Eucharistie, bénédiction et sacrifice dans l'Ancien Testament," *La Maison-Dieu* 123, 1975, pp. 7–28; J. Laporte, *La doctrine eucharistique chez Philon d'Alexandrie*, Paris, 1972).

Finally, let it be noted that "eucharist" is, for Justin, a technical term for the prayer and for the gifts over which the prayer is spoken. He writes in the *Dialogue with Trypho* 41:1 that the bread of the eucharist is handed down to us:

ἵνα ἅμα τε εὐχαριστῶμεν τῷ Θεῷ
ὑπέρ τε τοῦ τὸν κόσμον ἐκτικέναι
σὺν πᾶσι τοῖς ἐν αὐτῷ διὰ τὸν
ἄνθρωπον, καὶ ὑπὲρ τοῦ ἀπὸ τῆς
κακίας, ἐν ᾗ γεγόναμεν,
ἠλευθερωκέναι ἡμᾶς, καὶ τὰς

. . . so that we might give thanks to God, both for creating the world with all things that are in it for the sake of man, and for freeing us from the evil in which we were born, and for accom-

ἀρχὰς καὶ τὰς ἐξουσίας
καταλελυκέναι τελείαν κατάλυσιν
διὰ τοῦ παθητοῦ γενομένου κατὰ
τὴν βουλὴν αὐτοῦ.

In 1 *Apology* 66: 1–2 he writes:

καὶ ἡ τροφὴ αὕτη καλεῖται παρ'
ἡμῖν εὐχαριστία, ἧς οὐδενὶ ἄλλῳ
μετασχεῖν ἐξόν ἐστιν ἢ τῷ πισ-
τεύοντι ἀληθῆ εἶναι τὰ
δεδιδαγμένα ὑφ' ἡμῶν, καὶ
λουσαμένῳ τὸ ὑπὲρ ἀφέσεως
ἁμαρτιῶν καὶ εἰς ἀναγέννησιν
λουτρόν, καὶ οὕτως βεοῦντι ὡς ὁ
Χριστὸς παρέδωκεν, οὐ γὰρ ὡς
κοινὸν ἄρτον οὐδὲ κοινὸν πόμα
ταῦτα λαμβάνομεν.

plishing a complete destruction
of the principalities and powers
through him who suffered according to his will.

And we call this food "thanksgiving"; and no one may partake
of it unless he is convinced of
the truth of our teaching, and
has been cleansed with the
washing for the forgiveness of
sins and regeneration and lives
as Christ handed down. For we
do not receive these things as
common bread or common
drink. . . .

Texts: A. Hänggi and I. Pahl, *Prex Eucharistica*, pp. 70, 72. *Translation:*
R.C.D. Jasper & G. J. Cuming, *Prayers of the Eucharist*, pp. 17, 19.

As a single act of thanksgiving over both bread and cup, probably
the oldest eucharistic prayer we have is given in the *Apostolic Tradition* of Hippolytus:

Gratias tibi referimus, Deus, per
dilectum puerum tuum Iesum
Christum, quem in ultimis tem-
poribus misisti nobis salvatorem
et redemptorem et angelum
voluntatis tuae; qui est verbum
tuum inseparabilem, per quem
omnia fecisti et beneplacitum
tibi fuit, misisti de caelo in mat-
ricem virginis quique in utero
habitus incarnatus est et filius
tibi ostensus est, ex spiritu
sancto et virgine natus. Qui
voluntatem tuam complens et
populum sanctum tibi adqui-
rens extendit manus cum pateretur, ut a passione liberaret eos
qui in te crediderunt. Qui cum-

We give you thanks, Father,
through Jesus Christ, your beloved
Son, whom you sent in this end
of the ages to save and redeem us
and to proclaim to us your will.
He is your Word, inseparable from
you. Through him you created all
things, and in him take delight.
He is your Word, sent from
heaven to a virgin's womb. He
there took on our nature and our
lot and was shown forth as your
Son, born of the Holy Spirit and
of the Virgin Mary. It is he, our
Lord Jesus, who fulfilled all your
will and won for you a holy people; he stretched out his hands
in suffering in order to free from

que traderetur voluntariae passioni, ut mortem solvat et vincula diabuli disrumpat, et infernum calcet et iustos inluminet, et terminum figat et resurrectionem manifestet, accipiens panem gratias tibi agens dixit: Accipite, manducate, hoc est corpus meum quod pro vobis confringetur. Similiter et calicem dices: Hic est sanguis meus qui pro vobis effunditur. Quando hoc facitis, meam commemorationem facitis.

Memores igitur mortis et resurrectionis eius, offerimus tibi panem et calicem, gratias tibi agentes quia nos dignos habuisti adstare coram te et tibi ministrare. Et petimus ut mittas spiritum sanctum in oblationem sanctae ecclesiae: in unum congregans des omnibus qui percipiunt sanctis in repletionem spiritus sancti ad confirmationem fidei in veritate, ut te laudemus et glorificemus per puerum tuum Iesum Christum tibi gloria et honor patri et filio cum sancto spiritu in sancta ecclesia tua et nunc et in saecula saeculorum. Amen.

suffering those who trust you. It is he who, handed over to a death he freely accepted, in order to destroy death, to break the bonds of the evil one, to crush hell underfoot, to give light to the righteous, to establish his covenant, and to show forth the resurrection, taking bread and giving thanks to you, said: Take and eat: this is my body, broken for you.

In the same way also the cup, saying: This is my blood poured out for you. Do this for the remembrance of me. Remembering, then, his death and resurrection, we offer this bread and cup to you, giving you thanks that you have made us worthy to stand before you and to serve you. And we ask you: Send your Spirit upon these gifts of your Church; gather into one all who share this bread and wine; fill us with your Holy Spirit to establish our faith in truth, that we may praise and glorify you through your Son Jesus Christ. Through him all glory and honor are yours, Almighty Father, with the Holy Spirit, in your holy Church both now and forever. Amen.

Text: B. Botte, op. cit., p. 12. *Translation:* altered from the *Lutheran Book of Worship, Ministers' Edition* (Minneapolis & Philadelphia, 1978), p. 226.

Reconciliation

H. Karp remarks (in *Die Busse; Quellen zur Entstehung des altkirchlichen Busswesens*, p. xv): "In the early epoch the concept of keeping the community of saints pure is on the whole predominant." This statement should be stressed. The holiness of the community was a centrally important aim in the ancient exercise of penance and reconciliation; therein was expressed the faithfulness to the way of the Lord that one had taken on through the confession of faith at baptism. This is why the baptismal theme stood out so clearly in the celebration of reconciliation. The early church was confronted with a burning pastoral problem—how to respond to sinners in the assembly of the Lord, to unfaithful and weak people. It seems that this problem arose quite strikingly in the period when the final coming of the Lord to redeem his persecuted community was earnestly expected. There were many people who apostasized out of fear when they were faced with the choice for the Lord and its consequences—suffering and martyrdom.

The sources for our knowledge of penance and reconciliation in this period are principally: *The Shepherd of Hermas;* Clement of Alexandria (*Strom.* II; *Ped.* I; etc.); *Didascalia* (c. 6); Tertullian (*De paenitentia; De pudicitia*); Cyprian (letters); and the Council of Elvira (306 A.D.; text in J. D. Mansi, *Sacr. Conciliorum Nov. et Ampl. Collectio,* vol. 2, repr. Graz, 1960, pp. 5–19). For a collection of texts see H. Karp (op. cit.).

The impossibility of forgiveness for certain sins, although held by such rigorists as Tertullian, was no general churchly opinion. Already very early there existed a sort of catalogue of sins in which murder, apostasy, and adultery were always considered grave offenses. Forgiveness for these grave sins was possible, but only once in one's lifetime, after completion of the penance imposed by the church. This penance consisted in public actions of repentance over a certain period of time. The central theme here was not so much the need for God's forgiveness as for the maintenance of the holiness of the church. If one had committed a public sin, then the holiness of the congregation was affected; reparation was accomplished by public penance, visible to all and directed toward readmission to the community. The church itself was also active in the penitential process by its intercession for the sinner, in union with the sinner, an intercession Tertullian identifies with the pleading of Christ before the Father that does not go unheard. In this process, sins were most likely not confessed publicly but the penance was visible: rigorous fasting, "sackcloth and ashes," numerous prayers, and exclusion from the eucharist. When the penance was completed, readmission to the community included proclamation of God's forgiveness.

This entire complex of conversion was called *exomologēsis,* confession, upon which reconciliation followed; then participation in the eucharist was allowed. This practice of penance was to become much more developed in later periods.

Ministry and Ordination
The *Apostolic Tradition* comes from about the middle of the third century. From its text we may conclude that by about 250 A.D. in Rome (and perhaps also elsewhere), ecclesiastical office existed in a threefold heirarchical division: bishop, presbyter, and deacon. The bishop was the head of the congregation and had a precisely delineated function.

The threefold ministry can be traced back even further, however. In the letters of Ignatius of Antioch (Pseudo-Ignatius?), that threefold division is clearly present. The principal references are: *Magn.* 6:1–2; *Eph.* 3–5; *Philad.* 4; *Trall.* 3:1–2; *Smyrn.* 8:2. In these texts, the figure of the bishop comes to the fore; he carries on the task of the apostles for the sake of the congregation. The bishop must proclaim the faith and keep it untainted. Together with the college of presbyters, he is the sign of unity within the congregation, and by the bond with other bishops he is the sign of unity between the congregations. Unity was an important goal, since it was apparently already threatened by schism. In any case, the heirarchical structure of office in the church was already a fact in the mid-second century in Asia Minor—if we follow the dating of R. Joly (see p. 17).

The heirarchical structure seems not to be traceable back to the New Testament or to the time directly following it. In the first decades, office in the Christian congregations was much less clearly structured. There was no *episcopos* in the sense of "bishop." The function of *episcopē*, of oversight and leadership, along with *diakonia*, service, was attributed to a group of elders or presbyters. At the beginning leadership in the communities was democratic and collective (but not precisely structured). Perhaps it paralleled the makeup of civil government in the cities. It seems certain that office was adapted to the congregation, the house church, the brotherhood and sisterhood. With the consolidation of the "church" a single-headed leadership began to develop, with the elders acting as counselors. The elders' task remained vague, however, and slowly became meaningless. In the west the presbyter would not begin to operate in any modern sense as an independent officeholder in a local congregation until the twelfth century.

Deacons and deaconesses were important in the congregation, and the office was aspired to among Christians. They arranged practical

48

affairs and, probably for this reason, deacons were also charged with the finances. *Diakonia* and economy have since gone hand in hand, not always to the benefit of the former.

The *Apostolic Tradition* has been mentioned already and should be consulted. Material in Tertullian (see Dekkers, p. 74) and Cyprian (see Saxer, pp. 72–105) essentially agrees with the image of congregational office presumed in the *Apostolic Tradition*.

We include here the text of the prayer for the consecration of a bishop from the *Apostolic Tradition*. Since the third century, it has been in use in all the eastern traditions and since the Second Vatican Council has also been used in the Roman rite. It is a genuinely ecumenical text.

Deus et pater domini nostri Iesu Christi, pater misericordiarum et deus totius consolationis, qui in excelsis habitas et humilia respicis, qui cognoscis omnia antequam nascantur, tu qui dedisti terminos in ecclesia per verbum gratiae tuae, praedestinans ex principio genus iustorum Abraham, principes et sacerdotes constituens et sanctum tuum sine ministerio non derelinquens, ex initio saeculi bene tibi placuit in his quos elegisti dari: nunc effunde eam virtutem, quae a te est, principalis spiritus, quem dedisti dilecto filio tuo Iesu Christo, quod donavit sanctis apostolis, qui constituerunt ecclesiam per singula loca sanctificationem tuam, in gloriam et laudem indeficientem nomini tuo.

God the Father of our Lord Jesus Christ, Father of mercies and God of all consolation, you dwell in heaven, yet look with compassion on all that is humble. You know all things before they come to be; by your gracious word you have established the plan of your Church. From the beginning you chose the descendants of Abraham to be your holy nation. You established rulers and priests, and did not leave your sanctuary without ministers to serve you. From the creation of the world you have been pleased to be glorified by those whom you have chosen. So now pour out upon this chosen one that power which is from you, the governing Spirit whom you gave to your beloved Son, Jesus Christ, the Spirit given by him to the holy apostles, who founded the Church in every place to be your temple for the unceasing glory and praise of your name.

Da cordis cognitor pater, super hunc servum tuum, quem elegisti ad episcopatum, pascere

Father, you know all hearts. You have chosen your servant for the office of bishop. May he be a

49

gregem sanctam tuam, et prima-
tum sacerdotii tibi exhibere sine
reprehensione, servientem noctu
et die, incessanter repropitiari
vultum tuum et offerre dona
sancta(e) ecclesiae tuae, spiritum
primatus sacerdotii habere po-
testatem dimittere peccata secundum mandatum tuum, dare
sortes secundum praeceptum
tuum, solvere etiam omnem
collegationem secundum potes-
tatem quam dedisti apostolis,
placere autem tibi in mansue-
tudine et mundo corde, offer-
entem tibi odorem suavitatis, per
puerum tuum Iesum Christum,
per quem tibi gloria et potentia
et honor, patri et filio cum
spiritu sancto et nunc et in
saecula saeculorum. Amen.

shepherd to your holy flock, and
a high priest blameless in your
sight, ministering to you night and
day; may he always gain the
blessing of your favor and offer
the gifts of your holy Church.
Through the Spirit who gives the
grace of high priesthood grant
him the power to forgive sins as
you have commanded, to assign
ministries as you have decreed,
and to loose every bond by the
authority which you gave to your
apostles. May he be pleasing to
you by his gentleness and purity
of heart, presenting a fragrant offering to you, through Jesus
Christ, your Son, through whom
glory and power and honor are
yours with the Holy Spirit in your
Holy Church, now and forever.
Amen.

Text: B. Botte, pp. 7–10. *Translation: The Rites of the Catholic Church,* vol. 2
(New York, 1980), pp. 95–96.

5. IMAGES
Reference should be made again to F. van der Meer and Christine
Mohrmann, *Atlas of the Early Christian World,* in which is reproduced
much of the oldest iconography of baptism, the eucharist, the death
of the Christian, and the vision of the life to come. One finds there
the basic practice that became normative for Christian art: the symbolic representation of the mysteries, the veiled imaging of what
Christians believe, expressed in Old and New Testament metaphors,
the whole expressing trust in God's continuing faithful care for the
people.

CONCLUSION
Although direct information about worship in the first three centuries
is sparse, we may nonetheless conclude that it was at this time that
Christian worship was basically shaped in both form and content.
Later ages would add and change and make more precise, but the

structure, the shape, of worship may already be discovered in the pre-Constantinian period. This shape is attractive to us in its simplicity, intelligibility, pluriformity, and freedom of formulation. The period after the peace of the church, the period of reconciliation between church and state, will change much of this, not always for the better. What will in fact practically disappear is the most profound trait of this period, that is, the dynamic expectation of the kingdom of God in the coming of the Messiah, for whom many shed their blood out of the assurance that he would indeed come to bring all things to fulfillment. It was they who celebrated the meal of the Lord "until he comes."

Chapter Two

Worship in the Church of the Empire (312–600)

In this chapter, we shall attempt to place side by side the principal historical, cultural, and liturgical facts from both the east and the west in order to obtain a general overview of the development of worship in these important centuries. The facts are numerous and comprehensive. Here completeness cannot be our goal, but a sketch of the important development of the rites and of their significance certainly can be.

I. HISTORICAL OUTLINE

Literature

H.-G. Beck, *Geschichte der orthodoxen Kirche im byzantinischen Reich* (Göttingen, 1980).

H. Chadwick, *The Early Church* (London, 1967).

J. Daniélou & H. Marrou, *The Christian Centuries*, vol. 1 (New York, 1964).

M. Deanesly, *A History of Early Medieval Europe, 476–911*, 2nd corrected ed. (New York & London, 1963).

J. Gaudemet, *L'Eglise dans l'empire romain (IVe-Ve siècles)* (Paris, 1958).

H. Jedin, ed., *History of the Church*, vol. 2 (New York, 1980).

R. Kottje & B. Moeller, eds., *Alte Kirche und Ostkirche, Oekumenische Kirchengeschichte*, vol. 1 (Mainz, 1970).

J. Meyendorff, *Byzantine Theology: Historical Trends and Doctrinal Themes* (New York, 1974).

G. Ostrogorsky, *History of the Byzantine State*, rev. ed. (New Brunswick, N.J., 1969).

J. Pelikan, *The Emergence of the Catholic Tradition* (Chicago, 1971).

C. Pietri, *Roma christiana*, 2 vols. (Rome, 1976).

A. van der Aalst, *Aantekeningen bij de hellenisering van het christendom* (Nijmegen, 1974).

F. van der Meer, *Atlas of Western Civilization*, 2nd rev. ed. (London & New York, 1960).

F. van der Meer & C. Mohrmann, *Atlas of the Early Christian World* (London & New York, 1959).

A. THE WEST

1. CHURCH AND STATE

The emperor Constantine the Great has gone down in history as the liberator of the Christian church from the oppression of the preceding centuries. The persecutions during those centuries did not prevent the church in east and west from experiencing great growth, but the Christians were without legal rights. With Constantine's victory (312) and the misnamed "Edict of Toleration" of Milan (313), all of this changed. Here began the history, with all its ups and downs, of the relationship of church and state. Close behind the legal recognition of the church followed other decisions that were intended to achieve the freedom of the church and the abolition of pagan practices. Better treatment for slaves, the prohibition of execution by crucifixion, and the partial prohibition of gladiatorial games were all promulgated. Bishops became high government officials and magistrates. A separate legal process was established for clergy, who were also freed from military service and from paying taxes. Constantine acted as patron of the arts and presented to the church of the east and west magnificent great basilicas (Rome, Trier, Constantinople, Jerusalem, Bethlehem).

The church lived in and was "reconciled to time" (G. Dix, *The Shape of the Liturgy*). It was a long way from the church in hiding to the conspicuous basilica in the middle of the city, and it had been traveled very quickly. The consequences have been far-reaching. Many regard this time as the beginning of the church as a powerful secularized institution, tied hand and foot to the state. Perhaps this opinion is too one-sided and accentuates too greatly the break with the first centuries, but what indeed were the consequences? For one thing, the Church could act publicly. It could freely make converts and take its place in the public cultural life. Eventually, where foreign elements infiltrated society, the Christian church became the bearer and the protectress of the old Roman culture that she had taken upon herself, christened, and adopted. Furthermore, in this publicly recognized church, a liturgy could develop that was a delight for the eyes. Everything became more majestic, more open, more ostentatious, as large groups of people entered the church simply because of the social situation.

The recognition of Christianity and, later, its status as the official religion of the state, gave many people a reason for entering the church. Without church membership, it was difficult to get a position in the state. This reason for remaining merely on the threshold, a minimal convert, was to cause many serious problems for Christendom. There were both positive and negative sides to the church's growing popularity. The bishops complained that although the churches were indeed full, the number of the actually committed, that is, those who submitted to baptism, was small. Christianity became the religion of many people, but Christian practice was less evident! What is more, faith and magic went hand in hand. In short, the post-Constantinian church was a two-sided coin.

Generally, the successors of Constantine ruled over an empire that had been, since Diocletian, administratively divided in two parts (east and west). In the course of the coming decades it would, in fact, become divided into autonomous parts, but continue to exist for many centuries only in the east. After Constantine (d. 337 A.D.), the reign of Theodosius the Great (379–395 A.D.)—the last great single ruler of an undivided empire—was of the greatest importance for the Christianization of the empire: in 380, Christianity became the religion of the state. It was a time of the flowering of Christian arts and letters. The center of Theodosius's government was Milan, seat of the prefecture of Italy. Because of the turbulence of the times, the emperor Honorius (395–423 A.D.) transferred the imperial seat to the more secure Ravenna. Rebuilt as the imperial capital, the city was endowed with magnificent Christian structures that are still preserved (cf. *Atlas of the Early Christian World*, plates 218–236). The influence of Rome, as far as the emperor was concerned, grew ever smaller, but the city was regaining its influence through another great authority, the pope. Rome remained the metropolitan see of the west and of the western church, the protective bastion of the old Roman tradition.

Besides Rome and Milan, several other cities outside Italy were important for the history of the church. Several western provincial cities might be named: in Spain and Portugal—Cordoba (the bishop of Cordoba, Hosius, acted as advisor to Constantine), Elvira, Toledo, Braga; in old Gaul—Narbonne, Arles, Nîmes, Orange, Valence, Poitiers, Reims, Tours, Trier, Cologne, Maastricht; in northern Italy— Aquileia; in North Africa—Carthage, Milev, Hippo. The organization of the church was the same as that of the state. The bishop's seat was in a *civitas*, from which he exercised care over a *territorium* (a province).

2. THE BARBARIAN INVASIONS

Before the apparently invincible empire, with its two centers in Rome and Constantinople, loomed a great danger: the pressure of the barbarians upon the borders of the realm. The "barbarians" were nomadic peoples who pushed from as far as Mongolia and China through Kazakhstan to the west. They possessed extremely mobile armies that had good weapons at their command; the skillfulness and speed of their agile horsemen surprised the Roman legions. The empire could not turn aside this invasion of the barbarians. The western empire was flooded with alien peoples and taken over by their rulers, in spite of the counterattacks of the emperors. As a result, the political situation of the west was changed totally: the *pax romana* ended in a series of bloody wars. In the days of Pope Gregory the Great (590–604 A.D.), when the eastern Roman emperor attempted to restore order in Italy by battling the Lombards, southern Italy turned into an impoverished area of which only the pope took cognizance. Finally the papacy was separated from Byzantium and chose the side of the "barbarian kings."

The history of this turbulent time may be summarized as follows. The Goths invaded the Balkan peninsula and gave battle to Emperor Valens in 378 near Hadrianopolis, which was within easy reach of Byzantium. The emperor was killed. The Goths continued up the Danube, conquered parts of present-day Yugoslavia and Hungary, followed by almost the whole of Italy, and founded the kingdom of the Ostrogoths. The Visigoths came into southern France and Spain by skirting the borders of the eastern empire. They were Arians through their contacts with Constantinople, where some of the emperors had sided with the Arian party in the Christological conflicts. The Vandals cut diagonally from northern Poland through present-day Europe to Spain and then North Africa, destroying everything they encountered. The Burgundians, after roving about, ended up in the area of the French Alps and Clermont-Ferrand (Auvergne). The Franks took possession of the rest of Gaul and parts of Germany, that is, the left bank of the Rhine that had served as the natural boundary of the empire. Finally the Angles, the Saxons, and the Jutes migrated to Britain. All these peoples had thus established themselves within the boundaries of the empire and at the same time had experienced the culture of *romanitas*. A blending of cultures began that would form the basis of western European civilization. In this process, the Christian church in the west played a great role. The state had gone under; the political institutions no longer functioned well; the emperor ruled in distant, free Byzantium. The only institution that could and would safeguard continuity was the Christian church, which had grown up in the Roman empire, experienced its later blossoming, and was saturated with the culture of late antiquity. This church took the opportunity offered in the contact with the barbarians to preserve the old and at the same time to foster the new. The church "christened" these peoples. Perhaps this time was one of the most creative periods in the history of Christianity. A man like Pope Leo the Great (440–461 A.D.), and with him many other bishops, were the spiritual center at a time when all secular institutions had been dismembered and the authority of the emperor had been terminated.

3. THEOLOGY

Once the liberation of the church had been accomplished, growing controversies about doctrine and a considerable development in theoretical reflection on the meaning of the faith took place. In that development, the dictates and the power of the emperor made their clear mark. From the emperor's point of view this was understandable, for the tranquillity of the empire was at stake. In the Donatist controversy, for example, Constantine played an active role. In the west, much reflection (Augustine, Pelagius) was determined by the doctrine of grace. The questions of free will, God's grace, and predestination became the great points of controversy, in contrast to theological speculation in the east (see pp. 60–62). It is difficult to overestimate the influence of Augustine in the west, an influence that indirectly affected the liturgical texts.

4. MONASTICISM

The development of monasticism was of decisive influence in the west. There had been monks in the pre-Constantinian church, but now the monastic ideal brought about the great flight to the desert. "Monasticism arose as an almost unconscious and instinctive reaction against the secularization of the Church" (A. Schmemann, *Introduction to Liturgical Theology*, p. 102). A repugnance was felt toward the general laxity in a church with many catechumens and relatively few practicing, baptized Christians. Entrance into the monastic state was thus called a "second baptism." Consistent discipleship and the consistent imitation of the Lord were the principal goals; the lay monk had freed himself from the world, from marriage, and from

56

earthly pleasures. Monasticism was likened to the martyrdom of Christians in the earlier centuries; the monk had become the new witness to Christ through poverty and chastity. He lived in nearness to God and in expectation of the kingdom of God. As the faithful discovered and valued the radicality of these monks, their spiritual influence increased. The Christianizing of Europe is in large part due to the monks.

For the development of monasticism in the west, see *Atlas of the Early Christian World*, map 34. Well-known monks of this era include: Benedict, Augustine, Cassian, Columbanus, and Patrick. Monastic centers include: Subiaco, Monte Cassino, Lerins, Bobbio, Luxeuil, Tours, Bangor, Iona, Lindisfarne.

B. THE EAST

1. MEANING OF THE TERM

The reorganization of the Roman empire by Diocletian had great consequences for the church. By the division of the empire into two (eastern Roman and western Roman) and the consequent duplication of capital cities (Constantinople and Rome), later imperial history became a history of two kingdoms, two cultures, and two ways of being the church. The roots are the same but the flowers are different. And the same roots did not guarantee mutual peace; on the contrary, the mutual rivalry grew with the passing years until a complete break took place.

The term "east" must be carefully understood. The meaning first of all, of course, is found in the predominant position of the imperial city on the Bosporus, chosen by Constantine and quickly built to become a dazzling second Rome. From this city, the emperor ruled the eastern part of the empire. That included the *praefectura praetoris per Orientem* with these dioceses: Egypt, the "east" in a narrower sense (*Oriens*), Pontus, Asia, Thrace, and the capital city of Constantinople. The ancient democracy of Rome had given way to an autocratic imperial rule that rested upon a complete bureaucracy, an extensively worked out system of taxation that made the poor the primary victims, and an organized army that consisted not only of border troops but also of mobile units everywhere in the empire—*exercitus comitatensis*, the replacement of the old pretorian guard. Finally, after Constantine, government was closely bound to the church, gathering *Imperium* and *Sacerdotium* together in the person of the emperor as the divinely appointed leader.

At the heart of this realm was Hellenism, the culture of the

Greeks, yet for the Christians in the empire the word *Hellene* also signified "pagan." The Christians called themselves "Romans" (*Romaioi*), in the line of the old Roman imperial tradition. With the eclipse of the pagans under Justinian, only the "Romans" remained, that is, "Greeks" who had converted to Christianity. Later when the councils had established orthodoxy, "Roman" became a synonym for "orthodox" over against the heretics, who were mostly not Romans, *e.g.*, the Syrians. The heretics, for their part, identified the "Romans" (the Greek Christians) with the emperor; they called them "Melchites," that is, followers of the emperor (*malko* in Syriac), the symbol of the dominant state and culture. All of this also had great consequences for the church; the "Byzantine liturgy" took an imperial, that is, a dominant, place.

The east also included, however, that area that was called "Syria" by the Greeks and that embraced Palestine, Lebanon, Syria, Jordan, and Mesopotamia (Iraq). The Syrians were related by language and culture to the Jews and the Arabs (as the collective name "Semites" indicates) and lived in the empire principally on the threatened eastern borders (Edessa or Urfa), but also outside those borders in the Persian empire. From these locations on either side of the border arose the later terminology, East Syrian and West Syrian, which we shall meet in the liturgy. The city of Antioch, together with Jerusalem, the cradle of Christianity, was thoroughly Greek, but the countryside was Syrian. Over against the Greeks (the empire-minded, the "Melkites"), the Syrians always felt themselves the underdogs: powerless, inferior, suspicious, and more or less hostile. Therefore they did not choose the side of the Greeks, not even where orthodox doctrine was concerned. They became Nestorian or Monophysite and resisted the Greek state and church. It was they who welcomed Islam as liberator. But thereby they also lost much of their own identity (and liturgy), thus contributing to the predominant position of the Byzantine church and liturgy, which endured even when the Byzantine state disappeared under the violence of Islam.

Finally one can also use the term "eastern" to indicate Alexandria in Egypt, the rival of Constantinople, which collected the counterforces against the capital city and stimulated the peculiar characteristics of the people—the Copts. Here the ecclesiastical decision was for Monophysitism. One can also apply the term "eastern" to the Slavs in the Balkan peninsula, who settled there permanently in the middle of the sixth century.

Already then, by following the rough outlines of the meaning of the word "eastern," we begin to clearly differentiate the rites that are to be found in the east.

2. THE EASTERN ROMAN EMPIRE

The period that we are examining in this chapter counts, in Byzantine history, as the beginning of the Byzantine empire, the period of the development of basic principles and the laying of foundations for an empire that was to endure until 1453. We have just discussed the autocratic imperial rule; now we must note certain important facts and persons.

What is first of all remarkable is that, to the emperors and their subjects, it was a matter of great importance that the authority, the tradition, the privileges, and everything that had defined the old Rome should be continued and, if possible, even increased in the new Rome. In the early period, competition with the old imperial city was a primary concern of Constantinople. It was a history of touchiness. Both cities were distrustful of each other and did not yield to each other's claims. When Rome was nullified politically by the barbarians, the bishop of that city still maintained the old claims in unabridged form; time and again the pope became the adversary of the emperor. The "Byzantines" felt themselves exalted above the western barbarians, but these barbarians came through the dark tunnel of decay and advanced with such an élan that in the east suspicion and anxiety began to dominate, anxiety before so much creative energy. But all this would reach its height later. In the period that concerns us now, Constantinople still was preeminent because of the presence of the imperial court, the splendor of the new city, the rich trade, and the power of the imperial armies. It is obvious that this fact of superiority would also have great consequences in ecclesial affairs—the churches in east and west drifted apart.

The imperial armies were a necessity. Throughout its whole history, the empire was beleaguered, attacked, partly conquered, and made tributary. That happened in the north (by the barbarians in 376 in Illyria, Dacia, along the Danube, the natural border) and in the "east" (Armenia, Syria). Above all, the Persian princes again and again attempted to extend their territory. By pyrrhic victories and by negotiating, the Byzantine emperors were able to keep their heads above water until Islam brought them to their end.

The relation of church and state after Constantine (Edict of Toleration) and Theodosius (state religion) had changed profoundly from what it was in the preceding period. Christians took over powerful state positions from pagans. The influence of the pagans constantly lessened; after a short flourishing under Julian (361–363), paganism went into complete decline. It was in scholarship and education that pagans continued their leadership for the longest time, until Justinian in 529 took away from all pagans the license to teach and closed the pagan school for philosophers (the academy) in Athens. The learned then sought refuge in Persia. Absolute power in all areas was now the prerogative of Christendom under the leadership of the Christian emperor, "the image of God," who had been called to bring the world back to God in conformity with the way of the Logos. In the person of the emperor, both church and state were foreshadowings of the kingdom of God and were therefore very closely linked, practically a unity. The emperor was the central figure: he was interpreter of the Logos; he was himself norm and law by God's design. The ideal was unity of the state and unity of the church and "a fundamental interdependence of the Orthodox empire and the Orthodox church which together formed a single political and ecclesiastical entity" (G. Ostrogorsky, op. cit., p. 31).

The great emperors of the eastern Roman empire in this period were: Constantine, the founder of the realm; Theodosius I (379–395) who ruled both east and west and held them together until his death; and Justinian I (527–565) who dominated the sixth century by his politics of unity, his struggle with the barbarians, his treaties with the Persians, and his autocratic centralism. From his time come the great Hagia Sophia in Constantinople and the mosaics of San Vitale in Ravenna; linked to his name is the perdurable *Codex Justinianus* (529 and 533), *the* codex of civil law. His church politics were less fortunate: to maintain friendship with Rome, the Nestorians, the Monophysites, and the Orthodox all at the same time was an impossible task. Finally Maurice (582–602) must be named, the emperor known for his peace treaty with the Persians. His rule marks the transition from the late Roman polity to the medieval kingdom. The crowning of Heraclius in 610 finally rang out the old era. "Byzantium was to emerge from the crisis in an essentially different form, able to throw off the heritage of decadent political life and to draw on new and vigorous sources of strength. Byzantine history properly speaking is the history of the medieval Greek empire, and it is now that it begins" (G. Ostrogorsky, op. cit., p. 86).

3. THEOLOGY
In the Greek east at this period theology simply soared. The speculative spirit of the eastern "Romans" produced an unsurpassed synthe-

60

sis of faith and reason. The application of Hellenic thought patterns to the Christian faith to make it more understandable and more intelligible had already been under way, specifically in Alexandria and in the work of Clement and Origen. They had developed an intellectual Christianity in which philosophy, *gnosis*, and *theoria*, played a dominant role and were even overestimated. This faith-theory of Alexandria was taken over and enlarged by the great Cappodocians, the writers of the golden age of eastern theology. Their work was later carried on by Byzantine theology, which provided its philosophical foundation, in the work of Pseudo-Dionysius the Areopagite, Maximus the Confessor, Simeon the New Theologian, and Gregory Palamas, each with his own views, but all of them together creating a golden age of theology.

This theology is marked especially by the accent on contemplation, on *theoria*, a living vision. Theology is contemplation, gazing, spiritual seeing. (It is thus spoken of in visual terms.) Theology is the high point of human life. This contemplation, together with the doctrine of divinization, is determinative of Byzantine spirituality which, in its turn, is very closely linked to worship. What began in Alexandria continues to live. It is correct to speak about an unbroken theological tradition in the Byzantine church up to the present day.

The Syriac tradition presents another point of view that in the long run was not able to sustain its particularity against the Greek tradition. This theology was based principally upon the divine life through which we live. More than seeing, faith is the germ of life that is received by hearing. It is not knowledge and contemplation that is central here, but listening to the Word.

Unlike western theology at this time, theological reflection in the Greek east was largely determined by the doctrinal strife concerning God and Christ, the trinitarian and the christological controversies. Both the Arian and the Monophysite-Nestorian controversies profoundly influenced church life, resulting as they did in the establishment of the orthodox doctrine that was to remain definitive in the eastern churches. The decisions of the councils were, and still remain, the single most important key for the life of the church, and therefore they also have a clearly demonstrable influence on worship. For the specifics of these controversies, one should consult works of dogmatic history. Here we will only note that the "exaltation" of Christ, couched in such terms as "Son of God," "God," *pantokrator*, or "Most High," changed the external form of worship. Both the mediation of Christ and the eschatological subsoil of the old Christology ("messiah," "prophet") had to give way to worship and doxology directed to the Son of God, essentially the equal of the Father. "The image of Christ in this period was firmly outlined. The exalting and the establishing of the Christ-figure in the first six centuries had as a result that his humanity remained underexposed in Byzantine devotion, liturgy and theology" (van der Aalst, op. cit., p. 121). A certain one-sided tendency remains present in the Greek liturgy, derived as it is from Orthodox doctrine.

Another tendency was to be found on the boundary of the empire in the churches of the East and West Syrians. Through political developments, they had been separated from the Byzantine church and the Byzantine tradition, and they had persevered in Nestorianism and Monphysitism. This was facilitated partially by the peculiar character of the Syrian theological tradition, especially when it was marked by a "low" Christology. That is, its basic premise was that eschatological salvation was actualized in and through Jesus as messiah. The Syrian tradition has always had some difficulty in accepting Jesus as both Son of God and man, possibly because of its Jewish background.

4. MONASTICISM
The cradle of monasticism was in the east, in Egypt. Without monks, the history of the Byzantine church and of Byzantine theology would be unthinkable. Only in a later period would this become fully visible, but the roots of the monastic influence are found at this time. Characteristic of eastern monasticism was what Schmemann (op. cit., p. 104) calls "a longing for maximalism," which came to expression, for example, in ceaseless prayer. This practice of prayer, in expectation of the kingdom of God, called for renunciation of the world, "a departure out of life and its works for the sake of prayer" (ibid., p. 105). Time was filled with prayer; worship became "endless." The monk was solitary: he lived in celibacy and retreated into solitude (Syria). His life was austere, in some sense even dualistic, that is, suspended as it were between this world and the next. The monks came at last into the cities, increasing their influence. Bishops began to be chosen from among their number; even today the *typika*, the orders of service for eucharist and for the prayer of the hours, remain monastic in style; finally, the great theologians had close monastic ties (e.g., Basil learned communal monastic life from Pachomius).

Monasticism is of preeminent importance for Byzantine liturgy, as is apparent in the "Byzantine synthesis," the osmosis between "parochial" and monastic types of worship, all of which are treated at greater length in chapter 5.

C. ISLAM

Islam has already been mentioned. In fact, the great spread of Mohammedanism comes in the following period, but the beginning is traced to this time. The prophet Mohammed was born at Mecca in 570 A.D. He stands at the head of a movement that would sweep as a flood over its contemporary world around the Mediterranean basin (cf. *Atlas of Western Civilization,* map 16). Those who believed in the Islamic concept of "total submission" to God began the route of conquest in Medina, and that route finally led to the creation of a Mohammedan realm that was greater than the Roman empire at its greatest extent. The heartlands of ancient Christianity were subjected, and little of Christianity in this area survived except for small ghetto groups in Syria, Mesopotamia, and later Asia Minor (Turkey). North Africa came under the sway of Islam as did the greater part of Spain. The eastern Roman empire was able to maintain itself for several centuries, but on only a small territory (Byzantium, Greece, Sicily).

For Christians, Islam was and remained a mysterious, anti-Christian heresy, but "nonetheless, Islam made a decisive contribution to the cultural history of the West. For a part of the Hellenic heritage, especially in the fields of mathematics, astronomy, geography, and philosophy, came back to the Christian West at the end of the twelfth century via Spain and Italy in translations from the Arabic of works originally in Greek or in the translated works of Arabic scholars. . . . The world of Islam took away from Christianity her old cultural centers; she drove back the faith and the Empire; but she gave back the heritage of Hellas, revised and transformed, through these unexpected channels" (*Atlas of Western Civilization,* p. 54, translation corrected).

II. CULTURAL DATA

Literature

C. J. de Vogel, *Wijsgerige aspekten van het vroeg-christelijk denken* (Baarn, 1970).

C. Mohrmann, *Liturgical Latin: Its Origins and Character* (London, 1959).

P. Riché, *Education et culture dans l'Occident barbare, VIe–VIIIe siècles* (Paris, 1962).

A. van der Aalst, *Aantekeningen bij de helleniesering van het christendom* (Nijmegen, 1974).

F. van der Meer, *Atlas of Western Civilization*, 2nd rev. ed. (New York & London, 1960).

A. THE FOUNDATIONS

The foundations of the spiritual house in which we still live as believers, but also as westerners, were laid in the fourth and fifth centuries.

"The liturgy, with its feasts and hymns (in the West those of St. Ambrose); the Roman style of the prayers; the Roman ecclesiastical organization of the See of St. Peter; the great Scriptural commentaries; hagiography, and the systematization of Christian dogma and morality; the ascetic life . . . ; the basilicas with their decorations, and the appearance of symbolic, didactic, and expressionist art; finally, the Christian Platonism of the great Cappadocians, of Ambrose . . . and of Augustine, the spiritual father of the Middle Ages—such is the treasury which the Middle Ages, and we ourselves today, never cease to plunder. . . . Whoever compares the writings, art and above all, the personalities of the first Christian centuries with those of pre-Christian antiquity, is always struck by the presence of a new psychic factor—the Biblical factor. It is as if the human personality has received a new inner dimension, and it is immediately recognizable in a new imaginative idiom drawn from the Bible. It expressed itself in new emotions, new lines of approach, and a wholly new outlook on men and all things. The old *eros* has given way to *agape*; the superiority complex of the élite has given way to the feeling of human comradeship; man is revealed in the light of the Incarnation, and the gods have made way for the majesty of God." (*Atlas of Western Civilization*, pp. 34, 48.)

In regard to Christian art: the old technique and style remain in force but with a new symbolic, typological content, as may be seen in the sarcophagi, the mosaics, the old basilicas, and the cemeteries. This same typology is to be found in the extensive library we now possess of the works of the church Fathers, in liturgical sources, in preaching, and in catechesis. The heart of this typology is the faith in the future of the history of salvation. The present life of the community, its faith and worship, were experienced as the continuation of God's work of salvation that had begun in the past and that would come to full realization in the future. In the past lay the veiled signs of what was taking place in the present.

B. EDUCATIONAL SYSTEM

The Roman educational system, including the traditional programs of rhetorical study, was preserved in the west in spite of the barbarian invasions. This was so in Gaul up to the beginning of the sixth century, and in Italy up to the beginning of the seventh. When it was not possible to maintain the schools, their tradition was carried on in aristocratic families. The barbarians also frequently joined themselves to this instructional system. But then suddenly it stopped. By the beginning of the reign of Charlemagne, nothing was left of the old rhetorical system of education. A new type of education arose then that remained dominant into the twelfth century: education and study (almost entirely a privilege of monks and clerics) were concentrated on Bible and liturgy. The "people" remained devoid of education, as was most often the case in Roman antiquity, but the difference was that the place of the aristocracy in the schools was taken over by the clergy, the new aristocrats in the "maturing west."

C. LANGUAGE

See C. Mohrmann, *Liturgical Latin: Its Origins and Character* (London, 1959). Koine Greek had been the language in which the Christian gospel was proclaimed in the first centuries, also in the west (and specifically in Rome). It was probably the language of the common people to whom Christianity primarily addressed itself. In the second half of the second century, however, Latin also appeared as the language of Christians (in North Africa), and from that time on it was used more and more widely in the west. It was Christian Latin, however, the language of a subgroup, a variant of classical Latin. In its formation certain social and spiritual factors played a role: the closed group (ghettolike) within the society of the day; concepts derived from the gospel, which made new words necessary. Christian Latin was determined by the Bible and by popular tendencies.

Neologisms with an exotic flavor (e.g., *sanctificare, vivificare, quoniam*) arose and continued in existence even as the language became more cultivated. Neologisms could be borrowed from Greek (*aposto-*

lus, ecclesia, evangelium, baptisma) or created from Latin. The formation of these words was semasiological (i.e., words are given a new meaning, *sèma*, as in *salus* = salvation, not health; *caro* = unredeemed existence, not flesh; *pax* = peace with God); or lexicological (a new word is created, as *carnalis, spiritualis, salvator, salutare*). In the third century, this peculiar popular Christian language developed into a literary language with its own terminology, its own syntax, and its own style.

In the fourth century, writers turned again to classical Latin, for the church was now recognized in society and was concerned with adapting to that new situation. The time of hiding was over, and it was now time to come out into the open with the greatest dignity possible in the face of paganism. The Latin Fathers, and especially Hilary of Poitiers, went about this task.

It was against this background that liturgical Latin arose. In Rome, Greek was initially preserved in worship and in official church documents. Only toward the middle of the third century did Latin find its way into the documents, and most likely it came only later (probably about the middle of the fourth century) into the liturgy. That the shift to Latin in liturgy occurred so late is to be ascribed to the desire for a sacred language in worship. The community consciously distanced itself from ordinary language; the stylized character of liturgy is enhanced by the use of a "foreign" language. The preservation of Greek in Roman worship, in the midst of a community that used Christian Latin, its ordinary group language, was an attempt to maintain the sacred character of worship. Nonetheless, when Latin was introduced into the liturgy, Christian Latin was the basic language, but solemn, classical expressions were added. Once again the classical "Roman" language was being used. Words like *preces, precari, beatitudo, pontifex*, and so on were introduced as replacements for *oratio, orare, refrigerium*, and *episcopus!* The Latin text of the Roman canon is a clear example: the old *gravitas* (with its synonyms and its juridical precision) is back. Liturgical Latin was thus a solemn, almost hieratic language that remained understandable, but strange rather than commonplace.

Besides this liturgical language, in the fourth and fifth centuries a poetic language arose that was lively, popular, and both Christian and classical (Ambrose).

The language question is more complicated in the east, where political and social factors played a role. Uniformity of language, as was the case for so long with Latin in the west, was not known in the east. Of course, the most influential language was Greek, the language of the imperial court (although not always of imperial decrees; the "Romans"—the *Romaioi*—kept Latin as the official language). The imperial officials in the eastern part of the empire thus used Greek, and as a result it also became the language of the church and the liturgy. The original liturgy was in koine Greek in Jerusalem, Antioch, Alexandria, and Constantinople. The most important texts are Greek texts. The great theologians wrote in Greek. Although the "Romans" remained faithful to the old culture of the Roman empire in thought and word, it was the culture of an aristocracy, the leading class, that enjoyed education and had been initiated into rhetoric. Greek was *the* language of eastern Christianity during this period. It unconsciously claimed a monopoly and thereby evoked countermovements, especially among the Syrians. The Greeks learned no other language, but rather expected that others should speak their language.

At the same time, it must be said that Syriac is an important source for the knowledge of the liturgy, and that is so precisely because it is through Syriac writings that one has an opportunity of reaching older levels of liturgy, of discovering the local character of that older liturgy, and of encountering tendencies that, in reaction to the Greek spirit, tried as much as possible to maintain the characteristic Syriac tradition.

D. IMPERIAL CULTURE

The influence of the state on Christian worship was also felt in still other ways. The vesture of the clergy both in and outside the liturgy (the old garments of officials), certain utensils (candles, thuribles), courtly practices (bowing the head, kneeling before important persons, kissing the hand), solemn entrances (processions) in the magnificent church buildings: all of this witnesses to the influence of the "imperial" culture.

III. THE LITURGY:
ORDERS OF SERVICE AND TEXTS

Literature

In addition to the literature listed in chapter 1

Jerusalem

H. Leeb, *Die Gesänge im Gemeinschaftsgottesdienst von Jerusalem* (Vienna, 1970).

R. Zerfass, *Die Schriftlesung im Kathedraloffizium Jerusalems* (Münster, 1968).

The West

GENERAL

K. Gamber, *Codices liturgici, latini antiquiores* (Freiburg, 1963).

C. Vogel, *Introduction aux sources de l'histoire du culte chrétien au Moyen Age,* repr. (Spoleto, 1975).

DAILY PRAYER

H. Leeb, *Die Psalmodie bei Ambrosius* (Vienna, 1967).

P. Salmon, *L'office divin; histoire de la formation du bréviaire* (Paris, 1959).

———, *L'office divin au moyen age* (Paris, 1967).

G. Winkler, "Über die Kathedralvesper in den verschiedenen Riten des Ostens und Westens," *Archiv für Liturgiewissenschaft* 16, 1974, pp. 53–102.

THE YEAR

B. Botte, et al., *Epiphanie, retour du Christ* (Paris, 1967).

R. Cabié, *La Pentecôte* (Tournai, 1965).

O. Casel, "Art und Sinn der ältesten christlichen Osterfeier," *Jahrbuch für Liturgiewissenschaft* 14, 1938, pp. 1–78; trans. *La fête de Pâques dans l'Eglise des Pères* (Paris, 1963).

J. G. Davies, *Holy Week. A Short History* (London, 1963).

M. de Soos, *Le mystère liturgique* (Münster, 1958).

J. Pascher, *Das Liturgische Jahr* (Munich, 1963).

H. Wegman, *Het paasoktaaf in het missale Romanum en zijn geschiedenis* (Assen, 1968).

INITIATION

L. Ligier, *La Confirmation* (Paris, 1973).

L. Mitchell, *Baptismal Anointing* (London, 1966).

H. M. Riley, *Christian Initiation; A Comparative Study* (Washington, 1974).

A. Stenzel, *Die Taufe* (Innsbruck, 1958).

EUCHARIST

B. Botte, et al., *Eucharisties d'Orient et d'Occident,* 2 vols. (Paris, 1970).

———, *Le Canon de la messe romain* (Louvain, 1935).

——— & C. Mohrmann, *L'ordinaire de la messe* (Louvain, 1953).

O. Casel, *Das christliche Opfermysterium* (Graz, 1968).

PENANCE AND RECONCILIATION

J. Jungmann, *Die lateinischen Bussriten im ihrer geschichtlichen Entwicklung* (Innsbruck, 1932).

C. Vogel, *Le pécheur et la pénitence dans l'église ancienne* (Paris, 1969).

ORDINATION

C. Munier, *Les Statuta Ecclesiae Antiqua* (Paris, 1960).

L. Otto, *Das Weihesakrament* (Freiburg, 1969).

H. Porter, *The Ordination Prayers of the Ancient Western Churches* (London, 1967).

DEATH

E. Freistedt, *Altchristliche Totengedächtnistage und ihre Beziehung zum Jenseitsglauben und Totenkultus der Antike* (Münster, 1928, 1979).

J. Ndetika, *L'évocation de l'au-delà dans la prière pour les morts; étude patristique et de liturgie latines (IV–VIII siècles)* (Louvain, 1971).

MARRIAGE

K. Ritzer, *Formen, Riten, und religiöses Brauchtum der Eheschliessung im der christlichen Kirchen des ersten Jahrtausends* (Münster, 1962).

The East

GENERAL

Handbuch der Ostkirchenkunde (Düsseldorf,1971), see especially bibliography, pp. 766–817.

F. Heiler, *Die Ostkirchen* (Munich & Basel, 1971).

Liturgisch Woordenboek (see under "Boeken" and "Oosterse ritussen").

E. Pataq Simon, *L'expérience, de l'Esprit par l'église d'après la tradition syrienne d'Antioche* (Paris, 1971).

A. von Maltzew, *Die Liturgien der orthodox-katholischen Kirche des Morgenlandes* (Berlin, 1902).

DAILY PRAYER

Dimanche. Office selon les huit-tons (Chevetogne, 1972).

J. Mateos, *Lelya-Sapra; essai d'interprétation des matines chaldéennes* (Rome, 1959).

———, "The Origins of the Divine Office," *Worship* 31:8, 1967, pp. 477–485.

———, "The Morning and Evening Office," *Worship* 42:1, 1968, pp. 31–47.

E. Mercenier, *La prière des Églises de rite byzantin*, 3 vols. (Chevetogne, 1937–1965).

THE YEAR

G. Bertoniere, *The Historical Development of the Easter Vigil and Related Services in the Greek Church* (Rome, 1972).

EUCHARIST

B. Botte, et al., *Eucharisties d'Orient et d'Occident*, 2 vols. (Paris, 1970).

M. Edelby, *Liturgicon; Missel byzantin à l'usage des fidèles* (Beirut, 1960; German trans., Recklinghausen, 1967).

R. Kaczynski, *Das Wort Gottes in Liturgie und Alltag der Gemeinde des Johannes Chrysostomus* (Freiburg, 1974).

F. van der Paverd, *Zur Geschichte der Messliturgie in Antiocheia und Konstantinopel gegen Ende des vierten Jahrhunderts* (Rome, 1970).

R. Taft, *The Great Entrance; a History of the Transfer of Gifts* (Rome, 1975).

A. Tarby, *La prière eucharistique de l'église de Jerusalem* (Paris, 1972).

G. Wagner, *Der Ursprung der Chrysostomus liturgie* (Münster, 1973).

A. JEWISH BACKGROUND

There has already been a discussion in the first chapter of the Jewish background of Christian worship in the east and the west. In the succeeding centuries, this influence continued to be exerted, or so we may assume. There are no direct witnesses available, but neither is there a break with the past in Christian worship after the peace of the church. The liturgy continued to develop along the lines that came into being in previous centuries. Because of the development of doctrine, worship was also altered, but without a break; the Jewish background and even ongoing Jewish influence remained. One thing needs to be noted, however: this Jewish background was no longer recognized very precisely and practices were called Christian that at the outset had been actually Jewish Christian.

In the meanwhile, the relationship between Christians and Jews did not grow better after the peace of the church. There were few conversations, even less cooperation. Roles were reversed: in the early centuries it was the Jews who sometimes called the secular government for help against the Christians; after the peace of the church it was the Christians who made the situation of the Jews more difficult and sometimes untenable. There was enmity against the Jews and no patience for their *obstinatio* toward Christian teaching.

B. SOURCES

It is difficult to give an overview of the sources of the liturgy in this time. It can be established that there was great liturgical creativity in the fourth and fifth centuries, especially outside Rome, which because of its cosmopolitan character was for a long time more conservative, but there remain nonetheless few complete orders of service and actual texts. Indirect indications are to be found in greater number, so we shall make a distinction here between indirect and direct sources.

1. INDIRECT SOURCES

In Africa much is to be found in the writings of Augustine, especially his letters numbers 54 and 55 addressed to Januarius (PL 33:199; trans. in *Fathers of the Church*, vol. 9, New York, 1951, pp. 252–293), in which he describes the diversity of local liturgy (see also W. Roetzer, *Des hl. Augustinus Schriften als liturgiegeschichtliche Quelle*, Münster, 1930; and F. van der Meer, *Augustine the Bishop*, New York, 1962). Probably Africa had a sacramentary, a book with prayers for the president: Gennadius (d. 492) makes the remark that a certain bishop Voconius *"composuit etiam sacramentorum egregium volumen"* ("he composed in addition an admirable volume for the sacraments"). Such a number of prayers were composed, and such bad ones, that the councils of Hippo, Carthage, and Mileve(?) in 393, 397, and 416, respectively, required the official approval of such texts.

At this same time, there were Christian congregations in the Roman cities of Gaul, but little is known about them, save that a presbyter Museus (d. 469?) assembled a lectionary, a songbook (*responsoriale*), and a sacramentary. What they contained we do not know.

In Spain, the *Liber mozarabicus sacramentorum* and *Liber ordinum* are from a much later time, but the material in these books could stem from the fourth and fifth centuries. They were important collections in which old Roman material can be found. What is of greatest importance, however, is the diary of the pilgrimage of a Spanish woman, dated about 400 A.D.: *Peregrinatio ad loca sancta Egeriae* (C.C. 175, 32–106; trans. in J. Wilkinson, *Egeria's Travels*, London, 1971).

Of importance from north Italy are the writings of Ambrose (d.

392). Exceptionally valuable information about initiation is found in his *De mysteriis* and *De sacramentis* (*Sources chrétiennes* 25; English trans. of *De sacramentis* in E. Yarnold, *The Awe Inspiring Rites of Initiation*, Slough, 1973, pp. 99–153). Ambrose is known also for his poetry and hymns. There was a development of liturgical activity at Ravenna, but nothing remains except pieces of the *laus cerei* (*Exsultet;* cf. F. Sotocornola, *L'anno liturgico nei sermoni di Pietro Chrisologo*, Cesena, 1973). Pseudo-Maximus of Turin and his tractate on baptism (PL 77:771) should also be mentioned. Finally, there are remarks concerning worship here and there in the writings of Jerome.

In Rome, there was certainly liturgical activity, but no texts prior to the middle of the sixth century have been preserved. Of interest is a letter to Senarius (an official in the court of Theodoric at Ravenna) from the deacon John in Rome (later Pope John I [523–526?], PL 59: 399) that deals with the rites of baptism. Further information is to be found in writings of the popes:

1. Innocent I (401–417), who wrote a letter to the bishop of Gubbio in which he asks for unity in worship on the basis of the liturgy of Rome;
2. Leo I (440–461), known for his letters and sermons;
3. Hilarius (461–468), to whom perhaps may be attributed the organization of the *stationes*, the celebrations of the liturgy by the bishop of Rome together with the clergy and the faithful in various specially chosen churches of the city;
4. Felix II (483–492), who was the last to mention the intercessions of the faithful in the eucharist at Rome (PL 58:925);
5. Gelasius (492–496), to whom liturgical texts are attributed that are included in the *Sacramentarium Veronense*, which will be discussed later;
6. Vigilius (537–555), of whom there are several texts open to reconstruction.

The most important figure for the church and for the liturgy of his time was Pope Gregory the Great (590–604), from whose works much information about worship can be drawn.

For Egypt, one can find indirect information in the writings of Athanasius and Cyril of Alexandria (e.g., in their paschal letters), and we should also mention Pachomius' rule for monks in which liturgical material is to be found.

For Syria, with Antioch as its center (together with Jerusalem the heart of the beginning of Christianity), information can be obtained indirectly from both the Greek and the Syriac traditions. Although there are numerous patristic works, we shall limit ourselves to the works of the following:

Eusebius, *Ecclesiastical History* (*Sources chrétiennes* 31, 41, 55; text and English translation in *Loeb Classical Library*, vol. 1, Cambridge, 1965, pp. 153f.) contains precious data (e.g., concerning Easter);

Cyril of Jerusalem, twenty-four catechetical lectures of which the five "mystagogical catecheses" are an explication of Christian initiation rites (PG 33:331–1180; *Sources chrétiennes* 126; text and English translation in F. L. Cross, ed., *St. Cyril of Jerusalem's Lectures on the Christian Sacraments*, London, 1966);

Theodore of Mopsuestia, catechetical homilies concerning Christian initiation, of great significance for their content (Syriac text and translation in A. Mingana, ed. and trans., *Woodbrooke Studies*, vol. 6. Cambridge, 1933; cf. R. Tonneau & R. Devreesse, *Les homélies catéchétiques*, Vatican, 1949; E. Yarnold, op. cit., pp. 173–263).

John Chrysostom (cf. F. von der Paverd, op. cit.) whose works, especially his initiation catecheses, are rich in information (cf. E. Yarnold, op. cit., pp. 155–171; P. W. Harkins, *St. John Chrysostom: Baptismal Instructions*, Westminster, Md., 1963) as are his festal homilies (we shall come back to the liturgy that bears his name);

Nestorius, homilies;

Narsai, homilies (R. Connolly, *The Liturgical Homilies of Narsai*, Cambridge, 1909);

Ephrem, the inexhaustible hymn writer (see the homilies in E. Beck, ed., *Corpus Scriptorum Christianorum Orientalium* (*CSCO*), Louvain, 1903ff., 305–306, 311–312, 320–321, 334–335, 412–413, and the Easter hymns in *CSCO*, 248–249).

The paschal homilies of, among others, Hesychius and Basil of Seleucia (*Sources chrétiennes* 187).

This list of indirect sources is, to be sure, incomplete. As we have said, scattered facts can be found in virtually all the Christian writers as well as in the decrees of the councils and synods.

In Asia Minor, where theology reached such heights at this time, the writings of the following great church Fathers are also indirect sources for the liturgy. We may list: Asterios Sophistes of Cappadocia (cf. H. J. Auf der Maur, *Die Osterhomilien des Asterios Sophistes*, Trier, 1967), of interest for the history of Easter; the Cappadocians, including Basil the Great, to whom there is attributed a liturgy, about which more later. His other work is just as significant for liturgical history (sermons and homilies, letters about worship). Finally, let us mention Gregory of Nazianzus (*orationes* or sermons) and Gregory of Nyssa (sermons, *Vita Macrinae*).

2. DIRECT SOURCES

The West

A direct source for the Roman liturgy is the *Sacramentarium Veronense*, a book of prayers intended to be spoken by the president at the eucharist or at rites associated with the eucharist such as ordinations and baptism. With this book, a sacramentary had come into being out of the tradition of the so-called *libelli missarum*: little, easily manageable books containing one or several "mass formulae," that is, the prayers that were spoken by the bishop or priest during the service (usually an opening prayer, a prayer over the gifts, a proper preface, and a postcommunion prayer). There were probably several *libelli* for the various festivals and other days during the year. Originally the liturgical leader himself composed the texts for the liturgy. One year he would formulate the material in a certain way, another year in yet another way. In such a manner a great quantity of material was originated and preserved.

Most likely because improvisation soon became a burden, liturgical leaders began to exchange texts with one another. Texts were eagerly borrowed, especially from those who were gifted writers or who were of great authority, such as the bishop of Rome. Soon all this had gone so far that a fixed collection of good texts could be compiled.

Such a collection of *libelli,* ordered according to the months of the year, has been preserved in the *Sacramentarium Veronense*, which had earlier been called the Leonine Sacramentary or the *Leonianum* after Pope Leo I, who was initially thought to have been the author. This is an immensely valuable document that informs us about the liturgy in the sixth century. It is unfortunately incomplete: the first part (from January through early April) is missing and so are the prayers for the liturgy of Easter. The document is no official sacramentary such as we shall later encounter, but a private collection of "mass formulae" of which a great part goes back to bishops of the fifth and sixth centuries (Pope Vigilius, Pope Gelasius, etc.). Somewhere outside Rome the redactor collected and arranged the Roman *libelli.*

This book takes us as far back as possible in the history of the

Roman liturgy and lets us see into the culture of Latin prayer that distinguished between *preces* (consecratory formulae), *orationes fidelium* (intercessions), and *orationes* (short prayers after a song or a reading).

Edition: Sacramentarium Veronense, L. C. Mohlberg, ed., 2nd rev. ed. (*Rerum Ecclesiasticarum Documenta, Series Maior, Fontes* I) (Rome, 1966). *Studies:* See the introduction to the Mohlberg volume; and D. M. Hope, *The Leonine Sacramentary: A Reassessment of Its Nature and Purpose* (Oxford, 1971). *Contents:* Mass formulae for festivals of the saints (among others, John the Baptist, Peter and Paul in June), for Pentecost and Christmas, for ordinations (in September, formulae XXVIII), etc.

The East

Direct sources for the liturgy in the east are primarily related to the liturgy of Jerusalem, which was of widespread influence. Jerusalem and Palestine generally had been since Constantine the Christian pilgrimage places par excellence: there pilgrims visited the holy places, marked as they were by the great churches built by the emperor and the empress. There a local liturgy had developed that seems to have become extensively known and imitated.

The second important center in the east was Antioch.

ITINERARIUM AETHERIAE
Translation: J. Wilkinson, trans., *Egeria's Travels* (London, 1971).

About 400 A.D.: a detailed description of worship in Jerusalem, especially in the great basilica (*Martyrium*) and the rotunda of the Resurrection (*Anastasis*). The texts of the liturgies do not appear in Egeria's work.

THE ARMENIAN LECTIONARY
Text and translation: A. Renoux, *Le codex arménien Jérusalem 121, Patr. Orient.* 163, 168 (Paris, 1969, 1971); cf. J. Wilkinson, op. cit., pp. 253–277.

An extremely important document that shows the organization of the celebration of the church year, a schedule of readings, and a list of the church buildings chosen for the liturgy, all of this relating to Jerusalem of about 420–450 A.D.

THE GEORGIAN LECTIONARY
Text: M. Tarchnischvili, *Le grand lectionaire de l'église de Jérusalem (5e–8e siècles),* CSCO, 188–189, 204–205 (Leuven, 1959–1960).

The roots of this lectionary go back to the fifth century, although the total work is from a later time (eighth to ninth centuries). This manuscript material in printed form is valuable for comparison with the Armenian Lectionary.

CONSTITUTIONES APOSTOLORUM
Text: F. Funk (Paderborn, 1905; repr. Torino, 1962). *Translation: The Ante-Nicene Fathers,* Buffalo, 1886, vol. 7, pp. 391–508.

Probably from the fifth century and containing information about the church order of Antioch. Liturgical material takes up an important part of this book. Book VIII is of interest because of its detailed description of the eucharist (the so-called *Missa Clementina*), the text of the anaphora, and the prayers for ordination to office.

TESTAMENTUM DOMINI NOSTRI JESU CHRISTI
Text: I. Rahmani (Mainz, 1899). *Translation:* J. Cooper & A. J. Maclean, *The Testament of our Lord* (Edinburgh, 1902).

From the fifth century, Syrian, Monophysite: under the guise of a report of the teaching of the apostles (a frequent practice in these days), the book includes information about the arrangement of the church building and about ordinations, eucharist, and initiation.

THE EUCHOLOGION OF SERAPION
Translation: L. Deiss, *Springtime of the Liturgy* (Collegeville, 1979), pp. 184–200.

The so-called *Euchologion* of Serapion, bishop of Thmuis (c. 350), contains among other things three prayers for ordinations, a blessing of oil, and a prayer at a burial. Especially interesting in form and content is the eucharistic prayer, the "anaphora of Serapion."

C. SUMMARIES OF THE LITURGICAL DATA

1. THE LITURGY IN JERUSALEM

In the preceding chapter, prior to a detailed discussion of the data of Christian worship, a reference had to be made to the fundamental influences of the Jewish liturgy. Now we encounter an analogous situation: the fourth- and fifth-century liturgy in both east and west was more or less determined by the liturgy of Jerusalem, the holy city, which had gained new prominence in the time of Constantine and since then had become a center for pilgrimage. Here then is a short overview of the outstanding characteristics of the liturgy of Jerusalem.

Three practices of the Jerusalem church became models for Christian worship: (1) the structure and organization of the daily hours of prayer, (2) the celebration of festivals throughout the year, and (3) Christian initiation (baptism-anointing-eucharist).

Daily Prayer

In the journal of her travels, Egeria gives a detailed account (in chaps. 24ff.) of the services of prayer during the week and on Sundays. She describes the vigil with psalms and hymns that was concluded by morning prayer with its *"ymni matutini."* The Sunday morning service was preceded by the reading of the gospel account of the resurrection by the bishop in the Anastasis. The assembly was concluded with intercessions and the blessing by the bishop. As the bishop departed, the faithful took leave of him by kissing his hand. Among the "morning hymns" were Psalms 148, 149, and 150, which, in the common tradition in east and west, always recur in morning prayer. It should be noted that only on Sundays was the reading of scripture made part of morning prayer; otherwise, the character of morning prayer was determined by psalms of praise and intercessions.

Further, Egeria mentions prayer at the sixth and ninth hours, sext and none. These "hours" consisted of psalms and antiphons and concluded with the prayer and the blessing by the bishop.

Finally, Egeria describes vespers (toward the end of the afternoon), called here *lucernarium* (*lucernare, licinicon*). The lights were lit from the light that always burned in the grotto of the Anastasis. The "vesper hymns" (Psalms 130 and 141) were prayed; the second had been widely used in the church from early times. Then, in the presence of the bishop, other evening hymns (among them probably the *phos hilaron*) were sung. The intercessions with the diptychs followed, that is, the naming of those who were to be especially remembered. The bishop concluded with a prayer and the blessing of the catechumens and the faithful, and then he dismissed them all. The prayer, the blessing, and the dismissal were repeated in the atrium and in a little chapel. The assembly ended at dark.

This is a greatly abbreviated version of Egeria's description, but what it shows is that first of all Jerusalem had become a pilgrim city in which many people were constantly gathering. Because of this, daily services were possible and necessary. We see the way special festivals were celebrated: the services were held in churches that were built at the holy places—the *"stationes."* The assembly took place at the most beloved spots—in the basilica on the hill of Calvary (the Martyrium); in its nearby rotunda, the Anastasis, connected by a colonnade; and near the Chapel of the Cross between the Martyrium and the Anastasis, where the relics of the cross were reputed to have been found. It was Constantine who had constructed this magnificent building, a large complex where the liturgy was celebrated daily. No wonder pilgrims were profoundly impressed and, on their return home, adopted the Jerusalem practices. The worship life of the holy city came to be known everywhere.

Furthermore, it must be noted that Egeria speaks of a genuinely communal celebration of the liturgy wherein the bishop, the presbyters, and the deacons fulfilled proper roles but always in close connection with the faithful who were present. The bishop was a universally honored man and everyone took leave of him at the end of the services, but this is not to be construed as a "clericalization" of worship. Everything points rather to a "corporate" celebration.

In the midst of the faithful a group was present who are especially named by Egeria: the "monazontes et parthenae," male and female "monks," with whom some "fiery" lay people associated themselves. It was they who during the vigil prayed the psalms and who, on Sundays, remained in the church after morning prayer for communal prayer until the celebration of the eucharist. Monks in the city! Very likely they had their own residence in the city, but it is clear that they fulfilled a role in the life of the whole church and were closely connected to its life. These were no anchorites who had withdrawn to the desert in order to "seek salvation" in solitary fashion; they were people of communal life close to the tumult of the city. This fact has been of very great importance for the development of worship both in the east and in the west (cf. A. Schmemann, *Introduction to Liturgical Theology,* pp. 101–113, 146–166).

A third conclusion can be drawn from Egeria's description: the liturgy developed from the basic worship of the previous period. There was no break with the time before Constantine; there was rather a continuous evolution. This means that the fundamental characteristics of morning and evening prayer remained. In the morning and the evening, praise was sung to God (*eucharistia*) by the community of the church and intercessions were made for the needs of the congregation. This combined prayer of praise and petition was preserved. Because it was a prayer of the whole community, the texts were invariably a fixed series of psalms fitting to the time of day, well-known hymnic texts, short responses and invocations that could be easily remembered by the faithful, and the same text material time and again. This situation changed when the clergy, in Jerusalem, in Constantinople, in Rome, stimulated by the emperor, proceeded to elaborate the liturgy and thus began to take the primary role in it. It was then that the monks introduced their ideal of prayer into corporate worship. Clergy and monks changed the liturgy, but did not necessarily improve it.

Besides this "eucharistic" morning and evening service (eucharistic in the literal sense of praise and thanksgiving), there was in Jerusalem another sort of service to which R. Zerfass, *Die Schriftlesung in Kathedraloffizium Jerusalems* (Münster, 1968), has called attention. He speaks of a *Verkündigungsgottesdienst*, a service of proclamation in which holy scripture was read and the saving deeds of God were extolled. This pattern of worship had already been followed in the word service of the eucharist and in the Easter vigil, but it was now employed more widely. A so-called "festival office" arose (order of service for the feasts of the Lord, the *Theotokos*, the martyrs). Once again Jerusalem was the cradle for this development. At the place of the resurrection on Sunday mornings before morning prayer, the resurrection pericopes were read by the bishop. In the city and in Bethlehem, at places associated with the life of Jesus, the appropriate lections were read aloud. The consequences of this development were twofold: on the one hand, the prayer of the hours on festivals was enriched with variable texts, that is, with appropriate scripture readings in pericope series and with the associated texts of songs. On the other hand, there came to be a mixture of praise and proclamation (reading). One must not forget that both east and west had different but highly nuanced views of these practices. The reading need not have been only the holy scripture but also nonscriptural material (such as stories of the martyrs, famous homilies, etc.).

Finally we should mention an aspect of the congregation's participation in worship. Egeria speaks about "*ymni,*" about responses and antiphons and short invocations in morning and evening prayer. We lack information about how this was done, but it is probable that these responses included communal singing, which was most likely still an integral part of worship and not simply reserved to a choir. Praise and thanksgiving is most aptly expressed in song, but what "singing" was must be conceived broadly; it was singing but it was also "speaking" in song.

The Festivals
Egeria's description of the yearly festivals is accurate and detailed and is confirmed by the Armenian Lectionary (edition by A. Renoux) that also described the Jerusalem liturgy. It is remarkable that a practically complete pericope series for festivals had already been developed by the beginning of the fifth century. Which festivals? We

cannot give complete details except to note that in Jerusalem the celebration of the so-called church year had become more prominent than before. As to the earlier practice, we are certain only of the celebration of Sunday and of Easter. Now there were feasts of the Lord celebrated "in place" (i.e., at the places associated with the life of the Lord) of the *Theotokos,* and of confessors and martyrs. For all of these feasts precise lections were provided.

It is not surprising that the festival practices of Jerusalem and of Palestine came to be normative. The city was flooded with pilgrims who wanted to visit the holy places (above all the Martyrium, the place of Jesus' death). The memorial of the life of Jesus was celebrated at the places where he had lived and worked, where he had died and was raised. The consequence was that the celebration of the one mystery of Christ was divided into a remembrance of *historical places.* The unity of the original Sunday and Easter celebrations gave way to the multiplicity of celebrations of the "drama of salvation." "Gradually there arose a form of worship designed to help the participant relive—psychologically and religiously—the events or series of events with which the place was connected . . . this historicity gradually acquired a mysteriological formulation. . . . We see here an unwavering tendency to 'detailization' " (Schmemann, *Introduction to Liturgical Theology,* pp. 96–97).

Several festivals took place in Jerusalem. Egeria records Epiphany with its octave (the continuing eight-day celebration of great feasts); a fast of eight weeks (excluding Saturdays and Sundays); and the celebration of Holy Week, i.e., Palm Sunday, Holy Thursday, Good Friday, Holy Saturday, and Easter Sunday. These last three days were a single celebration, tied together from hour to hour with short pauses for rest, each part celebrated at the appropriate place and furnished with a complete cycle of readings. Ascension and Pentecost were also celebrated, as well as September 14 (memorial of the dedication of the great churches of Jerusalem). Besides the several memorial days of apostles, martyrs, and confessors, the Armenian Lectionary has readings for August 15 as the feast of the *Theotokos* in Bethlehem.

In short, in Jerusalem the festival calendar in the fourth century had been enlarged. This festival calendar, with variations, became the norm in both the east and the west.

The Sacraments
Christian initiation: We encounter baptism-anointing-eucharist in both the direct and the indirect sources for the Jerusalem liturgy: in

Egeria's diary, in the catecheses of Cyril of Jerusalem, in the Armenian Lectionary, and in a reconstruction of the anaphora (eucharistic prayer) of Jerusalem.

Baptism is treated in Egeria and in Cyril. The attention is focused on those who enrolled themselves at the beginning of the fast for baptism and anointing in the paschal night, who wanted to turn, *pros anatolēn, tou photos to chōrion* (*Mystagogical Catechesis* 1:9), "toward the east, the region of the light." The time of preparation is thus called *photizomenate*. The candidates were enrolled at the beginning of the fast to the accompaniment of the prayer of the congregation. Exorcisms, "*emphusēma*," the insufflation of the Spirit who drives out the demon, and the signing with the cross on the forehead were all parts of the initiation rites. The candidates solemnly received the handed-over "*symbolum*." The meaning of this creed was explained in detail by Cyril in several catecheses (*Myst. Catecheses* 6–18). The preparation ended on Holy Saturday afternoon. The candidates renounced Satan turned toward the west; then having turned toward the east, they confessed their faith, i.e., the "*redditio sumboli*": the confession in the presence of the church. In the meantime the paschal vigil had begun. After the traditional readings of the memorable night, the candidates went to the baptistery, undressed ("putting off the old man"), were anointed from head to foot with oil as a participation in the "good olive-tree" and the abundance of Christ and as an exorcism for the driving away of the power of evil (*Myst. Catechesis* 2:3), descended into the font filled with consecrated water, made the saving confession, *tēn sōtērion homologian* (*Myst. Catechesis* 2:4), and were immersed or had water poured over them three times. The immersion exemplified Paul's theology of baptism: one dies, is buried, and rises with the Lord in whom one is newborn (*neophytos*). Baptism is *tōn tou Christou pathēmatōn antitupon* (*Myst. Catechesis* 2:6), a representation—an antitype—of the sufferings of Christ, "a sanctifying mystery . . . a means of rising by way of initiation from the profane to the sacred, from the material to the spiritual, from the sensual to the noumenal" (Schmemann, p. 100).

The paschal night is regarded as the night of initiation into the mysteries, which in some sense differs from the earlier view that baptism was primarily a way of conversion, the way toward the messianic kingdom.

Anointing was inextricably connected with baptism in water, forming with it one single whole. Forehead, ears, nose, and breast were anointed: now one was a Christian, that is, an anointed one. This anointing was an indelible seal of the Holy Spirit (*sphragis*).

The eucharist is described in its essence by Cyril in *Mystagogical Catechesis* 5. He does not mention the service of readings, probably because the readings during the night vigil sufficed for the readings at the mass. But for the rest, Cyril gives the complete structure of eucharistic prayer (without the institution narrative), the subsequent Our Father, the *ta hagia tois hagiois* (holy things for the holy people), the communion song, and the manner of receiving communion (*Myst. Catechesis* 5:21).

An example can still be found, more or less preserved for us, known as the anaphora of James. It is traceable in manuscripts back to the ninth century (*Cod. Vaticanus graecus* 2282). A. Tarby, *La prière eucharistique de l'église de Jerusalem* (Paris, 1972), has made a convincing attempt at a reconstruction of this prayer. We give here Tarby's reconstruction in the translation found in R. C. D. Jasper and G. J. Cuming, *Prayers of the Eucharist*, 2nd ed. (New York, 1980):

PRAISE TO THE FATHER

"The bishop, bowing, says: It is truly fitting and right, suitable and profitable, to praise you, to bless you, to worship you, to glorify you, to give thanks to you, the creator of all creation, visible and invisible. You are hymned by the heaven of heavens and all their powers; the sun and moon and all the choir of stars; earth, sea, and all that is in them; the heavenly Jerusalem, the church of the first-born written in heaven, angels, archangels, thrones, dominions, principalities and powers, and awesome virtues. The cherubim with many eyes and seraphim with six wings, which cover their own faces with two wings, and their feet with two, and fly with two, cry one to the other with unwearying mouths and never-silent doxologies, (aloud) with clear voice the triumphal hymn of your magnificent glory, proclaiming, praising, crying, and saying"*:

SANCTUS

"People: Holy, holy, holy, Lord of Sabaoth; heaven and earth are full of your glory. Hosanna in the highest. Blessed is he that comes and will come in the name of the Lord. Hosanna in the highest."

EMBOLISM OF THE SANCTUS

"And the bishop, standing up, seals the gifts, saying privately: Holy you are, King of the ages, and Giver of all holiness; holy too is your only-begotten Son, our Lord Jesus Christ, and holy too is your holy Spirit, who searches out all things, even your depths, O God."

"And he bows and says: Holy you are, almighty, omnipotent, awesome, good, with sympathy above all for your fashioning. You made man from the earth and granted him the enjoyment of paradise; and when he transgressed your commandment and fell, you did not despise him or abandon him, for you are good, but you chastened him as a kindly father, you called him through the law, you taught him through the prophets.

"Later you sent your only-begotten Son, our Lord Jesus Christ, into the world to renew your image. He came down and was made flesh from the Holy Spirit and Mary, the holy virgin Mother of God. He dwelt among men and ordered everything for the salvation of our race."

ACCOUNT OF THE INSTITUTION

"And when he was about to endure his voluntary death, the sinless for us sinners, in the night when he was betrayed, for the life and salvation of the world,

"Then he stands up, takes the bread, seals it, and says: he took bread in his holy, undefiled, blameless hands, showed it to you, his God and Father; he gave thanks, blessed, sanctified, and broke it, and gave it to his disciples and apostles, saying,

"And he puts the bread down, saying aloud: 'Take, eat; this is my body, which is broken and distributed for you for forgiveness of sins.' *People:* Amen.

"Then he takes the cup, seals it, and says privately: Likewise after supper the cup, he mixed wine and water, blessed, and sanctified it, and gave it to his disciples and apostles, saying,

"And he puts it down, saying aloud: 'Drink from it, all of you; this is my blood of the new covenant, which is shed and distributed for you and for many for forgiveness of sins.' *People:* Amen.

"Then he stands and says privately: 'Do this for my remembrance; for as often as you eat this bread and drink this cup, you proclaim the death of the Son of Man until he comes.'

"And the deacons present answer: We believe and confess.

"People: Your death, Lord, we proclaim and your resurrection we confess."

ANAMNESIS

"Then he makes the sign of the cross, bows, and says: We therefore, remembering his death and his resurrection from the dead on the

third day and his return to heaven and his session at your right hand, his God and Father, and his glorious and awesome second coming, when he comes to judge the living and the dead, when he will reward each according to his works, we offer you, this awesome and bloodless sacrifice, that you deal not with us after our sins nor reward us according to our iniquities, but according to your gentleness and love for man to blot out the sins of your suppliants, *aloud,* for your people and your Church entreats you.

"People: Have mercy on us, Father, the Almighty."

EPICLESIS
"And the bishop stands up and says privately: Have mercy on us, Lord, God, Father, the Almighty; and send out upon us and upon these holy gifts set before you your holy Spirit, *he bows,* the Lord and giver of life, who shares the throne and the kingdom with you, God the Father and your Son, consubstantial and co-eternal, who spoke in the law and the prophets and your new covenant, who descended in the likeness of a dove upon our Lord Jesus Christ in the river Jordan, who descended upon your holy apostles in the likeness of fiery tongues *aloud* that he may come upon them, and make this bread the holy body of Christ, *People:* Amen.

"And this cup the precious blood of Christ, *People:* Amen.

"The bishop stands up and says privately: that they may become to all who partake of them for forgiveness of sins and for eternal life, for sanctification of souls and bodies, for bringing forth good works, for strengthening your holy Church, which you founded on the rock of faith, that the gates of hell should not prevail against it, rescuing it from every heresy, and from the stumbling-blocks of those who work lawlessness, until the consummation of the age.

"The clerics alone answer: Amen."

Then follows a great series of intercessions (diptychs) in the form "Remember, O Lord, . . ." and a concluding doxology.

In regard to the content of this prayer we should note the measured trinitarian structure and terminology, the image theology (the human person as image of God), the unique character of Christ's sacrifice, and the activity of the Holy Spirit.

In regard to the characteristic elements of this anaphora we should note these. First, the anaphora belongs to the Antiochene type, that is, it is a West Syrian anaphora that can be clearly distinguished from the Alexandrian type. An Antiochene anaphora is structured as follows:

praise of God continuing into the Sanctus;

remembrance of God's saving acts (thanksgiving), with the institution narrative as central point;

Jesus' command, in the narrative, "Do this in remembrance of me" is followed by the anamnesis in which the formula *memnēmenoi prospheromen*, "remembering we offer," explicates the congregation's action with bread and cup by reference to Jesus' death and resurrection;

there follows the epiclesis, the invocation of the Holy Spirit on the faithful and their gifts;

intercession and a concluding doxology fill out the prayer.

Second, the transition from the words of the institution to the anamnesis is here made by *memnēmenoi*. Another possible transition is made from "you proclaim the death of the Lord" (1 Cor 11:26) to "*kataggellontes . . . proethēkamen*," "proclaiming . . . we have offered" (anaphora of St. Mark). Memorial and proclamation are very close to each other.

In conclusion we may say that from a relatively large number of sources we know the liturgy of Jerusalem in the fourth and fifth centuries, especially in its principal aspects: daily prayer, festivals, initiation. Furthermore, it is well established that the liturgy of the city was more or less a model for further liturgical development in east and west. This assertion is not intended to be exclusive; the particular circumstances of Rome and Constantinople were also of importance. But nonetheless, it is striking that the structure of worship in Jerusalem, changed not a little in relation to the previous period, is found reflected practically everywhere. The holy city had exercised a great power of attraction on pilgrims and especially on the bishops. Jerusalem had for a long time ceased to be a political center—a position first held by Antioch, later by Constantinople. But it had been made into an ecclesiastical center by the emperor, and a center whose influence radiated greatly.

2. MONASTICISM AND WORSHIP

In Jerusalem, according to Egeria, the monks took part in communal worship together with the clergy and the people. This indicates that they had returned from silence and solitude in the desert to life in the city. In Jerusalem at least we can no longer speak of "anchorites," solitaries who lived apart from the world. Was this a consequence of a development in monasticism toward *koinonia*, toward the formation of groups? The monks could maintain themselves in the city because they formed a community (a convent in the broad sense of the word). Groups inclined toward encratism, like "the sons and daughters of the covenant" in Syria, had already been forming.

Probably, genuine *koinonia* among monks, the cenobites, was a creation of Pachomius in Egypt in the course of the fourth century. It is well known that the influence of this movement in monasticism was great: Basil took it over in Cappadocia. (Through the monks the theological inheritance of Alexandria—think of Origen—continued to live on.) The Cappadocian monks came to exercise great influence in Constantinople. Cassian so glorified the Egyptian monastic ideal that his Gallic colleagues could not ignore it; they simply had to adjust. In this way, the great influence of monasticism continued to grow in both east and west, but especially in the east.

The varieties of monasticism would require a separate study. In general, it is dangerous to assert that *the* monk thought or acted in such and such a way. The influence of the Monophysite monks of Syria and Egypt is demonstrable, however, particularly in their rejection of Constantinople, that is, of the emperor and "his" orthodoxy. Their anxiety to live in a perfect way in this world and their awe for the holy toward which they strove gave their life a certain dualism and impelled them toward practices of austerity and abstinence. These are elements that also penetrated the "Byzantine" liturgy. Moreover, one may assume that the presence of monastic influences in the liturgy is a consequence of cenobitism and especially of the communities in the cities. The monks were involved in the theological ferment; the preferred leaders of the church were chosen from their ranks. As advisors and religious guides, monks were involved in the life of the church and society through their own community life.

In regard to worship, A. Veilleux, *La liturgie dans le cénobitisme pachômien au quatrième siècle* (Rome, 1968), has demonstrated, perhaps somewhat one-sidedly, how closely monastic life "according to the teaching of Pachomius" was bound up with the life of the local church to which the monks were still attached. They pursued the ideal of the gospel within the community of which they were part, albeit living separately. They celebrated the eucharist (on Saturday and Sunday) as much as possible with the local congregation or with a priest assigned to them by the bishop. They gathered for the paschal night and for baptism. They accepted the church's authority in penance. In other words, they formed a *koinonia* within the church.

We can say with virtual certainty that the monks added elements to Christian worship that have changed its character. First, the liturgy had been essentially a celebration of a community; the monks added to that (at least in the long run) an individual dimension directed toward one's own salvation. Monastic piety individualized participation in worship; the contemplation of the holy was to receive sometimes more attention than the communal proclamation of God's grace.

Second, the asceticism of the monks began to determine worship. In monasticism, according to the rules that now began to appear, all the available time of day and night was filled with long and meditative prayer. Communal worship was lengthened and came to occupy the principal hours of the day. Time had significance only as "time for prayer." Christian worship thus came to be regulated by an ascetical discipline.

Third, the most significant monastic addition was a constantly changing and repeated use of scripture. Not only the psalms but also the other parts of the Old and New Testaments were read aloud, listened to, and meditated upon at certain hours of the day (according to Pachomius, in the morning and the evening), so that once again the ascetic ideal is evident. Responses and antiphons had accompanied psalms or other parts of scripture from ancient times, thus forming a sort of brief commentary and interpreting the text of the Old Testament in the light of the New Testament. These responses grew slowly into independent texts, poems, and hymns, extending well beyond the scriptural text. The later Byzantine lauds (morning prayer) may stand as an example. Hymns did not originate among the monks, but they were developed by them into endless, repetitive meditations on the *Kyrios*. The eastern rites in general have preserved this monastic characteristic and breathe the piety of the monks, which has become popular piety.

3. THE RITES OF EAST AND WEST

It is in the period we are considering that the "eastern" and "western" rites appear, that is, the distinct but not separate liturgical families mostly grouped around an important center. In the previous period, it was not yet possible to make a distinction between liturgical families because data were lacking and also because the variety of practices in local churches was still too great. Worship was probably then much more dependent upon certain persons and their talent for improvisation. But slowly there arose a tendency toward greater unity, toward the formation of a group of local churches around a central church, a tendency, thus, from diversity toward unity (which did not signify uniformity). This resulted in what we presently call the rites of east and west.

"Rite" must not be conceived too narrowly. It does not mean only and primarily "order of service," the course of events and the exterior routine in worship. By "rite" must be understood the total spiritual heritage of a certain church, that is, the liturgy, the popular piety, the spirituality, the discipline, as well as the theology hidden therein. One does not understand an eastern rite simply by knowing in fine detail the exterior forms. More is necessary, especially a great ability to imaginatively and sympathetically enter into the spirit of the very rite itself. It is clear that for a western believer, it is on the whole not possible to genuinely "know" an eastern rite, precisely because he or she is a western believer. The opposite is also the case. The theologians and jurists of the Roman patriarchate have forgotten this all too often. They have sometimes acted as if only one genuine rite existed: the Roman rite. As a result, there has been a tendency toward latinizing the rites of those eastern Christians united with Rome. The Second Vatican Council spoke out in favor of the authenticity of the eastern rites, as appeared in the Constitution on the Church (no. 23), the Decree on Ecumenism (nos. 14–17), and the Decree on the Catholic Eastern Churches.

The Eastern Rites
The following description is based on I. Rahmani, *Les liturgies orientales et occidentales* (Beirut, 1929); *Handbuch der Ostkirchenkunde* (Düsseldorf, 1971); and I. Dalmais, *Les liturgies d'Orient* (Paris, 1959; English translation, *Eastern Liturgies*, New York, 1960).

ALEXANDRIA
This metropolis of Egypt was an important center of the church, even during the previous period. The church in Egypt was divided by the Monophysite controversy (451): the orthodox yielded their independence and conformed to Constantinople and its liturgy; the Copts (who were Monophysites), maintained their particularity, but fell under a certain influence of the Syrian Monophysites. The old Alexandrian tradition is to be found among the Copts. Allied to the Coptic church, also in its liturgy, was the Ethiopian church (cf. J. Leroy, *Les manuscrits coptes et coptes-arabes illustrés*, B.A.H. xcvi, Paris, 1974).

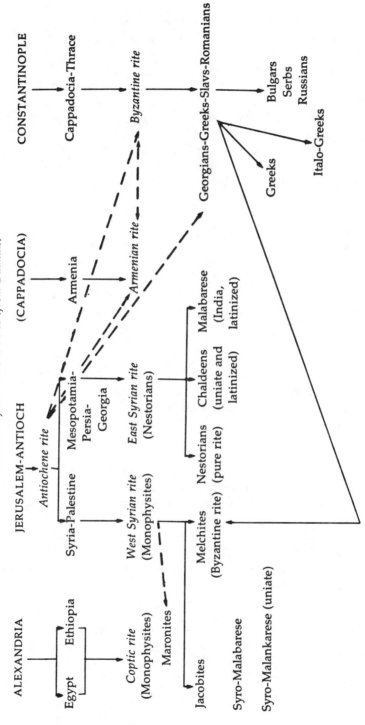

Overview of the Eastern Rites (from Dalmais)

ANTIOCH

This Greek city in Syria was a political center for a long time and therefore of great significance in the church. In this "capital of the eastern world" a particular rite developed that had a great, spreading effect and especially influenced Constantinople.

In 451, the church of Antioch was divided into the orthodox ("Melchites," followers of the emperor), who remained connected to Constantinople and took over the liturgy of this imperial city, which was originally Antiochene, and the Monophysite rite of the Jacobites (named for Bishop Jacob Baradai) in which the old Antiochene tradition, the West Syrian tradition, lived on. Christians of India (Malabar) took over this West Syrian tradition in the seventeenth century. And the influence of the West Syrian tradition on the Copts was not negligible.

The rite of the Maronites (Lebanon) originated in 681 in connection with Monotheletism and belongs to the Antiochene tradition. When the Maronites later united with Rome, they maintained their Syrian tradition but it became strongly latinized (cf. M. Hayek, *Liturgie maronite*, Paris, 1963; P. Naaman, *Théodoret de Cyr et le monastère de Saint Maroun; les origines des maronites*, Kaslik, 1971).

PERSIA

This land came into contact with Christianity most probably via Antioch and primarily Edessa, the border city of the eastern Roman empire. Already in the third century, established Christian communities in Persia are mentioned. These communities directed great mission efforts toward the far east. Christianity in Persia was Syrian, the East Syrian tradition that had developed its own characteristics and customs, partly because of the isolation of these Christians who lived outside the Roman empire. The Persian church became Nestorian and almost entirely cut itself off from the other churches at the end of the fifth century. The study of the East Syrian liturgy is of great importance because in it are preserved probably the oldest layers of Christian liturgy, and the mentality of the Jewish-Christian community can still be recognized there (e.g., the theology of the Name and a "low" christology) (cf. J. Leroy, *Les manuscrits syriaques à peintures*, B.A.H. lxxvii, 2 vols., Paris, 1964).

CONSTANTINOPLE

The new Rome, rooted in the old traditions of Thrace, Pontus, and Asia, experienced the ecclesiastical influence of Antioch and the determinative theological influence of Cappadocia (Gregory of Na-

90

zianzus was the archbishop of Constantinople). As the power of the emperor's own city grew, so did its ecclesiastical influence grow steadily until it surpassed Antioch and Jerusalem.

The Byzantine rite is a remarkable synthesis that came into being in the city that incarnated orthodoxy and, as a church center, united several traditions.

"For within this church the contribution of all the churches of the *oikoumene* of the time (which amounted to eastern Christendom, for the west, prey as it was to the barbarians, lived to itself) was sifted, with orthodoxy constantly triumphing over all errors, and the church, after every crisis, appearing even richer. Therefore the thought, the prayer, and the Christian life of the church of Constantinople is to be identified with the thought, the prayer, and the Christian life of all the orthodox Fathers, and her spiritual heritage is not to be limited to the contribution of one province or only a few authorities. This remarkable, balanced assimilation of all the riches of the Eastern churches gradually gave to the church of Constantinople a beauty and a radiance through which she became an example for all the churches who intended to follow her and through which her religious experience was of influence in the whole east" (Raquez, *Liturgisch Woordenboek*, vol. 2, cols. 2011–2012; cf. J. Meyendorff, *Byzantine Theology*, pp. 115–120).

One can truly assert that what is today called the eastern liturgy is principally the Byzantine liturgy. In Alexandria, in Antioch, in eastern Europe, even in the Syrian, Coptic, and Armenian traditions, Byzantine influence is felt. There is a clear parallel with the influence of the Roman liturgy in the west. By the reception and assimilation of many traditions, the Byzantine tradition became the expression of eastern Christianity, "the Byzantine synthesis" (Schmemann).

The Western Rites
In the west, there is actually only one rite, the Roman. What is meant by this will be described in the following chapter. Nonetheless, there were also distinctive rites in the western churches. These rites were probably not as particularized as were those in the east, but one can still speak of the "spiritual heritage of the local churches in the west." Just as the Byzantine rite became the recapitulation of the "eastern" heritage, so the Roman rite became the synthesis of the "western" heritage. The rest of this book will make this clearer.

Here we give only a short description of the western rites and suggest sources of further information (cf. *Liturgie de l'église particulière et liturgie de l'église universelle*, Saint Serge, 1975; Rome, 1976).

ROME

From the beginning, Christianity established itself in the capital of the empire. Through the emperor, it was granted a unique place in Rome after the peace of the church. The splendor of the imperial donations enhanced its image. The status of the bishop of Rome grew, and as a result the worship over which he presided took on its own stately character. In fact, this liturgy was the local, city of Rome liturgy, but its attractiveness was understandably great. For Rome was the only city in the west with a grand tradition. No wonder, then, that many came to be inspired by the liturgy of the city. But one must not forget that in the long run two kinds of worship developed in Rome: a city or parish liturgy and a more solemn, papal liturgy. This last is the best known and reflected its associations with the imperial court. To the extent that the bishop of Rome grew in importance, to that extent his liturgy became more impressive. Eventually the papal liturgy surpassed all others (cf. S. Pietri, *Roma christiana*, 2 vols., Rome, 1976).

MILAN

The origin and history of the rite that grew up in the important political and ecclesiastical center of Milan still lie in obscurity. Is the rite of Milan an adaptation of the Roman rite? Or were eastern rites and customs adapted for use in Milan and thereby did a new rite come to be? Is the influence of Milan to be traced to Gaul? There are sufficient Milanese sources and particular Milanese customs to enable scholars to speak of a rite. The name of Ambrose is connected with the rite but he was not its creator. Currently the rite has lost much of its proper character (cf. F. H. Dudden, *The Life and Times of St. Ambrose*, 2 vols., Oxford, 1935; J. Schmitz, *Gottesdienst in altchristlichen Mailand*, Cologne & Bonn, 1975).

CARTHAGE

It is doubtful that a true rite of Carthage ever existed; rather there seem to have been local adaptations of the Roman rite. It appears to be certain, though, that originally eastern influences also were present and that Africa (Carthage, Hippo) had an influence on the Spanish rite. There are few facts and these often point in the direction of Rome (cf. A. Hamman, *La vie quotidienne en Afrique du Nord au temps de Saint Augustin*, Paris, 1979).

SPAIN

The origin of the old Spanish or Visigothic rite is obscure: influence from Africa, old Roman sources used in the Spanish rite, and elements from Byzantine worship must all be considered, but a detailed description of the origin is not yet available. Many councils and synods concerned themselves with regulating worship. In 573, Toledo became the capital and center of the kingdom and, due to its influence, the rite was unified in structure and content. Important in this development were Leander, Peter of Lerida, Ildefonsus of Toledo, and Isidore of Seville. The euchology of the old Spanish rite is rich. In order to make the western liturgy uniform, this rite was forbidden by Pope Gregory VII. It lives on now—mutilated, it is true—in the Corpus Christi chapel of Toledo (cf. J. Fontaine, *L'Art préroman hispanique*, 2 vols., Paris, 1973, 1975).

GAUL

In a certain sense one can speak of a "Gallican rite" in the time before the Carolingians. But Gaul never had a genuine ecclesial center around which a rite could form. The term "rite" must therefore be used carefully. What is more, the political situation from the fourth to the seventh centuries was very unstable. Perhaps there were eastern influences; certainly the influence of the Roman rite was felt in the Roman cities of southern France, but there was no uniformity. Knowledge of Gallican practices is hard to come by because of a lack of source material. There are indirect sources (e.g., in the works of Caesarius of Arles and in the Gallic Councils), but for the writing of a history they are insufficient (cf. *L'Art gaulois*, 2nd ed., Paris, 1964, pp. 279–283).

What is called the "Celtic liturgy" can be determined with even less certainty. Probably it was an old Gallican rite that was mixed with Celtic customs. Certainly Celtic and Irish piety later becomes of great significance in the west. Forms of private prayer, devotions, the use of the Bible, the cult of the saints, confession of sins, all point to this piety, without, however, giving us lines of direct access to historical facts (cf. M. and L. de Paor, *Early Christian Ireland*, London, 1978).

Summary

Our short descriptions of the eastern and western rites may serve as sketches of the maze of liturgical practices. In the following pages, the contours of the rites and of the various orders of service will become sharper. The description was intended primarily as a witness to the pluriformity of the heritage of the churches, which were nonetheless one in the faith. The study of this heritage is important because it allows us to see how the dogma of the church was experienced and lived in the assembly of believers.

4. CHURCH ARCHITECTURE

Archeological discoveries have brought to light much information about the architecture of churches in the fourth and fifth centuries. The ground plan of the basilica was simple and the interior was adaptable to various purposes. There were constant elements, for example, the table (the "altar"), the ambo, the cathedra, perhaps also the "*cancelli.*" But only later in the fifth century did these elements take on the character of immovable monuments. The exterior of the basilica was unremarkable, but its interior was beautiful, in part because of the ornamentation on the floor, in the apse, and over the arches. The interior was intended for the initiates, who were admitted to participation in the rites. Initially the basilica was built along the longitudinal axis; rotundas were of a later date (Syrian?).

The floor plan of the basilica shows that the liturgy was a communal celebration in which everyone took part in his or her own way and in which the leaders fulfilled *ministeria*, serving roles in the midst of the faithful. The floor plan of the basilica continued as a feature of later western architecture, and that on a magnified scale, but the communality withered away (cf. C. J. A. C. Peeters, *De liturgische dispositie van het vroeg-christelijke kerkgebouw*, Assen, 1969).

5. DAILY PRAYER

The heart of daily prayer in the Christian community of the time was twofold: praise in the morning, lauds, and in the evening, vespers. The origin of this practice we discovered already in the previous period.

The structure of these two hours of prayer was elaborated according to the schema of the church of Jerusalem in the time after the peace of the church. This meant that "cathedral" (i.e., "congregational") and monastic elements grew together. The main thing was that morning prayer (*luce incipiente*), which was designed for the whole congregation, retained its popular appeal. The monks added parts of their own, especially night prayer, preceding the more popular morning prayer. The same is true of vespers, which was also designed for community participation.

Now that the church could move freely in society and could even affect social life to an important degree, the duty of participation in communal morning and evening prayer was even more impressed upon clergy, monastics, and the people. Synods of the time regularly returned to this theme (J. Jungmann, *Christian Prayer through the Centuries*, pp. 25ff.). If it was not possible for someone to participate in the morning and evening prayer in the church, then certainly there had to be prayer at home—the Lord's Prayer and the Creed. Many would have been able to recite by heart the fixed morning and evening psalms, having often heard them recited in the daily prayer in the church. In the morning, Psalms 148, 149, and 150 were said, and probably also Psalms 63 and 51 and several canticles, such as Exodus 15, Deuteronomy 32, and Daniel 3. Later an extensive hymnody was added. In the evening Psalms 141 and 142 were said, preceded (or followed) by the offering of incense, and finally the hymn *phos hilaron.*

From early times these psalms had been known as morning and evening psalms. They formed the heart of the hours of prayer and were prayed in a responsorial fashion (with responses and acclamations by the people) and concluded by a short summary prayer. In the prayers of the monks, the psalms were sometimes also read by one person while the others listened meditatively. Characteristically, the hour of prayer was concluded by intercessions (the litany with *kyrie, eleison* as response) and the Lord's prayer. The eastern practice of singing the Trisagion at the end of vespers is also very old. In other words, psalm and prayer–intercessions–Lord's prayer is the framework that would then be filled out with hymnic and meditative texts. In cities with a large number of active clergy and monks, this liturgy of the hours was probably held in every church. It is also possible that various churches took turns in holding a given hour of prayer, mornings and evenings (*statio;* cf. P. Salmon, *L'office divin*, pp. 69–97). The most important thing is that the Jewish-Christian practice of praising God in the morning and the evening was maintained in the Christian communities of the fourth and fifth centuries.

The West
That this tradition of morning and evening prayer was preserved is largely due to the monks. In regard to the west, we are best informed about Rome. Ascetics and monastics in Rome experienced a speedy rise in numbers and importance, perhaps under the influence of Egypt by way of Athanasius, who was in Rome for some time, and probably also through the influence of Augustine, Jerome, and Cassian. In the first half of the fifth century, cloisters were built by the popes near the Roman basilicas. The monks from those cloisters took charge of daily prayer in the basilicas of the city—in the morning, in the evening, and throughout the day. The monks even went to prayer in the late night or early morning before the morning office. For this, the Egyptian tradition would have been the primary model.

Thus we see the first contours of a fully developed daily prayer at fixed hours: the late part of the night, the morning, the third, sixth, and ninth hours, the evening, and later also perhaps midnight prayer. There was also prayer before the beginning of work (prime) and before sleep (compline). In other words, we see the beginning of a complete *officium divinum*, divine office, as it will later be called technically, meaning: "the duty of glorifying God by prayer."

The influence of the monks is to be noticed in the increase of psalmody, the introduction of the Old and New Testament canticles, the organized reading of the scripture, lives of the saints, and writings of the Fathers, and, above all, in the practice of matins, the night office before lauds. This night office was a daily vigil divided into several "nocturns" and filled with psalmody and reading. The Rule of St. Benedict collected and codified these early monastic customs of the Roman basilicas, and was probably inspired by them. By way of Benedict's rule, this monastic practice of prayer became known widely in the west and had great consequences for Christian liturgy, for the daily office eventually became so clericalized that it lost its popular character. The monks prayed in the name of the community, which began to participate less and less. The morning and evening prayer of the people became privatized into pious practices at home.

Important sources are: *The Rule of St. Benedict*, ed. & trans. J. McCann (Westminster, Md., 1952); or *La règle de S. Benoît, Sources chrétiennes* 181–186 (especially 182, chapters 8–19, and the commentary in 185 by A. de Vogüé). *The Rule of the Master*, ed. L. Eberle et al. (Kalamazoo, 1977); or *La règle du Maitre, Sources chrétiennes* 105–107. Jean Cassien, *Institutions cénobitiques, Sources chrétiennes* 109.

The East

The church in the east underwent a development parallel with that of the west. The old, simple structure of morning and evening prayer was preserved but was amplified by monastic additions. The influence of the monks was probably greater in the east, but it did not result in weakening the participation of the congregation as had begun to take place in the west. The monastics, who consecrated their lives to prayer, remained tied to the congregation and vice versa; a deep division in spirituality did not come about in the east.

Morning and evening prayer as the prayer of a congregation gathered in the church is described in *Constitutiones Apostolorum* (see list of sources): praise and thanksgiving in the morning ("that the

Lord has sent you light, that he has brought you past the night and brought on the day") and in the evening ("that he has given you the night to rest from the daily labors," VIII:34:2,6). These hours of prayers were supplemented by prayers at the third, sixth, and ninth hours, and *in gallorum cantu* (the cockcrow, the latter part of night; see above, regarding the Roman monks). Moreover, these "hours" were held in the church or, if that was not possible, in small groups at a certain house or privately. As a result, these other hours took on the character of communal prayers.

The structure of morning and evening prayer coincides with that of Jerusalem: morning or evening psalm (63 or 141), intercessions, concluding prayer by the bishop, and dismissal (VIII:35,37). From early texts we know that the prayer of the bishop was an anamnetic act of praise. The psalmody consists not only of psalms but also of hymns. This information gleaned from the Apostolic Constitutions is confirmed by Theodoret of Cyrrhus (*Ep.* 145:PG 83:1377C), by John Chrysostom (baptismal catechesis 8:17–18: *Sources chrétiennes* 50: 256–257; homily on 1 Tm 2:PG 62:530) and Eusebius of Caesarea (on Ps 64:PG 23:640B). The *Testamentum Domini* (ed. Rahmani, p. 145) notes all the times of prayer during the day, especially in the morning and evening, but according to the text the prayers at those times were offered privately by the people. Finally, we should note that in *Const. Ap.* 2:59 a vigil, a service of the word, is provided for Sunday (and Saturday) before morning prayer, just as in Jerusalem: in the latter part of the night, people assembled to pray three psalms and to hear the proclamation of the resurrection account. It is possible that this service of the word in later times was joined to the liturgy of the word in the celebration of the eucharist.

In regard to the monks, in Cappadocia, the monks joined the prayer of the congregation in the morning and the evening; they observed the hours of prayer during the day and at night by themselves (in J. Matéos, "L'office monastique à la fin du IVe siècle: Antioche, Palestine, Cappadoce," *Or. Chr. Per.* 47, 1963, pp. 55–88). In Syria and Palestine, the monks assembled in the latter part of night and, after a short rest, in the morning. The prayers during the day and at vespers were well known. In Egypt, the monks held a service of prayer and reading both morning and evening. The prayers during the day are not described in the sources.

This short tour through the history of daily prayer has taught us that in the church of this period, daily prayer was continued and received an even clearer ecclesial character. Moreover, we have seen a sort of osmosis between the liturgy of the congregation and the liturgy of the monks. The developments in both east and west generally followed parallel courses.

6. FESTIVALS AND CELEBRATIONS THROUGHOUT THE YEAR

The yearly recurring memorial days (*anni circuli,* the year round) increased. In this period the calendar took on a Christian character that it maintained until the French revolution.

Sunday

In 321 A.D. Sunday became an official day of rest intended for gatherings of the church, for the *cultus.* Civil law supported this use of Sunday and church law began to regulate the day of rest and church attendance in some detail. The keeping of Sunday was a proof of good Christian behavior, and not keeping it came to be included in the catalogue of sins. Old Testament sabbath laws were used as an argument for this, with Sunday being regarded now as the Christian sabbath. The result was that the celebration of the resurrection was deemphasized.

For Sundays and for feast days throughout the year, lists of scripture readings were compiled. Especially for the feasts there are sometimes remarkable correspondences in choice of readings found in the traditions of both east and west. The principle of selection must have been more or less the same (see pp. 121–122, "The Service of the Word").

Wednesday and Friday kept their character as weekly fast days. On those days, services of the word were held (in Rome and Alexandria) or the eucharist was celebrated (in North Africa and Jerusalem). In the east Saturday was drawn to Sunday: a eucharist was held and vigil kept.

Easter

The feast of Easter underwent development and, at the same time, maintained the traits of the previous period. For sources one should refer especially to the representative texts assembled by Cantalamessa (*Ostern in der alten Kirche*).

On the grounds of the sources, we can now distinguish three traditions—the Greek, the Syrian, and the Latin.

In the Greek tradition, the spiritualizing interpretation of Origen, passed on through Athanasius and the Cappadocians, continued to exercise its influence. But an osmosis took place: the *diabasis* idea was inserted into the older *pascha* tradition so that the theology of the passover lamb was preserved. At the same time, in Alexandria very clear distance was kept from the Jewish passover: the yearly *pascha*, regarded as primarily a Jewish phenomenon, was downplayed to allow full emphasis to be placed on the weekly eucharist. In Asia Minor, Easter began to be celebrated as at Jerusalem, with great attention given to the course of events in Jesus' life, especially the memorial of his resurrection. To keep Easter was to observe the resurrection, to commemorate the risen Son of God, consubstantial with the Father. Less attention was given to Christ's suffering and dying.

The Syrian tradition had its own unique character. Here the Christian passover was understood and celebrated on the basis of the synoptic tradition. Easter was the eating of the passover lamb, and that meant celebrating the eucharist, the sacrament of the death of the Lord and thus the memorial of the death of the new passover lamb. Thursday and Friday were joined: in the night from Thursday to Friday the memorial of the last supper and of Jesus' death on the cross was celebrated. Friday was the paschal day par excellence. It is possible that in the Syrian tradition two night vigils were kept— one from Thursday to Friday and one from Saturday to Sunday, this last as a memorial of the resurrection. Instructive in this regard is the *Twelfth Demonstration* of Aphrahat.

The Latin tradition preserved a view of Easter from the previous period: *pascha* is *passio*, the memorial of the passion. Ambrose evidences some influence by Origen, with a tendency to give baptism (Ex 13–14) more emphasis than the death of the passover lamb (Ex 12) and the eucharist, but this was not finally determinative. It was the genius of Augustine that added a dimension to the feast by reinterpreting the term *pascha/transitus*. He explained the term by reference to John 13:1—the *transitus* of Jesus out of the world to the Father. "Christ has passed through suffering from death to life and he has set out the way toward his resurrection for us who believe, that we too may pass over from death to life" (*Enar. in ps.* 120:6). The *transitus per passionem* is a synthesis of all the various ideas around this central feast of the Christian congregations. The passover of Jesus and the passover of the congregation are held together as a single event.

In all three traditions the views of Easter of the preceding period continued to be important and were elaborated upon. In order to sample this sense of the feast, one ought to read the texts in the Cantalamessa collection. In addition, one might read the resurrection hymns of Romanos the Melodist (*Sources chrétiennes* 128; for the English translation, see *Kontakia of Romanos* of M. Carpenter), which show an Easter feast concentrated on the Sunday of the resurrection, with all attention given to the glory of the God-Man (here the passover lamb theme has disappeared). Also important is a striking text from the early Roman liturgy, a preface (the first, variable part of the old Roman eucharistic prayer) that contains the thought both of Augustine and of Pope Leo the Great. This text, which follows, is found in the *Sacramentarium Gelasianum* (no. 466), which will be discussed in chapter 3.

Vere dignum . . . te quidem omni tempore, sed in hoc praecipue die laudare, benedicere et praedicare, quod pascha nostrum immolatus est Christus. Per quam in aeternam vitam filii lucis oriuntur, fidelibus regni caelestis atria reserantur et beati lege conmercii divinis humana mutantur. Quia nostrorum omnium mors cruce Christi redempta est et in resurrectione eius omnium vita resurrexit. Quem in susceptione mortalitatis deum maiestatis agnoscimus et in divinitatis gloriam deum et hominem confitemur. Qui mortem nostram moriendo distruxit et vitam resurgendo restituit: Iesus Christus dominus noster. . . .

It is indeed right . . . to praise you, to bless you, to proclaim you at all times, but especially on this day, for Christ our paschal lamb has been sacrificed. Through him the children of light are risen up to eternal life, the entrance to the kingdom of heaven is unlocked to believers, and the human is transformed into the divine according to the law of the happy exchange. For the death of us all is redeemed by the cross of Christ and in his resurrection the life of all is risen. In his taking of our mortality we acknowledge him as the majestic God and we confess him in the divine glory as God and man. Dying he destroyed our death and rising he restored life: Jesus Christ our Lord. . . .

What was the actual celebration of Easter in this period? We have described the undertone of the three traditions, but in all three the ritual expression was similar. Perhaps under the influence of the Jerusalem liturgy, with its emphasis on the events of Jesus' life, Easter came to be the *festa paschalia*. *Pascha* was now in the plural. Good Friday, Holy Saturday, and Easter Sunday were all celebrated, each with its own accent, and the last as the greatest day. So there came to be *pascha* in three days, a triduum for the commemoration of the suffering, burial, and resurrection of the Lord. At this time there also originated the celebrations of Ascension and Pentecost, the fortieth and fiftieth days, respectively, of the great fifty days after Easter. The Thursday before the triduum, later called Maundy Thursday, was the last day of the fast, the day for the reconciliation of penitents.

Thus the unity of the *pascha* was separated into a celebration of three days. This did not occur by conscious decision but by evolution, a developing experience of the meaning of the saving acts of the Lord. This evolution occurred in each of the three traditions we have described. The influence of Origen's exegesis is perceptible in this evolution, as is that of the Jerusalem liturgy, a processional liturgy that moved from one holy place to another in commemoration of the events of the triduum. It is also possible that late classical religious conceptions and ritual practices had some influence. The liturgy took on traits of a mystery cult. It imaged the Jesus story by means of rites. Rite and myth went hand in hand. The liturgy of the church became more and more retrospective as it mediated a salvation that was ritually portrayed and so experienced anew. This development would exercise a sustained influence on Christian worship in both east and west. The Jewish roots of Christian worship were now quite deeply hidden.

Lent

The time of preparation for Easter is Lent, and it was during this period of liturgical history that Lent was given the structure that long continued. We are not certain about the development of Lent, but there is a difference to be noted between eastern and western practice. Here and there the earlier two-day fast (Friday and Saturday) before the paschal vigil had already been extended to a week. This had been the practice in Alexandria and perhaps also in Rome. In his church history, Socrates (PG 67:633B) mentions a fast of three weeks. These three weeks preceded Easter, although it is uncertain how they were observed: a fast of three weeks in a row or of three separate weeks within the forty days. The forty-day fast was in vogue from about 350 A.D. The number forty in the Old Testament (Moses, Elijah) and the New Testament (Jesus) played a decisive role in its origin. Eusebius, *De solemnitate Paschali* 4, 5; Athananius' paschal letters; Cyril of Jerusalem's baptismal catecheses; Jerome, *Ep.* 24:4; Augustine's sermons and catecheses; the monks and their rules: these all prove the existence of this fast.

In the east, seven weeks were counted, or eight, as at Jerusalem (cf. Egeria), with Saturdays and Sundays excepted—thus forty days.

To that period was added the fast on Holy Saturday, determined by very ancient tradition. In Alexandria, the forty-day fast was the sequel to Epiphany (the celebration of the baptism of Christ). In the west, six weeks were counted (including Sundays) to and including Maundy Thursday, and so also forty days were kept. But the fasting (also on Sundays) had a somewhat different character and was seen as a time of conversion. In the time of Gregory the Great, the beginning of Lent was moved to Wednesday (later called Ash Wednesday). By excluding the Sundays and including Good Friday and Holy Saturday, the number forty was preserved. Also at this time, Lent began to be regarded as preparation for Easter Sunday, not any longer for the triduum. Pre-Lent (Septuagesima, Sexagesima, Quinquagesima) slowly came to be observed in Gaul through influences from the east, and the practice was later followed in Rome.

East and west agreed that the forty-day period was a time of *metanoia*, but also of the preparation of those who had given in their names at the beginning of Lent in order to be baptized in the paschal night, as is demonstrated by widespread data on the organization of initiation in those days. In Jerusalem, such a structure was already fully developed in the fourth century, as appears in the catecheses of Cyril.

We should mention especially the Lenten liturgy in Rome. At the beginning of the fifth century, the custom arose of keeping *stationes* during Lent: that is, the bishop, the clergy, and the faithful gathered at a specified church in the city to celebrate the eucharist. A key element of the *statio* was the procession to the church so beloved by the people. Lists of *stationes* were preserved for centuries and were even adapted to suit the local conditions of the churches outside Rome. In this stational celebration, the pericopes from holy scripture were chosen with an eye to the church where the assembly occurred and with the express intention of harmonizing the readings, a practice that was in some details followed in the later liturgy, especially in the old *Missale Romanum*. At the same time in Rome, the preparation for initiation was introduced into the observance of these *stationes*. Themes of fasting and conversion, of penance, of reconciliation, of initiation from both Old and New Testaments, were interlaced within the texts of the Roman books and formed a rich and varied whole. Basic material included John 4, 6, 9, and 11 and a selection of short and pointed antiphons (chosen from, among other sources, Psalms 1–26 and Ezekiel). In pithy and concise formulation, with a profound sense of typology and in richly varied readings and hymns from scriptures, the Roman liturgy for Lent, triduum and paschaltide was never commonplace and was often surprisingly effective (cf. J. P. Kirsch, *Die Stationskirchen der Missale Romanum,* Freiburg, 1926; H. Wegman, "Procedere und Prozession; eine Typologie," *Liturgisches Jahrbuch* 27, 1977, p. 28).

Christmas and Epiphany

At this time, the celebration of Christmas and Epiphany preceded by Advent as a time of preparation began to develop into the second great festival cycle of the church year. There is a great deal of traditional material that relates to the history and content of both feasts. We must limit ourselves here to a brief discussion, making reference to B. Botte, *Les origines de la Noël et de l'Epiphanie* (Louvain, 1932); and B. Botte et al., *Noël Epiphanie, retour du Christ* (Paris, 1967), in which the relevant texts are thoroughly explored.

The oldest mention of Christmas (December 25) as a Christian feast is found in the west at Rome in the *Chronography* of 354, based on a calendar that goes back to about 336. Thus, Christmas may have been known in Rome by 330 or earlier. There may have been some connection with the building of St. Peter's on the Vatican hill where, in one of the tombs, a mosaic of Christ as the *sol iustitiae* (sun of righteousness) had been discovered. The texts of Christmas often refer to Christ the light of the world and the sun of righteousness. In any case, it is practically certain that Christmas in Rome originated as a Christian appendage to (or perhaps replacement of) the pagan *Natalis Invicti,* the festival of the unconquered sun at the winter solstice. The syncretistic ideas of the emperor Constantine may also have been related to this development. There are extant Christmas sermons of Leo the Great (PL 54; *Sources chrétiennes* 22); Optatus of Milevis; Augustine (no. 202); Philaster of Brescia; Maximus of Turin; and of the eastern Fathers (Gregory of Naziarzus, PG 36, 336; John Chrysostom, PG 48, 703). It appears that the festival of Christmas was adopted in the east from Rome, probably in the last quarter of the fourth century in Constantinople and in the middle of the fifth century in Egypt.

The festival celebrated the birth of the Lord—his *natale* or his *manifestatio,* his *apparitio,* his *adventus*—all terms related to the Greek *epiphaneia.* The birth of Jesus is the appearance of the Lord in the midst of humanity as the sun of righteousness. In the liturgy, texts were read from Titus 2:11: "The grace of God has appeared (*epephanē*) for the salvation of all," and 2:13, "the appearing (*epephaneian*) of the glory of our great God and Savior Jesus Christ." The song texts (antiphons), known to us from later books but resting on old tradition, spoke of the royal appearance of God in human form (Psalm 110). The opening prayer of the night Mass of Christmas read:

Deus, qui hanc sacra-
tissimam noctem veri
luminis fecisti illustratione
clarescere: da, quaesumus;
ut, cujus lucis mysterium
in terra cognovimus, eius
quoque guadiis in caelo
perfruamur.

O God, who hast made this most holy night to shine with the brightness of the true light: Grant, we beseech thee, that as we have known on earth the mystery of that light, we may also come to the fullness of his joys in heaven.

The true light of God's glory (*kabod*) breaks into this world in the birth of Jesus. The textual material (preserved in both missal and breviary) of the Roman liturgy for Christmas is worthy of a thorough analysis. One will discover then a carefully considered and biblical sense for the mystery of Christ's nativity.

The feast of the Epiphany (January 6) is in all probability a feast of eastern origin. Even before the time of Athanasius it was known in Egypt as the festival of the baptism (and the birth) of Jesus. In Jerusalem, it was known in the time of Egeria at the end of the fourth century as the festival of the birth of the Lord. In Cappadocia, an alteration in the celebration is to be noted: in about 370, Epiphany was still the feast of the birth of Jesus, but a decade later the birth was celebrated on December 25 and the baptism in the Jordan on January 6. Such was also the case in Constantinople. The titles of these feasts were *theophania* or *ta genethlia* for December 25 and *ta phōta* for January 6. Still, it can be concluded from the sermons of Gregory of Nazianzus and Gregory of Nyssa that January 6 had the oldest rights to being the festival of the birth. By way of Gaul, the western church came to adopt the January 6 festival, but with a different end in view, to celebrate the adoration by the wise men. Mentioned also within the context of the feast are the baptism of Christ in the Jordan and the "first sign" at Cana in Galilee.

The eastern tradition of Christmas and Epiphany is rich with liturgical and homiletical material. The themes of light (one should note the connection with Easter), of the incarnation of God and the divinization of humanity, and of the role of the mother of God are disclosed in constantly new ways, especially in the hymnody.

The preparatory time for Christmas, Advent, originated in the west in the course of the second half of the fourth century, but was known in Rome only toward the end of the sixth century. The central theme was the coming of the Lord in glory (*adventus*) and the coming of the messianic kingdom, which explains the considerable place that is given to readings from Isaiah and Deutero-Isaiah. In the east, Advent stressed more strongly the preparation for the feast of the birth of the Lord.

Finally we should also note, alongside the Easter and Christmas cycles, the ember days, days of fasting at the change of the seasons (June, September, December, the days in March are of more recent date), known in Rome probably since the last quarter of the fourth century. The ember days of September have best preserved the old theme of the harvest. Some relationship may exist here to the Jewish feast of the Tabernacles.

Martyrs and Confessors
Besides the great festival cycles that were centered on the mystery of Christ, the time after the peace of the Church saw the rise of other festivals: the memorial days of the apostles, of the martyrs and confessors, and of the *Theotokos*. In the long run, these days assumed a very important place in what came to be called the celebration of the church year (cf. P. Harnoncourt, *Gesamtkirchliche und teilkirchliche liturgie*, Freiburg, 1974).

The remembrance (*memoria*) of the dead and the burial customs of the pagans were also practiced by Christians. Whether or not the bishops wished it, pagan practices and folklore continued to work within the Church. Probably no element of Christian folk piety has been so long-lived and so unchanging right into our own days as the cult of the dead. The pagan practices were Christianized. The meal for the dead was resolutely rebaptized by the bishops into a celebration of the eucharist. But that does not mean that the meals for the dead (*refrigeria*, meals of "refreshment") disappeared; traces of these meals may be found here and there up to our times.

What were some of these mortuary customs? The grave of the dead person was decorated with flowers and burning oil lamps were placed there. People came together near the grave in a chamber or in the open air to hold a meal with the dead person. The central chair reserved for the person was left empty. During the meal, wine was poured on the grave. What is more, objects were brought into contact with the grave and then carefully preserved (relics). The grave was provided with a memorial stone, if affordable, with all sorts of inscriptions. Epigraphy, the decoding of these stones, is important for our knowledge of the life of those days. In general, the

Christian funerary inscriptions were characterized by a great serenity due to the hope and expectation of a place of refreshment, light, and peace (*locus refrigerii, lucis et pacis* in the formulation of the Roman canon). Symbols of this life with the Lord are to be found on the sarcophagi of the time (cf. E. Dasmann, *Sündenvergebung durch Taufe, Busse und Märtyrerfürbitte in Zeugnissen frühchristlicher Frömmigkeit und Kunst,* Münster, 1973).

There was, however, one typically Christian custom: the memory of the dead person was celebrated not on his or her birthday (*natale*) but on the day of death, which was then also called *natale.* A confession of faith was thereby made in the resurrection and the life in which the dead person would share. Moreover, after the death, people gathered on the third, seventh, and thirtieth days for a memorial—especially on the third day, associated as it was with the resurrection of Christ. Finally, Christians also practiced the remembrance of several of the dead together, as, for example, all the deceased bishops of a local church (the pagans spoke of *cara cognatio,* the celebration of beloved relatives). The feast of the Chair of Peter (February 22) is an example of this. In Rome, the church recalled on that day all the dead bishops of the city. (The "chair" may then refer not only to the bishop's chair but also to the empty chair at the *refrigerium;* cf. T. Klauser, *Gesammelte Arbeiten,* Münster, 1974, pp. 97–120.)

These funerary customs were also anciently carried over into the remembrance of the martyrs, as for example in the memorial of Polycarp of Smyrna. In Rome, the memory of Peter and Paul was celebrated, and there is a further list dating from 354 of bishops and martyrs. In Lyons, the local martyrs were held in honor. In fact at the outset martyrs were only memorialized at the place or in the neighborhood of their martyrdom. After the peace of the church, churches called *martyria* were built over their graves. (Several of them are preserved in Rome.) A monument marked the grave, above which was built an altar for the celebration of the eucharist (cf. A. Grabar, *Martyrium,* 2 vols., Paris, 1946, repr. London, 1972).

Eventually the memory of the martyrs came to be celebrated in other places besides the burial places and their basilicas. Relics of these witnesses of the Lord were sought and, through what was thought to be divine guidance, were always and very easily found! Whether the relics in fact belonged to the martyr in question may be doubted. Moreover, honor came to be paid to "martyrs" who existed only in popular fantasy. Relics were transferred (*translatio*) to churches in the cities so that eventually all the churches became *martyria* harboring relics. The remembrance of the dead then began to assume the form of a hero cult, supported by fantastic tales of the courage of the saints and their disdain of death. Soon, deceased ascetics, virgins, and bishops came to be honored along with the martyrs.

For a knowledge of this veneration of the saints, the *calendaria* and the *martyrologia* (the oldest perhaps from 431) are of great significance. The *Missale Romanum* offers examples of the liturgy for martyrs in the section called Common of Martyrs.

The feasts of the *Theotokos*, whose veneration got underway after the Council of Ephesus in 431 (cf. *Lexicon der christlichen Ikonographie*, vol. 3, pp. 154–161), really originated in the east: August 15, *Koimysis*, or the Dormition; March 25, Annunciation; September 8, Birth. In the Christmas cycle, moreover, we find *Hypapantē* (the "Meeting of God" or the Presentation, at first celebrated on February 14, later on February 2). *Koimysis* was known in Jerusalem in the middle of the fifth century (Armenian Lectionary). The great spread of these feasts in the east took place by way of Constantinople. In Rome, the feasts were adopted only later, in the second half of the seventh century under the influence of Gaul. The oldest western feast of Mary was probably January 1, *Natale S. Mariae*. That day has a famous series of vespers antiphons that were taken from the Greek liturgy. The first antiphon is this:

O admirabile commercium: Creator generis humani, animatum corpus sumens, de Virgine nasci dignatus est: et procedens homo sine semine, largitus est nobis suam deitatem.

O wonderful exchange! The Creator of the human race, taking a human body, has humbled himself to be born of a virgin; coming forth a man without seed he graces us with his own divine life.

7. THE SACRAMENTS

Baptism and Confirmation in East and West

It is already clear from the description of initiation as it took place in Jerusalem that after the peace of the church the catechumenate underwent a significant change. Originally a time of continuous personal conversion toward a Christian style of life, now it became the step that was compulsory for a person if he or she wanted to count in society. People took this step as far as it was necessary: they became catechumens, but for the most part a deeper engagement or authentic conversion did not follow. As a catechumen, a person was officially a member of the church, but at the same time he or she was free of the burdens that were borne by baptized Christians. The quality of commitment in the Christian congregations soon decreased. The catechumenate was no longer a time of testing but a half-Christian state of life. The consequence was that baptism was put off and that children were not baptized unless parents themselves had dared to be baptized.

The reception into the catechumenate was simple. A person was given catechesis about the principles of Christian faith and was then "enrolled" during a ceremony in which the cross was signed on the candidate's forehead (*signatio*) and a laying on of hands took place. The evil spirit was exorcised (by *insufflatio*, "blowing it away"), and the candidate received a little salt to taste—as a rite of welcoming, as a sign against corruption and sin, and as a prefiguring of the eucharistic meal. The catechumens were then allowed to participate in the service of scripture readings, but before the intercessions they were dismissed: the liturgy of the eucharistic table was intended only for the baptized, the initiated.

However, other catechumens did want to undergo a conversion in their baptism and be taken into the congregation: these were the *electi* or *competentes* (west), the *photizomenoi*, the "illumined" (east). Every year during the Lent, they were taught the creed and Christian ethics and led step by step through prayer and the rites leading toward baptism at the paschal vigil. The gatherings for the *electi* during Lent were called *scrutinia*. Initially the intention of these "scrutinies" was to inquire after the candidate's manner of life, but they soon took on more and more the character of ecclesial ritual acts whereby the church stood by the baptismal candidates in their battle against Satan. The exorcistic rite of the church accompanied the personal conversion of the candidates. It is true that the candidates' choice of Christianity had become existentially less demanding; society was becoming more and more "Christian" and the pagan environment was less pervasive than it had been in previous years. But a conversion to the gospel continued to be necessary, and it followed that even at this time the decision of an adult to be baptized still signaled the beginning of a kind of ascetic life with clear ethical implications.

Two or three of these Lenten scrutinies were especially important. They took place most likely during the liturgy of the Sundays of

Lent—specifically the fourth, fifth, or sixth Sunday—and on the morning of Holy Saturday. There were local differences, but in general east and west followed a common practice. During these scrutinies, the creed (and perhaps also the Lord's prayer) was handed over (*traditio*) to the candidates. They were expected to learn these texts so well that at a following gathering they could recite them in the presence of the congregation; the texts could be "given back" (*redditio*). On Holy Saturday in the east, the *apotaxis* and *syntaxis* (the renunciation of Satan and the adherence to Christ) took place. In the west, it was likely that the *redditio* (Augustine) or a final exorcism, called *apertio aurium,* opening of the ears, was part of the rite.

The actual initiation by the water bath, anointing, and the eucharist took place in the paschal night, which in this period developed into the celebration of the baptism of the neophytes, the ones newborn "of water and the Spirit." That the paschal vigil had become a baptismal celebration was due to the influence of Pauline baptismal theology: initiation is dying and rising with the Lord and that is ritually celebrated and imaged.

The principal sources of our knowledge about initiation are not complete orders of the baptismal service, but a series of mystagogical catecheses or sermons that the bishops gave during the week after the vigil in order to further introduce the newly baptized into the *mysteria* in which they had participated, the saving signs of the Lord. Among these sources are the catecheses of: Augustine; Ambrose; Cyril of Jerusalem; John Chrysostom; Theodore of Mopsuestia; *Const. Ap.* VII, 39–45; the letter of the Roman deacon John to Sennarius; and Narsai (homily 22). (For further information see Riley, *Christian Initiation;* Whitaker, *Documents of the Baptismal Liturgy;* and especially, E. J. Yarnold, *The Awe-Inspiring Rites of Initiation: Baptismal Homilies of the Fourth Century.*)

These indirect sources present a baptismal liturgy that had undergone a definite development since the days of Hippolytus. This development consisted especially in the increasingly important status of the ritual activity of the church. It is remarkable how strongly the ritual battle against Satan had been developed: besides the renunciation of Satan, exorcism by the church had come more to the fore. This could have been connected with remnants of paganism in the present society, or perhaps there are other, sociological explanations for the phenomenon.

Here is a summary of the outline of the ritual of baptism according to the various sources:

AUGUSTINE

Renunciation, confession of faith, immersion; anointing and laying on of hands; handing over of the white baptismal garment.

AMBROSE

Exorcistic anointing, renunciation (turned toward west, then the turning to the east); blessing of the baptismal water; confession of faith, immersion (threefold); anointing of the head with *myron;* foot washing; baptismal garment; laying on of hands with prayer, *sphragis* (called *spiritale signaculum*).

It is not clear whether or not this *sphragis* was a ritual act. What could be meant is that through the prayer (accompanied by the laying on of hands) the Holy Spirit is given as a *signaculum* and the baptized is marked.

CYRIL OF JERUSALEM

Outside the baptistry: *apotaxis–syntaxis* (facing west, then east); in the baptistry: stripping, anointing with oil of exorcism; confession of faith and immersion (threefold); anointing with *myron* on forehead, ears, nose, and breast; this anointing is like what is elsewhere called *sphragis:* the sign on the forehead by which one can be recognized as a Christian. Cyril does not mention laying on of hands.

JOHN CHRYSOSTOM

Apotaxis ("apotassomai," "I renounce you, Satan," which is a primitive formula) and *syntaxis* (both were then expanded ritually by spitting at the devil and by confession of faith during the *syntaxis*); anointing with *myron* in the sign of the cross on the forehead, called *sphragis,* followed by the stripping and anointing of the whole body immediately before the immersion; threefold immersion with baptismal formula and laying on of hands; Lord's prayer and kiss.

THEODORE OF MOPSUESTIA

Apotaxis–syntaxis (pact, contract); anointing of the forehead with the sign of the cross (*sphragis*); before the bath, stripping and anointing of the whole body; blessing of the baptismal water; immersion with laying on of hands and the baptismal formula; the white garment; *sphragis* on the forehead (perhaps a later addition).

SYRIAN DOCUMENTS

Anointing (*sphragis*), immersion.

CONST. AP. VII, 39 ff.
Apotaxis–syntaxis (at the same time, confession of faith); anointing; blessing of baptismal water; immersion; anointing.

NARSAI OF NISIBIS
Apotaxis–syntaxis; anointing of the forehead with chrism and thereafter anointing of the whole body; blessing of the baptismal water; threefold immersion with baptismal formula ("Name . . . is baptized. . . ."); clothing; reception into the congregation.

It is clear that the baptismal theory and practice of the *Traditio Apostolica* of Hippolytus are still viable. The greatest change is found in the development of the *apotaxis–syntaxis* rite in the east (actually a doubling of the baptismal act) and the replacement of the threefold confession of faith by the baptismal formula, spoken by the bishop. Both changes indicate a growing ecclesiastical (official, priestly) action on behalf of the candidate.

One of the most difficult problems of liturgical history is the place of the laying on of hands and the anointing, in the course of initiation, as the gift of the Holy Spirit. Such rites as water bath, laying on of hands, and anointing developed differently in east and west. In the west, laying on of hands and anointing split off from *baptisma* and began to develop into an independent sacrament, confirmation, ministered by the bishops (see pp. 182–183). In the east, anointing with *myron* has remained part of the baptismal ritual, ministered by the priest who has also carried out the immersion. Moreover, eventually the laying on of hands came to be replaced by (or joined with) the anointing.

But one can posit that at this time, initiation was still seen as one single whole—as immersion and participation in Christ's dying and rising *and* as laying on of hands–anointing–*sphragis* and gift of the Holy Spirit (*teleiōsis,* fulfillment). The rites may have differed but the meaning was the same: Christian baptism is a gift of the Holy Spirit by which one is anointed to be a follower of the Lord and a participant in the messianic kingdom.

Once initiatied, the baptized were welcomed into the congregation by the kiss of peace. They were now members of the family and were allowed to share in the table of the Lord (cf. Augustine's Easter homilies). The rites of baptism included this participation.

There is little direct liturgical material from this time. In the *Euchologion* attributed to Serapion, one finds a few texts of an idiosyncratic theological character. A few prayers of blessing can also be found in *Const. Ap.* VII, 39–45. This period seems to have been still a time of improvisation. In those days, both eastern and western writers viewed baptism as initiation into the mysteries of the Lord through the rites of the church. These mysteries are represented sensibly through ritual immersion, anointing, and exorcism.

Eucharist
The material on the development of eucharistic celebration is abundant and the commentaries so numerous as to defy brief summarization. We refer, however, to the following works. For the western liturgy of the eucharist: J. Jungmann, *The Mass of the Roman Rite*, 2 vols. (New York, 1951–1955), outline of the development, analysis of the Roman rite; G. Kunze, *Die Gottesdienstliche Schriftlesung, Stand und Aufgabe* (Göttingen, 1947); A. Hänggi & I. Pahl, *Prex eucharistica* (Freiburg, 1968). For the various eastern liturgies: F. Brightman, *Liturgies Eastern and Western* (Oxford, 1896, repr. 1965, 1967); the work of Hänggi & Pahl above (which includes an extensive collection of eastern anaphoras); A. Raes, *Introductio in liturgiam orientalem,* (Rome, 1947). A somewhat dated book that is nonetheless still worth reading is N. Maurice Denis and R. Boulet, *Eucharistie ou la messe dans ses variétés, son histoire et ses origines* (Paris, 1953), a sort of travel guide for the history of the celebration of the eucharist, beginning in the twentieth century and going back to the gospels.

With these studies, one is introduced to the research that has been done on the ritual course of the eucharistic celebration. What becomes evident is that the core of that celebration, which we found described by Justin Martyr (about 150 A.D.), came to be surrounded by other rites, and that secondary rites took on independent life and were charged with new significance. Knowledge of the course of ritual is not sufficient; just as important, if not more important, is the study of the texts themselves: anaphoras or eucharistic prayers of east and west, the hymns and antiphons that were sung during the service, and so on. In these pages we will limit ourselves to an overview of anaphoras after a description of the outline of the celebration and of the structure of the liturgy of the word.

THE COURSE OF THE EUCHARISTIC RITUAL
We can give here only the highlights of the course of the eucharistic liturgy, which will assume definitive forms later in both east and west.

Jerusalem. Cyril (see p. 73): Liturgy of the word with readings (Old Testament?), psalm singing, gospel, homily; dismissal of the catechumens; eucharistic prayer; Lord's prayer, *Sancta sanctis* (*Priest:* "Holy things for the holy people." *People:* "One only is holy, one is the Lord, Jesus Christ!"); communion from bread and cup.

Cappadocia. Gregory of Nazianzus; Basil: Liturgy of the word (Old Testament, apostle, psalm, gospel, homily); prayer for and dismissal of the catechumens and the penitents; intercessions (litany led by a deacon) and kiss of peace; eucharistic prayer; Lord's prayer and fraction; communion.

Antioch and Constantinople. John Chrysostom: entrance of the bishop and greeting (*pax*); liturgy of the word (Old Testament, apostle, psalm, gospel, homily); litany, blessing, dismissal of catechumens, repeated for penitents and for people regarded as possessed; closing of the doors; intercessions with concluding prayer and kiss of peace; eucharistic prayer; Lord's prayer and fraction; *Sancta sanctis*; communion; dismissal by the deacon.

Commentary.

1. Dionysius the Areopagite, *Hier. eccl.*, 3, II, expressly notes the censing of the altar and of the congregation by the bishop. Later this function was taken over by the deacon. The text accompanying the censing of the table in today's Byzantine liturgy is as follows (note especially the last phrase):

Ἐν τάφῳ σωματικῶς, ἐν ᾅδου δὲ μετὰ ψυχῆς ὡς Θεός, ἐν παραδείσῳ δὲ μετὰ λῃστοῦ καὶ ἐν Θρόνῳ ὑπῆρχες Χριστὲ μετὰ Πατρὸς καὶ Πνεύματος πάντα πληρῶν ὁ ἀπερίγραπτος.

Christ, you were in the tomb bodily and in hell by your soul as God, in paradise with the thief and on the throne with the Father and the Spirit *filling all things, you unencompassed one.*

2. It is to be noted that the deacon had a proper role in prayer: he gave out the intentions to which the congregation responded (cf. Chrysostom, *In ep. II ad Cor. Hom.* 2, 5–8). This litany form is still maintained in the Byzantine liturgy (cf. v. d. Paverd, op. cit., pp. 140–221, especially p. 141, n. 1).

3. The *trisagios hymnos*, the Trisagion (to be distinguished from the *aggelikos hymnos*, the Gloria, and from the *epinikios hymnos*, the Sanctus), was probably placed in the liturgy about 450 A.D. It had already become part of the prayer of the hours, and as an ejaculatory prayer of the faithful had been in use for a much longer time. For the Byzantine tradition it was trinitarian in expression, and the Monophysitic reinterpretation (*ho staurōtheis di' hēmas*, "who was crucified for us") had no success in Constantinople, although it did among the Jacobites in Syria. The role of the Trisagion at the beginning of the service, at the entrance of the celebrant, is evident: it was a popular refrain to the psalm that was sung to accompany the entrance procession.

4. The *troparion ho monogenēs huios* may have been written by Emperor Justinian.

5. The liturgical interpretations of Theodore of Mopsuestia, that is, his mystagogical catecheses, seem to have been of great importance in the development of the Byzantine liturgy, for the entrance with the gifts, for the later *proskomide*, and for the theological reflection on the eucharist. We give here several quotations in the translation of A. Mingana, *Woodbrooke Studies* (Cambridge, 1933, vol. 6, pp. 79–86; cf. also the French translation of R. Tonneau and R. Devreesse and the English translation in E. Yarnold, *The Awe Inspiring Rites of Initiation*, pp. 176ff.):

"It is indeed evident that (this eucharistic food) is a sacrifice, but not a new one and one that (the priest) performs as his, but it is a remembrance of that other real sacrifice (of Christ). Because the priest performs things found in heaven through symbols and signs, it is necessary that his sacrifice also should be as their image, and that he should represent a likeness of the service of heaven. . . . These things, however, we expect to receive in reality through the resurrection at the time decreed by God, and now it is only by faith that we draw nigh unto the first fruits of these good things: to Christ our Lord and the high priest of the things that belong to us. We are ordered to perform in this world the symbols and signs of the future things so that, through the service of the Sacrament, we may be like men who enjoy symbolically the happiness of the heavenly benefits, and thus acquire a sense of possession and a strong hope of the things for which we look. . . . Those who have been chosen priests of the New Testament are believed to perform sacramentally, by the descent of the Holy Spirit, and for the confirmation and admonition of the children of the Sacrament, these things which we believe that

114

Christ our Lord performed and will perform in reality. . . . One is the sacrifice which has been immolated for us, that of Christ our Lord, who suffered death for us. . . . All of us, everywhere, at all times, and always, observe the commemoration of that sacrifice. . . . (This Sacrament) contains an image of the ineffable Economy of Christ our Lord, in which we receive the vision and the shadow of the happenings that took place. This is the reason why through the priest we picture Christ our Lord in our mind, as though in him we see the One who saved us and delivered us by the sacrifice of Himself; and through the deacons who serve the things that take place, we picture in our mind the invisible hosts who served with that ineffable service. It is the deacons who bring out this oblation— or the symbols of this oblation—which they arrange and place on the awe-inspiring altar, (an oblation) which in its vision, as represented to the imagination, is an awe-inspiring event to the onlookers. We must also think of Christ being at one time led and brought to His Passion, and at another time stretched on the altar to be sacrificed for us. And when the offering which is about to be placed (on the altar) is brought out in the sacred vessels of the paten and the chalice, we must think that Christ our Lord is being led and brought to His Passion . . . when they bring out (the Eucharistic bread) they place it on the holy altar, for the complete representation of the Passion, so that we may think of Him on the altar, as if He were placed in the sepulchre, after having achieved His Passion. This is the reason why those deacons who spread linens on the altar represent the figure of the linen clothes of the burial. . . ."

In these quotations, the sacramental representation of Jesus' suffering and death in the action of the church (and especially of the hierarchy: the bishop, called here "priest," and the deacons) comes clearly to expression. Liturgy is a sign-action and is seen as the "likeness of the service of heaven," as the making present of what has happened and of what will happen as the commemoration of Jesus' sacrifice. Theodore places great stress on the extension of the liturgical vision into the future, toward the completion of salvation history—an essential trait of eucharistic typology.

Of concern for us is the development of the presentation of the gifts (and of the later *proskomide* before the beginning of the service). Here is a clear example of a secondary rite taking on greater significance. Very little was changed in the ritual or elements of the anaphora, determined as it was by tradition and already recognized in the fourth and fifth centuries as an inheritance worthy of reverence. In contrast, less important rites were "solemnized" and given a certain independence. This occurred in the east earlier than in the west. The preparation and bringing of the gifts had been in itself a practical action: after the liturgy of the word the gifts were placed on the table in order that the prayer might be spoken over them (cf. Justin's description). Now this rite became a solemn offering, a solemn procession with the gifts to the sanctuary, and thus for the onlookers it became a sign of the suffering, death, and burial of the Lord. The visual aspect of worship, the visual participation of the faithful, grew in significance. Less attention was paid to the memorial of the death and resurrection as essentially tied to the memorial prayer, or perhaps unconsciously, the prayer came to be regarded as no longer sufficient. Something had to be made visible by actions: Jesus' suffering and burial had to be seen in signs, in images. A remarkable doubling of the celebration of the *"memoria passionis"* came about. The eucharistic prayer (including the institution narrative) was supplemented by the offering rite, which because of its visual and active solemnity became more and more central (cf. R. Taft, *The Great Entrance*, pp. 16–52, especially pp. 35–38).

There was a second element: the signs of the earthly liturgy represented the divine reality, that is, the *mysteria* of the glorified Christ, who willed to continue to be the slain lamb for his congregation. But this enacting of the presence of the heavenly in the earthly signs was so magnificent that the liturgy itself became something holy, untouchable, withdrawn from earthly eyes, only accessible to the spirit. The Lord has done great things for us (*Theod.* catechesis 15:24), which we represent in the liturgy. Our liturgy becomes therefore also holy and exalted. In this sense, it follows that the offertory procession became also a welcoming of the Lord of all things, *Pantokrator*. The deacons were the angels before the throne; the bishop the image of the *Kyrios*. In this context, the *cheroubikos hymnos*, the cherubic hymn, must be understood:

"We who mystically represent the cherubim singing the thrice-holy hymn to the life-giving Trinity, let us set aside all earthly cares that we may receive the King of the universe invisibly escorted by the angelic hosts. Alleluia."

It is clear what the offertory was: one welcomes the King of all things; the earthly liturgy is an image of the heavenly liturgy. This holy character of the liturgy would eventually lead to the holy words

116

of the anaphora being said in silence in the sanctuary, to which only ordained ministers had access; only they could stand at the altar, the throne of the lamb.

Here we see the later Byzantine liturgy already prefigured; ritual details were elevated to become holy signs of the heavenly Lord.

We may complete the image of the eucharistic celebration in the east by referring to the canonical compilations, such as, in the first place, the *Apostolic Constitutions* (books II, VII, VIII; ed. Funk, pp. 159ff., 411ff., 479ff.). Therein are rather complete descriptions that more or less reflect the state of affairs in Syria about 400 A.D. There is a correspondence with the rite of Antioch. Book VIII of the *Apostolic Constitutions* is known as the *missa clementina*: the authority of the text was heightened by attributing it to bishop Clement of Rome, regarded as having been very close to the apostles. The *missa clementina* is well known because of its long anaphora (English translation in R. Jasper and G. Cuming, *Prayers of the Eucharist*, 2nd ed., pp. 71–78), which was composed in the Antiochene style. Eucharistic data are also to be found in *Testamentum Domini Nostri* and the *Euchologion of Serapion* (anaphorae in Jasper and Cuming, op. cit., pp. 39–41, 80–82).

This overview shows that the central structure of the eucharistic celebration, such as described by Justin, still existed. Liturgy of the word and liturgy of the table formed a complementary whole. But there were additions: the entrance rite; psalmody between the lessons; an offertory procession (Antioch) by the clergy; a clearly defined eucharistic prayer; an elaboration of the communion rite. We should also especially mention the dismissal of the catechumens and penitents, who were excluded from participation in the eucharist.

In the east, then, the eucharist manifested an ancient and clear form along with a tendency, especially in Antioch and Constantinople, to embellish it with details and additions. This is understandable when one recalls that Constantinople was the imperial city with an imperial court ritual (incense, a strong hierarchy, court apparel, and concern with the mysticism of light) and was profoundly dedicated to the maintenance of orthodoxy. This was evident in holy liturgy, especially in the confession of the *Christos–Kyrios* as one in being with the Father.

THE WEST

The data, from widely spread sources, give no complete order of service for this period, neither in Rome nor in Spain and Gaul.

Gaul and Spain. While there were differences among the various local liturgical practices, especially in Gaul, the fundamental structure of the eucharist was maintained: liturgy of the word (probably three readings, one of which was from the Old Testament) and liturgy of the table (with a eucharistic prayer called *contestatio* or *illatio;* see pp. 166, 168). The song between lessons is known as *"psallendum."* The Trisagion before the readings seems to have been "imported" from the east, probably in the first half of the sixth century, but we do not know precisely how. The diptychs (memorials of the living and the dead in prayer form) were read before the eucharistic prayer and were concluded with the *oratio post nomina.* The *Sancta sanctis* is demonstrable in an adjusted form:

Sancta cum sanctis. Coniunctio corporis et sanguinis Domini nostri Iesu Christi sit edentibus et sumentibus in vitam aeternam (*Liber Ordinum,* col. 249).	Holy things be with the holy people. May the joining of the body and blood of our Lord Jesus Christ be for those who eat and drink for eternal life.

Those who did not commune, and there were steadily more of them, left the church before the end of the service. The bishops resisted this practice but finally had to give in: those who left early were nonetheless given the blessing (*Liber Ordinum,* col. 241).

Rome. In the writings of several popes, data are found that cast light on the celebration of the eucharist and, at the same time, show a certain development in the celebration. For example: Innocent I, in a letter of 416 A.D., speaks of the kiss of peace before communion and the diptychs within the eucharistic prayer; Leo the Great (440–461), to whom several liturgical formulations were ascribed; Hilarius (461–468) and Simplicius (468–482), who were responsible for the organization of the *stationes* in the various churches of Rome; Gelasius (492–496), to whom certain texts have been attributed and who introduced the litany into the Roman celebration at the expense of the typical Roman intercessions; and, above all, Gregory the Great (590–604), who placed the Lord's prayer before the breaking of bread and linked it to the eucharistic prayer, and who probably had something to do with the present shortened form of the *Kyrie-Christe-Kyrie* (cf. Jungmann, op. cit., pp. 37–45).

But these data touch on details of a celebration that was still very sober and that preserved the ancient structure. This structure contained the following elements:

118

1. Opening prayer (later preceded by the Kyrie), perhaps intended as a conclusion of the entrance;
2. The liturgy of the word contained, in contrast to the general tradition elsewhere, two readings: one from the apostle and one from the gospels. There was psalmody between the lessons;
3. The dismissal of the catechumens and penitents;
4. The intercessions were replaced by a litany on the eastern model that was then later transferred to the beginning of the liturgy;
5. The bringing of gifts by the faithful during the liturgy, with a concluding prayer (*oratio super oblata*);
6. The eucharistic prayer with a variable part (the preface) and an invariable part (the canon);
7. Lord's prayer and kiss of peace with the fraction (originally in reversed positions);
8. Communion and a prayer after communion (*postcommunio*);
9. Prayer of blessing over the faithful (*oratio super populum*) and dismissal.

We note here in passing that the ritual of the "papal mass," the *statio* of the bishop of Rome with his clergy and the faithful, will be described in the following chapter. The heart of this mass, however, probably went back to the times we are now describing.

1. Two readings were proclaimed in the Roman liturgy. The first was taken from any one of the New Testament writings except the gospels; the second was from the gospels. There may have been on some occasions an Old Testament reading preceding those two readings (cf. *Leiturgia*, vol. 2, p. 141). Why the Roman liturgy fixed upon two readings can no longer be exactly determined.

2. It is striking that the Roman liturgy had three prayers, each of which occurred at the end of a "procession": the entrance, the offertory, and the communion processions, during which the congregation (or the presider during the entrance) would have been in movement. These three prayers are typically Roman in style, content, and form. The style is both ceremonious and concise, somewhat aloof, and requires a practiced ear. The content is sometimes remarkably biblical, laden with important scriptural concepts. On the other hand, there are cases where the style becomes too personal, too emotional, or too flat. The form is always recognizable: the "address" to God; the remembrance of the saving deeds; the supplication; the conclusion (doxology). This structure recalls Jewish prayer (*berakah*) (cf. E. Bishop, "The Genius of the Roman Rite," *Liturgica Historica*, Oxford, 1918, pp. 1–19).

3. It is not evident from the contemporary sources that the faithful presented the gifts of bread and wine during the celebration, but this could be deduced from the prayers *"super oblata,"* as for example:

Propitiare, Domine, supplicationibus nostris: et has oblationes famulorum famularumque benignus assume; ut quod singuli obtulerunt ad honorem nominis tui, cunctis proficiat ad salutem (*Gel. V.* 1180).	Deign, O God, to listen to our supplications and mercifully receive the offerings of your servants and handmaids, that what each one offers to the honor of your name may culminate in the salvation of all.

This prayer presumes a communal celebration in which both clergy and faithful participate in their own way.

4. It is striking that the kiss of peace no longer concludes the intercessions but comes after the Lord's prayer and the fraction and thus is directly related to communion. This may have resulted when the intercessions were replaced by the litany.

5. Just as in the east and in Gaul, song appears to have had a place in the liturgy of Rome. Initially, singing occurred in responsorial or antiphonal form: to the cantillation of the lector(s) or cantor(s) the faithful answered with one response or two refrains. The cantillation was itself midway between singing and speaking: a recitative. Of later date and probably of monastic origin was the antiphonal form, carried out by two choirs standing facing each other who had to know the psalms well in order to be able to recite them alternately. The antiphon, a text often taken from the psalm itself, established the melody and was also often an interpretation of the psalm (cf. the Byzantine *hirmos*). Musical development was due to the cantors. In later centuries, these cantors formed the *schola cantorum* that originated in the cloisters attached to basilicas as early as the fifth century. The music itself is discussed in *Geschichte der katholischen Kirchenmusik*, K. G. Fellerer, ed., vol. 1. (Kassel, 1972), and E. T. Moneta-Caglio, *Lo Jubilius e le origini della salmodia responsiale* (Venice, 1976–1977; see also literature list, p. 68).

It is evident that the Roman rite maintained the fundamental structure of the eucharist that we found in Justin. Service of the word and table service are recognizable as the pillars of the celebration. The additions made by Rome were still modest ones; the total impression is one of simplicity. There is little evidence of an "allegorical" expansion of the liturgy or of an accentuation of details. "The genius of the Roman rite" was sobriety and transparency; only later, in contact with the Frankish-Germanic style, would changes appear.

THE SERVICE OF THE WORD IN THE EUCHARIST

From the above description of the various rites, it is evident that the liturgy of the word was marked in general by the same traits in both east and west. There was a reading from the Old Testament (later—sixth century—this ceased to be the practice at Rome except on certain days). From the New Testament there was a reading from the "apostle" and one from the gospel. The readings were linked by song; the gospel was introduced by the Alleluia (which, however, seems to be of more recent date). After the gospel reading a homily was given. We know the homilies of the great Fathers of the church; but what was preaching like in the local churches outside the cities? It is difficult to answer but it may be assumed that the interpretation of scripture occupied a not insignificant place in the life of the clergy: they were after all the co-workers with the bishop, and the bishop was the interpreter of holy scripture, which was inherited from the apostles and was the foundation of orthodoxy. The *parathêkê*, the fixed, "written" tradition, was now determinative.

How was scripture read? With some probability one can say that at the Sunday eucharist there was not a *lectio continua* of a certain bibilical book. This would have been the case in special services, for example, at the midday service of readings. Such a continuous reading would have been carried out only in monastic and ascetical circles. From the writings of Augustine and Chrysostom, two ancient preachers from whom a great number of sermons has been passed on to us, it is not clear whether or not a complete system of pericopes had yet been developed for the whole year. On festivals and during the paschal cycle, there were readings from certain books (e.g., from the Pentateuch and from the gospel of John) and from certain passages of those books (pericopes or *capitula*) but there was no comprehensive system. It is likely that the bishops, and above all the "great" bishops, made their own choices for the Sundays. From this practice, the complete pericope cycle grew slowly, with significant differences in east and west. But both traditions agreed on the fundamental principle: for the eucharist, "pericopes"—short pieces from an Old or New Testament book best suited to the time, the place, and the occasion—were chosen. We should finally note that there is very little trace of any direct Jewish influence on this development, as might be expected given the low estimation of Jewish practices in this period.

In short, the reading of scripture was the foundation of the Christian assembly; even the catechumens were admitted during the reading in order to enable faith to grow in them. But the choice of readings was not yet systematized; it is in Rome, at the beginning of the seventh century, that a coordinated series of pericopes began to appear.

THE EUCHARISTIC PRAYER

A critical introduction to the many studies of "the great prayer" can be found in the collection *Prex eucharistica* (PE) by A. Hänggi and J. Pahl. A fine collection and introduction in English is R. Jasper and G. J. Cuming, *Prayers of the Eucharist, Early and Reformed*, 2nd ed. (New York, 1980). We will attempt to systematize the data. The differences between the rites of east and west are suggested primarily by the variants in the eucharistic prayers, in the study of which one encounters the traces of certain liturgical families that go back to the period that we are describing in this chapter. It is true, however, that of all the prayers in the west only the Roman canon remains in use, while in the east it is primarily the anaphorae of Chrysostom and Basil in the Byzantine liturgy that predominate practically everywhere.

In the east, the eucharistic prayer was called anaphora (*anapherein*, to present, to offer) that is, the prayer of offering, containing the memorial of Jesus' offering, or *eucharistia*, thanksgiving. In the west, one spoke of *oratio sacrificii* or *oratio oblationis*, as well as simply of *oratio* or *prex*. *Canon actionis* (the rule determining the action) is typically Roman; *illatio* and *contestatio* are old Spanish and Gallican titles.

ORIGIN

About the origin of the anaphora very little can be said with complete confidence, but one can study recent reconstructions that appear to be solidly based since the knowledge of Jewish prayer and Jewish meal liturgy has increased so significantly. Scholars such as W. Bousset (who studied the blessing in *Const. Ap.* VII, 33–38), A. Baumstark, H. Lietzmann, and others, with remarkable knowledge of the sources, inaugurated the study of the eucharist and of the origins of the anaphora. Nowadays, many authors, especially the following as well as many others unnamed here, have worked toward a synthesis.

J. P. Audet. "Esquisse du genre littéraire de la bénédiction juive et de l'eucharistie chrétienne," *Revue biblique* 65, 1958, pp. 371–399; "Genre littéraire et formes cultuelles de l'eucharistie," *Ephemerides Liturgicae* 80, 1966, pp. 353–385; cf. E. Bickerman, "Bénédiction et prière," *Revue biblique* 69, 1962, pp. 524–532: the genre of the eucharistic prayer goes back to the Jewish blessing and shows the same traits, that is, praise and thanksgiving. R. Ledogar, *Acknowledgement* (Rome, 1968), carefully nuances this opinion on the basis of a thorough analysis.

T. Talley. "From *Berakah* to *Eucharistia*: A Reopening Question," *Worship* 50, 1976, pp. 115–137, exercises a strong critique (by way of careful analysis especially of the meal prayers of the *Didache* and the anaphora of Addai and Mari) on the rather widely accepted thesis of Audet. Talley demonstrates that Audet builds his thesis on an ideal *berakah* and thus generalizes too much and, further, he shows that in the earliest Christian congregations the word *eucharistia* could have taken on a specifically Christian connotation, not to be made equivalent to *eulogia*, blessing. Earliest Christian anaphorae are in the tradition of the Jewish meal prayers but with a radically new accent on thanksgiving (cf. G. Rouwhorst, "Bénédiction, action de grâces, supplication," *Questions liturgiques* 61, 1980, pp. 211–240; and H. Wegman, "Généologie hypothétique de la prière eucharistique," in ibid., pp. 263–278).

G. Dix. The Shape of the Liturgy demonstrates that the fundamental actions of the eucharist go back to Jesus' last supper, which was a genuine Jewish meal. Jesus took the bread, spoke the blessing, broke, and gave; and so also, after the meal, the cup. The seven actions of the Lord (taking, blessing, breaking, giving; taking, blessing, giving), Jewish in setting, became the four actions (taking, blessing, breaking, giving of bread and cup together) developed ritually into the Christian eucharist: the preparation of the gifts, the prayer of blessing, the breaking of the bread, the communion. Moreover, Dix points out the influence of the meal rites of the Jews, especially the *kiddush*, the blessing at the beginning of a sabbath or feast day, and the *birkat ha-mazon*, the blessing after supper.

L. Bouyer. Eucharist (Notre Dame, 1968), goes further along the line of Dix and relates Jewish prayer in detail—the *berakoth* at table, the *berakoth* of the Shema, and the *tephillah*—to the origin of the anaphora. Here and there Bouyer's analytic method could be improved: his comparisons are sometimes too overdrawn.

L. Ligier. "From the Last Supper to the Eucharist," in L. C. Sheppard, ed., *The New Liturgy* (London, 1970, pp. 113–150); "The Origins of the Eucharistic Prayer," in *Studia Liturgica* 9, 1973, pp. 161–185. Ligier has made an especial contribution in researching the place of the institution narrative in the eucharistic prayer. He points to the parallel in the *birkat ha-mazon*, in which narrative or supplicatory additions (embolisms) could also occur (in the prayer's second paragraph, *birkat ha-aretz*, on Hanukkah and Purim, and in the third paragraph, *birkat ha-Ierushalayyim*, on Passover). Ligier proposes the possibility that in the oldest state of the anaphora (i.e., until about 100 to 150 A.D.), its character as table prayer was better expressed because of the lack of the Sanctus and even of the institution narrative.

It seems to me that the insertion of the institution narrative with its anamnetic "command" into the eucharistic prayer and the development of the anamnesis (and eventually the epiclesis) make this prayer an anaphora, an offering prayer with a ritual basis. The institution narratives were apparently handled in a free way and actions "of the Lord" were even added (e.g., "he lifted up his eyes to heaven") as a basis for ritual "performance." It is possible that in the fourth century, the representation of the Mystery outshone the proclamatory memorial in a way that was analogous to the evolution we found in the ritual of the paschal vigil and baptism. The "pictorial" and dramatized institution narrative with anamnesis and epiclesis became the central act of the eucharist. This fourth-century tendency would determine the theology and spirituality of the eucharist through the ages. We refer again to the view of Theodore of Mopsuestia about the offertory, which underwent an analogous development. The development of eucharistic theology goes from thanksgiving to representation of the "mystery" of the death of the Lord, who is both High Priest and sacrifice, both *archihiereus* and *thusia*.

It must be remembered, however, that the anaphora of Hippolytus, probably the oldest that we know at present, already contained an institution narrative within the table prayer, although its use is much more "anamnetic" in character.

Several fundamental elements of the anaphora are described below (see pp. 84–85).

1. *The glorification of God's Name*, of God as God. This element of *eucharistia* is found in all anaphorae, usually at the beginning (cf. Pss. 92:2; 33; 147), but in a variety of ways: by the use of adjectives with the *alpha negans* (*anekphrastos*, inexpressible; *akataleptos*, inconceivable) or by a prayer to God for the ability to speak the divine glory (for who is able to praise God?) or by the stating of God's own revelation: we are able to praise God because God is revealed to us through the Son and the Spirit. These three ways of praising are to be found in the anaphorae, but the trinitarian doxology is especially prominent in the anaphora of Basil.

2. *The anamnesis in a broad sense*, which is the memorial of the great saving deeds of God. This memorial sometimes includes the creation of all things and of humanity, the fall, and God's mercy for sinful humanity, which is re-created in God's image through the law and the prophets and finally through Jesus the Son, whose incarnation, life, passion, and resurrection are recalled. In this anamnesis, the institution narrative is sometimes also included.

In the oldest anaphorae praise, thanksgiving, and anamnesis are often found mixed together and not strictly differentiated. Moreover the anamnesis is not yet so strongly developed theologically (e.g., the anaphorae of Addai and Mari, of the Twelve Apostles, of John Chrysostom). In "elevated" compositions, such as the anaphorae of Basil or of James (Jerusalem), one finds those various elements distinguished and the contents tightly formulated.

The significance of the anamnesis is doxological (praising and thanking) and also theological (confessing). The prayer may confess the unity of God's plan of salvation, of creation, and re-creation. Or it may confess the holiness of God over against the sinfulness of humanity, whereby the eucharist is given a penitential character. Finally, because of the anamnesis, the celebration of the eucharist is not seen in its particularity but rather as rooted in salvation history and, above all, in the dying and rising of the Lord. Eucharist can only exist by being the *memoria mortis Domini*, and it is rooted in the unique event, the historical, "once for all" of Jesus' death.

This rooting is expressed primarily in what is called the anamnesis in the strict sense. The institution narrative closes with the words: "Do this in remembrance of me." This command is "carried out" in the prayer that has come to be immediately connected to it: "Therefore we remember the death and resurrection of the Lord and we offer to you, Father, these gifts, which you have yourself given us" (memores . . . offerimus, *memnēmenoi toinun . . . prospheromen*). Eucharist is *thusia* only as a memorial of the sacrifice of the Son that is proclaimed in the congregation; but as memorial it is also really an act of the congregation which presents gifts and prays.

3. The epiclesis, a prayer for the fruits of the celebrations (unity, peace, health, life) like the supplicatory prayer at the end of the Jewish *birkat ha-mazon*. From this originated the prayers of supplication and the memorials of the living and the dead that were frequently introduced into the anaphorae. In the eucharistic prayers known to us, however, the epiclesis is primarily a prayer asking the Holy Spirit to sanctify the gifts of the faithful who participate at the holy table, that the gifts may become the body and blood of the Lord, or (what is the same thing) for the changing of human, sinful gifts through the memorial of Jesus' sacrifice. It is through the Holy Spirit that the celebration of the congregation is made the memorial of the death and resurrection of the Lord.

The anaphorae are listed below according to ritual type. The abbreviation "PE" refers to the collection *Prex Eucharistica*. The abbreviation "PEER" refers to *Prayers of the Eucharist Early and Reformed*.

THE EAST

The eastern anaphorae have one thing in common: they have no variable parts.

A selection of the East Syrian anaphorae follows.

1. *The anaphora of the apostles Addai and Mari* (PE 375ff., PEER 26ff.). This anaphora is one of the oldest known texts, probably from the third century, and is striking in its lack of the institution narrative. It contains later additions such as the Sanctus with an introduction and perhaps the epiclesis. It is a strophic prayer that is Semitic in color, style, and content (glorification of the Name; mention of the sinfulness of humanity and of the grace of the saving dispensation of God) and still resembles table prayer proclaimed even today. The text is magnificent in its simplicity.

2. *The anaphora of the apostle Peter* (called *sharar*; Maronite; PE 410ff., PEER 29ff.). This prayer must be considered in relation to the foregoing anaphora, for they both may stem from a common source, but have been developed through insertions and additions. It is primarily addressed to Christ, probably a sign of antiquity.

3. *The anaphora of Theodore of Mopsuestia* (PE 381ff.).

4. *The anaphora of Nestorius* (PE 387ff.). These two anaphorae are influenced by the West Syrian ("Jerusalem") tradition. (Nestorius especially seems to have used the anaphora of Chrysostom as a model.) In regard to structure, the supplications (*intercessions*) in these anaphorae come before the epiclesis.

A selection of the West Syrian anaphorae follows. The centers of this tradition were Jerusalem-Antioch, Caesarea (Cappadocia), and Constantinople. The texts were originally Greek, later also Syrian (translations from the Greek or original compositions). This tradition included many anaphorae of which we will mention only the foremost representatives.

1. *The anaphora of the Twelve Apostles* (PE 265; PEER 93ff.).

2. *The anaphora of St. John Chrysostom* (PE 223; PEER 89ff.). The texts of these two anaphorae are related to each other and seem to go back to an older common original text dating from the beginning of the fourth century (Antioch). This original may have shown some resemblance to the anaphora of Addai and Mari and probably had neither Sanctus nor a passage introductory to the Sanctus. The authorship of Chrysostom is controverted, with most scholars denying it. Recently G. Wagner, *Der Ursprung der Chrysostomusliturgie* (Münster, 1973), has tried to prove that Chrysostom was indeed the author. The original in the course of the years was subject to several theological additions.

The structure demonstrates that in the first part, praise (possibly trinitarian from the beginning) and thanksgiving were mixed together. The Sanctus and its introduction seem indeed to be a later addition: in both anaphorae, this passage interrupts the flow of the composition. After the Sanctus, one sentence makes the transition to the narrative of the institution. Then follow the anamnesis, the epiclesis (the prayer for the Holy Spirit "over us and the gifts"), the supplications, and the doxology. The structure is simple and typically Antiochene (in comparison with the Alexandrian family mentioned before).

3. *The anaphora of Basil* (PE 230, 347; PEER 98ff., 34ff.). Of this anaphora there is a long Byzantine Greek version and a shorter Alexandrian version. The latter is probably the oldest, coming from Cappadocia in the early fourth century. It is possible that Basil used this text in the composition of the Byzantine version which, as is generally assumed, was from his hand. It is not certain that Basil also

wrote the shorter Coptic version before he reworked it into the longer form. Both texts, and especially the Byzantine text, are majestic compositions, balanced in structure and rich in content (Trinity, the God-Man, the Spirit). It is a genuinely Greek anaphora that has lost every Semitic trait and in which harmony and theological reflection stand out prominently.

The structure is Antiochene: praise, which is possible for humanity only through the Son and in the Spirit (trinitarian hymn) leads into the Sanctus; the anamnesis of the saving deeds of God in creation and re-creation that is the work of the Son; the institution narrative, summary and center of the prayer, followed by the anamnesis in a strict sense (memorial and offering); the epiclesis, which is strongly developed (conscious of its sinfulness, the congregation prays for the Spirit); the intercessions (very harmonious in formulation); and the concluding doxology.

This dry summary does an injustice to the beauty of this prayer in which theology comes to expression as prayer. The Coptic version excels by its directness, and while it is simpler in content is not of lesser quality.

Of interest is the threefold occurrence in the anamnesis of re-membrance–offering–praise:

Μεμνημένvι οὖν δέσποτα καὶ ἡμεῖς
τῶν σωτηρίων αὐτοῦ παθημάτων,
τοῦ ζωοποιοῦ σταυροῦ, τῆς
τριημέρου ταφῆς, τῆς ἐκ νεκρῶν
ἀναστάσεως, τῆς εἰς οὐρανοὺς
ἀνόδου, τῆς ἐκ δεξιῶν σοῦ τοῦ Θεοῦ
καὶ Πατρὸς καθέδρας καὶ τῆς
ἐνδόξου καὶ φοβερᾶς δευτέρας
αὐτοῦ παρουσίας,

Τὰ σὰ ἐκ τῶν σῶν σοὶ
προσφέροντες κατὰ πάντα καὶ διὰ
πάντα.

Σὲ ὑμνοῦμεν. . . ."

Therefore, Master, we also, re-membering his saving passion, his life-giving cross, his three-day burial, his resurrection from the dead, his ascension into heaven, his session at your right hand, God and Father, and his glorious and fearful second coming;

Aloud: offer[ing] you your own from your own, in all and through all,

People: we hymn you. . . .

4. *The anaphora of James (of Jerusalem)* (PE 244; PEER 60ff.). For a discussion and the text, see pp. 82–85 under the liturgy of Jerusalem. This anaphora is to be counted, along with that of Basil, as the best that is known in the east. It possesses a carefully elaborated structure and is, in content, different from the Basil anaphora but just as interesting (especially in its working out of the trinitarian dogma

128

throughout the text). No epiclesis is as rich as that of the anaphora of James.

5. *The anaphora of Sahag* (PE 332). Known to us from the Armenian liturgy, but clearly inspired by and of the same structure as the anaphora of Basil.

6. *The anaphora of Gregory of Nazianzus* (PE 327, 358). Known to us in both Armenian and Egyptian versions but originally from Syria; the authorship of Gregory is doubtful. The prayer in the Egyptian version is entirely directed to Christ and for the most part is cast in the first person singular.

7. *The anaphora of the Apostolic Constitution VIII: 12, 4–51* (PE 82; PEER 71ff.). This is a very long prayer with an extended anamnesis marked by weighty and balanced composition. The part before the Sanctus—the blessing of the Name of God who has created all things and is present to all things in Wisdom—is reminiscent of the Tephillah of Yom Kippur (cf. L. Ligier, NRT 82, 1960, 40–55).

The anaphorae of the West (and East) Syrian tradition all have the same Antiochene structure. There are texts among them that indicate both how deeply the controversies concerning God and the Son of God cut into the life of the church and how deeply they determined the spirituality of the east. It is also to be noted that in a text like that of Addai and Mari, the terminology of offering is missing and the proclamation of the death of the Lord stands forth, while in the later texts the anamnesis of Christ's sacrifice in the action of the church has become pivotal.

A selection of the Alexandrian anaphorae follows. The Alexandrian tradition differs from the Antiochene especially in the structure of the anaphora. Most notable is the placing of an epiclesis before the institution narrative while also preserving the epiclesis at the end of the prayer (thus a twofold epiclesis). Furthermore, the formulation of anamnesis in the strict sense is to be noted: "Proclaiming the death of your Son and confessing his resurrection, we have offered (*proethēkamen*) before you from your own gifts." The Aorist is typical and, what is more, the anamnesis is in the form of proclamation (*kataggellontes*).

1. *The anaphora of Mark* (PE 101, 116, 120; PEER 48ff., 43, cf. 44). This anaphora was written in Greek; the Coptic translation is known as the anaphora of Cyril of Alexandria (PE 135). The structure of the prayer is as follows:

praise and thanksgiving to God who created the world and humanity (image theology: humanity was created and re-created according to God's image); this praise takes form in the sacrifice—*eucharistountes prospheromen tēn logikēn kai anaimakton latreian* ("we give thanks to you and offer this reasonable and bloodless service");

the intercessions for the church and the peoples and all in need;

Sanctus and its introduction;

first epiclesis, the word "full" in "heaven and earth are full of your glory" connects this expression with "Fill, O God, these gifts also with your blessing through your Holy Spirit";

institution narrative with anamnesis;

epiclesis (with the language about the Holy Spirit strongly developed);

doxology.

2. *The anaphora of the papyrus Dêr-Balyzeh* (PE 124; PEER 45).

3. *The anaphora of Serapion* (PE 128; PEER 39ff.). A remarkable text in which the *Didache* is quoted and the institution narrative is divided in two. The epiclesis refers to the Logos, which involves the Spirit also. Maybe Serapion knew an earlier and simpler form of the anaphora of St. Mark rather than that of the received text (cf. G. J. Cuming, "Thmuis Revisited," *Theological Studies* 41, 1980, pp. 568–575).

The Ethiopic rite also has its own anaphorae, but these are of more recent date and demonstrate a definite decline in style and content: they are exuberant and awe-filled before the sacred mystery (cf. "apologies," expressions of sinfulness).

It should be understood that only the actual reading of these texts prepares one to weigh their values. By knowing the structure, one can easily distinguish the Alexandrian from the Antiochene anaphorae.

THE WEST

The western church possesses as heritage a multiplicity of eucharistic prayers. The old Spanish and old Gallican liturgies are the sources of many texts. In contrast with the Roman tradition, new texts were constantly composed in Gaul and Spain. Their structure was rather "loose" and their content variable. The total harvest of texts is rich and worth a special study because it expresses the faith of the church outside of Rome. These old Spanish and old Gallican eucharistic prayers are no longer used because the Roman liturgy conquered the west. For further study of these traditions, the reader is referred to PE 461 and PEER 106f. (old Gallican texts); to PE 494 and PEER 110f. (old Spanish texts); to H. Büsse, "Das eucharistiche Hochgebet der altspanischen Liturgie," *Liturgisches Jahrbuch* 23, 1973, pp. 42–55; and to A. Thaler, *Das Selbstverständnis der Kirche in den Gebetstexten der altspanischen Liturgie* (Frankfurt, 1975). The Roman canon (PE 424, prefaces 438 ff.; PEER 120ff.) is a unique composition both in form and content. It consists of two parts: (1) the preface, including the opening dialogue, the *vere dignum* (a variable text, composed for each feast and for many Sundays, which is always concentrated upon Jesus' saving work) and the Sanctus; and (2) the actual canon, the heart of which is formed by the institution narrative preceded by a prayer for the acceptance and change of the gifts and followed by the anamnesis, the epiclesis, and the doxology; several further prayers and memorials are added.

We call to the attention of the reader the prefaces, of which good examples exist (e.g. *Sacr. Veron.* nos. 177, 217, and the texts preserved in the *Missale Romanum*).

The canon is one of the oldest parts of the Roman liturgy. In essentials it is known already in the writings of Ambrose (*De Sacramentis* IV, 5, 21; 6, 26–27; cf. PEER 112ff.), in an anonymous Arian fragment (L. Mohlberg, *Sacramentarium Veronense*, no. 1543–1544), and in an old Spanish fragment (*Liber sacramentorum*, ed. Ferotin, no. 1440; for these last two, cf. PEER 115ff.). Because of the quotations found in Ambrose, one may assume that the text was already widely known in the middle of the fourth century. The author is unknown, but it is practically certain that its original language was Latin, not Greek. There have been attempts to reconstruct the oldest form of the text (among others by C. Vagaggini, *The Canon of the Mass and Liturgical Reform* (1967, pp. 28–34), and by Jasper and Cuming (PEER, pp. 115ff.), but these remain hypothetical.

The prayer is a venerable liturgical piece and, at the same time, an unusual composition whose structure is not clearly discernible. Rather, the Roman canon is a grandiloquent *and* solemn prayer asking God to accept the gifts of the congregation so that the sacrifice of Christ may be celebrated. In this canon there is no emphasis on praise; there is no epiclesis (as it is known in the east), nor any mention of the Holy Spirit. It is precisely remembrance of the sacrifice of the Lord and proclamation of his death and resurrection. But above all, there is a preoccupation with the celebration of the congregation (the *familia Dei*), which must become an epiphany of the saving deeds of Christ. It is toward this epiphany that the canon is directed, and thus the consistently repeated prayer that the hallowing of the gifts of the congregation may cause them to become the sacrament (sign) of Christ's dying and rising for the salvation of humanity and the praise of his Father. The eucharist is seen as God's gift to the congregation through Christ and also as the gift of the congregation to the Father through Christ. A double movement is effected in the celebration: the presentation of the gifts and receiving them back again, both praise and the reception of grace in and through the Son. More than any anaphora of the east, the Roman canon focuses on the participation of the (local) church, and on the gifts offered, both for the celebration and for mutual service (*diakonia*). This human contribution forms, as it were, the stakes for the memorial of Jesus' sacrifice. So the Roman canon is a chain of prayers asking God to look with favor upon the gifts of the faithful and upon their *diakonia*, making them into a sign of the sacrifice and *diakonia* of the Son. The Roman canon presupposes an action—each member of the congregation putting in what is needed to celebrate the memorial of Jesus' sacrifice. The emphasis on this phase of the canon is a bit one-sided and the scope of the prayer is limited, but it must be said that the fundamental thought of the canon is biblical (cf. Rom 12:1; Heb 13:9–16). The Roman canon presumes the unity of liturgy and *diakonia*, of the celebration of Jesus' sacrifice and the self-engagement of the participants (see also H.-J. Schulz, *Ökumenische Glaubenseinheit aus eucharistischer Uberlieferung*, Paderborn, 1976, especially pp. 56–71).

SUMMARY

This concludes our overview of the anaphorae and the development of the celebration of the eucharist at a time when a great deal of improvisation was still going on. There are nonetheless extant several texts that give us an insight into the way the Lord's meal was experienced in those days. In regard to the genealogy of the anaphorae, see H. Wegman, "Généologie hypothetique de la prière eucharistique," *Questions Liturgiques* 61, 1980, pp. 263–278. We may say generally that if an anaphora is tightly composed, clear and harmonious in style, and theologically reflective (trinitarian, christological), it is probably a later text, from the time of the flowering of the genre. The anaphorae of Basil and James are good examples of this. Other texts are more archaic and demonstrate the growth of the anaphora as, for example, the anaphora of Addai and Mari, of which we here give the text in a reconstruction and translation (cf. H. Wegman, "Pleidooi voor een tekst: de Anaphora van de Apostelen Addai en Mari," *Bijdragen* 40, 1979, pp. 15–43; PEER 27f.). Words that I have italicized are important for further analysis and take us back to the old Syrian, Jewish-Christian world of faith.

"*First strophe:* Worthy of *glory* from every mouth and *thanksgiving* from every tongue is the adorable and glorious *Name*. . . . He *created* the world through his grace and its inhabitants through his kindness; he *saved* men through his mercy; and gave great grace to mortals . . . (seal or doxology).

"*Second strophe:* . . . Lord, we . . . give you thanks because you have given us a great grace which cannot be repaid. For you *put on our human nature to give us life* through your divine nature; you exalted our lowliness; you redressed our fallen state; you revived our mortality; you forgave our debts; you justified our sinfulness; you *enlightened our intelligence*. You, our Lord and our God, conquered our enemies, and *made the lowliness of our weak nature to triumph* through the abundant mercy of your grace . . . (seal or doxology).

"*Third strophe:* You, Lord, through your many mercies which cannot be told, *be graciously mindful* of all the pious and righteous fathers who were pleasing in your sight, in the commemoration of (your) body and blood . . . which we offer to you on the pure and holy altar, as you taught us. And grant us your tranquility and your peace for all the days of this age. Amen.

"*Seal or doxology:* And because of all your wonderful *dispensation* toward us, with *open mouths and uncovered faces* let us give you thanks and glorify you without ceasing in your Church, which has been redeemed by (your) precious blood. . . . Amen."

Finally, we add to this a reconstruction of the Roman canon (from C. Vagaggini, *The Canon of the Mass and Liturgical Reform*):

I. Dominus vobiscum.	I. The Lord be with you.
Et cum spiritu tuo.	And with you.
Sursum corda.	Let us lift up our hearts.
Habemus ad Dominum.	We have raised them up to the Lord.
Gratias agamus Domino Deo nostro.	Let us give thanks to the Lord our God.
Dignum et iustum est.	It is right and fitting.

II. *Dignum et iustum est, aequum et iustum est nos tibi super omnia gratias agere, Domine, Sancte Pater, omnipotens aeterne Deus, qui incomparabili tuae bonitatis honestate lucem in tenebris fulgere dignatus es mittens nobis Iesum Christum suspiratorem animarum nostrarum, qui nostrae salutis causa humuliando se ad mortem usque subiecit, ut nos ea quae Adam amiserat immortalitate resistutos efficeret sibi heredes et filios.

III. Cuius benignitatis agere gratias tuae tantae magnanimitati quibusque laudibus nec sufficere possumus petentes de tua magna et flexibili pietate accepto ferre sacrificium istud, quod tibi offerimus stantes ante conspectum tuae divinae pietatis per Iesum Christum Dominum et Deum nostrum.

IV. †Per quem petimus et rogamus, omnipotens Pater ut accepta habeas et benedicere digneris haec munera et haec sacrificia illibata quae tibi in primis offerimus pro tua sancta ecclesia catholica, quam pacificare digneris per totum orbem terrarum diffusam (una cum beatissimo papa nostro illo et omnibus orthodoxis atque apostolicae fidei cultoribus).

II. It is right and fitting, good and just, that we should always give thanks to you for all things.

Lord, holy Father, almighty eternal God, who in your incomparable goodness were pleased to make light shine in darkness when you sent Jesus Christ to us as protector of our souls. For our salvation he humbled himself, and subjected himself to death, so as to restore to us that immortality which Adam had lost, and to make us God's heirs and sons.

III. For such goodness and generosity we can never praise and thank you sufficiently, and so we ask you in your great love and compassion kindly to accept this sacrifice which we offer you in the presence of your divine goodness, through Jesus Christ our Lord and God.

IV. Through him we humbly ask and pray you, almighty Father, to accept and to bless these gifts, these pure offerings. We offer them to you, first of all, for your holy catholic Church: be pleased to give peace to her, spread over all the earth. (We offer them to you at the same time, for our blessed bishop, N., and for all the bishops faithful to true doctrine, who are the guardians of the apostolic faith.)

* Anonymous Arian fragment. Cf. Mohlberg, Sacr. Veronense, p. 202 (nos. 1543–1544).

† Mozarabic fragment. Cf. Liber sacramentorum (ed. Férotin), no. 1440.

Memorare etiam, quaesumus Domine, servorum tuorum, qui tibi in honore sanctorum tuorum N.N. reddunt vota sua Deo vivo ac vero pro remissione suorum omnium delictorum.

Remember also, Lord, your servants who address their prayers to you, the living and true God, in honor of your saints, N.N., for the forgiveness of all their sins.

V. (Emitte, Domine, Spiritum tuum Sanctum de caelis) quorum (et horum) oblationem benedictam, ratam rationabilemque facere digneris, quae est imago et similitudo corporis et sanguinis Iesu Christi filii tui ac redemptoris nostri.

V. (Send, Lord, your Holy Spirit from heaven) and mercifully bless and accept this offering which is the image and likeness of the body and blood of Jesus Christ your Son, our redeemer.

VI. *Qui pridie quam pateretur in sanctis manibus suis accepit panem, respexit in caelum ad te, Sancte Pater, omnipotens aeterne Deus, gratias agens benedixit fregit fractumque apostolis et discipulis suis tradidit dicens: accipite et edite ex hox omnes hoc est enim corpus meum quod pro vobis confringetur.

VI. For on the day before he suffered, he took bread into his holy and blessed hands, looked up to heaven, to you, holy Father, almighty eternal God, and giving thanks, blessed and broke it and gave it to his apostles and disciples, saying "Take and eat this, all of you, for this is my body that will be broken for you."

Similiter etiam calicem postquam caenatum est pridie quam pateretur accepit respexit in caelum ad te sancte Pater, omnipotens aeterne Deus gratias agens benedixit, apostolis suis et discipulis tradidit dicens: accipite et bibite ex hoc omnes hic est enim sanguis meus, qui pro vobis et pro multis effundetur in remissionem peccatorum. Quotiescumque hoc feceritis toties commemorationem meam facietis donec iterum adveniam.

In the same way, on the day before he suffered, after he had eaten, he took the cup into his holy and blessed hands, looked up to heaven, to you, holy Father, almighty eternal God, and giving thanks, blessed and gave it to his apostles and disciples, saying "Take and drink of this, all of you, for this is my blood which shall be poured out for you and for everyone to take away all sins. Each time that you do this, you will do it in memory of me until I return."

* Ambrose, *De sacr.* 5, 21–27.

VII. Ergo memores gloriosissimae eius passionis et ab inferis resurrectionis et in caelos ascensionis offerimus tibi hanc immaculatam hostiam incruentam hostiam hunc panem sanctum et calicem vitae aeternae.

VII. That is why, mindful of his most glorious passion and of his resurrection from the dead and ascension into heaven, we offer you this spotless victim, this unbloody victim, this holy bread and cup of eternal life.

VIII. Et petimus et precamur ut hanc oblationem suscipias in sublimi altari tuo, per manus angelorum tuorum, sicut suscipere dignatus es munera pueri tui iusti Abel et sacrificium patriarchae nostri Abrahae et quod tibi obtulit summus sacerdos tuus Melchisedech.

VIII. And we ask and pray you to accept this offering carried by your angels to your heavenly altar, as you wished also to accept the gifts of your just servant Abel, the sacrifice of Abraham, father of our race, and the offering of your high priest Melchisedech.

IX. (Obsecrantes ut per gratiam Spiritus Sancti in munere tuae caritatis firmemur, et quod ex tua hac benedictione acceperimus, aeternitatis gloria consequamur.)

IX. (We ask you that through the grace of the Holy Spirit the gift of your love may be confirmed in us, and that we may possess in eternal glory what we already receive from your goodness.)

X. Per Dominum nostrum Iesum Christum, in quo tibi est, cum quo tibi est honor, laus, gloria, magnificentia, potestas, cum Spiritu Sancto a saeculis et nunc et semper et in omnia saecula saeculorum. Amen.

X. Through our Lord, Jesus Christ, in whom and with whom honor, praise, glory, might, and power are yours with the Holy Spirit from the beginning, now and always, for ever and ever. Amen.

Reconciliation
Fundamentally little was changed in the practice of penance and reconciliation in comparison with the previous period. The church continued to hold onto the principle that penance was allowed once after baptism, and this principle very likely became stricter than before (see F. van de Paverd, "Disciplinarian Procedures in the Early Church," *Augustinianum* 21, 1981, pp. 291–316).

The course of penance was as follows. All those who had committed a serious sin were formally expelled (*excommunicatio*) and, if they desired reconciliation, had to come back and ask for admission to penance. It is, however, to be noted that sometimes the excommunication coincided with the admission to penance. The penitent was received among the other penitents and the bishop assigned the penance according to the sin. During the penance the penitent was excluded from communion (*akoinonia*). To have been received among the penitents was for the congregation the proof that a person recognized himself as a sinner and let it be known openly. The public character of the reception was, however, not only directed toward the conversion of the sinner but was also an invitation to the congregation to stand by the sinners and to pray for them. Reception was accomplished by the bishop's laying on of hands. The penitents received ashes on their heads and wore special penitential garments.

After the reception the actual time of penance began. The penitent had to fast, give alms, abstain from meat, and offer help to others. Most difficult were the many prohibitions: the penitent could not serve in the army or engage in trade; could bring no case before the civil court; and, above all, had to forgo marital intercourse during the penance and thereafter during the rest of his or her life. Should the penitent's partner have died, the penitent could not marry again. "In face of the various texts it becomes evident that in making himself a penitent the sinner placed himself in a definitive state that did not end with reconciliation. . . . After having been solemnly received as a penitent the sinner had to begin a new life—a life of expiation before reconciliation, a life of holiness in refound innocence after the day of pardon" (translated from C. Vogel, *Le pecheur et la penitence dans l'Eglise ancienne*, Paris, 1966, pp. 38–39).

On account of this enduring character of penance, even after the actual time of penance, people began to change the age for doing penance. One had to be mature to be able to undertake penance. Hence a paradox: the church made the practices of the "one-time" penance so strict that it had to be postponed until one's later years.

After the time of penance the *reconciliation*, ministered by the bishop, took place in the midst of the congregation, usually on Maundy Thursday before the celebration of the paschal festival that would begin on Good Friday. This reconciliation signified reintroduction into the congregation in which and through which the forgiveness of God was confessed. As a later prayer would formulate it:

. . . et manum pietatis tuae manui nostrae subpone, ut, per manus nostrae impositionem, te co-

. . . and support our hands by the hand of your compassion so that through your co-operation and the imposition of our hands, the grace of the

operante infundatur eis	Holy Spirit may be poured out upon
spiritus sancti gratia,	them and your celestial benediction de-
descendat super eos	scend upon them. . . .
caelestis benedictio . . .	
(OR. 50, C. XXV, 49).	

But in the burdensomeness of the penitential practice lay the causes of its decay. People, with the exception of ascetics, for whom it was not intended in the first place, avoided penance. The order of penitents turned into a sort of "third order." In the following period the practice would change under the influence of the monks, who from early times had played a great role in attending to penitents.

Ministry and Ordination

The Latin word *ordo*, "corps," was applied to officeholders in the church, thus distinguishing them from the people. The Latin term was a civil expression: the Senate was called *ordo clarissimus* and that corps governed the city (*ordo populusque*). The term *ordo*, then, was taken over and used to indicate the clergy (the corps of the consecrated), who were differentiated from the people and who then were supposed to serve the people (*ministerium*). A person was taken into this *ordo* by means of *ordinatio*, which in the liturgy meant a consecration by laying on of hands and prayer. In Greek a distinction was made between *cheirotonia* (appointment and installation, *katastasis*) and *cheirothesia* (laying on of hands). This latter was a consecration into the order.

THE EAST

The *Constitutiones Apostolurum* is a direct source for the later rites of ordination in the east (both Antiochene and Alexandrian). Of interest also is the *Euchologion* of Serapion, which contains ordination prayers (*cheirothesia katastaseōs episkopou*—laying on of hands at the consecration of a bishop: Funk II, 189).

The data are to be found in *Const. Apost.*, VIII, 4, 2–5, 12 (Funk, 472–477), consecration of a bishop; VIII, 16, 2–5 (Funk, 521–523), of a priest; VIII, 17, 2–3 (Funk, 523–525), of a deacon; VIII, 21, 2–4 (Funk, 525–527), of a subdeacon; VIII, 22, 2–4 (Funk, 527), of a lector (psalmist).

In these ordinations the *Const. Apost.* agrees with the *Apostolic Tradition*, which was discussed in the previous chapter. At the consecration of a bishop, there were at least three bishops who consecrated, just as the Council of Nicea stipulated (canon 4, Kirch no. 404). What is new is the laying of the gospel book on the head of the one being consecrated, an epicletic act we shall also meet later in the west. The prayer of consecration is an expansion of that found in the *Apostolic Tradition:* he who is ordained bishop within a local church (*no vacua manus impositio*) serves a new cult that is prefigured in the Old Testament. The ordination of priests and deacons remained simple: laying on of hands and prayer. At the ordination of a priest only the bishop laid on hands. A new development, which was connected with the importance of churchly office in the society of the time, was the consecration of the subdeacon (acolyte) and lector (psalmist), who were earlier only "installed."

Common to all eastern rites for ordination is a sort of "installation formula" that is at once a summons to prayer and an introduction to the prayer of consecration. It probably goes back to the fourth century (Antioch) and since then has been used in all ordinations:

Ἡ θεία χάρις, ἡ πάντυτε τὰ ἀσθενῆ Θεραπεύουσα καὶ τὰ ἐλλείποντα ἀναπληροῦσα προχειρίζεται τ̓ δεῖνα . . . εἰς πρεσβύτερον· εὐξώμεθα οὖν ὑπέρ αὐτοῦ ἵνα ἐλθη ἐπ̓ αὐτὸν ἡ χάρις τοῦ παναγίου Πνεύματος.	Divine grace, which always heals what is sick and weak and fills up what is lacking, chooses this N. as presbyter. Let us pray for him that the grace of the all-holy Spirit may come upon him.

THE WEST

We are concerned here with the old Roman ritual for ordinations. The Roman ritual was simple and still directly connected to the praxis of the *Apostolic Tradition.* The essence of the ritual continued to be the laying on of hands with prayer for the Holy Spirit. An important addition was the congregational prayer (litany) before the prayer of consecration. Most likely the ordinands also received the clothing proper to their ordination (the *planeta* for the presbyter, the *stola* or *orarion* for the deacon). After the ordination the kiss of peace took place and the celebration of the eucharist continued.

Most interesting are the ordination texts of the Roman tradition from the last quarter of the sixth century, to which time they are traceable in written form, that have been in use until our time in an unbroken tradition. Their age is, however, even greater (fifth century). The texts are found in *Sacramentarium Veronense* (ed. L. Mohlberg): nos. 924–947, *consecratio episcoporum;* nos. 948–951, *benedictio super diaconos;* nos. 952–954, *consecratio presbyteri.* By using the collections of texts of H. B. Porter, *The Ordination Prayers of the Ancient Western Churches* (London, 1967), it is possible to make a comparison with other ordination rites in the west (Gaul, Spain).

In these prayers a central place is given to the hierarchy, that is, the rank of ecclesial office established according to the command and grace of the Lord God (*Deus honorum dator*) and of the Son, God's power and wisdom, for the purpose of serving and upholding the church. The fullness of the ministry takes form in the episcopacy, with which the presbytery participates as *cooperator*, as *secundi meriti munus*, in analogy to the leadership of Moses and his helpers and the priestly ranks of Aaron and the Levites. Both bishop and presbyter are charged to lead and to accompany God's people as good shepherds, and to deepen faith by the preaching of the word of God. The deacon is regarded as the helper of the bishop in his cultic and social task.

It is interesting to note that these Roman prayers are structured according to the schema of the *orationes:* address to God; memorial of God's saving action; epiclesis; concluding doxology. Once again we discover the Jewish *berakah* schema.

As an example here is the *consecratio presbyteri* (*Veronense*, no. 954, translation from Porter, op. cit., pp. 25–29):

Domine, sancte pater, omnipotens aeterne deus, honorum omnium et omnium dignitatum quae tibi militant distributor, per quem proficiunt universa; per quem cuncta firmantur, amplificatis semper in melius naturae rationabilis incrementis per ordinem congrua ratione dispositum. Unde sacerdotales gradus et officia leuitarum sacramentis mysticis instituta creuerunt; ut cum pontifices summos regendis populis praefecisses, ad eorum societatis et operis adiumentum sequentis ordinis uiros et secundae dignitatis elegeris. Sic in heremo per septuaginta	O Lord, Holy Father, Almighty, Everlasting God, bestower of all the honours and of all the worthy ranks which do thee service, thou through whom all things make increase, through whom everything is made firm, by the ever-extended increase to the benefit of rational nature by a succession arranged in due order; whence the priestly ranks and the offices of the Levites arose and were inaugurated with mystical symbols. Thus when thou didst set up high priests to rule over thy people, thou didst choose men of a lesser order and secondary dignity to be their companions and to help them in their labour. Likewise in

uirorum prudentium mentes Moyse spiritum propagasti; quibus ille adiutoribus usus in populo, innumeras multitudines facile gubernauit. Sic et Eleazaro et Ithamar, filiis Aaron, paternae plenitudinis abundantiam transfudisti, ut ad hostias salutares et frequentioris officii sacramenta sufficeret meritum sacerdotum. Ac prouidentia, domine, apostolis filii tui doctores fidei comites addedisti, quibus illi orbem totum secundis praedicatoribus impleuerunt.

Quapropter infirmitati quoque nostrae, domine, quaesumus, haec adiumenta largire, qui quanto magis fragiliores sumus, tanto his pluribus indigemus. Da, quaesumus, pater, in hos famulos tuos presbyterii dignitatem. Innoua in uisceribus eorum spiritum sanctitatis. Acceptum a te, deus, secundi meriti munus obtineant, censuramque morum exemplo suae conuersationis insinuent. Sint probi cooperatores ordinis nostri. Eluceat in eis totius forma iustitiae, ut bonam rationem dispensationis sibi creditae reddituri, aeternae beatitudinis praemia consequantur; per . . .

the desert thou didst spread out the spirit of Moses through the minds of seventy wise men, so that he, using them as helpers among the people, governed with ease countless multitudes. Likewise also thou didst impart unto Eleazar and Ithamar, the sons of Aaron, the richness of their father's plenty, so that the benefit of priests might be sufficient for the salutary sacrifices and the rites of a more frequent worship. And also by providence, O Lord, thou didst add, to the Apostles of thy Son, teachers of the faith as companions, and they filled the whole world with these secondary preachers.

Wherefore, we beseech thee, O Lord, to grant these assistants to our weakness also, for we who are so much frailer need so many more. Grant, we beseech thee, O Father, the dignity of presbyters unto these thy servants. Renew in their inward parts the Spirit of holiness. May they obtain and receive of thee, O God, the office of second dignity, and by the example of their conversation may they commend a strict way of life. May they be virtuous colleagues of our order. Let the pattern of all righteousness show forth in them, in order that, rendering in time to come a good account of the stewardship committed unto them, they may obtain the rewards of eternal blessedness; through . . .

Liturgy at Death
See pages 105–107.

Marriage
The first signs of a liturgical celebration on the occasion of a Christian marriage appear in this period. The crowning (in the east), the joining of the hands, the *velatio* (in Rome), none of which are specifically Christian, come to be accompanied by the prayer of the church's minister. We refer to Paulinus of Nola, Carmen XXV, 199–232 (CSEL 30, 244–245) and to the *Sacramentarium Veronense* (ed. Mohlberg), nos. 1105–1110, *velatio nuptialis*. No. 1110 provides a blessing of the bride that retained its popularity in later years.

See further on pages 237–238 and 295, and K. Ritzer, *Formen, Riten und religiösen Brauchtum der Eheschliessung in der christlichen Kirchen des ersten Jahrtausends* (Münster, 1962; LQF 38).

CONCLUSION

"Worship in the Church of the Empire" is known to us from many direct and indirect sources, as we have shown to the extent possible in this book. This form of worship came to be determinative for the later celebration of the liturgy: from then on the structures would remain the same although they sometimes became less visible through added embellishment. It is about these structures that this chapter has been concerned. What we discovered primarily was a development toward the public *cultus:* signs began to play a great role as did the "presentation" of the invisible mystery. Moreover, "today" (*hodie*) began to be a characteristic mark of the liturgy; the expectation of the kingdom of God became more vague. This is not remarkable if one recalls that the christianizing church became "reconciled to time" (Dix) and found that its task lay in the contemporary world, its inspiration in Hellenism, its sensibility in the neo-platonic approach to reality, for "Plato too understood divine transcendence" (Barlaam, *Second letter to Palamas,* cf. J. Meyendorff, *Byzantine Theology,* p. 13).

Chapter Three

The Roman-Frankish-Germanic Liturgy in the West: From Gregory I (590–604) to Gregory VII (1073–1085)

The period described in this chapter is of great importance for worship in the western church. There are now available to us a multiplicity of sources that disclose orders of service that were no longer purely Roman (*stadtrömisch*), but that evidenced a mixture of "Roman" and "northern" traditions. We will attempt to describe this mixture as accurately as possible, for at this time the liturgy developed a character that was to remain essentially unchanged over the ensuing centuries. The following chapter is intended as an invitation to careful study of these sources and a thoroughgoing analysis of these orders of service.

I. HISTORICAL DATA

Literature

H. Jedin, ed., *Handbook of Church History*, vol. 3: *The Church in the Age of Feudalism* (New York, 1969).

A. Mirgeler, *Geschichte Europas* (Freiburg, 1964).

———, *Kritischer Rückblick auf das abendlandische Christentum*, Herder Bücherei 329 (Freiburg, 1969).

C. Morris, *The Discovery of the Individual; 1050–1200* (London, 1972).

R. W. Southern, *The Making of the Middle Ages* (London, 1953, repr. 1978).

———, *Western Society and the Church in the Middle Ages*, Pelican History of the Church, vol. 2 (Harmonsworth, 1970).

A. THE CAROLINGIANS

The barbarian invasion of the west Roman empire was described in chapter 2. As a result of that invasion, many features of the empire were totally changed and the emperors were unable to exercise any further influence in the west; they withdrew to the eastern part of the empire.

In Spain (and in central and southern France, the heartlands of the Roman empire outside of Italy), the Visigoths had established themselves since 416 A.D. This Visigothic empire disappeared in Spain only in the eighth century under the occupation by Islam. From the fifth to the eighth centuries there was a flourishing church life in Spain with a great deal of writing, practically nothing of which has remained.

Italy (an anachronistic term) was a football in the hands of several leaders: the east Goths, who established an independent kingdom under Odoacer (476–493) and Theodoric (493); the emperor, who wanted to keep Italy for the empire; and the pope who, as bishop of Rome, was the moral leader of the region. In 568 the land suffered under new invasions, this time from the Lombards, who were not assimilated into the autochthonous population. These Lombards were nonorthodox so that relations with the local population were all the more harsh and inimical. The invaders quickly took mastery in Italy, and thereby the south was brought to ruin through wars carried on by desperate emperors attempting to restore their authority in the old *Imperium.* They did not succeed: even Ravenna, the city of the exarch, fell into the hands of the Lombards, so that only the pope in Rome remained as representative of the old culture. Thereby his moral authority increased and his position in relation to the east grew more independent.

The growth of this independent position was hastened by the fact that between 681 and 715, "Syrians" (especially monks) fled to Rome before the advance of Islam. The city received the refugees and they stimulated the movement toward independence from the emperor, for they were disgruntled with his meddling in church affairs. There were even a number of these easterners who came to sit on the papal throne. Not only did they introduce their own customs into the liturgy (one thinks of the *Improperia* for Good Friday) but they also turned to another secular authority, that in the north, where the Carolingians came to power in the eighth century and where St. Boniface, the apostle of Germany, had restored the church after the disorder of the sixth and seventh centuries.

The Frankish kingdom consisted of Neustria (from the Scheldt to the Loire) and Austrasia (between the Meuse and the Rhine), with later extensions to the south, to the Pyrenees, and to the other side of the Rhine (Frisians, Saxons, Hessians, Bavarians). The kingdom came into existence after the arrival of the Franks, who penetrated from the north and kept penetrating further south into the cities and settlements along the important Roman imperial highway (Rome–Genoa–Aix-en-Provence–Vienne–Burgundy–Metz–Trier–Cologne) with its branches to Poitiers and Tours. Through this penetration an assimilation took place between the old Roman culture in the cities and the "barbarian" culture, and this encounter was the very germ of western civilization. In the process of assimilation the church played a significant role.

Assimilation was advanced by the conversion to Christianity of the Merovingian Clovis (481–511). He stimulated both the growth of the land and the cultural influence of the church. With the Merovingians, who ruled primarily in Neustria (Paris and environs), there began the process of stabilization and unification that would be completed under the Carolingians.

We ought not, however, imagine the conditions before and during the Merovingians in such rosy hues. It is not for nothing that those days are called the "barbarian centuries." There was, to be sure, a great expansion of labor in which the countryside was developed and the center of gravity came to lie outside the cities, but this countryside was in the possession of the landed aristocracy who had serfs at their disposal. Each lord was an absolute ruler. He had his own land, his own church, and most likely also his own priest—matters about which the bishop in the city had little to say. Organization of the kingdom and the church did not amount to much. The church was principally, if not totally, structured on a local basis, with, as a consequence, widespread disorganization and chaos. Previously the church was organized on the basis of the old division of the Roman empire, but this soon decayed. The consequences were incalculable: in politics there were the mutually warring lords; in the church there was a sort of vacuum. This situation continued until the Carolingians began to centralize their power.

The Carolingians, who came from Austrasia, established a strong kingship by attracting and commanding the loyalties of the nobility. In such a way they succeeded step by step in taking over and consolidating the power in both parts of the Frankish kingdom: thus began the blossoming of the Frankish kingdom and the Carolingian renaissance. The anointing of Pippin as king by Boniface was the first sign of this renaissance; the coronation of Charlemagne as emperor was its high point. The Frankish kingdom began to measure itself against the powerful empire in the east, which in the meanwhile had to defend itself against Islam. Western Europe had become a reality and along with it came into existence a truly western liturgy.

The center of gravity of the Frankish kingdom under the Carolingians and their direct successors, the Ottonians, lay in the Rhineland, but with a tilt toward the south (Bavaria, Switzerland, Austria). Central cities were Aachen, Trier, Cologne, and Mainz. The western part (France) would need decades before unity could be forged from the splinters of feudalism.

England and Ireland were of great significance for Europe and for the church: the Anglo-Saxon and Irish monks provided a new *élan*. The Irish monastic church is known to us from the fourth century; that there had been contacts with the east is practically certain. It was a tightly organized, somewhat closed church, ruled by the abbots of the many cloisters. The conquest of England by the barbarians (Angles, Saxons, Jutes) only increased that tightness. "Ireland grew above all into a (one is tempted to say) museum of the old Christian literary tradition but also into a center for the spread of a sociological form of Christianity which was distinguishable in essential points from the Roman tradition. The principal distinction of the two forms rested doubtless in the imbedding of Irish Christianity in the indigenous tradition of clan and people" (Mirgeler, *Geschichte Europas*, p. 12). The monasteries—the monks of which formed a closed, tight-knit community—put forth a great missionary activity with its own characteristics and its own culture, that was fruitful in the encounter with others, such as occurred on English soil.

In the beginning of the seventh century, Gregory the Great sent Roman missionaries, monks of the Benedictine rule, to England to bring about the conversion of the barbarian tribes. They met there the Irish monks who had come for the same purpose. This led initially to narrow-minded rivalry that was eventually put aside: as a result of the cooperation of both "parties," the building of the Anglo-Saxon church was begun and completed, a church with its own style (which is still perhaps to be encountered in the Anglican church), a profound culture, and a wide-ranging energy to accomplish practical results. For the ecclesiastical revival under the Carolingians, one has mostly the Anglo-Saxon monks to thank. They had come to Europe to convert the heathen but at the same time they brought to an end the chaotic conditions prevailing there in church life. They also created a firm link with Rome that would function as a model, which is easy to understand given the origin of the Anglo-Saxon church: Roman monks in Canterbury had traditionally preserved the link with Rome.

B. THE OTTONIANS

After the death of Charlemagne, his empire was divided into east and west. For the time being the west remained splintered and without influence, but the east gained considerable prestige under the Ottonians and the Salian dynasty (919–1106). Lorraine and Burgundy were joined to the eastern realm with the result that the Carolingian tradition could be continued. The Ottonians carried on the established church politics: they confirmed the already significant political power (*Stadtherrschaft*) of the bishops but, as the occasion arose, they nominated for bishoprics only those candidates who were favorably disposed toward the rulers. Here are to be found the roots of the decline of the bishop's office and of the investiture controversy, the controversy between emperor and pope that began because of too great an influence of the state on the church and ended with too great papal claims upon the state.

The Ottonians attempted to restore the old imperial tradition: Otto III was enthroned in Rome as a new Constantine. This meant that the emperor, with many ecclesiastical dignitaries in his retinue (monks and especially bishops), introduced to Rome the liturgy as he knew it. Rome was experiencing in the meanwhile a low point in its ecclesiastical life so that the implantation of the "northern" ideas took place all the more easily.

The Carolingians and the Ottonians are of great importance for the liturgy in the west. The Carolingians brought the Roman liturgy to the north; the Ottonians brought the Frankish-Roman liturgy to the south, as we shall see.

C. THE EUCHARISTIC CONTROVERSY

We should mention here the controversy about the eucharist that occupied the church in the west at this time and that deeply influenced the experience of this sacrament in subsequent centuries. The controversy came to a head on the question of symbol and reality and depended on two mutually exclusive ways of looking at the eucharist: the "realistic" and the "spiritual" (one should use these terms only with care). The controversy was carried on by the abbot Paschasius Radbertus (of Corbie) and his monk Ratramnus, about 825, but was continued in the fierce struggle around Berengarius of Tours a century and a half later, at which time the realistic view gained the upper hand. Radbertus argued for the actual, real presence of Christ's saving life and death in the eucharist (*veritas*). Ratramnus defended the historical, thus past, dimension of Christ's life, which, therefore, could only be celebrated *in figura* in the eucharist. It was the nature of symbolic reality that was in question and the way that the notions *veritas* and *figura* were applied. For Radbertus *veritas* was the real presence of Christ, celebrated *in figura*; for Ratramnus the *veritas* was the past historical event that could only be present *in figura*. What is clear is that the "realistic" conception won the day in western theology and piety. A parallel development may be seen in the allegorical explanation of the eucharist by Amalarius of Metz, which we shall discuss below.

II. CULTURAL DATA

Literature

Atlas of Western Civilization, op. cit.

A. L. Mayer. *Die Liturgie in der europäischen Geistesgeschichte.* Darmstadt, 1971 (a collection of a series of articles from the *Jahrbuch für Liturgiewissenschaft*).

The sixth, seventh, and eighth centuries were chaotic. The old was no longer viable; the new was not yet in existence. The church— especially the clergy (the bishops) and the monks—was the central focus of renewal and assimilation.

"It is however this same torso of the Old Empire, populated by barbarized Romans and with Christianized Germans on its frontiers, that was to be the cradle of mediaeval Christianity. And it is partly due to the new element, the Barbarians, that this Christianity developed such a great vitality that it eventually overshadowed the Arab world, its antithesis, and the Byzantine world, its counterpart— two worlds which seemed at the moment to be so immutably superior. This is a fact which from now on becomes increasingly evident. In contrast to a Byzantium preoccupied with constantly repetitive, dignified clichés and elegant and subtle variations on older themes, comes the barbarian but soon to be Latinized West, with its spontaneous and startlingly original creations. In the VIIth and VIIIth centuries there are the Celtic miniatures, insular script, and the 'high crosses' in England. In the ninth century there was the scholarly but bold adoption of the whole late Latin heritage that was still available—script, miniatures, ivories, architectural types, scholastic authors and all. In the Xth century the miniatures of Reichenau represent the flowering of the Christo-German expressionism. In the XIth and XIIth centuries there comes within a few decades a rapidly rising stream of artistic developments, all variants of the 'Roman' basilica: the portal, the richly turreted abbey church, the stained-glass window, and the rebirth of monumental sculpture—and then, immediately on top of that, the development of early Gothic. In the same period in a different field, we see the development of Latin poetry and Bernardine prose; in other words a living medieval Latin. Victorine and Bernardine mysticism flourishes beside the dialectic of Abelard and the later development of scholastic theology and philosophy. Finally, in the vernacular, we have the rise of epic poetry and the Provençal lyric" (*Atlas of Western Civilization*, p. 57).

Latin was preserved in the official documents of the church: it remained the vehicle of church affairs and the language of worship. As a consequence the role of the clergy in worship became steadily more important, for it was they who understood Latin. It followed almost automatically that the liturgy became primarily an action of the clergy and its language acquired that mysterious character that accentuated the sacred action. A development thereby set in that ran counter to the original liturgy of Rome: the worship of the north became both clerical and sacral.

Charlemagne's ideal was a Christian culture within a church-state, stimulated by competent bishops and monks and under his personal leadership. Leading figures were Theodulf, Paul the Deacon, Paulinus of Aquileia, Agobard, Angilbert, John Scotus Erigena, and Alcuin. The new culture made its own contributions to the old Roman culture on which it was modeled. The ninth, tenth, and eleventh centuries were above all "the centuries of the book" (and the book illustrated with miniatures) and consequently the centuries of the monks. The Carolingian culture after Charlemagne suffered irreparable damage from the Normans, the Saracens, and the Magyars, who attacked and plundered the west, but it was saved in the "German Empire": at Reichenau, St. Gall, Trier, Mainz, Echternach, Cologne. This all was followed then by Cluny, the mother abbey of more than 1,400 monasteries—the Cluniacs, the spiritual elite of western Christendom. From them came the reform of the Roman Curia, the reclaiming of Spain from Islam, Romanesque building, and most importantly, powerful support for the pope in the investiture controversy with the emperor.

In the eleventh century came "the resurrection of France": in this century of experiment we find early scholasticism in Paris, Chartres, and Tours, Romanesque style and monumental sculpture (Moissac).

III. THE LITURGY: ORDERS OF SERVICE AND TEXTS

Literature

A. Adam, *Lehrbuch der Dogmengeschichte*, vol. 2: *Mittelalter und Reformationszeit* (Götersloh, 1968).

A. Angenendt, "Religiosität und Theologie," *Archiv für Liturgiewissenschaft* 20/21, 1978/1979, pp. 28–55.

J. Bach, *Die Dogmengeschichte des Mittelalters*, vol. 1. (Vienna, 1873; repr. 1966).

A. Baumstark, *Missale romanum; seine Entwicklung, ihre wichtigsten Urkunden und Probleme* (Eindhoven, 1929).

W. Breuer, *Die lateinische Eucharistiedichtung des Mittelalters* (Düsseldorf, 1970).

P. de Clerck, *La "prière universelle" dans les liturgies latines anciennes* (Münster, 1977).

J. Fisher, *Christian Initiation; Baptism in the Medieval West* (London, 1965).

H. Geertman, *Mores veterum* (Groningen, 1975).

A. Häussling, *Mönchskonvent und Eucharistiefeier* (Münster, 1973), LQF 58.

A. Hughes, *Medieval Manuscripts for Mass and Office* (Toronto, 1981).

J. Jungmann, *The Place of Christ in Liturgical Prayer* (New York, 1965).

A. Kavanagh, *The Shape of Baptism* (New York, 1978).

A. King, *Liturgies of the Primatial Sees* (London, 1957).

————, *Liturgies of the Past* (London, 1959).

B. Kleinheyer, *Die Priesterweihe im römischen Ritus* (Trier, 1962).

T. Maertens, *Histoire et pastorale du rituel du catéchuménat et du baptême* (Bruges, 1962).

O. Nuszbaum, *Die Aufbewahrung der Eucharistie* (Köln-Bonn, 1979).

J. Pascher, *Das liturgische Jahr* (Munich, 1963).

"Penance: The Ministry of Reconciliation," *Resonance* 1/2, 2/1, 1965/1966.

R. Rutherford, *The Death of a Christian* (New York, 1980).

P. Salmon, *L'office divin au moyen âge* (Paris, 1967).

A. Santantoni, *L'ordinazione episcopale* (Rome, 1976).

D. Sicard, *La liturgie de la mort dans l'église latine des origines à la réforme carolingienne* (Münster, 1978), LQF 63.

C. Vogel, *Introduction aux sources de l'histoire du culte chrétien au moyen âge* (Spoleto, 1965).

————, *Le pecheur et la penitence au moyen âge* (Paris, 1969).

A. SOURCES

In describing the sources of western liturgy we will make use of C. Vogel, *Introduction aux sources de l'histoire du culte chrétien au moyen âge* and the editions of the *ordines romani* by M. Andrieu mentioned below.

1. THE ORIGIN OF WESTERN WORSHIP

In Rome there had come to be a *"stadtrömische"* liturgy that was celebrated by the bishop of Rome and also—but now accommodated to smaller groups—in the churches of the city. It is possible that in the fourth and fifth centuries, a differentiation grew up between the so-called papal liturgy and the liturgy in the "presbyteral" churches, but what is certain is that before all else the Roman liturgy was local, that is, it was under the leadership of the bishop. Worship was well-organized. There were books describing the orders of service. It must be noted, however, that the composition of new text material stopped almost entirely. Rather, the archives were consulted and old texts found and used. The sources of new texts had dried up, perhaps because of concern for "great affairs" and political unrest, with a resultant increase in a need for pastoral care. In any case, it is clear that there was a desire to set bounds to any too emotional or too controversial liturgical texts, evidently out of concern for a somewhat more objective liturgy (cf. J. Jungmann, *The Mass of the Roman Rite*, vol. 1, pp. 44–74).

The Carolingians set about the reorganization of church life in order to consolidate the unity of the realm. They turned to Rome and took over the Roman liturgy; indigenous liturgical uses and the old Gallican liturgy were suppressed, with more or less success. This was possible because the popular feeling was already slanted that way: the Anglo-Saxon monks had directed the eyes of the Franks toward the pope and the church of Rome and had stimulated contact with that church. Pilgrims, among them many bishops, journeyed to Rome and came home enthusiastic. They wanted to adopt the city's impressive worship in their own churches. So it was that the Roman city liturgy migrated to the north, to Aachen and from there to the whole realm, and became the "Frankish liturgy," a liturgy unified and romanized as much as possible.

151

The term romanization, however, must be carefully understood. The Roman rite was local and adapted to Roman conditions. Moreover, this rite was short, almost juridical in succinctness and was emotionally reserved. It was discovered that the Roman rite could not be adopted just like that—it spoke too little to the circumstances prevailing among other peoples. This was especially true of the *sacramentarium*, the Roman book that was sent by the pope to Aachen at the request of the emperor: it was too short. Elements from the tradition of the Frankish church began to be added to it, with the result that a hybrid liturgy arose: Frankish-Roman or Roman-Frankish. What is more, the German "spirit" played a great role in this blending. Finally this "romanizing" was clinched under the Ottonians: the practically definitive fusion of the Roman-Frankish-Germanic liturgy came about in Mainz in 950. This liturgy, this mixture, was taken by the Ottonians to Rome when they went there to put things in order, and it was then slowly but surely taken over by the popes. So it was that western liturgy came to be.

What is at present called Roman liturgy is not the old *stadtrömische* worship carried out by the bishop or the presbyters with the faithful ("papal" or "presbyteral") in the city, but the hybrid Roman-Frankish liturgy. In historical research one must always distinguish both components. And that has been done in a large number of source studies in the last decades: the old Roman and the Frankish elements have been clearly differentiated. It is significant that our liturgical sources were in fact written in Frankish territory. When analyzed paleographically it is clear that the manuscripts are not Roman.

2. SOURCES

Information concerning worship is found in the writings of several authors of this period. We list here some of the best known:

Chrodegang of Metz;

Alcuin (cf. G. Ellard, *Master Alcuin, Liturgist,* Chicago, 1956);

Theodulf of Orleans (*On Baptismal Liturgy:* PL 105, 223);

Hincmar of Rheims;

Amalarius of Metz (extensive descriptions of worship in *Expositio missae, Liber officialis, De ordine antiphonarii* available in an edition by J. Hanssens, 1948–1950);

Rhabanus Maurus (*De institutione clericorum libri III:* PL 107, 292);

Walafrid Strabo (the first historian of liturgy; d. 849; *De exordiis et incrementis quarundam in observationibus ecclesiasticis rerum:* PL 114, 919–966);

Florus of Lyons (the great opponent of Amalarius of Metz and his allegorical method);

Benedict of Aniane (introduction of the Benedictine rule and reworking of the Roman Sacramentary for Frankish use).

Besides these, other, more direct sources are as follows: sacramentaries and missals, pericope lists and lectionaries, antiphonaries, *ordines* and pontificals, and the non-Roman books.

Sacramentaries and Missals

A sacramentary is a book that contains the texts spoken by the president in the liturgy. Sometimes short ritual comments (called rubrics) are also included, but only by way of exception. The following types can be distinguished:

The Gelasian Sacramentary (Gelasianum Vetus) (ed. Mohlberg, Rome, 1960; Vatic. Regilat. 316, Bibl. Nat. cod. lat. 7193) was written about 750 near Paris and is unique of its kind. The *Gelasianum Vetus* is marked by division into three books and by the fact that before the *secreta* (prayer over the gifts), two prayers (*orationes*) are given that are much alike and perhaps were considered as options for the celebrant. In content the book is a mixture of Roman and old Gallican material. The Roman material probably goes back to the year 650 and was used both in and around Rome. It came to be known in Gaul and was used there extensively until 750. This material may have come to the north by means of pilgrims or monks. It is apparently a pre-Carolingian romanization due to private initiative.

The sacramentaria Gelasiana of the eighth century are sacramentaries that are partly Gelasian (see *Gelasianum Vetus*) but also include many Gregorian elements (see below). Many examples of this type have been preserved, all of which almost surely go back to an archetype that is lost. Several well-known examples of the *Gelasiana s. VIII (saeculi octavi)* are: the sacramentary of Gellone (end of the eighth century, from Cambrai, a beautiful manuscript, edited by A. Dumas, C. Chr. clix–ccxxa); the sacramentary of Angoulème (ed. P. Cagin, 1918); of Phillips (unpublished, Berlin); of St. Gall (ed. L. Mohlberg, 1939, LQF 42); Triplex (ed. O. Heiming, Münster, 1968,

LQF 46); of Rheinau (ed. A. Hänggi-A. Schönberg, Freiburg, 1970). All of these copies are associated with monasteries, and the lost original must have been Frankish, probably compiled under Pippin (751–768) during the visit of Pope Stephen II (754–760) to France, when the papal liturgy became an object of intense interest. The author of the archetype is not known. The goal appears to have been to unite the Gelasian tradition with the Gregorian (i.e., the papal) tradition and, at the same time, to couple the liturgical practices in France and Rome in an attempt at unification.

The *sacramentaria Gregoriana* represent another type: they have no three-part division as in the *Gelasianum Vetus*, but follow the days of the year. There are three principal subtypes to note: the *sacramentarium Paduense*, the *Hadrianum*, and the *Hadrianum* with Supplement.

The *sacramentarium Paduense* (ed. Mohlberg, Münster, 1927, LQF 11/12: Padua, Bibl. cap. D. 47) was probably compiled in Liège about 841–855 (the last part contains additions from a later time). The prototype was Roman and was written in 683 under Pope Leo II and, a short time later, was taken out of Rome by someone, probably a pilgrim who was impressed by the liturgy in St. Peter's, with which basilica this sacramentary is connected. There is a century and a half between the prototype and the present manuscript, during which much was added that was not purely Roman.

The *sacramentarium Hadrianum*: no attempt to introduce the Roman liturgy fully into the Frankish realm had yet succeeded. Charlemagne tried once again. He mandated Paul the Deacon, who was returning to Monte Cassino from Aachen, to ask Pope Hadrian (772–795) for a pure Roman sacramentary without extraneous additions. Only in 785 did the pope respond to this request: the "sacramentary of Pope Gregory in pure form" was sent to Charlemagne. This copy was preserved in the imperial library as a model, as the authentic exemplar for copying. The exemplar sent by the pope has not been preserved but we do possess what is probably a direct copy in the manuscript *Cambrai cod. 164* (ed. H. Lietzmann, Münster, 1911, LQF 2) and a still later recopying in the manuscript *Vat. Reg. lat. 337* (ed. Wilson, HBS, London, 1915). This sacramentary *"a s. Gregorio papa romano editum"* is an incomplete book: many formulae are lacking that occur in other sacramentaries, such as those for the Sundays throughout the year. It is clear that Pope Hadrian did not comply with the request of Charlemagne; he sent him an incomplete book that, moreover, was based entirely on the papal liturgy. Apparently in Rome they were at a loss as to how to comply with the emperor's request; the pope sent the most beautiful copy that he possessed, but it was incomplete. It was not one of Pope Gregory's books but one that had been used by an unknown pope for the liturgical celebrations in the various churches of the city (*stationes*), and it stems from the first half of the eighth century (735).

The sacramentarium Hadrianum with Supplement, until recently ascribed to Alcuin, probably goes back to Benedict of Aniane (ed. J. Deshusses, Freiburg, 1971). The supplement to the *Hadrianum* contained a series of prefaces, a series of episcopal blessing formulas, and, especially, formulas that were lacking in the papal station-sacramentary (ed. Deshusses, nos. 1020ff.). The supplement was most likely compiled in 810–815 from the *Gelasiana s. VIII*, from an older Roman book of which the original is not known, but which perhaps goes back to Pope Honorius or Gregory I, and from Gallican material. This extended *Gregorianum* from the hand of Benedict of Aniane spread widely in north Italy and France. Why the supplement? To make the papal sacramentary usable for the situation in the Frankish realm. This *sacramentarium Hadrianum* with Supplement finally was given a dominant place in the west; in the long run it supplanted all other types. And so, by way of the supplement, Gelasian and Frankish elements were preserved in the Western tradition (see further in J. Deshusses, *Le sacrementaire Gregorien*, 2 vols., Freiburg, 1971, 1979).

The accompanying illustration gives a synopsis of the development of the sacramentaries and their mutual relationships, partly following the reconstruction of J. Deshusses (op. cit., vol. 1, p. 51), together with use of the fundamental work of A. Chavasse, *Le sacramentaire gélasien* (Paris-Tournai, 1958), in which the mutual relationships of all the sacramentaries are studied and placed in a schema.

THE MISSAL: SEQUEL TO THIS HISTORY

If we follow this history still further we see that the road leads finally to the missal. The Gregorian Sacramentary with the supplement, a Roman-Frankish book, was taken to Rome by the Ottonians and adopted by the popes. The monastery of Reichenau was given the mandate by the popes to make a copy of this sacramentary every year for use at the papal court. Thus Roman prayer books, which had been brought north in the seventh century, returned to Rome in the tenth century as Roman-Frankish books and so formed the matrix for the missal.

Early on, a variety of books were used at the celebration of the eucharist: a prayer book (sacramentary), a book of readings, a song

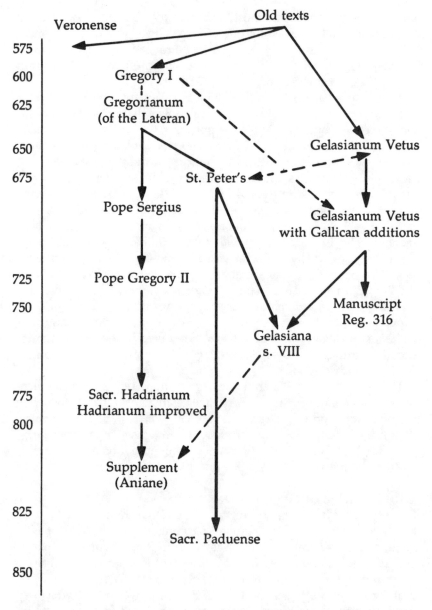

Veronense   Old texts

575

600   Gregory I

625   Gregorianum
(of the Lateran)

650   Gelasianum Vetus

675   St. Peter's

Pope Sergius   Gelasianum Vetus
with Gallican additions

725   Pope Gregory II

750   Manuscript
Reg. 316

Gelasiana
s. VIII

775   Sacr. Hadrianum
Hadrianum improved

800

Supplement
(Aniane)

825

Sacr. Paduense

850

(Dotted line indicates that at this place we are dealing with hypothesis.)

156

book, and an *ordo,* that is, a description of the course of the service. With the development of the office of priest, the growth in the number of churches, and (perhaps) the still to be discussed growth of the so-called "private mass," the need arose for one manageable book in which could be found everything necessary for the celebration of the eucharist every day of the year. The books needed for eucharist began to be put together into a single book, that is, complete mass formulae for every day were prepared in which the prayers, readings, songs, and rubrics were made into a unity. The resultant book was called the *Missale plenum,* which reached its final and definitive form in the *Missale Romanum* of the Council of Trent (see chapter 4).

Pericope Lists and Lectionaries
The choice of scriptural pericopes for certain days and festivals was already known in the previous historical period, especially at Jerusalem. Now this tradition came to full flower, and as a result, there are many extant lists of pericopes that appeared in the manuscripts.

Various methods were used to identify the pericopes. The pericope for a certain day might be noted in the margin of a page of scripture or separate lists were made, in which the verses were indicated along with the beginning and ending words of the reading. Or the pericopes could be written out in full and then assembled in a book (*lectionarium*). Or they could be written out fully along with the prayers and songs of the Mass (*missale plenum*). The four methods were in use from the sixth to fourteenth centuries.

For the study of the system of pericopes we refer to G. Kunze, *Die gottesdienstliche Schriftlesung* (Gotting, 1947); E. Ranke, *Das kirchliche Perikopensystem* (Berlin, 1847); S. Beissel, *Enstehung der Perikopen des römischen Messbuches* (Freiburg, 1907); T. Klauser, *Das römische Capitulare Evangeliorum* (Münster, 1935); W. H. Frere, *Studies in Early Liturgy, II. The Roman Gospel Lectionary* (London, 1934); *The Roman Epistle Lectionary* (London, 1935); A. Chavasse, "Les plus anciens types de lectionaire et de l'antiphonaire romain de la messe," *Revue bénédictine* 62, 1952, pp. 1–91.

For a good documentation of the pericope series in the manuscripts we refer to Vogel (op. cit., pp. 289–328). We will note here the principal sources for the Roman liturgy.

The *Epistolarium of Würzburg* (cf. G. Morin, "Le plus ancien comes ou lectionaire de l'église romaine," *Revue bénédictine* 27, 1910, pp. 41–47) is pure Roman and gives the series of epistles from about the time of Gregory or shortly after his death (600).

The Comes of Alcuin (cf. A. Wilmart, "Le lectionaire d'Alcuin," *Ephemerides Liturgicae* 51, 1937, pp. 136–197) is probably a Roman system from about 626 that was known to Alcuin.

The Capitularia Evangeliorum (gospel lists) are to be divided into four groups—the first purely Roman from about 645, the second Roman from 740, the third Roman from 755, and the fourth Roman-Frankish from 750 (ed. Klauser, 1935, LQF 28).

The Lectionarium of Murbach (cf. A. Wilmart, "Le Comes de Murbach," *Revue bénédictine* 30, 1913, pp. 35–69) is Roman-Frankish from the eighth century. For the first time we find in this book the pericopes of both epistles and gospels side by side for the whole year.

Antiphonaries

The *antiphonale missarum* contained all the sung texts for the celebration of the eucharist. The Roman antiphonaries were introduced into the Frankish kingdom under Pippin. The texts can be found in R. Hesbert, *Antiphonale sextuplex* (Brussels, 1935), in which the six principal manuscripts have been published, all six of which mostly agree with each other in structure and in the division of the church year. Later manuscripts can be found in the series *Paléographie musicale* (Solesmes-Tournai, from 1899) in which musical notation is included (e.g., St. Yrieix, St. Gall, Montpellier, Laon, Einsiedeln, Chartres).

For the sung texts of the liturgy of the hours (*antiphonale officii*), we are first of all dependent upon the work of Amalarius of Metz, published by J. Hanssens (*Liber de ordine antiphonarii*, vol. 1, pp. 363ff.). Other manuscripts have been published by R. J. Hesbert, *Corpus antiphonalium officii*, in the series *Rerum ecclesiasticarum documenta*, series maior, Fontes VII, VIII (Rome, from 1963); here one will find the so-called *cursus romanus*.

For the hymns see G. M. Dreves, C. Blume, eds., *Analecta hymnica medii aevi*, 55 vols. (Leipzig, 1886–1922). Cf. F. J. Raby, *A History of Christian Latin Poetry*, 2nd ed. (Oxford, 1953).

Ordines and Pontificals

THE ORDINES

The *ordines* are liturgical books with rubrics and descriptions of the course of the service. These rubric books are necessary together with the books of prayers (*sacramentaria*) in order to be able to study a service. They contain the staging directions. From the Frankish time very many manuscripts have been preserved: M. Andrieu has put together a sort of genealogy of these rubric books and indicated where purely Roman practices are being described and where a Roman-Frankish tradition is found. His edition of the *ordines* is indispensable for the study of western liturgy: M. Andrieu, *Les ordines romani du haut moyen âge*, vol. 1: *Les manuscrits;* vols. 2–5: *Les textes* (*ordines* 1–50) (Louvain, 1931–1961; cf. also C. Vogel, *Introduction aux sources*, pp. 109–113).

In Rome there existed anciently collections of rubric books (*ordines*) as well as collections of *libelli* (prayer texts for the eucharist). It is also certain that from these collections parts were brought to the north by pilgrims, monks, and bishops. There they appeared in new collections. Now the concern is to differentiate the purely Roman and the Frankish *ordines* from each other, for even the purely Roman documents are only known to us from Frankish manuscripts. Andrieu distinguishes a collection A and a collection B.

Collection A is purely Roman and contains *ordines* 1, 11, 27, 42, 34, and 13A. This collection must have been assembled about 700–750 (albeit the oldest copy known is from 800). These *ordines*, however, were joined into collection A after they had already been known for some time in the Frankish areas.

Collection B is a hybrid collection, a joining of Frankish and Roman *ordines*, in which the Roman ones were adapted and changed. The adaptation was necessary because the Roman *ordines* were written for the local situation at Rome and were thereby not usable in the north. Moreover there was no intention of totally forbidding or suppressing local practices. This collection includes *ordines* 13B, 1, 11, 28, 41, 42, and 37A. The collection was most likely compiled at the beginning of the ninth century in Lotharingia (Lorraine).

The Collection of St. Amand is a "gallicanized collection" first published by L. Duchesne and including *ordines* 4, 30B, 21, 39, 43, and 20. It was probably compiled under Pippin.

The *ordines* can be divided as follows:

for celebration of eucharist: *ordines* 1, 2, 3, 4, 5, 6, 7, 9, 10, 17 (15, 16, 17);

for baptism: *ordo* 11;

for ordinations: *ordines* 34, 35, 35A, 35B, 36, 39, 40A, 40B;

for burial: *ordo* 49;

for coronation of the emperor: *ordines* 45, 46, 47, 48;

for dedication of a church: *ordines* 41, 42, 43;

for celebration of the church year: *ordines* 50 (for the whole year); 22, 28 (Lent); 23, 24, 26, 27, 28A, 29, 30A, 30B, 31, 32, 33 (Holy Week, liturgy of the hours); 30A, 30B, 31, 32 (the week after Easter); 25 (blessing of the paschal candle); 37A, 37B, 38, 39 (Quatember days); 20 (Candlemas);

for the liturgy of the hours and its readings: *ordines* 12, 13A, 13B, 13C, 13D, 14, 15, 16, 17, 18;

for the meal (monasteries): *ordo* 19;

for liturgical garments: *ordo* 8;

for the ceremony *diligentia*: *ordo* 44;

for the greater litany: *ordo* 21.

A further description of several ordines follows:

ordo 1: "qualiter missa celebratur"; an important document describing the papal mass (stational celebration) in Rome about the time of Pope Gregory (600). The short recension of this *ordo* is the oldest and is purely Roman; the longer is Roman-Frankish;

ordo 5: the same *ordo* as 1 but now Frankish, intended for the bishop's liturgy in the north. The compiler made use of *ordo* 1 and of the writings of Amalarius; second half of the ninth century;

ordo 7: careful statement of the ceremony that was to be carried out during the Roman canon; end of the ninth century. Of importance for a study of the development in the text of the canon;

ordo 11: the Roman baptismal *ordo*. Important for the evolution of baptism. The *ordo* is probably dependent on the baptismal *ordo* in the *Gelasianum Vetus*. Ca. 650–700 (one of the oldest *ordines*);

ordo 13: in a variety of recensions. Summary indications of the readings from scripture and the nonscriptural readings during vigils (matins). Recension A is purely Roman (Lateran?) from the eighth century;

ordo 23: description of the services during Holy Week in Rome (*Triduum Sacrum*) by a Frankish pilgrim who attended the liturgy;

ordo 24: Holy Week, including the paschal vigil: most likely Roman and used in one or another Roman basilica;

ordo 34: a purely Roman *ordo* for ordinations to office (acolyte, subdeacon, deacon, priest, bishop);

ordo 36: second half of the ninth century; a Frankish-German *ordo* for ordinations;

ordo 49: a Roman *ordo* for burial (eighth century), probably going back to very old tradition in Rome.

For a full picture of the development of western liturgy we must still refer to the origin of the *pontificale* and the *rituale*, books that are still being used currently in the Roman liturgy but that go back to developments in the seventh to eleventh centuries.

THE PONTIFICALE

A *pontificale* is a book containing orders of service together with prayers for all the liturgical celebrations except the eucharist (such a collection for the eucharist is to be found in the missal). The prayers that belong to other celebrations than eucharist were gathered from the sacramentaries and brought within the *ordines,* or the other way around: the *ordines* were brought into the *sacramentaria.* Thus a development occurred analogous to that of the missal: there was a desire for a manageable book in which the orders of service together with all prayers and readings would be readily available. The term "pontifical" is, however, of more recent date (fourteenth century). First attempts to produce such books are known in the ninth century (cf. the list of manuscripts in Vogel, op. cit., pp. 185–186).

The most important representative of the genre is the *Pontificale romano-germanicum* (ed. C. Vogel & R. Elze, Rome, 1963), also called the "Ottonian Pontifical" or the "Mainz Pontifical" after the age and place of origin. This pontifical is a joining, a compilation of didactic (juridical and theological) and liturgical material in one book. It is known to us in some fifty manuscripts that all go back to one original that was apparently Germanic. The compilation is voluminous and contains complete orders of service and prayers with commentary between. The orders of service are Roman or Roman-Frankish in origin.

The book was composed in the St. Alban cloister in Mainz. Mainz was then an eminent episcopal see in the empire of the Ottonians; the archbishop of Mainz was chancellor to the king. This archbishop and other bishops around Otto I are known to have been concerned with the renewal of worship. That is also evident from the compilation of this pontifical, which we must date about 960–963 and attribute to a team of redactors in the cloister at Mainz under the leadership of the archbishop. It is most likely that constant improvements were made thereafter while the general structure of the work was maintained. That the Pontifical of Mainz spread throughout Europe is primarily due to the authorities that stood behind it—the archbishop of Mainz and the emperor.

The most interesting fact, however, is that this book came to Rome and was there accepted by the pope, under pressure from Otto I. Rome was experiencing a scandalous chaos in church life that the emperor wanted to bring to an end. His successors (including, among others, Henry II, 1004–1024) continued this pressure so that popes came to be accustomed to the "imported" liturgy and began to use it for themselves. It is known, however, that the canons of the Lateran and of St. Peter's were less disposed to give in—for a long time they still continued faithful to the old Roman liturgy. But the *Pontificale romano-germanicum* had in fact won.

Through the controversy between emperor and pope—the so-called "investiture controversy," which concerned the rights and duties of state and church in relation to each other—the popes began to centralize in Rome the power over ecclesiastical affairs. The popes then wanted also to withdraw worship from imperial influence. The *Regula canonica* (in the name of Gregory VII) said it straightforwardly:

Romani autem diverso modo agere ceperunt, maxime a tempore quo Teutonicis concessum est regimen nostrae Ecclesiae. Nos autem et ordinem romanum et antiquum morem investigantes, statuimus fieri nostrae Ecclesiae sicut superius praenotavimus, antiquos imitantes patres.	The Romans began to act in another way, chiefly from the time that the supervision of our Church was granted to the Germans. We, however, having ascertained the *ordo romanus* and ancient custom, have decided, as we noted before, that it is more fitting for our Church to imitate the ancient fathers.

Gregory wanted to restore the old customs of the city. But what he in fact restored was not the old Roman liturgy; actually it was the Roman-Frankish liturgy, as it had been brought to Rome under Otto I, which had been taken over at the papal court under the name "Roman."

After Gregory, during the eleventh and twelfth centuries, liturgical books were compiled, all of which, however, were dependent upon the *Pontificale romano-germanicum*. This family of Roman books is called the *Pontificale romanum* of the twelfth century. The most important thing about them was that copyists in Rome abbreviated the book from which they worked; the didactic pieces were left out along with old *ordines;* rites were shortened and simplified; all superfluous ballast in both prayers and rubrics was thrown out. It became a Roman book: cool, businesslike, precise, "curial." This Roman edition came to be known in Europe between 1198 and 1216, that is, during the reigns of Gregory VII and Innocent III, especially because several popes during that time sojourned outside Rome. This matter is treated in the following chapter.

Just as the missal was built upon the Roman-Frankish liturgical books, so the pontifical is to be traced to the same sources: the Roman-Frankish *ordines.* This mixed liturgy was later declared binding by the Council of Trent. Thus, what now is called "Roman liturgy" is the Roman-Frankish-Germanic liturgy, not the *stadtrömische* worship of the fifth century.

THE RITUALE
In the long run, it became the practice to include in the pontifical only the services led by a bishop. But provision also had to be made for the services in which a priest could preside, for example, baptism, penance, marriage, anointing of the sick, and burial. For these ceremonies a manageable book was needed. After a complicated history the so-called *rituale* came into being. It contained orders of service and prayers; it was no "handbook" (*manuale, pastorale*). Research into the medieval *ritualia* has only begun. Through it we should be able to trace local or regional practices.

The first signs of genuine *ritualia* are found in the eleventh century when collections of certain *ordines* (*collectaria*) were collated into books. Well-known examples are the *Ritualia of St. Florian* (ed. A. Franz) and the *Ritualia of Rheinau* (ed. Hurlimann).

The Non-Roman Books
We have limited ourselves here so far to the Roman-Frankish-Germanic liturgical sources. Besides these sources there exist books in which the liturgies unique to Gaul, Spain, and the Celts are described. These are all rather recent but nonetheless valuable for knowledge of worship outside of Rome. The euchology is frequently richer and more effusive. These books are therefore of great significance for a comparative study of the content of western liturgy. We list here the most important liturgical books; a fuller overview is given in C. Vogel, *Introduction,* pp. 90–92, 223–234 (with bibliography).

GALLICAN LITURGY

Expositio antiquae liturgiae gallicanae, ed. E. Ratcliff (London, 1971); early eighth century (?), Ps.-Germanus of Paris (?).

Lectionarium of Lexeuil, ed. P. Salmon (Rome, 1944).

Missale Bobbiense, ed. Lowe (London, 1920), PL 72, col. 351–574; eighth century.

Missale Francorum, ed. Mohlberg (Rome, 1957); eighth century.

Missale Gallicanum Vetus, ed. Mohlberg (Rome, 1958); eighth century.

Missale Gothicum, ed. Mohlberg (Rome, 1961); with an appendix including the so-called Masses of Mone, pp. 61–91; seventh-eighth centuries.

CELTIC LITURGY

Antiphonal of Bangor, ed. Warren (1893–1895).

Missal of Stowe, ed. G. Warren (London, 1906–1915); eighth century.

MOZARABIC LITURGY

Antifonario de Léon, ed. J. Vives & A. Fabrega (Madrid, 1953).

Liber commicus sive lectionarius, ed. Perez de Urbel e Gonzales, 2 vols. (Madrid, 1940–1955).

Liber mozarabicus sacramentorum, ed. Férotin (Paris, 1912); tenth century.

Liber ordinum, ed. Férotin (Paris, 1904); eleventh century.

Oracional visigotico, ed. J. Vives (Barcelona, 1946).

MILANESE LITURGY

Capitulare evangelorium, ed. P. Borella, in *Ambrosius* 10, 1934, pp. 220–223.

Sacramentarium of Ariberto, ed. A. Paredi (Bergamo, 1958); eleventh century.

Sacramentarium of Bergamo, ed. A. Paredi (Bergamo, 1962), LQF 49; tenth-eleventh centuries.

Sacramentarium of Biasca, ed. O. Heiming (Münster, 1968), LQF 51; ninth-tenth centuries.

Sacramentarium of the chapter of Milan, ed. J. Frei (Münster, 1974), LQF 56.

Sacramentarium Triplex, ed. O. Heiming (Münster, 1968), LQF 46.

B. A GLOSSARY OF TERMS

Here follows an alphabetical arrangement of several terms that are used in the Latin liturgy and are of significance for its understanding. See also F. L. Cross, *The Oxford Dictionary of the Christian Church,* 2nd ed. (Oxford, 1974).

abrenuntiatio: renunciation of Satan; a part of the baptismal rite at least from the time of the *Traditio Apostolica* of Hippolytus. Originally closely connected with the baptismal act of immersion; later separated by intervening rites such as the blessing of the water.

absolutio: conclusion (closing prayer or concluding rite); or acquittal or exoneration (formula for forgiveness of sins in penance); also preserved in *absoute,* the last prayer for the dead person before burial.

antependium: a vesture for the front side, or church side, of the altar.

antiphona: antiphon, or the praying of a psalm or a group of psalms in double choir, facing each other. Connected with the foregoing, also an appropriate psalm verse with its own melody that is sung before and after a psalm (originally after each verse of the psalm) establishing the *leitmotiv* of the psalm. Verses were also taken from the gospels or from free texts. These antiphons are important for the Christian interpretation of the psalms, and their melodies frequently suggest the mood of a given feast. See *responsorium.*

apologia: confession of sin; declaration of unworthiness in prayer form.

benedicere: to praise and thank ("bless God") or bless (call God's blessing upon something); also both senses combined, as in the *benedictio aquae,* the blessing of baptismal water: praise of God (and thanksgiving) together with a prayer for his blessing upon the water and upon those who shall be baptized therein.

Benedictus: song of Zechariah (Lk 1:68–79), sung or prayed in the Roman morning office. See *canticum.*

Breviarium: a liturgical book in which the hours are included, that is, the prayers, songs, and readings that must be prayed at the indicated hours every day; now called *liturgia horarum,* liturgy of the hours.

calix: chalice, the history of which is interesting, suggestive of the development in eucharistic piety and experience. (See further in *Lexicon der christlichen Ikonographie.*)

canticum: biblical song of praise, as distinguished from the psalms. The term refers especially to the three canticles from the gospel of Luke: the songs of Zechariah, Mary, and Simeon. Well-known canticles from the Latin liturgy: Ex 15:1–19 (Moses) and Dn 3:57–88 (three young men in the fiery furnace). For contemporary use one should consult morning and evening prayer in the new breviary.

capitulum: short scriptural reading in the hours, after the psalms.

chrisma: scented oil for anointing. Anointing with chrism takes place after the immersion in water at baptism. The anointing of the baptized by the bishop is called confirmation (*confirmatio*). The history of this practice will be found in the various chapters under "baptism."

ciborium: canopy over the altar; also and especially used, however, for a large chalice in which the hosts (consecrated bread) for the faithful are kept. *Ciboria* in chalice form are known since the thirteenth century; before that the gifts were kept in a box (e.g., in the form of a eucharistic dove). The history of the *ciborium* also demonstrates the development of eucharistic experience and piety.

comes: a book containing the scriptural pericopes to be read at a service.

commendatio animae: a group of prayers by the community of the faithful for a dying person and after death in which he or she is "commended" to God.

commune sanctorum: texts for eucharist and for the hours that are used for festivals of saints that have no proper texts. There are a "common of martyrs," "common of confessors," "common of virgins," etc. used according to the saint remembered.

communis oratio: intercessions.

competentes: catechumens who are in the last stage before baptism, i.e., those who have been accepted for baptism; also called *electi*.

confessio: confession, praise; also used to indicate the space around the tomb of a martyr or the altar over the tomb.

consecratio: consecration, dedication, sacring. One thinks of the eucharistic consecration: the hallowing of the gifts to be the body and blood of the Lord through and in the eucharistic prayer (anaphora).

contestatio: eucharistic prayer in the old Gallican rite.

cursus: the distribution of the psalms among the hours throughout the week. In the present breviary, there is a four-week distribution of the psalms.

Dominus vobiscum: frequently recurrent greeting in worship (cf. Lk 1: 28). *Dominus* should be understood here as Jesus Christ. The formula has been used since apostolic times in both east and west. The response of the faithful to the greeting is *"Et cum spiritu tuo"* ("and with thy spirit," which is to say, "and also with you"). This "spirit" was later interpreted to mean the Holy Spirit, whom the liturgical leader received through ordination to office.

elevatio: the lifting up of the gifts during the consecration in the celebration of the eucharist: generally practiced in the Roman liturgy since the beginning of the thirteenth century.

embolism: insertion into a prayer or an elaboration of a liturgical prayer (e.g., the prayer "Deliver us . . ." connected to the Lord's prayer in the Roman eucharistic liturgy).

epiclesis: technical term for the invocation of the Holy Spirit upon the gifts and the people in the eucharistic prayer (anaphora, canon); a general tradition in both east and west. In the Roman liturgy, however, the epiclesis has lost its character as invocation of the Spirit.

epistolarium: a book including the scriptural readings (pericopes) for the eucharist except for the gospels, ordered according to the church year (cf. *missale*). At present it is no longer in use but replaced by the *lectionarium* (lectionary).

evangelarium: gospel book (book with the four gospels complete) or a book with the gospel pericopes for mass for each day of the year.

exorcism: casting out of the devil (especially in the baptismal rites, cf. *abrenuntiatio*); very old practice and especially significant in the baptismal rite of Hippolytus, *Traditio Apostolica*.

Exsultet: opening word of the hymn welcoming the light of the paschal candle in the celebration of the Easter vigil (consisting of a preface and an act of praise and anamnesis). This text is important for the understanding of the Easter festival.

extrema unctio: last anointing before the death of a believer. It placed a strong accent on the forgiveness of sins. It is now seen in the light of *unctio infirmorum* (anointing of the sick), a sacrament of the church that gives a ritual center to pastoral care for the seriously ill and that is given to the sick so that they might be strengthened in bearing suffering.

fermentum: consecrated bread that the bishop of Rome sent to the priests who along with their communities celebrated the eucharist in the *tituli* ("parish" churches); intended as a sign of unity—one celebration at several places, one family of the church. See *statio*.

graduale: song between the lections, a response to the reading from the scripture, anciently sung in responsorial form.

gratiarum actio: praise and thanksgiving (*eucharistia*).

illatio: eucharistic prayer in the Visigothic rite.

improperia: the "reproaches"—a song in the liturgy of Good Friday containing the lament of the Lord concerning the unfaithfulness of his people; probably of Syrian origin.

intinctio: a manner of receiving communion by dipping the bread in the cup.

lectio congrua: a reading that is adapted to the situation (the festival, the place of celebration, the occasion).

lectio continua: the ongoing reading of a part of the Bible (e.g., the Pentateuch) in the liturgy.

lectio currens: a kind of *lectio continua* but with the exclusion of certain sections so that a continuous narrative results and so that difficult parts are left out. Scripture has always been read with great freedom in the liturgy and not always in accord with what "exegesis" might properly demand.

lectionarium: the liturgical book in which the scripture readings (pericopes) for the liturgy are collected. The present Roman Sunday lectionary contains three readings: one each from the Old Testament, from "the apostle," and from the gospel.

litaniae: a prayer of beseeching consisting of a series of bids followed by an acclamation or response (cf. the *ektenia* in the Byzantine liturgy). The "intercessions" in the liturgy (cf. *preces*) are litanic in character, intentions for prayer announced by the leader and a response by the people. In the western tradition there are also litanies that are made up only of invocations and responses, e.g., the litany of the saints or of the Mother of God (*litaniae lauretanae*). These are an important source for a knowledge of biblical and popular piety.

lucernarium: blessing of the light at evening; evening service (vespers).

missa: dismissal with its ceremonies, such as the benediction; also simply a service. In the Roman rite since the Middle Ages the term has been used for the celebration of the eucharist.

missale: the mass book, the book that contains the texts for the celebration of the mass—both the invariable texts (*ordinarium* or *ordo missae*) and the variable texts such as the prayers, songs, and readings arranged for various occasions.

168

natale: anniversary—memorial of the deceased on the day of death; also *natale episcopi*—memorial of the consecration of a bishop.

offertorium: the service of preparation of the gifts before the eucharistic prayer in the mass; also, the song during this preparation.

oratio: a prayer, e.g., at the opening of the service, *collecta;* after the preparation of the gifts, *super oblata;* after communion, *post communionem.* The Roman *orationes* are examples of pithy formulations with a specific structure.

planeta: a chasuble, the liturgical overgarment for the president. There were several forms and models of the chasuble in the course of history. Such liturgical vesture is intended to stylize the celebration.

praefatio: the dialogue before the eucharistic prayer; the term is also applied to the first (variable) part of the Roman eucharistic prayer (the canon).

preces: intercessions; supplications; the term is now used primarily for the intercessions in morning and evening prayer. See *communis oratio.*

proprium: the proper texts for a feast in the celebration of eucharist and the hours, as contrasted with *commune.* See *commune sanctorum.*

prosa: a text that is sung with the melisma at the end of the alleluia. The final vowel of alleluia was frequently extended into a series of notes (melisma) and these were then filled up with the *prosa* text (*sequentia*). The historical basis of the *prosa* is still obscure; research into its origin will certainly demonstrate the great creativity and inventiveness in the several liturgical centers (e.g., those that existed in the time of the Ottonians).

prosula: a short *prosa* text. See *prosa.*

responsorium: a sung "answer" to a reading or to the *capitulum* (see *capitulum*) in the liturgy of the hours. The structure is: *responsum–versus–responsum* (etc.). Originally the word indicated the responsorial performance of, for example, a psalm: the psalm was sung or sung-spoken by the *psalmista,* the cantor, and answered by those present in a fixed refrain.

Sanctus: the "thrice-holy" song in the Roman canon (between preface and canon), an act of praise that is introduced with a reference to the heavenly liturgy (the Cherubim and Seraphim before God's throne).

sequentia: in the first instance a *prosa* text (see *prosa*) after the alleluia; later (since the twelfth century) developed into a kind of hymn, with a regular structure and rhyme in strophes. In the Middle Ages sequences were written for every feast. Well-known examples in the present liturgy include: *Victimae paschali laudes* (for Easter); *Lauda Sion; Veni Sancte Spiritus.*

signaculum: a sign by which one is marked (*sphragis*); seal. The signing with a cross (whether or not with oil) is intended, as in the baptismal rite and in confirmation (anointing with the Holy Spirit). *Signaculum* is also the term for the kiss of peace. (See the extensive discussion in J. Ysebaert, *Greek Baptismal Terminology,* Nijmegen, 1962.)

signatio: signing with the cross on the forehead (confirmation).

statio: the oldest meaning is fasting and doing penance on certain days in the week (Wednesday and Friday). Later, especially in Rome, it came to mean a liturgical celebration (eucharist) of the whole congregation under the presidency of the bishop. The celebration took place in a designated church. The *statio* demonstrated that the many churches in a city were nonetheless one (*koinonia*) under the leadership of the bishop (one eucharist, one altar, one bishop). See *fermentum.*

Te decet laus: an old doxological text.

Te Deum: a festival hymn (doxology).

Te igitur: the opening words of the Roman canon (fourth century?).

tractus: a psalm that is read or sung by a soloist or a choir without interruption (as for example, by a response).

Vidi aquam: an antiphon sung during the sprinkling with water on the Sundays in Easter.

C. SUMMARIES OF THE LITURGICAL DATA

1. DAILY PRAYER

In the previous chapter we indicated that at Rome the practice of daily prayer was entrusted to monks. Cloisters were established at the great basilicas—at the Lateran and at St. Peter's, for example. The abbot of St. Peter (the *primicerius* or *archicantor*) had a prominent function in the city, including a role in the papal mass, according to *Ordo Romanus* I. It seems that at the basilicas the custom of the daily office, using the entire psalter every week, gradually came into prominence. Moreover, it became the custom to remember the saints by praying an office that was devoted to memorializing their lives. All of this was most likely known to Benedict when he composed that part of his *Rule* that governed the daily office of the monks. Such rules became common in other monastic communities.

In the *Rule of Benedict*, a great deal of attention is paid to the *officium divinum*, to the *disciplina psallendi*, which is ordered by *discretio*, to the customs of the churches in Rome to which the monks are bound, and to the reading from holy scripture. Daily prayer was thus completely structured; for details see J. G. Tarruell, "La nouvelle distribution du psautier dans la *Liturgia Horarum*" (*Ephemerides Liturgicae*, 87, 1973, pp. 325–382), who makes clear that there are differences between the "Benedictine" and the "Roman" cursus of psalmody. The general form of the monastic office was as follows:

night office: an introduction (Psalm 95) and a hymn;

Sundays: six psalms followed by four lessons; six more psalms followed by four more lessons; three canticles with four lessons; *Te Deum;* hymn; blessing;

weekdays: two groups of six psalms each, each group followed by two or four lessons;

morning prayer: introduction (Psalms 67, 51); two psalms and a canticle followed by Psalms 148–150; short reading with a responsory; hymn; song of Zechariah; intercessions; Lord's prayer and concluding prayer;

evening prayer: almost identical with morning prayer, but with four psalms and the song of Mary; the psalms were chosen from Psalms 110–147;

little hours: hymn; three psalms; short reading with responsory; Lord's prayer and concluding prayer.

The elements of daily prayer that have already been discussed are clearly present here: psalmody, song, readings, and prayer. Hymns have been given a fixed place. Of primary interest is the fact that daily prayer was prayed in common. At various hours, determined by tradition, the monks assembled for communal prayer, a task assigned to them by the church. This means that there was a growing conception that the monks (and later also the clergy) had to fulfill the church's task of prayer. Still one step further was the idea that they did this in the name of the faithful, whereby the difference between them and the faithful would become still greater.

This old Benedictine office was significant for western liturgical development. Through the Frankish monks (Benedict of Aniane), it became the model outside Rome; in adapted form, it was followed by the clergy in Carolingian times when rules were set up to protect the dignity of the clerical office. The clergy was urged to "live canonically" (*canonice vivere*) by making their residences "priestly monasteries." One of the expressions of this common life was daily prayer, a model for which was found in the Benedictine office (*Rule of Chrodegang of Metz*, c. 753).

There were certainly protests—the clergy resisted being transformed into monks! The will to carry out this daily monastic prayer decreased still more when it was lengthened and augmented in the monasteries by all sorts of additions (prayers for the dead; an office for the Mother of God and for certain saints; the penitential psalms). The daily burden became too great for the clergy. What is more, the communal character of this prayer was not successful among the clergy. One should note in this respect the moral and liturgical decadence of the tenth century, which affected especially the daily office of the clergy. The Gregorian reform stimulated anew a regular style of life as in the days of Chrodegang. Out of this renewal arose the first contours of the later "breviary," a prayerbook collecting together the Roman-Benedictine tradition of the preceding centuries.

The sources of the breviary were the *psalterium*, the *collectarium* (or *sacramentarium*), the *lectionarium*, and the *antiphonale*. From these books one manageable book was assembled (cf. J. Jungmann, *Christian Prayer through the Ages*, pp. 58–95). The antiphons and the responsories of the breviary are especially important to us for a sound knowledge of the liturgy (as well as for a meditative use of the scripture!).

2. FESTIVALS AND CELEBRATIONS
THROUGHOUT THE YEAR
It is striking that Sunday, the Christian day *par excellence*, came to acquire a new meaning, i.e., the celebration of the trinity. An example of this change is to be found in the introduction of the preface *De Trinitate* into the Sunday liturgy, a short, correct, but hardly hymnic formation of the trinitarian dogma. The origins and authorship of this preface are still discussed. We give here the text of the preface:

Vere dignum et iustum est, aequum et salutare, nos tibi semper et ubique gratias agere, Domine, sancte Pater, omnipotens aeterne Deus: qui cum unigenito Filio tuo et Spiritu Sancto unus es Deus, unus es Dominus: non in unius singularitate personae, sed in unius Trinitate substantiae. Quod enim de tua gloria, revelante te, credimus, hoc de Filio tuo, hoc de Spiritu Sancto sine differentia discretionis sentimus. Ut in confessione verae sempiternaeque Deitatis, et in personis proprietas, et in essentia unitas, et in majestate adoretur aequalitas. Quam laudant Angeli atque Archangeli. Cherubim quoque ac Seraphim, qui non cessant clamare quotide, una voce dicentes: Sanctus, Sanctus, Sanctus.

It is truly meet and just, right and salutary, that we should at all times and in all places give you thanks, O Lord, holy Father, almighty and eternal God, who with your only begotten Son and the Holy Spirit are one God, one Lord: not in the singleness of one person but in the Trinity of a one substance. For that which we believe from your revelation concerning your glory, that also we believe of your Son and of the Holy Spirit, without difference or distinction. Thus, in confessing the true and everlasting Godhead, we adore the persons as distinct, their unity in being, and their equality in majesty. This the angels praise together with the archangels, cherubim, and seraphim; day by day they cease not to cry out as with one voice: Holy, Holy, Holy.

We know from the lectionaries that series of pericopes were provided for the Sundays within and outside the festival cycles and for Wednesdays and Fridays. These series remained in use in the western church with few appreciable changes. They were principally made up of New Testament texts and were unchangeable—each Sunday every year had the same scripture readings. The selection from scripture was limited, probably because it was affected by the local Roman stational liturgy, which was also limited in the use of scripture. Other series are known to us from Gaul and Spain. We do not know exactly how and why the selections were made. Sometimes the epistle and gospel in all these series were clearly related to each other (especially on feast days), but it is also true (especially in the formularies for the "green" Sundays) that the series of epistles and gospels were not interrelated, and any connection was coincidental.

The paschal observance underwent a change that did not bode well for a unitary vision of the mystery at the heart of this celebration. Lent was now reckoned as including Holy Saturday and was preparatory for Easter Sunday, regarded as the undisputed high point of the triduum. A kind of disjuncture of the three days arose, each day having an independent character. The spirit of the time was expressed clearly in the dramatic presentation of the passion and resurrection of the Lord in the Passion and Easter plays. The people loved the expressive rites of Holy Week because of their apotropaic power (the fire, the candle, the water, the palm branch, Easter bread, etc.).

The *Ordines Romani*, which we have summarized, give a description of the actual liturgical services: the blessing of the fire; the consecration of *chrisma*; the solemn reservation of the consecrated gifts on Maundy Thursday; the veneration of the cross on Good Friday, which became yet more expressive (especially through the so-called *Improperia*, God's reproaches of those who have turned from him); the twelve lessons after the Easter proclamation (Exsultet); and the blessing of the baptismal water with its accompanying ceremonies in the Easter vigil.

We must unfortunately omit here an analysis of the actual orders of service—the material is too extensive. Nonetheless, two facts should be mentioned. First, the texts usually refer to Good Friday as *in passione Domini*. This rests in a very old tradition that goes back to the second century. *Pascha* was understood with the Greek *paschein* in mind and came to mean "suffering," a word taken to include the death of Jesus as the heart of the Christian *pascha*. *Pascha* and *paschein* stand behind the Latin *pati, passio*, "suffering." The later name for Good Friday, *in passione et morte Domini* was seemingly more catechetically precise (because more complete), but it might also be regarded as a breaking of this venerable tradition. The oldest tradition of the paschal festival, the celebration of the death of Jesus as paschal mystery, echoed into the Middle Ages in a responsory at matins of Holy Saturday in the Roman breviary. The text is probably from the eighth century but contains very ancient notions:

Recessit pastor noster, fons aquae vivae, ad cuius transitum sol obscuratus est: Nam et ille captus est, qui captivum tenebat primum hominem: hodie portas mortis et seras pariter Salvator noster disrupit. *V.* Des-

Our shepherd, the fount of living water, is gone, at whose passing the sun was darkened: for he is taken captive, who took captive the first man: today our Savior burst asunder both the gates and bolts of death. *V.* He destroyed

truxit quidem claustra inferni,	the prisons of hell, and overthrew
et subvertit potentias diaboli.	the might of the devil. For he is
Nam et ille. . . .	taken. . . .

The death of the Lord (his *transitus,* cf. John 13:1) is reflected upon in this text (a responsory is a meditative response to what has been read aloud to the community) as the imprisoning of evil, as the breaking of the bolts of the underworld to which the Lord descended in order to destroy the power of evil. The subject here is thus the descent into hell and the liberation of humanity from the power of death and Satan. This idea is to be found in the early Christian tradition (with Jewish-Christian roots) as, for example, R. Murray, *Symbols of Church and Kingdom* has demonstrated (Cambridge, 1975, pp. 228–236, 324–329). It is worthy of note that the *Improperia* (*Popule meus, quid feci tibi*) of Good Friday probably originated from the same environment. Syrian ideas became known in the west by way of Constantinople. Even more important is the fact that the vision of the second century still influences the paschal observance in the eighth century.

Second, the Easter vigil in this period coincides with that of the previous period: the vigil was the celebration of baptism, the night of initiation into the mystery of Christ (see pp. 177–183). *Pascha* was divided into three days in the midst of which the night vigil took place for those who were ready for baptism. This vigil consisted of a number of readings (as had been customary for centuries) in which the saving deeds of God for his people were proclaimed. Then followed baptism. The celebration of baptism provided the transition to the eucharist—thus was one completely initiated. Because the rest of the faithful also took part in this eucharist, a special word service was provided for it. In other words, much of the tradition was still to be found here: the vigil provided the transition to the celebration of the resurrection of Jesus by means of the eucharist. But there was one great change: this vigil was steadily moved back earlier and earlier on Holy Saturday and thereby the sense of the night vigil lost its force. What is more, baptism finally disappeared from the vigil, and Easter Sunday was given its own matins, yet another night vigil! This all signified a continuing disintegration of the Easter vigil that continued in the Roman liturgy until 1955 (see the Appendix, p. 346).

The same discontinuity that we find in the triduum is also to be found in Holy Week and Paschaltide. There was an attempt to imitate the historical acts of Jesus' last days as much as possible. Palm Sunday and Maundy Thursday were thereby given a full treatment. Paschaltide moved into the background: the Sundays in Easter came to be called the Sundays after Easter instead of the Sundays of the great fifty days. Ascension and Pentecost were made independent, less clearly connected with Easter. In short: the church year was losing its earlier unitary vision; instead a chain of festivals was being developed.

This growing disintegration becomes even clearer when one studies the calendars of the saints. The civil year was being "churched," just as social life in general was coming to be determined by the church. Ecclesiastical festivals filled the year and provided for the necessary days off. Every city had its own saints. The feasts of the saints increased as a result of the translations of relics into the churches, thus also increasing the number of altars where the relics of the saints were honored (see A. Häussling, *Mönchskonvent und Eucharistiefeier*).

Christmas, preceded by an Advent of four (or five) weeks with its especially rich responses and antiphons, came to occupy a place almost out of all proportion in the devotion of the people. Deep emotion was centered on the memorial of Christ's birth against the background of the solstice festival of the rising of the sun in the midst of the dark winter. Old Germanic popular and magical religion was now shaped by the liturgy of the church, from Martinmass (November 11) to Epiphany, and it is still working in our secular society.

A further detailed description must be omitted here. But we can include two final remarks. First, we have already seen the interest the Jerusalem liturgy displayed in the historic course of Jesus' life. It is possible that this pattern came to be known in the west and was the more eagerly taken over because it corresponded so well to the Frankish-German mentality, with its sense for detail, allegory, and spontaneity. All of this was in contrast to the old *Romanitas*. Therefore, it was difficult for the Roman Curia to accept the Ottonian liturgy, which had been imported from beyond the Alps; its profuseness seemed an eyesore. Rome soon began to trim down the Frankish-German rites, with the result that many popular elements once again disappeared. It must be said, however, that the Frankish-German rites were no models of clear and flowing structure, nor of sobriety and brevity. On the other hand, it is clear that the visual and the bodily, the nonrational participation of the people, came into its own in this form of worship. The piety of western Christians has been strongly stimulated by this fact.

Second, this description has thus far been limited to a discussion of the exterior evolution of the Roman rite. To reach the heart of the matter, the texts themselves must be consulted: the choice of readings, the texts of liturgical songs, the prayers.

In conclusion, a short remark should be made concerning liturgical drama, from which western dramatics may generally be traced. People began sometimes to surround the church's Latin liturgy with dramatic "sketches" drawn from the Bible and eventually translated into the vernacular. A good example of this was the Easter play with its visit of the women to the sepulchre. As the plays came to be deeply loved, the distance between them and the clerical, Latin liturgy of the church grew ever greater. In these plays, one tastes something of the real character of medieval Christians. For further information we refer the reader to: K. Young, *The Drama of the Medieval Church*, 2 vols. (Oxford, 1933; repr. 1955); W. Liphardt, *Lateinische Osterfeiern und Osterspiele*, 7 vols. (Berlin, 1975ff.); R. Jonsson, ed., *Corpus Troparum: tropes du propre de la messe*; vol. 1: *Cycle de Noël* (Stockholm, 1975); *Dimensioni drammatiche della liturgia mediaevale, Atti del i convegno di studio* (Viterbo, 1976); O. Hardison, *Christian Rite and Christian Drama in the Middle Ages* (Baltimore, 1965). For a description of Holy Week and the rest of the liturgical year in which the official liturgy was joined with extraliturgical drama, see especially: A. Kurzeja, *Der älteste Liber ordinarius der Trierer Domkirche; ein Beitrag zur Liturgiegeschichte der deutsche Ortskirchen* (Münster, 1970), cf. esp. pp. 480–494; for music: *The Play of Daniel*, Pro Cantione Antiqua. Argo IRG 900.

3. THE SACRAMENTS

The data are here summarized in outline. Details will be found in the sources listed below:

Baptism and Confirmation

An especially important work is: J. Fisher, *Christian Initiation: Baptism in the Medieval West; A Study in Disintegration of the Primitive Rite of Initiation* (London, 1965).

The sources for baptism and confirmation are: *Gelasianum Vetus*, ed. Mohlberg, nos. 283–328 (pp. 42–54) and nos. 419–452 (pp. 67–74); the letter of the deacon John to Senarius (ed. Wilmart, 1933; cf. Whitaker, *Documents*, pp. 154–158); *Ordo Romanus XI*, ed. M. Andrieu, vol. 2, pp. 380ff.

This source contains the old elements that had characterized the baptismal rite for centuries, but also later Frankish-Roman practices. The oldest parts speak about *infantes* (neophytes), a term applied to the newly baptized without reference to age (thus also applied to adults). More recent parts speak of *parvuli* (little children, babies), indicating the infant baptism that in this period had become the usual practice.

The rites of baptism took place throughout Lent. The catechumenate had no significance, having become simply a ritual and not a real period of testing, as in the first centuries. Nonetheless the first part of the rite is still called *ad caticumenum faciendum* (making catechumens), but the further title *orationes super electos* (prayers over the elect) indicates that there was no longer any recognizable difference between catechumens and *electi*. A person was enrolled (*scribuntur nomina infantum*) as a catechumen to be baptized during the Easter vigil. The enrollment was paired with a welcoming and exorcistic rite: the giving of salt. During Lent the catechumen was supported by prayer and exorcisms in the midst of the assembly. The exorcism of the devil occurs through the laying on of hands and prayer (perhaps also through blowing).

On the third, fourth, and fifth Sundays in Lent there were special services called *scrutinia* of the *electi*, the content of which is already largely known to us from the previous period.

Third Sunday: *"Incipit expositio evangeliorum in aurium apertionum (apertionem) ad electos;"* "here begins the exposition of the gospel into the opened ears of the elect."

Fourth Sunday: *"Incipit praefatio symboli ad electos,"* "here begins the handing over of the creed (*symbolum*) to the *electi*" (in both Greek and Latin).

Fifth Sunday: *Item praefatio orationis dominicae,* the handing over of the Lord's prayer together with a short catechesis.

It should be noted that the handing over of the gospels and of the Lord's prayer were not Roman but came into the *Gelasianum* from outside Rome. The meaning of the act of handing over was explained to the elect. This explanation soon became a ritual, stereotypical text, which would indicate that these acts of *traditio* had become less important through the growth of the baptism of infants.

In the *Ordo Romanus* XI, discussed on pages 181–183, such was certainly the case.

It may be that the title *in aurium apertionum* was intended to indicate a time span, i.e. both the handing over and the "giving back" of the creed, the gospels, and the Lord's prayer. Before the handing over, the ears of the candidate were first "opened" by an exorcism; that is, by prayer and laying on of hands the catechumen was withdrawn from the power of evil so that he or she could listen and understand the words of the gospel, the Lord's prayer, or the creed, and so that he or she could ponder them and at the proper time give them back.

On Holy Saturday morning, the "giving back" (recitation, confession) of the creed took place. This "giving back" was again paired with an exorcism (the text addresses Satan personally: *"Proinde, damnate, da honorem deo vivo et vero,"* "Therefore, damned one, give honor to the living and true God") that reached its high point in the ephphatha rite. The nose and ears of the candidate were touched with saliva while these words were said:

Effeta, quod est adaparire, in odorem suavitatis. Tu autem effugare, diabole, adpropinquavit enim iudicium dei.	Ephphatha, which is be opened, unto the odor of sweetness. You however, devil, flee, for the judgment of God has drawn near.

The text was inspired by Mark 7:34–35 and in the spirit of the times it was literally applied: the candidate was "exorcised" with spittle, freed from the bond of Satan so that he or she could listen, understand, and speak. That speaking was, in the first place, the confession of faith, but it was also the renunciation of Satan and his works that directly followed. This renunciation was paired with an anointing of breast and shoulders as a sign of strengthening (massage) in the battle against Satan. In other words there was very concrete thinking and acting in this rite: baptism is a choice for Christ and against Satan, a choice which takes form in the words of the rite. The whole action was called *apertio aurium* and was clearly connected with the rites of earlier days.

But there was a negative side to this development: the renunciation of Satan was separated from the baptismal questions, that is, from the confession of faith just before the immersion, with the result that the candidate's choosing during the act of baptism came to be expressed less richly.

The paschal vigil in the *Gelasianum* contains the *benedictio cerei*, the song of praise of the light, the paschal candle. This is followed by readings from scripture, together with strikingly fine prayers, and the celebration of baptism–confirmation–eucharist; thus initiation is evidenced as a whole. In the readings, the paschal theme and the baptismal theme are interwoven.

After the readings *"procedunt ad fontes,"* they go to the font. Then the blessing over the water is pronounced, an anamnetic prayer that ends with this solemn epiclesis:

Discendat in hanc plentitudinem fontis virtus spiritus tui et totam huius aquae substantiam regenerandis fecundet effectu. Hic omnium peccatorum maculae deleantur. Hic natura ad imaginem tuam condita et ad honorem sui reformata principiis cunctis vetustatis squaloribus emundetur, ut omnis homo hoc sacramentum regenerationis ingressus in vera innocentia nova infantia renascatur: per dominum nostrum . . . (ed. Mohlberg, no. 448).	May the power of your Spirit descend in fullness upon this font so that the water may be fruitful for regenerating God's people. Here may the sins of all be blotted out. Here may human nature created according to your image and recreated from the evil brought upon it by human sin be renewed so that every person entering into this sacrament of regeneration may truly be reborn into a new state of innocence in accord with human dignity. Through our Lord. . . .

Then follows the baptismal questions: the creed in dialogue form together with the thrice-repeated immersion. The immersion is then completed by anointing with chrism by a presbyter. The baptized are then led before the bishop: "the neophytes themselves are signed by the bishop, receiving the sevenfold gift of the Holy Spirit as he puts chrism upon their foreheads" (*consignantur ipsi infantes ab episcopo, dum accipiunt septem dona gratia spiritus sancti, mittit chrisma in frontibus eorum*). The bishop lays his hands upon the baptized, anoints them, and signs their forehead with a cross, all regarded as a single action in which the Holy Spirit is given (*donum Spiritus Sancti*, "the Holy Spirit which is given").

The baptismal liturgy is concluded with the hymn *Gloria in excelsis*, signifying the transition to the celebration of the eucharist (liturgy of the word and liturgy of the table) in which the baptized may now participate since they now belong to the *familia Dei*, the family of God. This eucharist has its own readings: Colossians 3:1–4 and Matthew 28:1–7.

The *Gelasianum Vetus* agrees entirely with the baptismal rite of the third-century *Traditio Apostolica* of Hippolytus. Even the typically Roman practice of double anointing with chrism after baptism (by a presbyter and by the bishop) is still found there. Immersion and anointing are indissolubly linked; there is still no sign of confirmation as a separate sacrament. And it is especially clear that the paschal vigil still retains its authentic form—a vigil with baptism and the eucharist as the transition to the celebration of Easter.

ORDO ROMANUS XI

This source provides another baptismal liturgy in which the most important change is this: in contrast to the *Gelasianum Vetus*, it proceeds from the presupposition of a universally practiced baptism of infants. The description of this Roman-Frankish initiation ritual is very extensive and still contains all the essentials of the old rite. But it is without adaptation, that is, the ritual of the baptism of adults, in which the active choice and participation of the candidate is presumed, has not been adapted to the circumstance of the baptism of infants. The rite is an exceptionally precise order of service for initiation, a showpiece of liturgy, on which great care has been spent and in which nothing is left to chance. But it still misses its goal: it is really unusable for infant baptism. Despite this fact, it has made its influence felt even into the 1980s.

It is not necessary to analyze this *Ordo;* its principal parts are identical with those of the *Gelasianum.* We refer to just one important change: the three scrutinies, the Sunday services for the *electi* that have just been described, were moved to weekdays and increased to seven on the grounds of number symbolism. Here we can see a clear form of ritualization. Seven times during Lent the parents and the godparents had to bring the child to the church for a repeated exorcism. The word *scrutinium* had lost its original meaning. There was no longer any "inquiry" regarding the life and conduct of the candidate. (How could there be in the case of babies?) What remained was a solemn action of the church on the child's behalf, to free it from the clutches of the Evil One, from sin that as an inheritance weighs upon every person. Of these seven scrutinies, the second, fourth, fifth, and sixth were identical and rather simple: laying on of hands and an exorcistic prayer over the children. The first, third, and seventh had a more ceremonial tone, containing as they did the old rites: the enrollment with the gift of salt and the *apertio aurium* as described above. Baptism itself, with the laying on of hands and anointing with chrism, took place during the vigil, moved now to an earlier time on Holy Saturday.

Ordo Romanus XI makes evident the anomaly inherent in the ritual for the baptism of infants. A change in this situation took place in the Roman rite only after Vatican II, in 1969 (see pp. 352–359). For further implications, see A. Angenendt, "Taufe und Politik im frühen Mittelalter," *Frühmittelalterliche Studien* 7, 1973, pp. 143–168.

Confirmation in the *Gelasianum Vetus* is still of a piece with the immersion, the act of baptism. The twofold anointing (as described in the *Traditio Apostolica*, see pp. 34–39) by presbyter and bishop was typically Roman and intended for the local situation of the city of Rome, where the presbyters celebrated liturgy in close connection to the pope, who was *the* liturgist. This rite was taken over in the north, but the situation beyond the Alps was different. Pastoral care was reaching out from the cities to the countryside and was taking on its own characteristics. This was especially so in southern France. In the celebration of initiation there was not always a bishop present. Moreover, in Gaul the double anointing after baptism, as in Rome, was unknown. One anointing with chrism was practiced and that was done by the presbyter; the laying on of hands, in contrast, was reserved to the bishop.

The priests in southern France then began to omit the anointing after baptism and, under the influence of the Roman practice, to leave this for the bishop to do. This practice was disapproved by the bishops, especially at the Council of Orange in 441 (see canon 2). They determined that anointing with chrism by a priest or deacon must take place in the context of the baptism itself. The bond with the bishop would be protected by the fact that the chrism would have been blessed by the bishop. The bishops thus emphasized this particular Gallican practice: one chrism anointing in the context of the baptism by the ministering priest or deacon. A double anointing as at Rome was superfluous, according to them, and the one anointing had to take place at the baptism (cf. L. van Buchen, *L'homélie pseudo-eusébienne de Pentecôte; l'origine de la 'confirmatio' en Gaule Méridionale et l'interpretation de ce rite par Fauste de Riez*, Nijmegen, 1967; A. Angenendt, "Bonifatius und das *Sacramentum initiationis*," *Römische Quartalschrift für Christliche Altertumskunde* 72, 1977, pp. 133–183).

On the other hand there had anciently been a laying on of hands after baptism as bestowal of the Holy Spirit. In both Rome and Gaul this was the prerogative of the bishop. It is certain that from at least the sixth century, this laying on of hands was called *confirmatio*, a confirming of baptism by the personal mediation of the bishop. This remained the case, but as a result of the growth of infant baptism and the development of rural pastoral care, this confirming was detached from baptism because the bishop could not be everywhere at once. In other words, from the middle of the fifth century it became the practice to separate the bishop's laying on of hands from the celebration of baptism. Furthermore, the old Roman practice of anointing by the bishop was carried on nonetheless, with the result that confirmation arose as an independent sacrament, i.e. anointing–laying on of hands–signing with the cross by the bishop, separate from baptism administered by the priest with its immersion–anointing.

The complicated, still not entirely clarified, history of confirmation demonstrates in any case the growing disintegration of Christian initiation through which baptism, confirmation, and eucharist were distinguished from one another. The practice of infant baptism was partly the cause of this. One of the consequences was that baptism was seen less as the bestowal of the Holy Spirit than rather too exclusively as the forgiving of original sin. A second, even more farreaching consequence was that the place of the Holy Spirit in the life of the western church began to diminish; the faithful tended to see the Spirit as too much tied to the infrequent visits of the bishop.

Why the laying on of hands in baptism was reserved to the bishop (in contrast to the east where the presiding priest "confirms") remains a puzzle. Was there a desire to preserve the Roman practice? Was there the intention to strengthen the awareness of the unity of the local churches in the person of the bishop?

Eucharist

The sources for a knowledge of the eucharist in this period are numerous. In the first place there are the diverse *sacramentaria*, which contain collections of prayers. Then there are the *lectionaria* and the *antiphonaria*. Here we will limit discussion to the order of the service together with a short commentary upon it.

THE SO-CALLED PAPAL MASS

The ritual for the eucharist in the west goes back to the so-called papal mass as this was celebrated by the pope, the *clerus*, and the faithful c. 600 (and probably even earlier) in designated churches of the city of Rome. An extensive description of this liturgy is found in the *Ordo Romanus* I (ed. Andrieu, *Les ordines romani*, vol. 2). The course of the service was as follows:

Nos. 24–54—The great entrance procession and the opening of the liturgy: Clad in liturgical garments the pope enters the basilica with his retinue in a solemn procession accompanied by the antiphonal singing of a psalm—the introit, the antiphon of which establishes the character of this Sunday service. Then follow the Kyrie, the Gloria in excelsis, and the *oratio,* which is introduced by the greeting *pax vobis* ("peace be to you") or *Dominus vobiscum* (the response is: *et cum spiritu tuo*) and the call to prayer, *oremus* ("let us pray"). The *cathedra* (the presiding chair of the bishop) stands in the center of the apse. This first part of the ritual is focused upon the person of the pope and is marked by a rich ceremonial, reminiscent of the imperial court, with much candlelight and incense. What is more, there is evident a great reverence for the "sacred space" of the altar and for the book from which the reading is done.

Nos. 55–66—The service of readings: There are two readings from the New Testament; various pericope series can be found in the sources. The reading of the gospel by the deacon is surrounded by great ceremonial (especially candles and incense). The gospel book is considered a sign of the presence of the Lord; it is richly decorated and after the reading it is solemnly put away in a *capsa* (box). There is no mention of a homily nor of the *communis oratio* (the prayers of the faithful).

Nos. 67–126—The service of the altar: Altare est Christus ("the altar is Christ") goes an old saying; it is also a sign of the presence of the Lord, surrounded with reverence just as was the gospel book during the service of readings. The influence of court ceremonial and of the Byzantine liturgy is certainly present here. The service of the altar has been harmoniously built up and extended. The offertory is in fact a great procession of the aristocracy to the pope and of the faithful to his assistants to present the gifts for the celebration and for the poor. The requisite gifts of bread and wine are placed on the altar by the deacon, and the gifts of the pope are added to them. The procession is concluded with an *oratio super oblata* (synonyms for *oblata* include *munera* and *sacrificia,* that is, "gifts which are intended for the celebration of the sacrifice"). The canon, the text of which was discussed in the previous chapter, is spoken by the pope alone: *"surgit pontifex solus in canone, episcopi vero, presbyteri, diaconi, subdiaconi permanent inclinati"* ("the pope alone rises for the canon, but the bishops, priests, deacons and subdeacons remain bowed"). Does this also mean that the canon is prayed in complete silence? This rubric with its direction about *"permanent inclinati"* places great emphasis upon the holiness of the event that occurs at the *"conse-*

cratio," the heart of the eucharistic prayer in which the gifts are blessed and consecrated (the institution narrative). The communion is preceded by the Lord's prayer, the breaking of the bread, and the mingling of the bread in the cup (we pass over the details of this complicated rite). The communion is the counterpart to the offertory: now there is a procession to the altar in order to receive the sanctified gifts from the hands of the presider. It is as if it were a ritual expression of the concept *commercium,* exchange, that is used several times in the Roman texts. The communion concludes with another *oratio,* the *postcommunio.*

This papal mass is very solemn, a fact that coincides with the function and the authority of the bishop of Rome, who for many years had replaced the emperor in the west. Nonetheless the essentials of the eucharist have been carefully preserved: the liturgy of the word and the liturgy of the table are clearly recognizable though they have been placed in a broader context. There is no extravagant excess. It must be noted though that the bishop of Rome plays a very central role: he is the most important person, the presider *par excellence.* The faithful stay somewhere in the background next to the dazzling clerical ceremonial. Finally it is significant that in such detailed ritual there is no mention of the homily. Did the pope have other worries besides the preparation of his homily?

This ritual of the papal mass profoundly influenced the future of the eucharistic celebration in the west. The bishops from north of the Alps who visited Rome regarded it with wonder, took it home with them, and adopted it, albeit not slavishly. It was changed and adapted. This adaptation went further than just the exterior ritual; the idea changed. In the first place, the old communal service tended to become a cultic concern of the clerics who knew Latin and the rites, and it had only indirect contact with the faithful. Worship became thereby hieratic and separated from the people. Furthermore the symbolic thought and feeling that had marked the liturgy up to that time had to make way for an analytic manner of thought. "Mystery" no longer meant "sign that points beyond itself" or symbol, but "incomprehensible" and "invisible." The view of God's salvation and God's grace became more material and thinglike. Sacraments tended to be thought of as "channels" of grace, with the result that the relationship between faith and sacrament became less obvious. As a further consequence, the internal dynamic of worship was bent toward a more static experience of the liturgy in which the faithful participated receptively rather than actively.

The Frankish redaction of the ritual of the papal mass is found in the long version of *Ordo Romanus* I and in the *Ordines Romani* IV and V (in Andrieu, vol. 2). Here we will discuss only the more significant differences.

Now the presider is not the pope but the bishop or abbot, and now priests are beginning to take over the functions formerly assigned to the many minor assistants of the pope. Especially the office of the deacon begins to disappear, being assumed by the priest, a fact that may be due to the increase in the number of priests, even among the monks. All of this led to a vagueness about the various functions, a vagueness that would continue into subsequent periods.

The monastic influence is evident in the increase of hymnic texts in the eucharist such as tropes and sequences (see R. L. Crocker, *The Early Medieval Sequence*, Berkeley, 1977).

Characteristic of the Frankish and Germanic peoples is the increase of the dramatic in the ritual: the ritual action of the presider becomes more demonstrative and thus emphasizes the words that he speaks. This is apparent, for example, in the many gestures of consecration during the canon and in the ritual expansion of the offertory. On the other hand, all of this resulted in a certain impoverishment and narrowing of the essential rites of the service. The communion of the faithful decreases drastically, with the result that the communion of the presiding minister is all the more conspicuous and his role in the service becomes still more a solo affair (see P. Browe, *Die haüfige Kommunion im Mittelalter*, Münster, 1938). The bread is reduced to a host and the plate exchanged for a *ciborium* that can contain many such hosts (see Nuszbaum, op. cit.). As a result of a sacral conception of the presence of the Lord, communion is received upon the tongue. This narrowing is also to be found in the canon, prayed in silence and visually accentuated, now considered to be especially focused upon "the words" over bread and cup, the words of the Lord himself, through which the consecration takes place and the sacrament is "confected." In the later missals these words of consecration would be written in capital letters. The presence of the Lord in bread and wine through the consecration now becomes the predominant fact. The consecratory action by the priest in the sight of the faithful in the long run obscures in some sense the celebration of the memorial of the saving deed of the Lord. Nevertheless, throughout the western church there flourished a deeply rooted and very specific eucharistic piety and experience that still is to be felt among Roman Catholics of today.

What were the underlying causes of all this? Most likely one ought to consider here the deep change in mentality in the west, which is to be traced back to the Franks and the Germans and their "dark ages." Maybe (but indirectly) there was some "eastern" influence. The change in mentality has been characterized in this way: in this period philosophy and theology were failing and, as a result, religious piety developed uncriticized. "In this sense one may dare to say that religion has never so massively penetrated into Christianity" (Angenendt, "Religiosität und Theologie," loc. cit., p. 31).

One final striking change that the Roman papal mass underwent in the north concerned the arrangement of the church building, the orientation of the edifice. The construction of a church toward the east, on the east-west axis, was already old. Pagan peoples prayed facing east. Christian authors had christened this practice: facing the east was facing Christ, the rising Sun (cf. F. Dölger, *Sol Salutis*, Münster, 1925). Such "orientation" is found already in the church buildings completed during Constantine's reign.

In the old church buildings two types of orientation are to be distinguished. Type 1 was employed in the "eastern" tradition almost exclusively from the sixth century. Type 2 is found mostly, although not exclusively, in the west in the Constantinian period (e.g., the basilica of St. Peter in Rome).

Plan of the Church Floor

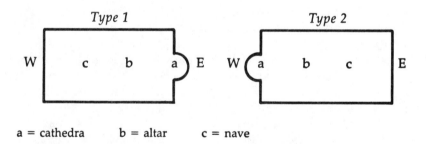

a = cathedra   b = altar   c = nave

Assuming that one prayed facing the east, this meant for the eucharistic rite that in type 1 the president had to turn around during prayer (especially the eucharistic prayer), since while seated on the *cathedra* he faced west toward the people. During prayer then he stood "with back toward the people."

In type 2 churches, the president stood at the *cathedra* facing both the east and the people.

It is this latter arrangement of the church interior that is presumed in the description of the papal mass in *Ordo Romanus* I elaborated

187

upon above. The apse stands in the west; the pope sits on the *cathedra* in the apse, looking toward the east and toward the faithful gathered in the nave.

In the Frankish description of the papal mass, the orientation of *Ordo Romanus* I is not presumed, but rather the "eastern" manner of orientation, that of type 1 in which the apse is directed toward the east and the façade of the church to the west. As a consequence, there were very definite ritual changes, above all in the posture of the president at prayer, who now turned to the east during the prayers. During the canon he stood with his back to the faithful in the nave as he did also at the beginning of the Gloria and during the *oratio* after the entrance and after communion. In other words, we find here a clear adaptation of the papal ritual to the local situation. This Frankish practice of orientation, which corresponded to that of the eastern church, in later times (tenth century) became general in the west, even at Rome. Why this type 1 orientation was introduced in Gaul cannot be said.

We will go a step further: how it happened we do not know for sure, but the fact is that the *cathedra* came to be less important. Did this correspond to the "crisis in preaching" during this period? Or with the fact that vernacular preaching was no longer done around the altar area, where Latin had exclusive rights, but the pulpit placed closer to the people? In any case it came about that the altar was moved to the apse; the president stood there with his back to the people. The *cathedra* was then no longer a pulpit but a token of honor for the bishop and his church (the "cathedral," the church where the *cathedra* is), placed most usually to the right of the altar. The altar space became the "choir," the place of the clergy who inherited this prerogative from the monks. The monks had had in their churches a place for the communal office—two rows of benches facing each other for antiphonal song, i.e., with two answering choirs. So there gradually arose the medieval arrangement of altar, priest-choir, and nave. The tendency was for the choir to be more and more separated from the rest of the church. Finally, a misarrangement of the church building took place when a so-called "communion altar" was placed between the choir and the faithful, a table from which communion was distributed to the people but without any clear connection with the eucharistic action.

HISTORY OF THE ORIGIN OF THE MASS

The Frankish *Ordines* IV and V do not mention several facts about the origin of the *Ordo Missae*, of the private mass, and of the so-

188

called *expositiones missae* (mass commentaries), all of which are of
great importance for the further history of the eucharist.

THE "ORDO MISSAE"
See A. Nocent, "Les apologies dans la célébration eucharistiques," in
Liturgie et rémission des péchés, (Rome, 1975, pp. 179–196).
The term
ordo missae refers to the unchangeable texts of the Roman (western)
celebration of the eucharist. Anciently included were: the prayer
Kyrie, the hymn Gloria in excelsis, the greeting addressed to the
congregation, *Dominus vobiscum*, with its answer *et cum spiritu tuo;*
the dialogue introductory to the preface; the preface, Sanctus,
and canon.

Added to the old unchangeable texts in this period were certain
characteristic prayers that might be classified under the title "apologies" or expressions of unworthiness, confessions, statements of sinfulness and guilt. These prayers consisted of the sinner's confession
before God with interior prayer that the merciful God might make
the petitioner worthy to celebrate the mysteries. There is a parallel
practice in the Byzantine and other eastern rites. These "apologies,"
which can vary endlessly on the same theme, were priestly prayers,
framed in the first person singular.

This sort of prayer took place before the beginning of the liturgy,
during the walk to the altar (the Confiteor together with the use of
Psalm 43 is the best-known example), as preparation for the proclamation of the gospel (the well-known *Munda cor meum et labia mea*),
the prayers during the offertory (at the preparation of bread and cup
and during the hand washing), before communion, and then before
the blessing at the end. In all these prayers the same thought is
expressed—the prayer that the unworthy one might become worthy
to approach the sanctuary.

The origin of this series of apologies is to be found in the Frankish-German church, not in Rome. Irish–Anglo-Saxon monastic sensibility played a large role in this. The prayers arose in the monasteries
of Reichenau, St. Gall, and the Rhineland. Research into the manuscripts demonstrates that the so-called *Rhineland Ordo Missae* was of
decisive significance. Here is another example of the influence of the
German church under the Ottonians (Mainz, Reichenau, and St.
Gall) that had assumed the responsibilities of the Frankish church
after Charlemagne.

B. Luykx, *De oorsprong van het gewone der Mis* (Utrecht, 1955, pp.
13–14), gives a characterization of the *Ordo Missae:*

"More strongly than in Rome, where the indigenous liturgy had been further developed in the atmosphere of court-ceremonial, the priests north of the Alps felt that it behooved them to offer the most holy sacrifice with the utmost piety and devotion. . . . So we see that along with the gradual establishment of the Roman liturgy in the north there was at the same time the emergence of a subjective element. The *Ordo Missae*, which would grow in a long ripening process, was, then, not influenced by the courtly ceremonial, the external splendor and complicated structure, that were so evident in the liturgy at Rome, but by the desire to deepen the personal piety of the celebrant and ministers at mass. Thus, a new and important element came into the liturgy north of the Alps. While *Ordo Romanus* I remains the description of an actual liturgical ritual for the most part inspired by the imperial court ceremonial and intended for the group participation of all the clergy and the faithful, the *Ordo Missae* is a prayer schema intended for the personal devotional experience of the celebrant alone. Thus we encounter here a phenomenon of express clericalization in the liturgy."

Here are several examples from the *Missale Romanum* of priestly prayers for the celebration of the eucharist that have been used for centuries.

While going to the altar:

Aufer a nobis, quaesumus, Domine iniquitates nostras: ut ad Sancta sanctorum puris mereamur mentibus introire.	Take away our sins, we pray you, O Lord, so that with pure minds we may worthily enter into the holy of holies.

Before the gospel:

Munda cor meum ac labia mea, omnipotens Deus, qui labia Isaiae Prophetae calculo mundasti ignito; ita me tua grata miseratione dignare mundare, ut sanctum evangelium tuum digne valeam nuntiare.	Cleanse my heart and my lips, almighty God, as you cleansed the lips of the prophet Isaiah with a burning coal. In your mercy so cleanse me that I may worthily proclaim your holy gospel.

At the offertory:

Suscipe, sancte Pater, omnipotens aeterne Deus, hanc im-	Receive, O holy Father, almighty and eternal God, this spotless host

maculatam hostiam, quam ego indignus famulus tuus offero tibi Deo meo vivo et vero, pro innumerabilibus peccatis, et offensionibus et negligentiis meis, et pro omnibus circumstantibus, sed et pro omnibus fidelibus christianis vivis atque defunctis: ut mihi et illis proficiat ad salutem in vitam aeternam.

which I, your unworthy servant, offer to you, my living and true God, for my own countless sins, offenses and negligences; and for all present here, as well as for all faithful Christians both living and dead, that it may profit me and them as a means of reaching salvation in the eternal life.

Before communion:

Domine Iesu Christe, Fili Dei vivi, qui ex voluntate Patris, cooperante Spiritu Sancto, per mortem tuam mundum vivificasti: libera me per hoc sacrosanctum Corpus et Sanguinem tuum ab omnibus iniquitatibus meis, et universis malis: et fac me tuis semper inhaerere mandatis, et a te numquam separari permittas.

Lord Jesus Christ, Son of the living God, who by the Father's will and the cooperation of the Holy Spirit, through your death brought life to the world, deliver me by this, your most sacred Body and Blood from all my sins and from every evil. Make me always obedient to your commandments, and never allow me to be separated from you.

After communion:

Corpus tuum, Domine, quod sumpsi, et Sanguinem, quem potavi, adhaereat visceribus meis: et praesta: ut in me non remaneat scelerum macula, quem pura et sancta refecerunt sacramenta.

May your Body, O Lord, which I have eaten, and your Blood, which I have drunk, cleave to my inmost being. Grant that no stain of sin may remain within me, now that I am refreshed by this pure and holy sacrament.

At the end of mass:

Placeat tibi, sancta Trinitas, obsequium servitutis meae: et praesta; ut sacrificium, quod oculis tuae majestatis indignus

May the homage of my service be pleasing to you, O holy Trinity. Grant that the sacrifice which I, unworthy as I am, have offered in

obtuli, tibi sit acceptabile,	the sight of your majesty, may be
mihique et omnibus, pro quibus	acceptable to you, and through
illud obtuli, sit, te miserante,	your mercy may it win favor for
propitiable.	me and for all those for whom I
	have offered it.

One should note that these are the individual prayers of the priest; they indicate both that he feels unworthy and sinful and that he celebrates the sacrifice for the sake of the faithful. By attentive reading one discovers here the growing private dimension of the celebration of the eucharist that will become predominant.

THE PRIVATE MASS

This term is intended to indicate a celebration of the eucharist by a priest with one or two assistants, without the presence of the community of the faithful. This kind of celebration began in this period; its full development takes place in the later Middle Ages.

A. A. Häussling, *Mönchskonvent und Eucharistiefeier*, comes to the conclusion in his extensive and well-documented study that for the monks the Roman liturgy served as the model for the building of their churches and the arrangement of their liturgy. The monastic church with its high altar and the many chapels with their altars situated in the whole of the abbey were "a copy of the normative urban church, a representation of Rome . . . the many masses within the great monastery corresponded to the celebrations of the urban liturgy. These formed a unity just as the churches, chapels and altars of the monastic city formed a unity, one church family claiming to be a representation of the normative city" (pp. 313–314). The monks wanted to imitate the Roman situation in the building of their monasteries; that is, by the celebration of the eucharist at the central altar of the church as well as at the altars in the chapels they copied the local Roman liturgy, in which the pope held the one *statio* service and the presbyters celebrated the eucharist together with their people in the many *tituli* (unity in multiplicity). For the Carolingian monks Rome was the model, and behind Rome they saw Jerusalem. Furthermore, Häussling points to the influence of the Roman devotion to the martyrs and saints, in which it was the custom to celebrate the eucharist near the grave or the relics. The imitation of the Roman urban liturgy also in this regard furthered the multiplicity of masses in the north, but also contributed to the increase of the numbers of saints and relics (and, in general, the memorializing of the dead). In this accent on the devotion to the saints and in the associated increase of altars (and thus of "masses") there must have been also a rejection of iconoclasm that was just as radical in the west as in the east.

O. Nussbaum, *Kloster, Priestermönch und Privatmesse* (Bonn, 1961), seeks the cause of the origin of the private mass in the rapid increase of the number of priests among the monks. Roman monks who at the beginning of the seventh century had gone on the mission to the Anglo-Saxons needed priests in their midst. The English hierarchy was initially monastic. The practice of ordaining monks as priests then increased so rapidly that in a few decades it was generally agreed that the monk not only could be a priest, but should be a priest, and indeed must be a priest. The monasteries came to be populated with priest-monks, one of whom presided at the "conventual mass": he was the hebdomadary, the weekly presider (an idea taken up with some reference to Jewish temple service). The monk then experienced priesthood within the context of an ascetic ideal that was marked by individualism, by a sense of sin, by a concern for one's own salvation, and by a soul properly disposed for receiving the *bona gratia Dei* through means of the sacraments of the church. The eucharist was the center and high point of these sacraments, *the* gift of God's forgiveness and reconciliation. These monastic practices and outlooks were soon taken over by the secular clergy.

The many priests began to celebrate at many altars in the name of the faithful ("*Memento, Domine . . . pro quibus tibi offerimus*," "Remember, Lord . . . those for whom we offer to thee. . . ."). The people grew accustomed to the many priests and the many masses and began to register the intentions for which they "wanted to have a mass read": for the dead, for oneself after one's death, and for all kinds of other intentions. The full privatization of the mass is of a later date, but the practice started at this time along with the increase in the number of priests.

In addition to the above explanations of the origin of the private mass, yet a third can be added: the obscuring of liturgical functions. The pastor outside the city had no great host of assistants and singers available as did the bishop in his cathedral; often he stood alone at worship, with one or two assistants at most. This meant of course a more sober celebration and a significant change: the priest began to fill the role of the deacon, of the lector, of the psalmist. He became the sole "functionary" in the service. A book was developed in which the whole order of service was conveniently arranged—the pericopes from scripture, the sung texts, the prayers: thus, the so-called *missale plenum*. The priest became the sacred "minister," *der Gottesmann*, who alone could enter the sanctuary.

What we have called here the private mass would later prove to be the cause of a radical change in the celebration of the eucharist and in the piety of priests and people. In addition, the controversies over the eucharist altered the eucharistic experience in the west. We conclude here with C. Heitz, *Recherches sur les rapports entre architecture et liturgie à l'époque carolingienne* (Paris, 1963, pp. 245, 235): "But the liturgy itself changed. At the time of Charlemagne it was active, engaging a whole assembly of monks and of laypeople. In the tenth century, however, it became a liturgy of representation passively experienced. The deep cause for this was a change in spirit: laden with confused speculation the symbols were lost sight of; there was a drift toward allegory and the humanization of the divine. From mystery, formerly received through the veiled means of symbolic transformation, the liturgy passed to historical and soon even theatrical representation. It is a fact that the principal scenes of the resurrection were acted out as at a theatre. The choirs took turns at singing about the various episodes. Ultimately individual actors were selected from these choirs and the mystery already evoked by voice was similarly enacted in gesture. . . . The ancient liturgical spirit, the fruit of many centuries of collective fervor and active participation in the cult, was transformed little by little to become a liturgy practiced 'by delegation.' "

MASS COMMENTARIES (EXPOSITIONES MISSAE)

The term "mass commentary" denotes an exegesis of the celebration of the eucharist. One could of course call the mystagogical catecheses of the fourth century a "mass commentary," but the term is actually used to indicate a certain literary genre that had been developing since Carolingian times.

The first striking thing is the term "mass." We reported already in the previous chapter that since the second century the term "eucharist" became *the* title for the celebration of the supper of the Lord. Thereby the emphasis was laid upon the praise-full and thankful proclamation of God's saving deeds, above all in Jesus, whose sacrifice was recalled (memorial) in the celebration of the congregation. Although representation began to play a great role from the fourth century, nonetheless the liturgical texts put their greatest stress on the dynamic of God's continuing saving act in the Son who lives beyond death and who gives his Spirit.

The term *missa* is also old, signifying dismissal, an action that always went together with prayers (a blessing, for example) and ceremonies (such as the dismissal of the catechumens). From a part of the service the term was transferred to the whole service; *missa* then meant, generally, "service," "celebration." Finally in the singular it acquired the meaning "eucharist," "eucharistic sacrifice." This last meaning has been in use since Carolingian times and became current primarily through the works of Amalarius of Metz, who introduced the allegorical method in his mass commentary and who gave the term "mass" a wholly different set of connotations than the term "eucharist" anciently possessed.

The *expositio Missae* as a genre was intended for the clergy, who as we have seen played a predominant role in the celebration. It was a text book for their education for *the* priestly office, along with commentaries on the creed, the Lord's prayer, and baptism. These formed the minimum package of knowledge for the clergy in Carolingian times. Later these commentaries were also to develop into pious considerations (meditation books) or into learned, theological, encyclopedic exposés. The oldest mass commentary (Anonymous, *Primum in ordine*, ed. R. Wilmart, *E.L.* 50, 1936, pp. 133–139) was followed by a great number of other commentaries throughout the Middle Ages.

We mention the mass commentary here, however, principally on account of Amalarius of Metz (775–852), a disciple of Alcuin who is known for his *Liber Officialis* (823; a description of the church year, the mass, the hours, etc.). His name is tied to the allegorical interpretation of the liturgy, a method whereby the rites and texts of the eucharist were understood allegorically, and a method vilified by the deacon Florus of Lyons. In this method, consideration was no longer given to the common significance of a gesture or a word, but an exterior explanation was applied, intended to make the whole an instrument for catechesis. There was no use of typology, in which the dynamic of salvation history through the experience of symbols is primary; this allegory rather was an uncritical, static, outward, and rational explanation of innumerable *figurae*, circumventing the event and using the celebration for instruction.

Amalarius says in his *Expositio Missae*, for example, that the introit (entrance song) is an "image" of the choir of the prophets who announced the Messiah; the Kyrie images the prophets in the time of Christ; the Gloria is the choir of angels; the first *collecta* (opening prayer) is related to the twelve-year-old Christ in the temple; the epistle evokes the preaching of John the Baptist, etc. The actions and texts of the mass are an outward expression of the whole life of

Jesus without any internal connection with the actual content of the mass. What is imaged is the historical life of Jesus as presented to the individual believer in such a way that he or she can dwell upon the mystery of Jesus' life.

In the following centuries this allegorical method came to exercise great influence especially in its impact upon the faithful. The popular expressions of liturgical piety, especially at Christmas and Easter, must be understood as stemming from this "method." Add to all of this the development of a predominantly realistic view of the eucharist, which resulted from the theological controversies of the time, and it is evident that a radical change has taken place in the Christian mentality as regards sacrament (see above, pp. 186–194).

Penance and Confession

During the fourth to the sixth centuries, both the catechumenate as a preparation for baptism, and the reception into the *ordo poenitentium*, the order of penitents, took place at the beginning of the yearly fast. Later, the fast was set to begin on the preceding Wednesday (Ash Wednesday).

ADMISSION AS A PENITENT

A short service for reception into the order of penitents on Ash Wednesday is still to be found in the *Gelasianum Vetus*. To this reception then, after the penance and the *akoinonia*, which might last years, there corresponded a reconciliation, a new reception into the congregation during the liturgy of Maundy Thursday. Here is a selection of texts from the *Gelasianum*:

At the reception into the order of penitents (ed. Mohlberg, nos. 81, 82):

Domine Deus noster, qui offensionem nostram non vinceris, sed satisfactionem placaris, respice, quaesumus ad hunc famulum tuum, qui se tibi peccasse graviter confitetur. Tuum est ablutionem criminum dare et veniam prestare peccantibus, qui dixisti paenitentiam te malle peccatorum quam mortem. Concede ergo, domine, hoc, ut et tibi paenitentiam excopias

Lord our God, you whom our offenses cannot harm but are appeased by satisfaction, look graciously, we beseech you, upon this your servant, who confesses to you that he has sinned gravely. Yours is the power to grant the washing away of offenses and to bestow pardon upon sinners, for you have said that you desire the conversion rather than the death of sinners. Therefore, Lord, grant

caelebret ut correctis actibus suis conferre tibi ad te sempiterna [sic] gaudia caelebretur: per.

Praecor, domine, clementiam tuae maiestatis ac nominis, ut huic famulo tuo peccata et facinora sua confitenti veniam dare et praeteritorum criminum (debita) relaxare digneris. Qui humeris tuis ovem perditam reduxisti ad caulas, qui publicani precibus vel confessione placatus es, tu etiam, domine, et huic famulo tuo placare, tu eum praecibus benignus adsiste, ut in confessione flevili permanens clementiam tuam caeleriter exoret et sanctis ac sacris altaribus restitutus spei rursus aeternae caelestis gloria reformetur: per.

that he may bring such fruits of repentance before you and so engage in acts of penance that eternal joys may be celebrated to your honor.

I beseech the mercy of your majesty and name, Lord, that you would deign to grant pardon to your servant, as he confesses his sins and crimes, and forgive the debt of his previous sins. You, who on your shoulders have returned the lost sheep to the sheepfold and have been appeased by the prayers and confession of the publican, be pleased to look kindly on the prayers of your servant so that in the confession of his faults, through persevering pleading he may speedily experience your mercy and thus restored to (communion) at the holy and sacred altar with your saints, he may be renewed again unto hope in the glory of the heavenly kingdom.

At the reconciliation (after a question from the deacon and an address by the bishop) the following prayer (ed. Mohlberg, no. 358):

Deus humani generis benignissime conditor et misericordissime formator, qui hominem invidia diaboli ab aeternitate deiectum unici filii tui sanguine redemisti: vivifica itaque quem tibi nullatenus mori desideras, et qui non derelinquis devium, adsume corruptum. Moveat pietatem tuam, quaesumus, domine, huius famuli tui lacri-

O God, most kind creator and merciful sustainer of the human race who through the blood of your only-begotten Son have redeemed humanity's fall from eternal life by the envy of the evil one, restore life and be present to the sinner whom you in no way desire to die and whom you do not leave abandoned. May the sorrowful sighings of this servant

mosa suspiria. Tu eius medere vulneribus. Tui iacenti manum porrige salutarem, ne aeclesia tua aliqua sui corporis porcione vastetur nec grex tuus detrimentum susteneat, ne de familiae tuae damno inimicus exultet, ne renatum lavacro salutaris mors secunda possedeat. Tibi ergo, domine, supplices praeces, tibi fletum cordis effundimus. Tu parce confitenti ut imminentibus paene sentenciae quae futuri iuducii te miserante non incedat. Nesciat quod territ in tenebris, quod stridit in flammis, atque ab erroris via ad iter reversus iusticiae nequaquam ultra novis vulneribus saucietur, sed integrum sit ei atque perpetuum et quod gratia tua contulit et quod misericordia reformavit: per.

of yours, we beseech you, Lord, move you to be merciful. Heal his wounds. Extend your saving hand to the fallen, lest your church be destroyed in a portion of its reality as Christ's body, or your flock sustain a loss, or the enemy rejoice in the condemnation of a member of your family or lest the second death overtake one reborn in the saving waters of baptism. To you, Lord, therefore, we pour forth our suppliant prayers and the groanings of our heart. Spare the person who confesses sinfulness before you so that through your mercy he will not fall into the fearful sentence to come. May he not experience the terror of darkness where there is the gnashing of teeth in the flames of hell, but be brought back from the way of error to the road of justice so that he may in no way be further injured by new wounds but rather may he ever be made whole because your grace has sustained him and your mercy has reformed him.

The texts breathe a trust in the grace and mercy of God; the presider expresses this trust, which is that of the whole assembly. Here there is a fellowship in which the penitent does penance, is helped by communal prayer, and then is again received. This reception is at the same time a prayer for the forgiveness of God. One notes also the notions of "the enemy," judgement, hell, and darkness, which anticipate the famous romanesque tympans at church entrances.

The *Gelasianum Vetus* offered in the sixth and seventh centuries a complete reconciliation ritual breathing the spirit of the preceding centuries. The prayers give a view of sin and reconciliation as extensions of the forgiveness granted in baptism:

Lavant aquae, lavant lacrimae. Inde gaudium de adsumptione vocatorum, hinc laeticiae de absolutione paenitencium (ed. Mohlberg, no. 353).	The waters wash; tears wash. There is gladness at the reception of the called; here joy at the absolution of the penitents.

CHANGES IN THE RITE

This old rite underwent a change in the ninth century, influenced by the Frankish-German mentality that has already been discussed: texts and rites were added to heighten the drama of the *ordo*. These are to be found in *Ordo Romanus* 50 (ed. Andrieu, vol. 5, pp. 192f.); they were introduced practically unchanged into the *Pontificale Romanum* of the council of Trent.

What change had taken place? One was the underscoring of dramatic power of the vesting in the penitential garment and the putting of ashes on the head; the bishop blessed both and then put the ashes on the heads of the penitents who came to kneel one by one before him. During the action he then spoke the well-known text:

Memento homo, quia pulvis es, et in pulverem reverteris: age poenitentiam, ut habeas vitam aeternam.	Remember, O man, that you are dust and unto dust you shall return: do penance that you may have eternal life.

This text was inspired by Genesis 3:19–24. The celebration came to be buttressed with scriptural texts of which a dramatic action seemed to be part and parcel, texts that were literally construed to act as a basis for a "liturgical theater." Here the pressure toward visualization of the liturgy is obvious.

On the basis of Genesis 3:19–24, reception into the order of penitents took the form of a removal and expulsion from the church (*expulsio*). After the penitential psalms were prayed (a selection of psalms which at this time became current in the monasteries: Pss 6, 32, 38, 51, 102, 130, 143), the bishop preached, making clear that as Adam was cast out of paradise on account of his sin so sinners are cast out of the congregation. Then he took the first penitent by the right hand and, with the others holding each other's hands, they were led out of the church by the bishop. Then he said:

Ecce ejicimini vos hodie a liminibus sanctae matris	Behold, you are cast forth today from the household of holy mother church

| Ecclesiae propter peccata, et scelera vestra, sicut Adam primus homo ejectus est de paradiso propter transgressionem suam. | on account of your sins and crimes, as Adam the first man was cast forth from paradise on account of his transgression. |

The accompanying song was just as significant:

| In sudore vultus tuis vesceris pane tuo. | In the sweat of your brow shall you eat your bread. |

In other words, a person was not taken into the order of penitents within the congregation, but was first cast out of the congregation, out of the church. The drama was striking.

In regard to the reconciliation on Holy Thursday, the texts were the same ones known from the *Gelasianum* except for a few additions. As a counterpart to the ejection from the church, one finds now a procession in which the reconciled penitents were brought hand in hand into the church and, accompanied by prayer, were received again into the community.

This penitential practice, which we have just described relying upon the sources, fell into disuse for the following reasons. First, there was the severity of the practice, a severity from which everyone recoiled. Second, there was the growing conviction that every person is sinful and must do penance. As a result the ashes came to be placed on the foreheads of all those present on Ash Wednesday, since all were sinners. Moreover, a way was found by which this guilt could be expressed in private rather than in public, and it was the Irish monks who found this way.

PRIVATE PENANCE

Private penance was introduced into the Frankish-German church by the monks, and it engendered both great resistance and great approval. The totally new thing about this practice was that all who were aware of their sinfulness could receive forgiveness as often as they wished, and not, as formerly, just once in their lives. The sinner came to a priest (not only to a bishop, as in public penance), confessed his or her sins, and received an assigned penance (fasting and almsgiving) according to fixed rules (tariffs). It was understood that the forgiveness was bestowed by God as the penance assigned by the priest was completed. The whole process was private and secret, between penitent and priest. There was no order of penitents, no communal prayer of the congregation for the penitents, no liturgy of penance, but rather a privatized acknowledgment of sin and assignment of penance: confession. The goal? "In the texts we can see that often penance is thought of not as penalty justly due but as medicine for the malady of sin and for the restoration of moral health and social acceptance" (J. McNeill, *The Celtic Churches*, Chicago, 1974, p. 84).

It is difficult to imagine how radical this change was. Besides the secret and private character, the new thing in penitential practice was the "taxation" of sin, described with great color and detail! For each fault there was a precisely described penance. The origin of all of this must be sought in the (Irish) monastic environment, where we also find the first "penitentials" (mid-sixth century). These penance books were brought into northern Europe by the Anglo-Saxon monks. Pastorally, of course, this renewal was of considerable significance since many sinners who could not or dared not undertake public penance now could receive forgiveness through personal penance.

Public penance and private confession battled for the favor of the members of the church during Carolingian times. The hierarchy demanded public penance; the people asked for confession. It is understandable that most local pastors began to follow the latter practice. Initially public penance would still be required for great public sins, but for great secret sins confession was permitted. It was simply a matter of course that the practice of confession finally won the day, totally vanquishing public penance.

Ordinations

The development in the orders of service for ordaining bishops, priests (presbyters), and deacons was not slight. Here we will give the sources and major traits of the liturgies. The most important sources are the following:

The sacramentaries: *Gelasianum Vetus* (ed. Mohlberg, 23–29, 115–128); *Gregorianum* (ed. Lietzmann, 5–9);

Missale Francorum (ed. Mohlberg, 3ff.) and the *Statua Ecclesiae Antiqua* (ed. Ch. Munier, 75–100). The *Missale Francorum* gives the old Gallican practices that were influenced by those of Rome;

The *Gelasiana Saeculi Octavi*;

Ordines Romani XXXIV–XXXIX (ed. Andrieu, III); XXXIV gives the pure Roman order of service;

The *Pontificale Romano-germanicum* (ed. Vogel-Elze, I, 20ff.): a summary of Roman-Gallic practices.

Most of the sources show a mixture of Roman elements and Frankish-German customs. The consequence was that the characteristic sobriety and transparency of the Roman order of service disappeared, having been forced to yield to a more "dramatic" ritual. The Frankish-German additions were thus related to or were an expression of the spirit that we have already described.

The old central rite, the laying on of hands, continued to be practiced, as did also the old ordination prayer. But there was the tendency no longer to regard the laying on of hands with prayer as the central action, but to find that centrality rather in the handing over of the vestments and *instrumenta* that went with the office (e.g., the chasuble, the paten, and the chalice at the ordination of a presbyter; the stole (*orarium*) and the gospel book at that of a deacon). According to the Germanic conception, this handing over (*traditio*) of the tokens of honor and of the "uniform" signified the handing over of the office itself (cf. *Sacr. Angoulême* 150). In the old Roman rite, however, the conveyance (or investiture) was a simple rite before the ordination itself.

Still more important was the anointing of the priest's hands, which was probably of Irish or Anglo-Saxon origin, supported by Old Testament texts. This anointing indicates how all-important and sacral the presidency in the eucharist had become—for it was for the sake of the eucharist that the anointing took place. The bishop was anointed on forehead and hands (high priest!), the priest only on the hands.

Finally we should note that the Frankish-German books contained prayers from very different traditions; there are two invitations to the congregation to pray, two ordination prayers, two texts for the presentation of the candidate (which contradict each other). One cannot therefore speak of an optimal ritual. Nonetheless it was this ordination ritual, once again expanded in the twelfth century, that lasted for centuries.

Liturgy at Death

We note here the especially interesting *Ordo Romanus* XLIX, a document in which the old Christian view of death still echoes and one that apparently functioned as a model in the north.

The *Ordo* mentions *viaticum*, the communion for the dying, given as pledge of participation in the resurrection of the Lord. During the time of dying, the passion account of the Lord was read and at the moment of death there was the famous text, still in use:

| Subvenite sancti Dei . . . | Come, saints of God . . . may Christ |
| suscipiat te Christus | receive you. |

This was used together with the exodus psalm 114. The dead person was brought to the church accompanied by the antiphon:

In paradiso Dei ducant te	May the angels lead you into paradise
angeli . . . perducant te	. . . may they lead you into Jerusalem,
in civitatem sanctam	the holy city.
Hierusalem.	

There a wake was held and the burial followed.

Both the reality of death and suffering as well as trust for the future with the Lord are expressed. Once again it is apparent how remarkably right the old texts for worship can be.

CONCLUSION

This chapter has described the western form of worship resulting from the mixing of the old Roman urban liturgy with Frankish-German customs and mentality. This liturgy was connected with the growing western civilization that itself was also a confluence of different cultural streams. To call this liturgy "Roman" is a simplification of the matter. Certainly western worship is built on the solid foundations of Roman forms and prayers. These foundations were in fact so solid that they were able to bear the superstructure erected by the Carolingians and the Ottonians.

Chapter Four

Toward a Uniform Roman Liturgy:
From Gregory VII to the Council of Trent (1545–1563)

The center of gravity in the western liturgy, as became apparent in chapter 3, lay in the period from the sixth to the tenth centuries, during which that liturgy was formed through a mingling of both urban Roman and Frankish-German elements. That is not to say, however, that development of Christian worship in the west was now at an end. The Middle Ages added special theological and devotional elements; the Ottonian liturgy was changed, abbreviated, and systematized. In this chapter we wish to describe this "Roman" liturgy ultimately codified by the Council of Trent that became uniform throughout the entire west. Since it is the development of public worship in the west that is to be described, only indirect attention can be given to the piety of the faithful that, in fact, came more and more to be disengaged from the liturgy.

I. HISTORICAL DATA

Literature

C. H. Haskins, *The Renaissance of the Twelfth Century* (Cambridge, Mass., 1928).

E. L. Ladurie, *Montaillou; The Promised Land of Error* (New York, 1978).

A. Mirgeler, *Geschichte Europas* (Freiburg, 1964).

C. Morris, *The Discovery of the Individual* (London, 1972).

R. W. Southern, *Western Society and the Church in the Middle Ages*, Pelican History of the Church, vol. 2 (London, 1970).

A. GENERAL HISTORICAL SETTING

"The social and religious order . . . showed little sign of breaking up in the year 1050. Whether we look at western Europe's general economic condition, its religious ideals, its forms of government, or its ritual processes, there is little to suggest that a great change was at hand. And yet within the next sixty or seventy years the outlook had changed in almost every respect. The secular ruler had been demoted from his position of quasi-sacerdotal splendour, the pope had assumed a new power of intervention and direction in both spiritual and secular affairs, the Benedictine rule had lost its monopoly in the religious life, an entirely new impulse had been given to law and theology, and several important steps had been taken toward understanding and even controlling the physical world. The expansion of Europe had begun in earnest. That all this should have happened in so short a time is the most remarkable fact in medieval history" (Southern, p. 34).

There was a great economic development that reached a high point in the twelfth and thirteenth centuries. The cities came to new life, trade improved, transportation over better roads and rivers was possible, agriculture was stimulated by new methods, credit and the market blossomed. Wealth and possessions increased and the aristocracy was confronted with a new class in society. The ordinary person changed, no longer a slave to the landholder or to the church. The "supernatural" had less appeal because of the growing thirst for intellectual exploration: people wanted to understand. Indeed *ratio* determined the views of the time and sought out new ways of improving life. But there was also a growth of charismatic movements intended to protect religious values and human emotionality. Most likely various expressions of piety also formed a counterweight to the rational stream in society and church.

To sketch the church in the Middle Ages in a few lines is not possible and would do injustice to the rich variations in the life of faith in those days. But one point, important for the development of worship, should be made. The word "church" in this period must more and more be translated as "hierarchy." Hierarchy meant a definite ordering from high to low. The higher a person rose in the hierarchy, the greater his prestige, authority, and power. The highest authority was invested in the pope who was assisted by his "curia," his court. The pope's authority was greatly increased as a result of the investiture controversy and was maintained for a long time— until the fourteenth century when the French kings began to dominate the popes in Avignon. The pope ruled the church, and to achieve this highest goal, maintaining the *societas perfecta*, he made use of secular authorities. That the church thereby became very active in power politics was not considered disturbing, for everything was regarded as directed toward the honor of God and his church. There emerged from this leadership of the popes a great *élan* and a profound stimulation of churchly life, even though there was always the danger of secularization.

Only from the fourteenth century on did the popes pull back into the ecclesiastical citadel that they then anxiously defended. They demanded their rights in the face of both the secular authorities and the heretical movements. The popes felt it necessary to defend the inviolability of their authority, yet they did it without sufficiently attending to what it was exactly that they were proposing to do with their authority. The church was seen as static, as a fortress to be defended; every form of critical reflection was interpreted as faithlessness to the divinely instituted papal authority. These attitudes marked a period of decline for the church, characterized by the fact that the ecclesiastical pyramid had become top-heavy.

The bishops and the clergy also participated in the authority of the pope, albeit on a correspondingly lower rung of the hierarchical ladder. The tendency to clericalization continued at a quickened pace during this time. The supervision and daily leadership of local churches were in the hands of the clergy. From the countless and populous monasteries went out many of the monks to participate in church life. Thus the clerical costume became the *imago* of the church.

In addition we should mention the continuing power of attraction exercised by the city of Rome, the city of the pope who defended the status of the church against the state and who, with the support of the bishops, employed worship as a sign of unity. Yet we still cannot speak of genuine centralization at this period.

What is clear is that ecclesiastical hierarchy was of decisive importance during the Middle Ages, even in the liturgy. The faithful were reduced to onlookers; their piety had little to do with the "official" worship, but expressed itself in its own way. The liturgy of the hierarchy had difficulty in assimilating popular piety into itself, and the people's liturgy never again became genuine ecclesiastical liturgy.

The laity were excluded from the hierarchy, but that is not to say that they remained without influence on ecclesial life. Again and again there arose in the Middle Ages movements of more or less charismatic character that intended to carry out sweeping changes and make a thoroughgoing renewal of the church, all of which did give a new impulse to Christian piety. Frequently these movements came into conflict with the church, or else they came to be absorbed into the hierarchical scheme of things. There then remained only the wait for the next reform movement in which the same process would be repeated. These movements time and again pointed the church toward the evangelical foundation on which it was built: following the Lord, standing with the poor and the outcasts of society, waiting for the coming kingdom of justice. One thinks here of the "little brothers" of Francis, of the Friars Preachers, of the cathari, of the brothers of the *Devotio Moderna*, and of so many other movements, orthodox and heretical, in this turbulent period. It is to be noted, however, that a direct influence of the lay movements on worship is not demonstrable. Liturgy was apparently carefully protected by the many ordained officeholders. What the Franciscans did do, as faithful sons of the church of Rome, was to spread the curial liturgy throughout the west, as we shall see below.

B. "SYSTEMATIC COMPLETENESS"

The period before us was especially characterized by a certain "systematic completeness" that was attained step by step with staggering logic. Life was conceived as taking place within a coherent juridical and theological system. Under the great popes Gregory VII, Innocent III, Innocent IV, and Boniface VIII, canon law reached a high point: the code elaborated a tight, precisely worked out governmental system in which everything fitted together. Church life was confined within narrow and detailed rules. Moreover the period was characterized by theological thought that designed an all-inclusive system in which human dignity and human relationship to God were central. After about 1350, however, there was a marked decline in both canon law and theology; creativity broke down and gave way to imitation by epigones.

The stable structure of church and society and the great heights of spirituality were without doubt due to the church, not to the secular powers, who were engaged in life and death struggles (the Hundred Years War) and who were exhausting the resources of their countries.

C. MONASTICISM

The monks and monastic culture have given to the face of the west and the western church certain characteristic features. The Carolingian revival, the Ottonian renewal, the all-embracing spirit of Cluny are pillars on which rest the church in the west. Scholarship grew in the monasteries; counsel for kings and popes came from behind monastery walls; the liturgy blossomed into splendid services of worship in the tightly ordered, hierarchically ruled cloistered communities, which arose in order to give prayer a central place, but which did not always persevere in that life of prayer!

It is important to note that from the middle of the twelfth century on, the influence of the Benedictine monks of Cluny quickly decreased. This came about partly because of internal deterioration, denounced by Bernard of Clairvaux, and partly because of the evolution of the universities, which were not tied to the monasteries but took part in the tumultuous city life. The monastic liturgy was drastically shortened and adapted to life outside the cloister. The monastic church yielded to the "people's church" in the parishes of villages and cities, parishes that had originated in the twelfth century.

D. SACRAMENTAL THEOLOGY

It is in this period that we find the great development in sacramental theology.

In the patristic vocabulary *sacramentum* meant "proclamation" and thus the making present of a saving event from the past by means of repeatable rites. The saving event from the past is evoked in word and sign: for the believer—who reads the sign, understands the word, and believes both sign and word—salvation is present. Since the fourth century, "sacrament" has had also a cultic significance: the ritual action itself is called "sacrament." In short, in the patristic period "sacrament" related to the signified (the mystery of salvation to which the sign refers) and to the sign itself that presents this salvation as contemporary.

In early scholasticism (Hugh of St. Victor; Peter Lombard) theological reflection developed. Now it was not so much the sign character of sacrament nor the reference to a past event of salvation that were of primary significance, but the fact that Christ instituted the ritual action, that is, the sacrament. "Sacrament" was understood in an institutional sense: it is an institution that goes back to Christ himself. From this follows the efficacy of the sacrament. This efficacy is not primarily connected to the sign character of the ritual action but to the institution by Christ. Because Christ gave the sign to the church, grace is given through the sacrament, the recipient is sanctified. A salvation-history perspective on the sacraments was weakened, just as typology yielded to allegory. Following such a line of thought, people began to speak of *ex opere operato*, of the sanctifying work that is bound to the sign that comes from Christ himself and therefore is effective. What remained as a lively conviction was the sense that something created can "signify" the spiritual: a *sacramentum* is a holy sign, in some way containing the holy.

In high scholasticism the doctrine of the sacraments was developed further, especially by the introduction of the teaching concerning "matter" and "form." A sacrament is "made up" ("confected" even) of matter (e.g., bread and wine) and the essential formula of words, both being necessary for the sacrament to be valid. This theological concept was then fixed by the jurists into precisely defined liturgical rules. From Thomas Aquinas came the synthesis (so often forgotten after him), the elucidation of the vital relationship between the efficacy of the sacrament and the faith of the recipient.

The development of the doctrine of the sacraments in the Middle Ages, which is here only briefly sketched, is reflected in the actual celebration of the sacraments during this time, especially eucharist and penance. (For a fuller discussion of sacramental theology during the Middle Ages, see E. Schillebeeckx, *Sacramentele heilseconomie*, Bilthoven, 1952.)

II. CULTURAL DATA

Literature

Atlas of Western Civilization, op. cit.

F. van der Meer, *Keerpunt der Middeleeuwen* (Utrecht, 1950).

H. Nolthenius, *Duecento; zwerftocht door Italiës late Middeleeuwen* (Utrecht, n.d.).

J. Huizinga, *The Waning of the Middle Ages* (Harmondsworth, 1965).

A. NATIONALISM

Here is how a southern poet, Cecco Angiolieri of Siena, living among the Germans in the north thought of these "barbarians": "All Germans stink. . . . Here they set the table without linen and sit with seven fellows around one tureen. They wipe their dirty fingers on their soutanes while pork grease drips from their chins" (cf. H. Nolthenius, *Duecento*, p. 19). And what would a Frenchman have written about an Englishman during the Hundred Years War? The feelings of nationality were present very early. And nationality was now to give specific accents to culture.

B. PHILOSOPHIC CONTEMPLATION
AND LYRIC INSPIRATION

"Philosophic contemplation and lyric inspiration (in piety, architecture, sculpture and poetry) are indeed the hallmarks of the XII century, one of the most creative periods in human history. . . . We can say that the era of the traditional, conservative and strictly monastic culture that leaned on the old Christian culture is at an end, and that the modern popular and lyrical—in a word, 'Gothic'— culture has begun. Further, that the symbolic and predominately Platonic conception of the world associated with the masters of the school of Chartres . . . has given way to scholasticism with its concern for concreteness, realism and cause-and-effect. After 1130 scholastic theology dominates ecclesiastical life for centuries. It is neither the Fathers nor the liturgical symbols that count, but the new teachers with their reasons and their systems" (*Atlas of Western Civilization*, p. 102).

During this same time, Bernard of Clairvaux used his sharp pen to call his fellow monks to order. He demanded simplification and austerity. In his *Apology* he puts his finger on the darker side of the spiritual elite of his time. In a long, satirical discourse against laxity, he says: "Abstemiousness is accounted miserliness, sobriety strictness, silence gloom. On the other hand, laxity is labeled discretion, extravagance generosity, talkativeness sociability, and laughter joy." Gluttony and excess in food and drink are excoriated: "When a monk gets up from the table and the swollen veins in his temple begin to throb, all he is fit for is to go back to bed. After all, if you force a man to come to the office of vigils before his digestion is complete, all you will extract from him is a groan instead of a tone." After condemning abuse of the infirmary ("Is this the way Macarius lived? Is it Basil's teaching or Anthony's command?"), fashionable and expensive clothing, and the negligence and luxury of abbots, there follows this characteristic passage on the monastic church and on the cloister:

"These are only small things; I am coming to things of greater moment. I merely mention these minor details because they happen to be rather common. I shall say nothing about the soaring heights and extravagant lengths and unnecessary widths of the churches, nothing about their expensive decorations and their novel images, which catch the attention of those who go in to pray, and dry up their devotion. To me they seem like something out of the Old Testament; but let them be, since it is all to the glory of God.

210

However as one monk to another . . . 'Tell me, O poor men,' this is my question, 'tell me, O poor men—if you really are poor men . . . why is there gold in the holy place?' It is not the same for monks and bishops. Bishops have a duty toward both wise and foolish. They have to make use of material ornamentation to rouse devotion in a carnal people, incapable of spiritual things. But we no longer belong to such people. . . . Can it be our own devotion we are trying to excite by such display, or is the purpose of it to win the admiration of fools and the offerings of simple folk? . . . Listen to the marvels of it all. It is possible to spend money in such a way that it increases; it is an investment which grows, and pouring it out only brings in more. The very sight of such sumptuous and exquisite baubles is sufficient to inspire men to make offerings, though not to say their prayers . . . oh, vanity of vanities, whose vanity is rivalled only by its insanity! The walls of the church are aglow, but the poor of the church go hungry. The stones of the church are covered with gold, while its children are left naked. The food of the poor is taken to feed the eyes of the rich. . . . What excuse can there be for these ridiculous monstrosities in the cloisters where the monks do their reading, extraordinary things at once beautiful and ugly? Here we find filthy monkeys and fierce lions, fearful centaurs, harpies, and striped tigers, soldiers at war, and hunters blowing their horns. Here is one head with many bodies, there is one body with many heads. . . . All round there is such an amazing variety of shapes that one could easily prefer to take one's reading from the walls instead of from a book. One could spend the whole day gazing fascinated at these things, one by one, instead of meditating on the law of God. Good, Lord, even if the foolishness of it all occasion no shame, at least one might balk at the expense" ("An Apology to Abbot William," 28–29; cf. 16, 21, 23 in *The Works of Bernard of Clairvaux*, vol. 1: *Treatises I*, M. B. Pennington, ed., Spencer, Mass., 1970, pp. 63–66; cf. pp. 52–53, 57, 58).

C. TOWARD THE WANING OF THE MIDDLE AGES

In the thirteenth century theology reached a high point in the works of Thomas, Albert, and Bonaventure. Both lyricism and *ratio* worked together in the gothic cathedral. There was a charismatic renewal in the manner of life in the mendicant orders; they helped to reinvigorate pastoral care by establishing themselves in the cities, in the midst of the people. Thereby the popular pathos was given full attention, but outside of the hierarchical liturgy.

The fourteenth century was "a late afternoon; the sun has passed its zenith and is moving down the sky" (*Atlas*, p. 103). There was disappointment with the pope, who had gone into exile in Avignon. The disastrous western schism began and caused Christians to wonder where their allegiance lay and to what extent the church had come under the control of the French kings. It was a century in which the plague killed a large portion of the population and the Hundred Years War infected human spirits, leaving behind failed crusades and dead-end theologies.

This all led to the "waning of the middle ages" (Huizinga). F. van der Meer writes:

"It was a disillusioned world, obsessed with the consciousness of its own decline. . . . After 1400 very few believed any more in the ideals of the knight or the mendicant friar, and they no longer dreamed of an angelic Pope or of a great Christian Emperor comparable to Charlemagne. No one was any longer contented with society, the Church, or himself. What was worse, men felt the grotesque hollowness of almost all existing institutions and conventions, and this over-intense reaction to life expressed itself in exasperated violence or in torturous sophistication. . . . Time and again it is obvious that the two poles of medieval society, Pope and Emperor, are no longer a stabilizing force. . . . 'Christendom,' that sublime illusion, had ceased to exist, and became divided into separate nations each trying to get rich at the expense of others. . . . Monstrous scandals, peaceful devotion and solitary saints mark the religious life of the XVth century. Christianity has received the gift of tears, for it is the period of Pietàs and of the Man of Sorrows. . . . There are no great theologians any more, for theology is also on the wane" (*Atlas*, p. 116).

III. THE LITURGY: ORDERS OF SERVICE AND TEXTS

Literature

L. Braeckmans, *Confession et communion au moyen âge et au concile de Trente* (Gembloux, 1971).

P. Browe, *Die Verehrung der Eucharistie im Mittelalter* (Munich, 1933).

F. Clark, *Eucharistic Sacrifice and the Reformation* (Oxford, 1967).

E. Dumoutet, *Le Christ selon la chair et la vie liturgique au moyen âge* (Paris, 1932).

————, *Le désir de voir l'hostie et les origines de la dévotion au Saint Sacrement* (Paris, 1926).

A. Franz, *Die Messe in deutschen Mittelalter* (Freiburg, 1902).

F. Hannerl, *Mittelalterliche Frömmigkeit im Spiegel der Gebetbuch-literatur Süddeutschlands* (Munich, 1954).

P. Jounel, *Le culte des saints dans les basiliques de Latran et du Vatican au douzième siècle* (Rome, 1977).

V. L. Kennedy, "The Moment of Consecration and the Elevation of the Host," *Medieval Studies* 6, 1944, pp. 121–150.

A. Mayer, *Die Liturgie in der Europäischen Geistesgeschichte* (Darmstadt, 1971).

J. B. Molin & P. Mutembe, *Le rituel du mariage en France du XIIe au XVIe siècle* (Paris, 1974).

A. Stenzel, *Die Taufe* (Innsbruck, 1958).

R. Theisen, *Mass Liturgy and the Council of Trent* (Collegeville, 1965).

S. van Dijk & J. Hazelden Walker, *The Origins of the Modern Roman Liturgy: The Liturgy of the Papal Court and the Franciscan Order in the Thirteenth Century* (London, 1960).

L. Veit, *Volksfrommes Brauchtum und Kirche im deutschen Mittelalter, ein Durchblick* (Freiburg, 1936).

R. Zerfasz, *Der Streit um die Laienpredigt* (Freiburg, 1974).

A. GENERAL DESCRIPTION

From very early times there had been a distinction in the city of Rome between the liturgy of the *tituli* and the celebrations in which the pope presided. On account of the large number of churches, the pope had to delegate liturgical leadership to his clergy. But he remained united with his diocese by himself leading the services on certain days of the year in predetermined churches of the city. It goes without saying that because of the status of the pope the pilgrims to Rome gave much more attention to the papal celebrations, and it was these they attempted to copy, as we described in chapter 3.

In that same chapter it was pointed out that in the tenth century the Ottonians restored order in the midst of unimaginable chaos in the church at Rome. And they introduced into the city the Roman-Frankish-German liturgy. There was certainly resistance, especially from the canons of the Lateran and of St. Peter who desired to maintain the old Roman customs (and for a long time succeeded in doing so), but nonetheless there was general acceptance of the restored order. Those who complained about it did so only because it was the work of "Teutons." During the investiture controversy this became a tainted word. Since Gregory VII, people preferred to speak of the "classical Roman liturgy," but this classical liturgy was in fact nothing other than the mixture of both old Roman and Frankish material together with a Germanic spirit. Once again during this period this mixed liturgy was given a Roman cast, and this we mean to describe in the present chapter.

1. THE ROMAN CURIA

Beginning in the eleventh century and especially in the twelfth, the popes began to withdraw from direct pastoral work in the city: people began to speak of the "papal court," the *curia romana*," in the midst of which the pope lived and from which he received advice on policy. Soon the pope and his court began to go their own way, free from the local church of Rome because, it could be said, the pope had responsibility for all the churches! This meant in fact that the papal Curia began to identify itself more and more with *the* church, that is, not the local church but the universal church, of which the pope was the head, the vicar of the Lord. *Curia romana* came to mean *ecclesia romana*, that is, the pope, the head of the hierarchy, surrounded by his clerical court.

Along with having a court, the pope also had his own chapel, where he celebrated the liturgy isolated and closed off from the clergy and faithful of the city. This was especially the case with daily prayer (the breviary) and the eucharist, which was celebrated by the pope himself or by one of his court dignitaries (a bishop without diocese or a priest) in his presence. The celebration of eucharist by the pope with his clergy and all the faithful (the stational liturgy) gave way to the celebration of the pope with his court. Of Pope Leo IX (1048–1054) it is known that he prayed the liturgy of the hours together with an assistant in his private chapel, *Sancta Sanctorum*, part of the complex of the Lateran. For this papal liturgy special books were now assembled: a missal and a breviary in which all the orders of service and texts were gathered and conveniently arranged as concisely as possible. This meant that the "Ottonian liturgy" was now adapted to the papal liturgical requirements.

One of the most important popes of this period is Innocent III (1198–1216), "the supreme example of the man who sees the world in the clear-cut facts, readily recognizes all possibilities and knows his course of action" (van Dijk, *The Origins of the Modern Roman*

214

Liturgy, p. 91). He brought order to Rome on both the spiritual and economic planes; he renewed the liturgy; he fostered a simple style in life as well as in worship. It was under his leadership that the important Fourth Lateran Council (1215) took place, which among other things required the clergy to study theology, to pray the liturgy of the hours every day, and to be responsible for the cleanliness of the church buildings; made stipulations regarding annual confession and the Easter communion; and used the term "transsubstantiation" officially for the first time. This council was a "resplendent" confirmation of the spiritual power of the pope in the Middle Ages.

Innocent III had a book compiled that was very important for the future of worship: an *Ordinale* in which the organization and the course of the liturgy of the hours was clearly described in precise rubrics. This "ordinary" for daily prayer was quickly followed by a prayer book that included the prayers, the readings, the psalms and antiphons, and the responsaries together with the rubrics arranged systematically following the course of the year. Under Pope Honorius III (1216–1227) a book similar to the above was produced, but this time it was designed for the daily celebration of the eucharist in the papal chapel.

The later liturgical books of the Council of Trent are in fact derived from these liturgical books of the papal court. They contain the Roman-Frankish-German liturgy, but now much abbreviated and reorganized.

2. THE FRANCISCANS

Francis of Assisi and his followers were of considerable significance for the evolution of the western liturgy in the Middle Ages and thereafter, as the late S. van Dijk pointed out (see literature list above). The ideal of the little brothers was pastoral care, standing up for the outcasts of society. The friars lived amidst the turmoil of the cities and shared the poverty of the masses. It is no surprise that the monastic liturgy of the hours and the solemn celebration of the eucharist in the monasteries were not practical for these pastoral workers. Their churches called for orders of service more appropriate to their life.

They found the books they needed in the cathedral of Assisi, where the bishop had given his canons special liturgical books with short, sober, and intelligible offices for each day. They were in fact the books of the papal court: the breviary of Innocent III and the missal of Honorius III. This shows how widely the influence of papal chapel liturgy had been extended. Visiting bishops took copies of the papal books home to their dioceses. These books of the papal Curia were made obligatory for the Franciscans by the Rule of 1230. From the so-called *Regula* editions of missal and breviary, the papal liturgical books can be reconstructed.

Nonetheless even these papal books, no matter how enthusiastically they were adopted, were not suited to worship in the poorer and less-educated areas. The difference between the papal palace and the church in the slums was too great. The fourth general of the Franciscans, Haymo of Faversham (from Kent; died in Anagni in 1244), a practical and clear-thinking Englishman (cf. van Dijk, *The Origins of the Roman Liturgy*, pp. 280ff.), adapted the books. In the first place he gave, in *Indutus planeta* (1242), a description of the celebration of mass (based on an older document, the so-called *Paratus*; van Dijk, *The Origins*, pp. 248–253), and thereafter he published rubrics for the breviary and missal (1243, 1244).

These revised books, which still had about them the aura of the Roman Curia, soon spread throughout all of Europe. Here and there they were repeatedly changed and retouched to reflect local customs. Every diocese added texts, but fundamentally they remained recognizable as books of the papal Curia. What this meant was that the liturgy of the papal chapel, and not the old Roman stational service, became the model for liturgical celebration in Europe.

The western evolution thus proceeded along this route: the old urban Roman liturgy (principally the papal *statio* celebration) was imported among the Franks and there mixed with Frankish usages and Germanic ideas. This material was organized by "Ottonian" bishops and monks and imposed by the emperor. It was adopted reluctantly by the popes but then it was subsequently much abbreviated and systematized. The Franciscans took this liturgy of the papal chapel along with them, passing it on and spreading it throughout Europe, so that finally the moment came when one could speak of a unified western liturgy.

3. THE COUNCIL OF TRENT

There were repeated efforts at restoration and renewal both in church life and in worship during the Middle Ages. Gregory VII effected the "Gregorian reform," which promoted the integrity of the clergy through celibacy and common life, as well as promoted the authority of the pope and the "old Roman tradition." Innocent III renewed worship, on the basis of the "tradition of the apostolic see," and church life, through the work of the Fourth Lateran Council. The great scholastic, theologians who reacted against the *deliramenta* ("ravings") of the allegorical method used to explain the mass rites, determined to give a solid foundation to eucharistic faith. The Franciscans brought a new charisma and *élan* to pastoral care and adapted the liturgy to pastoral needs. The Fifth Lateran Council (1513) took place against the background of a program for renewal presented to Pope Leo X by Paolo Giustiniani and Pietro Quirini in which very precise proposals were made for improving the lamentable conditions in the church. The *Liber sacerdotalis* of Castellani (1523) was directly connected to this program and tried to bring about a changed mentality.

These movements are indicative of a precarious decline in both church life and worship, of ecclesiastical abuses, of loss of charism and overemphasis on the institutional aspect of the church. The decline in medieval worship must first of all be laid to clericalization and the related individualizing of the piety of the faithful, a piety that grew apart from the liturgy and covered church life with a thick layer of peripheral phenomena. The Council of Trent itself, falling at the end of the Middle Ages and in the time of the Renaissance, is to be considered one of the attempts at renewal in the life and teaching of the church. *Renewal* in this case meant primarily *restoration.*

The waning of the Middle Ages clearly had affected ecclesiastical life. To all appearances the church was flourishing: the whole society was pervaded by the liturgy of the church, but this liturgy was marked by an excess of feasts, by popular customs, and by details and superstitious practices that overlaid the heart of the faith. There were excesses in the cult of the saints, in indulgences, in the concern for personal salvation, in devotion to the Madonna and to the Blessed Sacrament. On the other hand there was the Reformation appealing to holy scripture and to evangelical freedom over against the traditions of the church (see chapter 6). The reaction against the Reformation came to mean that all effort at renewal was regarded with suspicion and was rejected. As a result only the reforms inaugurated by the Council of Trent were given legitimacy. The council took an important step and restored order, but its restorative character and its desire to maintain the old have in the long run seemed to be too powerful and inflexible. Thus a certain dynamism disappeared and with it also the tendency toward more radical renewal. The Council of Trent came to be too highly regarded as the ultimate norm.

The liturgy of the church was given ample attention in the decrees of the council. Whenever fundamentals are discussed, such as the relationship of scripture and tradition or the doctrine of justification, the theology of the sacraments is also involved. A sacrament is seen by the council as the instrument of God's distribution of grace to the believer by way of the church—that is, the hierarchy—that administers it; hence the importance of the objective and valid performance of the sign by the church. The faith of the participants is, to be sure, not forgotten but is given less attention; the office of the ordained minister of the church and the church's uniform liturgy are the salient things here. This meant that the council by no means called a halt to the process of clericalization. On the other hand, the council did put brakes on the subjectivization of the liturgy. In the long run the most obvious disadvantage that accrued from the work of the council would appear to be ritualism or "validism," the delusion about validity. The council rightly wanted to protect the "tradition," that is, *the given*, the gift of God by way of God's church, but the celebration of that gift was made too tightly and uniformly regulated.

The council took great pains to restore order to the chaotic life of the church. Centralization was not the purpose of this work but the preservation of the ecclesiastical traditions in which could be seen the guidance of the Holy Spirit. Every change in these traditions, as well as in the liturgical traditions, was regarded as an attack upon the life of the church and as faithlessness to what had been handed on under the inspiration of the Holy Spirit. By a somewhat strange application of this principle, the use of the vernacular was rejected and Latin was made obligatory, for Latin belonged to the tradition of the church. What is more, one could not simply change the rites of the church; that was reserved to the authority that alone stood as guarantor of the church's bond with tradition. It is this notion of tradition that also was behind the decision of the council to revise the liturgical books and, with the full authority of the Apostolic See, to disseminate them throughout the church in the west so that the perpetuation of the tradition could once again be guaranteed. Unity would become uniformity as this principle came to be further elaborated by jurists and rubricists.

Trent signified the termination of the development of worship according to the western rite. It brought about order, stability, objectivity, uniformity—virtues that have done the church much good but which, in later centuries, could come to be oppressive.

218

B. SOURCES

1. INDIRECT SOURCES
The following books are of significance for the liturgy:

Bernold of Constance, *Micrologus*, written about 1090, underscored the reform under Pope Gregory VII, and leaned on the old Roman tradition (PL 151, 579);

Ivo of Chartres, *Sermones de ecclesiasticis sacramentis* (c. 1100; PL 162, 505);

Rupert of Deutz, *De divinis officiis* (PL 170, 9);

Hugh of St. Victor (d. 1141), *De sacramentis*, a remarkable resource both for sacramental theology and for insight into the twelfth-century liturgy of the Victorines at Paris (PL 176, 41; English translation: *On the Sacraments of the Christian Faith*, R. Deferrari, trans., Cambridge, Mass., 1951);

John Beleth, *Rationale divinorum officiorum* (PL 202, 9);

Innocent III, *De sacrificio missae* (PL 217, 763);

Durandus (1237–1296), *Rationale divinorum officiorum* (ed. Ch. Barthélémy, Paris, 1854), a work that enjoyed great popularity and wide distribution (43 editions before 1500!). As bishop, Durandus, a widely read man and a canonist of the school of Bologna, wanted to instruct his clergy in the significance of the liturgical rites that they carried out. The book is an extensive work that marks the high point of the allegorical interpretation of the liturgy in the Middle Ages.

2. DIRECT SOURCES
See S. van Dijk, *The Ordinal of the Papal Court from Innocent III to Boniface VIII* (Freiburg, 1975); and S. van Dijk, *Sources of the Modern Roman Liturgy*, 2 vols. (Leiden, 1963). Here we will limit ourselves to the history of the official Roman liturgical books. But there is even more that could be done. The multitudinous local or regional adaptations are being sought out in cathedral libraries, but this research is not yet completed. An example of systematic research in this vein is the study by Molin and Mutembe (see the literature list on p. 213 above) on the marriage ritual in France from the twelfth to the sixteenth centuries. The same could be done for baptism or the anointing of the sick or penance. Then we might be able to form a picture of local or diocesan pastoral care and the place of the liturgy therein.

The Missale Romanum

This book is the incorporation of several books into one for the use of the president, called the "celebrant," the one ordained to this office. For any given Sunday, weekday, or feast day, the appointed prayers, readings, and song-texts are placed together in a so-called "mass formulary." To that are added directions for performance of the rites (rubrics), together with the unchangeable parts of every celebration of the eucharist. The mass formularies are arranged, first of all in the *temporale* (proper of the temporal cycle for Sundays and weekdays) and then in the *sanctorale* (the feasts of the Mother of God and the saints) and then, third, in the "common formularies" and "formularies for special occasions," the so-called votive masses. This is the division of the material in the *Missale Romanum* of 1570.

The direct predecessors of the *Missale Romanum* were the *missal for the Curia* of Honorius III (1216–1227) and the *Regula Missal* of the Franciscans. The *Missale Romanum* is the principal book of the Roman-western rite for the celebration of the eucharist.

The Pontificale

This is the book in which all celebrations are described (excluding the eucharist) in which the bishop presides, such as ordinations, the consecration of churches, etc. It is divided into three parts—consecrations of persons, consecrations of things, and *varia*. The history of this book has been fully described by M. Andrieu, *Le pontifical romain au moyen âge*, 4 vols. (Rome, 1938, 1940, 1941).

In the twelfth century the "Ottonian" pontifical (see pp. 161–162) was edited, abbreviated, and adapted to the court chapel of the pope. Best known to us is the *Pontificale of Apamea*. In the thirteenth century these followed yet another reworking under Pope Innocent III, and this Roman exemplar was quickly disseminated. Shortly thereafter came Durandus of Mende (see under "Indirect Sources," p. 219) with a new recension of the pontifical in which he included local practices. It was he who created the division into three parts we have just described. The pontifical of Durandus was of decisive influence. It was adapted and reworked by Piccolomini and Burckard (1487), the papal ceremonialists. There then followed editions in 1497 and 1520 (Castellani), until in 1596 the official *Pontificale Romanum* that had been proposed by the Council of Trent was published (Clement VIII).

The Ceremoniale Episcoporum

A rubric book for the liturgy in cathedrals. The first edition was in the year 1600 (Clement VIII).

The Breviarium Romanum

The breviary, containing the hours for each day of the year, consists of calendar and rubrics, the psalter divided over the seven days of the week, the changeable texts for Sundays and weekdays (temporal cycle), the changeable texts for the festivals of the saints (sanctoral cycle), and several additions (texts of prayers in honor of the Mother of God, hours of prayer for the dead, etc.).

The edition approved by the Council of Trent appeared in 1568 (Pius V): *Breviarium Romanum*. Small changes may be found in the succeeding editions: 1602, 1632. A radical change in the praying of the psalms took place in the 1914 edition: the old *cursus*, which went back to the seventh century, was abandoned for pastoral reasons.

The breviary too is the incorporation into one book of the several books that anciently had been used for the hours (as is still the usage in the east). The most important of these was the *psalterium* wherein in addition to the 150 psalms there were collected the psalm prayers (*collectae*) for concluding the psalms, the biblical canticles, and several hymns. The psalms were distributed among the hours of the week (initially by a sign placed by each psalm indicating when it should be prayed, later by arrangement in precise order according to the day). Along with the psalms, the antiphons, and responsories (originally song texts) came to be added. The breviary originated in an ambience of the renewal of the clergy; the Fourth Lateran Council, for example, stipulated the liturgy of the hours as part of the daily office of priests (canon 17). On the basis of this principle Pope Innocent III had an *ordinarius* compiled for his chapel—an ordinary for the daily liturgy of the hours. This *ordinarius* was adopted by the Franciscans and then revised by Haymo of Faversham in 1243–1244 (cf. S. van Dijk, *Sources of the Modern Roman Liturgy*). This last reworking was again adopted by the papal court and so became the source of the forementioned *Breviarium Romanum*. We must forego a discussion of many details. Only it should be noted that up to the twelfth century a great creativity marked the liturgy of the hours, especially in prayers, antiphons, and responses. Later when a manageable book was called for, there had to be an abbreviation, leaving out much that had been created. In the manuscripts, therefore, there is much more material to be found than in either the curial or Franciscan breviaries.

The Rituale Romanum

This book was used by the priest-celebrant at the celebration of the sacraments other than the eucharist (see *Missale*) and the liturgy of the hours (see *Breviarium*). The ritual contains prayers and rubrics together with pastoral comments for the celebration of baptism, penance, anointing of the sick, marriage, and death. Moreover there are numerous blessings.

While the missal and the breviary exemplify the high points of the church's worship and thus were regarded as more inviolable and exempt from local changes, the content of the *Rituale* was more open to change and local adaptations; it was less a universal book and more accommodated to pastoral care in the local church. This was even true of the time after the Council of Trent. It is significant that the renewal of the Roman liturgy in the twentieth century began in the rites of the *Rituale*.

In regard to the history of the *Rituale*, here again we see a collation together of material from several originally independent liturgical books. Early beginnings can be found perhaps in the eighth century, while from the ninth century we know of monastic excerpts from the great books. *Ritualia* for pastors date from the twelfth century. Later these *ritualia* were made obligatory for priests. A precise study of the highly diversified material in these books has only just begun.

Unity (not uniformity) in the *Rituale* came about only with the publication (with papal approval) and general distribution of the *Sacerdotale* of Castellani in 1523. After the Council of Trent this book was used by many bishops in the compilation of their own diocesan *ritualia* which, in turn, strongly contributed to the renewal of church life. But there was to be a long wait for that *Rituale* which, according to the spirit of the Council of Trent, was to be finally authoritative for the whole church. In 1575 such an edition was attempted (by Santorius), but the actual appearance of the *Rituale Romanum* came about only in 1614 (Paul V), though diocesan or regional *ritualia* could adapt the Roman book according to local needs.

The Ordinale

For a knowledge of medieval liturgy the *ordinalia* are of great signifi-cance, but a study of them has in recent decades been rather neglected. They were, to be sure, not official or strictly liturgical books. An *ordinale* (*liber ordinarius*) is a handbook for worship in which the course of the various liturgical celebrations in a monastery, a cathedral, or a collegiate church is described. By means of it one can, therefore, trace something of the evolution of worship in the tradition of a local church. Publication of the Benedictine *ordinalia* has begun in the series *Corpus consuetudinum monasticarum*. Several *ordinalia* have also been published by the Henry Bradshaw Society.

C. SUMMARIES OF THE LITURGICAL DATA

1. DAILY PRAYER

The Breviary
The ordering of the *vita canonica* for the secular clergy had no abiding success. For all kinds of reasons the clergy came to forsake the solemnity of the daily prayer in the church and to pray the office in small groups. That is possibly the reason why the breviary was successful. Pope Innocent III ordered the first codification of the liturgy of the hours. This was the beginning of that breviary tradition in the western church that was so widely disseminated by the Franciscans. This curial office slowly replaced the old Roman tradition, especially that of St. Peter's. What was the consequence of this abbreviated prayerbook? Because it was short and practical, it could easily be used by those who had to attend to their daily pastoral work, and it opened the door for the practice of private recitation. This practice was strongly stimulated by the advent of printing, with the resultant proliferation of books.

For the tenor and substance of the breviary one must refer to the book itself. It was an anthology out of a long tradition of prayer, still monastic in character but reduced to the medieval clergyman's need.

Popular Prayer
The evolution of the practice of prayer among the faithful in the Middle Ages must, in distinction to previous periods, be discussed separately. We refer to J. Jungmann, *Christian Prayer through the Centuries* (New York, 1978).

What is striking here is the emphasis on the concrete, especially in regard to events in the life of Jesus and their foreshadowings in the Old Testament. These events were graphically depicted and presented for meditation. People began to linger over, to meditate upon Jesus' life, which was so vividly portrayed. Such meditation, centered upon the cross and the passion of the Lord, was intended to lead the believer to share in Jesus' sufferings (Bernard, Francis). Just as important was the depiction of the birth of Jesus, which had a strong spiritual and emotional appeal. Along with this came the evolution in devotion to Mary: the "little office" of the Blessed Virgin was added to the liturgy of the hours. Marian hymns became popular as did litanies (among others the famous litany of Loreto). The Hail Mary originated at the end of the eleventh century, along with the *Salve Regina* and various antiphons. The best known popular prayer, based upon a repetition of the same texts, was the rosary, a replacement of the praying of the psalms, an oral prayer intended to stimulate spiritual meditation. Finally we should mention devotion to the saints, bearing witness as it does to a fertile imagination, in which relics played a great role. See further in *Lexicon der christlichen Ikonographie*, vol. 3, cols. 181–198, 212–233, 568–572, and vols. 5–8 passim.

This evolution had two sides. On the one hand, it is apparent that in spite of the clericalization of worship, popular piety continued to seek ways of expression. The faithful wanted to be interiorly affected, involved with heart and mind in the mystery of God's grace. This interior participation reached a high point in the *Devotio Moderna* (Thomas à Kempis). The mystery of God did not pass the faithful by—the whole social life of the Middle Ages was saturated with it. Moreover, further study would show that this piety was profoundly based on the scripture: people meditated upon the saving deeds of God made clear and illustrated on human scale. This posed problems, but the Bible was an open book, even for those who could not or might not read it. Unfortunately, the clergy did not satisfy the need for basing the daily prayer of the people on a sound foundation of biblical theology. Piety became overgrown with allegory and a kind of magic. This all calls into question the influence of preaching in those days. Was there inadequate knowledge on the part of the clergy? In any case there was undoubtedly a popular alienation from the genuine liturgy of the church.

"Popular piety lived more at a surface level than at the center of the gospel message. It was threatened more than in former times by superstitious practices shown particularly in an excessive trust in relics, in the punctilious performance of a set number of devotional practices and in the gaining of indulgences. . . . The tendency to dwell on the periphery and to indulge in excessive elaboration, appears most of all in devotion to the Mother of God; a devotion expressed in terms of sympathy with her in her sorrows in *Compassio*, in mourning with her which survives to this day in the *Stabat Mater*. . . . We see from the above what little contact popular piety in the later Middle Ages had with the central facts of the Christian order of salvation. The only explanation for this is that the official liturgy of the Church had become an unknown quantity to the rank and file" (Jungmann, *Christian Prayer through the Centuries*, pp. 124–126).

See also P. H. Vrijhof & J. D. J. Waardenburg, eds., *Official and Popular Religion* (The Hague, 1979); V. Turner & E. Turner, *Image and Pilgrimage in Christian Culture* (New York, 1978); J. Sumption, *Pilgrimage: An Image of Medieval Religion* (London, 1975).

2. FESTIVALS AND CELEBRATIONS THROUGHOUT THE YEAR

In this area there was no fruitful development. The celebration of the *mysteria Christi* was buried under details that distracted attention from the essential. Consider the stress on the historical details of Jesus' life or the extreme attention paid to Mary and to the numerous saints. It was evident that during the Middle Ages a disintegration was taking place in the liturgical celebration of the mystery of salvation. This meant not only that the attention that had been focused on Sunday, on the paschal mystery, and on salvation in Christ grew less, but that especially the feasts of Mary and of the saints no longer were centered in the Christ mystery but were growing independently. The saints became protectors of people in need, because they were already living in the glory of the Lord.

On the other hand we should not deny the "relativity" of the official liturgy. In each period Christian people have experienced in their own way the *communio sanctorum*. This experience shaped the "people's church." (Cf. also E. Mâle, *L'art religieux du XIIIe siècle en France*, Paris, 1902, especially pp. 306–432).

3. THE SACRAMENTS

Baptism
For a knowledge of the baptismal rite in the Middle Ages besides what we noted as sources in the preceding chapter, the following book, in which many medieval sources are listed, is of interest: E. Martène, *De antiquis ecclesiae ritibus libri quatuor* (Antwerp, 1736, photographically reproduced, 1967).

The principal development that took place at this time and that was concluded with the *Rituale Romanum* of the Council of Trent was this: the celebration of baptism was reduced to one assembly, one rite.

The background of this development was as follows: pastorally, infant baptism had become the normal practice. Baptism was perceived as the sacrament in which original sin was forgiven and washed away. Moreover, the theology of the sacraments played a role: concern was centered upon the valid use of matter (the pouring of water) and form (the speaking of the baptismal formula). The liturgy was looked upon as an essential rite that was then adorned in various ways. The heart of a valid baptism was considered first of all to consist in the removal of original sin and making the baptizand a child of God. Thus, baptism began to be administered as soon as possible after birth. Infant mortality was at that time still great. There was a desire to prevent a child dying unbaptized "with original sin" on its soul. In such circumstances it was impossible to maintain a baptismal ritual that extended over several weeks in Lent and it was necessary to reduce baptism simply to one occasion. One can still find in the sources listed by Martène orders of service in which one of the traditional "scrutiny days" was preserved (e.g., Wednesday in the fourth week of Lent), but this was a historical relic, since baptisms no longer took place only and exclusively during the paschal vigil.

What did this changed view of baptism mean for the order of service? What had happened before during Lent and at the paschal vigil was now joined together into a single rite, which attempted to preserve all earlier elements. That is, the old texts and rites were maintained even though they were intended for the baptism of adults and thus were inappropriate for the baptism of babies. What is more, nothing was scrapped, so that the ritual overflowed with repetitious prayers and rites.

The ritual for the baptism of infants looked like this according to the later *rituale of Trent*:

1. *Reception* into the catechumenate, i.e., the stating of the name; the signing with the cross on the forehead accompanied by an exorcism with prayer and blowing the evil spirit away; finally salt is placed on the child's tongue (the old welcoming rite);
2. *Repeated exorcisms* by laying on of hands and prayer; rites that go back to the days of the *competenti* (Lent), in pursuance of victory over evil. There follows the handing over of the creed and the

Lord's prayer, the old rite of *traditio* which now makes no sense. The confession of faith (the creed) made by the godparents in later times is more like the old *redditio*. It is interesting to note that at this point in some medieval *ordines* the reading of Mark 10:13–16 occurs (cf. the later Reformation orders for baptism!). Then follows the ephphatha rite (touching of the nose and ears with saliva, intended as exorcism) and the renunciation of Satan with an anointing. All of this takes place outside the baptistery;

3. *The actual baptism* consists of the profession of faith made by the godparents, the baptism itself by pouring (or immersion), the anointing with chrism, the giving of the white baptismal garment (and, as a later custom, of the baptismal candle). Initially, the eucharist was mentioned as concluding the rite, but even this mentioning finally disappears and thus it came about that children were not permitted to receive communion unless they were at least seven years old. The baptismal formula became *"baptizo te . . ."* ("I baptize you . . ."), and thereby the role of the priest was clearly accentuated.

An order for the baptism of adults was also compiled parallel in structure to this rite for infant baptism.

It should be noted that the medieval sources mention the anointing before the baptism as occurring before or after the renunciation of Satan; in both cases the intention is the same: to symbolize the battle against Satan. Furthermore, it should be noted that a differentiation is made in regard to the place of the celebration: in numbers 1 and 2 above the ceremonies take place *ad limen* (that is, in the porch or, later, the sacristy) of the church; in number 3 they take place in the baptismal room. Perhaps the old distinction between catechumenate and actual baptism is still playing a role.

Confirmation
The evolution of confirmation into an independent sacrament definitively continued during this period and, what is more, contemporary elements were added to the rite. The independence of confirmation made it necessary to adapt the rite. A first attempt is to be found in the *Pontificale* of the twelfth century. The Fourth Lateran Council (1215) determined that confirmation must be administered to children of seven years. The definitive rite for confirmation is given in the *Pontificale of Durandus* (ed. M. Andrieu, *Le Pontifical romain*, vol. 3, pp. 333–336).

This very short rite consists in:

1. An opening prayer (a sort of invitatory);
2. The collective laying on of hands; the *Pontificale* of the twelfth century has an individual laying on of hands, but Durandus makes it into a collective act (cf. the *Apostolic Tradition* of Hippolytus);
3. The anointing with chrism on the forehead of the confirmand, whose name is spoken. The text of the formula for confirmation runs:

Signo te signo crucis et confirmo te crismate salutis in nomine Patris et Filii et Spiritus Sancti	I sign you with the sign of the cross and confirm you with the chrism of salvation in the name of the Father and of the Son and of the Holy Spirit

and Durandus adds:

ut replearis eodem spiritu sancto et habeas vitam aeternam. Amen.	that you may be filled with that same Holy Spirit and may have eternal life. Amen.

4. The tap on the cheek (*alapa*) with the text: "*Pax tecum*" ("Peace be to you"). The greeting of peace is underlined by a "slap," a rather strange combination! Probably this was regarded as a sort of knight's dubbing whereby the confirmand was dubbed knight of Christ. This medieval explanation remained current for a long time but has little to do with the original substance of confirmation, which was the pouring out of the Holy Spirit.

Two elements ought to be further underscored. It appears that in the Middle Ages anointing became the central act of confirmation just as it is in the east. In the old Roman tradition the laying on of hands also belonged to the central act, if not exclusively then at least as a very important action. On account of its greater expressiveness and its biblical roots (anointing of priests and kings, being anointed with the Holy Spirit), anointing became the principal moment or, to use the terms of scholastic theology, the *materia* of the sacrament.

Once the rite for confirmation had been fixed, the anomaly of western initiation rites became more apparent. The Holy Spirit as gift to the church became an almost forgotten idea. That a child is baptized and born again in water and the Holy Spirit, that the child receives the Spirit in order to be child of the Father, in order to go the way of the Messiah: this vision, which is filled with great dynamism, disappeared into the background of the Christian consciousness in the western church. The consequences were great—the institution became more important than the Spirit, the carcass more honored than the breath that must awaken it to life.

The Eucharist
The standard work is that of J. Jungmann, *The Mass of the Roman Rite.*

THE RITE
The essential elements of the celebration, the pillars of which were still the service of the word and the service of the table, were maintained during the Middle Ages. But the service of the word took place in unintelligible Latin, and there were very few participants at the table, which was no longer a table in fact, but an altar. This altar was placed in the apse of the church and was given a superstructure (retables) displaying sculptures or paintings of Christ's death on the cross. The space for the plate and cup on the altar became smaller as the celebration more and more became the private action of the celebrant. He was the ordained representative of the church who alone could validly and effectively solemnize the sacrament before the faithful onlookers. Instructive in this regard are the rubrics of the mass, which describe almost exclusively the action of the priest. The people were no longer the *circumstantes* ("those standing around the table"); the faithful knelt at a distance. The separation between the ordained and the other believers had become definitive.

Moreover, the retable of the altar points to a change in the eucharistic experience. The mass was the sacred action whereby Christ's death was represented. This representation was very carefully explicated by the theologians: it was no repetition of Christ's sacrifice, which was once for all, but a re-presentation in signs of bread and wine. But in the experience of the faithful and in the explanation of the preachers, representation frequently became "repetition." The altar was Calvary, on which the cross was set; the consecrated host was Christ hanging on the cross—a mystery to be beheld at a distance and in holy silence. One might certainly expect to derive certain fruits from such a beholding for, as the preachers said, the fruits of the sacrifice of the mass were manifold.

Because the faithful had become onlookers and because the people of the gothic period were drawn to what appealed to the eyes, to drama and dramatic depiction, the rite of the mass underwent a change in some details, such as the following: the greeting of the altar with a kiss was repeated several times; the use of incense increased; the ritual of the offertory was extended; the silence during

229

the canon was broken by the ringing of a bell to indicate the moment of consecration. The genuflections, the numerous signs of the cross, the exuberant posture of prayer (with arms extended), the striking of the breast, the kneeling to receive communion on the tongue—all these were visible acts in the mass of the time. The repeated cleansing of the plate (replaced now by a small paten, only for the priest) and of the cup originated at this time. These activities demonstrate both the fondness for the dramatic and the perception of the holy eucharist as making the Lord present.

One of the most important changes in the celebration was the elevation of the sacred host after the consecration. When the formula of the sacrament (the *forma sacramenti*), i.e., "this is my body," had been spoken, the bread was changed into the body of Christ. He was then really present, visible directly in the now only exterior sign of the bread. Christ was shown to the faithful in order to be adored; the *eating* of the bread became an exception. Of central interest was *"le désir de voir l'hostie"* ("the desire to see the host," Dumoutet). The solemnity of the elevation of the host (as well as of the elevation of the cup) was enhanced by its taking place against the background of the dossal curtain, accompanied by the candle that had been lit at the consecration, together with the ringing of the bell. During the elevation the people knelt, struck themselves on the breast, and said a brief prayer.

This rite of elevation was prescribed by a Synod at Paris in 1209 or 1215 (Bishop Pierre de Nemours). There was a desire to underscore the precise moment of consecration (that is, at the utterance of the essential words) and at the same time respond to the visual needs of the faithful. After a few decades the practice of elevation had spread throughout all of Europe and had been generally accepted. The understanding of the mass has been determined by that action ever since then: as a widespread image of the eucharist one sees pictures of the priest elevating the host with a crucifix in the background.

The rite of elevation marked the beginning of what was to become a more widespread eucharistic devotion. The elevation was, as it were, extended by placing the consecrated host in a monstrance, which was then set upon a throne (exposition) for adoration and for the praise of Christ truly present. Soon processions began to take place with the celebrant carrying the most holy sacrament (i.e., the consecrated host) and then blessing the people with the monstrance. Feast days were declared in honor of the Blessed Sacrament.

Through all these changes the eucharistic celebration was maintained; the essential parts were still there, but because of the continued use of Latin, they had become almost unintelligible. Moreover, they had been buried under details that led to a new perception of the mass. This perception was based upon the doctrine of the real presence of Christ in the eucharist, now seen as being accomplished through a change in the gifts. Symbol yielded to concept. The symbolic character of consecrated bread and wine was overshadowed by the concept of transubstantiation that came to take its place. People began to commune spiritually, i.e., they gazed with faith upon the Lord present under the sacred species. The sign was only external; it was, as it were, the wrapping, *accidens;* but the heart of the matter, the substance, was changed into Christ's body. The bread, that was now only exteriorly bread, was no longer so much to be eaten as to be beheld and worshipped as the body of Christ.

For the ritual description of the medieval mass one should consult Haymo of Faversham, *Incipit ordo agendorum et dicendorum a sacerdote in missa privata et feriali juxta consuetudinem ecclesiae romanae* (1242), which was based upon the older *Paratus* text and was adopted by the missal of Trent (cf. S. van Dijk, *Sources of the Modern Roman Liturgy*, vol. 2, pp. 3–14).

POPULAR PIETY

Some of the best treatments of this subject are found in A. Franz, *Die Messe im deutschen Mittelalter* (Freiburg, 1902). Interesting material is to be found in the *Dialogus miraculorum* of Caesarius of Heisterbach (c. 1180–1240), an extensive collection of eucharistic miracles that occurred frequently in the Middle Ages and that made a great impression on the people, not least because of the preachers eager to make use of them.

The miracles in question were remarkable events that took place during the consecration or during the communion of the priest or of the faithful: miracles of light or miracles of taste or smell at communion; *Verwandlungswunder* or miracles that made clear how unworthy a person was to participate in the eucharist. These miracle stories make a good measuring stick of popular faith. They do indeed recount miraculous happenings, but at the same time they give evidence of a peculiar conception of the eucharist.

This time also saw the rise of the many mass parodies. On the one hand they reflect the popular view of the clergy, and on the other they demonstrate the ease with which people dealt with holy things in the Middle Ages (see Franz).

It is not possible to give here a summary of the theology of the eucharist. Still worthy of study is A. Vonier, *A Key to the Doctrine of the Eucharist* (London, 1925). This book showed the precision with which Thomas and other theologians of his time thought and wrote about the eucharist. They emphasized the sacramentality of the mass, the anamnesis of the sacrifice of the cross, which was not repeated but commemorated in sign. By means of the concept of "transubstantiation," they strove to give a theological foundation to the reality of Christ's presence in the signs, and at the same time to find a way that avoided either an extreme spiritualism (Berengarius) or similarly crass realism (such as often marked preaching and popular piety). And they succeeded in their task: Thomas' pages on the eucharist (for example, see *Summa* III, 22, 3 ad 2; III, 73, 4; III, 83, 1) are unequalled and full of profound faith. It is a pity that this theology did not more deeply penetrate the life of the church. Misconceptions about the eucharist could have been avoided and so could a centuries-long controversy between Roman Catholic and Reformation theology. See the hymns composed by Thomas— *Lauda Sion, Pange lingua,* and especially *Adorote,* the text of which follows:

Adoro te devote, latens Deitas Quae sub his figuris vere latitas: Tibi se cor meum totum subjicit, Quia te contemplans totum deficit.	I adore you, God hidden in mystery, under these sacramental signs. My heart belongs wholly to you and yet all human thought fails as it contemplates this mystery.
Visus, gustus, tactus in te fallitur, Sed auditu solo tuto creditur: Credo quidquid dixit Dei Filius, Nil hoc Veritatis verbo verius.	Seeing, tasting, and touching cannot open this mystery to us, only hearing and believing the word of life spoken by the Son of God opens the truth of this mystery for us.
In cruce latebat sola Deitas, At hic latet simul et humanitas: Ambo tamen credens atque confitens, Peto quid petivit latro paenitens.	I confess my belief in the crucified God who dies in the body of the broken man and with the good thief I seek to share in his kingdom.

Plagas, sicut Thomas, non intueor,	Thomas saw your wounds and
Deum tamen meum te confiteor:	believed; I believe in you, my
Fac me tibi semper magis credere,	Lord, without seeing. By your
In te spem habere, te diligere.	grace, may I come to believe in,
	trust, and love you more
	deeply.

O memoriale mortis Domini,	Christ's death remembered is
Panis vivus vitam praestans	the living bread that brings us
homini:	life in the midst of our death.
Praesta meae menti de te vivere,	May I cling to you to find life
Et te illi semper dulce sapere.	and strength always.

Pie pellicane, Jesu Domine,	Lord Jesus, faithful pelican,
Me immundum munda tuo	wash me unto life in your
sanguine,	blood for a single drop brings
Cujus una stilla salvum facere	salvation and takes away the
Totum mundum quit ab omni	sin of the world.
scelere.	

Jesu, quem velatum nunc aspicio,	Jesus, whom I now contemplate
Oro fiat illud quod tam sitio:	hidden in mystery, hear the
Ut, te revelata cernens facie,	prayer of one who longs to see
Visu sim beatus tuae gloriae.	you and grant that at last I may
Amen.	know the joy of your gaze of
	love for all eternity.

Confession

In the foregoing chapters the evolution of the sacrament of penance was described. The ancient practice of the church was public penance, supported by the prayer of the congregation, and public reconciliation. Under the pressure of pastoral practice a new idea had arisen: *pénitence tariffée*, penance according to tariffs fixed by the penitential books. This penance was a private event between the sinner and the priest. Forgiveness was regarded as bestowed by God when the penance had been completed. On this basis the practice of confession arose during the thirteenth century, as we shall see below.

The *pénitence tariffée* fixed a certain number of penitential exercises (e.g., fasting during a specific length of time) for various kinds of sins. But before long it became possible to buy oneself off from this penance by means of *redemptiones*. The *redemptio* took place by paying a certain amount of money, usually to the clergy. One of the customary practices was *comparare missas,* the "buying of masses." These penitential masses profoundly determined the image of pastoral care. The many masses required numerous priests. The task of some of these priests consisted mainly in the celebration of masses, even several times a day. There was also the *missa sicca* (a mass without consecration). When the faithful came to receive their penance, it was the priest himself who could determine the *redemptio* and collect the requisite money. A full purse made some people feel that they could allow themselves a few sins because they had enough money for the *redemptio.* The forgiveness of God was bought for money—a lamentable development that caused a blight on the life of the church.

In the first half of the thirteenth century there was a clear awareness of this abuse and an attempt was made to put a stop to it by means of the practice of confession. Confession was new in that penance and forgiveness were brought together into one celebration. We found a similar joining of originally separate liturgical elements in infant baptism (see pp. 225–227). Now for the forgiveness of sins a truly repentant confession was necessary. This was heard by the priest who, by speaking with the penitent, was able to inquire into his or her motivation. Confession, undergone as an act of humiliation, was at the same time the penance and was regarded as sufficient for the forgiveness. The absolution of the priest was the intercession of the church for God's forgiveness. Later the absolution—the exonerating, forgiving sacramental formula—became the essential rite of the sacrament.

It was presumed that the penitent whose sins had been forgiven by the absolution in confession would still do penance after confession as evidence of conversion. This penance was set by the confessor, but it often consisted of a number of masses for which the penitent would have to pay. Indulgences were also *redemptio* from penances that had been imposed. So the malignancy continued in the church in spite of the existence of confession!

Ordinations to Office

The most influential liturgy for ordination was that of Durandus of Mende in his *Pontificale* (ed. Andrieu, vol. 3). Durandus' clear and precise order of service was adopted without much change by the papal court (Avignon) and became the model for the Council of Trent. We will limit ourselves here to the ordination of priests.

Durandus' point of departure was the order of service of the *curia romana,* the papal court, in the twelfth century, but he added to that old Frankish rites and texts. These additions were not always successful since they "doubled" the rite in form and content (e.g., there were two ordination prayers) and the whole was too overladen. This impression is strengthened by the apparent desire for dramatization, whereby every prayer had to be accompanied by an action and vice versa. Especially notable in the ritual of Durandus are the hierarchical view of the priestly office and the consequent differentiation between ordination (reception into the hierarchy) and jurisdiction (the commission to preach and forgive sins). This meant that reception into the hierarchy was the principal element in ordination and not the *ministerium* in the midst of the congregation. Connected with this was the small place accorded to the faithful in the liturgy of ordination. This attitude is indicative of the clerical character of the medieval church. The choice of their pastor by the faithful was definitely a thing of the past.

We cannot describe and analyze the ordination rites *in extenso*, but can mention only a few details. The essential rite of ordination, i.e., the laying on of hands with the ordination prayer, was preserved unchanged. Only now the heart of ordination was not deemed to lie in the laying on of hands but in the handing over of the "official" instruments or in the anointing of the hands. A feature entirely new to Durandus' rite was the handing over of jurisdiction: at the end of the service the ordained say the creed, receive the commission to preach and to forgive sins, and promise obedience to their bishop.

We quote below two extracts from Durandus' text that were of Frankish origin. Attention should be paid to the way the priest is portrayed. First an excerpt from the address of the bishop to those about to be ordained priests:

Agnoscite quid agitis; imitemini quod tractatis, quatenus, mortis dominicae misterium celebrantes, mortificare membra vestra a vitiis et concupiscentiis omnibus procuratis. Sit doctrina vestra spiritualis medicina populo Dei. Sit odor vitae vestrae delectamentum ecclesiae Christi, ut praedicatione atque exemplo edificatis domum, id est familiam Dei, quatenus nec nos de vestra provectione, nec

Insofar as you are celebrating the mystery of the death of the Lord, recognize what you are doing, imitate what you are handling and mortify your bodies from participating in sinful acts and desires. Let your teaching be spiritual medicine for the people of God. Let the fragrance of your life be a delight to the church of Christ so that you may edify by preaching and example the house, that is the family of God. Thus neither we

235

vos de tanti officii susceptione damnari a domino sed remunerari pocius mereamur. Quod ipse nobis concedat per gratiam suam (Andrieu III, pp. 336–337).

by promoting you to office in the church nor you by receiving so great a task will merit to be condemned by the Lord but rather to be rewarded abundantly. May the Lord grant us this through his grace.

From the second (Gallican) ordination prayer:

Deus sanctificationum omnium auctor . . . super hos famulos . . . munus tuae benedictionis infunde . . . ut in lege tua die ac nocte meditantes, quod legerint, credant, quod crediderint, doceant; quod docuerint, imitentur. . . .

O God, source of all graces . . . pour forth upon your servants . . . the gift of your blessing so that meditating day and night upon your law they may believe what they read, teach what they believe, and imitate what they teach. . . .

The Sick and the Dying

The anointing of the sick and the dying assumed the character of final forgiveness of sins (*extrema unctio*). As a result the seven penitential psalms came into use as well as formulas for the anointing such as the following:

Per istam sanctam unctionem et suam piisimam misericordiam parcat tibi dominus quidquid oculorum vitio deliquisti.

Through this holy anointing and his faithful mercy may the Lord forgive you whatever evil you may have committed by sins of sight [of hearing, touching, etc.].

See further A. Chavasse, *Etude sur l'onction des infirmes dans l'Eglise latine du IIIe au XIe siècle* (Lyon, 1942); and M. Andrieu, *Le Pontifical romain au moyen âge*, vol. 2, pp. 490–492, 493–495, 495–505.

Death

The view of death changed in the course of the Middle Ages. The hope for the resurrection and eternal rest was supplemented by a concept on a more human scale: death decided the battle between good and evil in a person; death was the judgment. Images of the last judgment are still to be seen over the portals of the cathedrals. The hymn *Dies irae* expressed this theme very graphically (cf. C. Vellekoop, *Dies irae, dies illa; Studien zur Frühgeschichte einer Sequenz*, Bilthoven, 1978).

The sense of the transitoriness of human life was strong: every beauty is fleeting, nothing of it remains, for the body rots away. Death takes everyone away (the dance of death; cf. *Lexicon der christlichen Ikonographie*, vol. 4, cols. 344–347) and before death all are equal. One can best prepare for death by a continuous meditation on the judgment, on heaven and hell (the *ars moriendi*; cf. *Lexicon der christlichen Ikonographie*, vol. 1, col. 188).

A ritual for funerals is to be found in the Roman *Pontificale* of the thirteenth century (Andrieu, vol. 2, pp. 505–513). See also van Dijk, *Sources*, vol. 2, pp. 386–397; J. Huizinga, *The Waning of the Middle Ages*, pp. 140–152; and R. Rutherford, *The Death of a Christian*, pp. 53–87.

Marriage

There are data indicating that from early times the church has participated in the ritual concluding a marriage by means of a priest's presence. In the fourth century a prayer of blessing was spoken over the couple while a veil was placed over the heads of both bridegroom and bride (*velatio*). It appears that under Germanic influence in later times, this custom was kept only for the bride. The old text for the *velatio*, as found in the *Sacramentum Veronense* (nos. 1105–1110), was read during the celebration of the eucharist before communion. There was also an old practice of blessing the bedroom. Most likely from the ninth century on, the priest was involved at the house on the occasion of a wedding in such customs as the giving of the bride to the bridegroom by the father of the bride, the giving of gifts to the bride (especially the ring, a Roman custom), and the solemn entrance into the marriage chamber, which the priest was asked to bless.

From that time on, the place of the church in the accomplishment of the marriage grew steadily more important. The reason for this is that the church wanted to guarantee and protect the free consent of the bride, thereby recognizing the fundamental right of the woman. Moreover, the church wanted to see to it that the marrying couple were not related, a grounds so frequently used for annulment. Both of these motives stimulated the presence of the church. House customs were moved to the *limen ecclesiae*, the threshold or porch of the church; the troth was plighted before the celebration of eucharist. Thus the rite of the sacrament of matrimony grew into being. England and Normandy provide early data; "Anglo-Norman" liturgists gave a form to the ritual. From them comes the oldest formula with which the bridegroom promised faithfulness to his bride:

De isto anulo te sponso, et de isto auro te honoro, et de ista dote te doto (Molin & Mutembe, p. 292).

With this ring I espouse you, and with this gold I honor you, and with this gift I gift you.

Thus we see the structural elements of the wedding ritual: both the blessing over the couple during the eucharist and the mutual exchange of consent symbolized by the gift of the ring, at all of which the priest is present. There was sometimes a tendency to have the priest assume the role of the father of the bride, but this never resulted in clericalization of the wedding ceremony.

In the north the rite took place in front of the door of the church, in the south (southern France and Italy), in the church before the altar. Many variations were introduced into the basic ritual from region to region, thus indicating both unity and diversity in ritual practice.

Details are given in the study by J. Molin and P. Mutembe, *Le rituel de mariage en France du XIIe au XVIe siècle* (Paris, 1974).

Chapter Five

The Byzantine Synthesis:
The Byzantine Liturgy after 610 A.D.

In chapter 2 the liturgy of the church of the empire was described, and there we encountered great diversity of liturgical traditions, all of which resulted from the evolution of the patriarchates in the east and the influential position of Rome in the west.

In chapters 3 and 4 the liturgy of the Roman rite was presented. The Roman liturgy was perceived as the result of an osmosis of several traditions that then evolved into *the* liturgy in the western patriarchate.

In this chapter we will describe the history of the Byzantine liturgy. This liturgy is also a synthesis of many traditions as well as *the* sign of orthodoxy, and therefore by far the most important form of worship in the east. The Byzantine rite united in itself many elements but at the same time overshadowed the other rites in the east: a remarkable parallel with the development in the west. The cause for this is not hard to find: Constantinople was the city of the emperor and of the patriarch and the center of the Byzantine empire. Thereby the liturgy of the imperial city was disseminated widely. In describing "the eastern liturgy," we may justly limit ourselves to the Byzantine rite as the summary of eastern worship and spirituality. We have noted other rites (see above pp. 88–91, 126–130) but their dissemination was not as extensive. The source material for the Byzantine rite is still not completely available and the history of the rite shows several important *lacunae*.

I. HISTORICAL DATA

Literature

H.-G. Beck, *Geschichte der orthodoxen Kirche im byzantinischen Reich* (Göttingen, 1980).

F. Heiler, *Die Ostkirchen* (Munich, 1971).

K. Onasch, *Grundzüge der Russischen Kirchengeschichte* (Göttingen, 1967).

G. Ostrogorsky, *History of the Byzantine State* (New Brunswick, N.J., 1969).

A. Schmemann, *The Historical Road of Eastern Orthodoxy* (Chicago, 1963).

E. von Ivánka, ed., *Handbuch der Ostkirchenkunde* (Düsseldorf, 1971).

A. HISTORICAL PERIODS

The internal strength of the Byzantine empire along with its ability to resist and survive strike everyone who is concerned with the written history of the *Imperium*. These traits must have been the result of a profound culture in which both the Greek and Latin spirits, both the fine sense of measured life and the tight structuring of society, converged. The result was a society that could resist the ravages of time and repel the assaults made against it from all sides by its enemies. The Byzantine state had a history that, after the initial period (Theodosius, Justinian), ran from the year 610 to 1453, from the great emperor Heraclius (610–641) to Constantine XI (1449–1453), who died at the hands of the Turks at the fall of the imperial city. In those long centuries there were always powers of restoration at work and the emperors knew how to neutralize the results of the many wars by means of a powerful internal organization of the realm, by both improvisation and the weight of tradition. It is an impressive history of an empire not plagued by feelings of inferiority!

The Byzantine empire was the eastern inheritor of the Roman empire, uniting in itself the Greek and the Latin spirits in its own creative way, a way that became most evident in the period we will now discuss. From the seventh century on, the empire developed independently and expanded to become a great medieval power. As such it served as a buffer for western culture, as a protective wall against the devastating attacks from the east. At the same time the empire absorbed many values into its own world view.

The first period (610–711) was ruled by the dynasty of Heraclius. Politically, its main concern at this time was the partially successful protection of the empire from the Persians (conquest of Jerusalem), and resistance to the Islamic Arabs against whom the empire was no match. It lost Syria, Palestine, Egypt, and Armenia to Islam. As a result both nationalistic and Monophysite tendencies in those lands grew rapidly. This meant that Orthodoxy came to be even more closely connected to Byzantium and that church communities in the lands conquered by Islam were identified with heterodoxy and came to be isolated. Added to this, in the west (Italy, North Africa) the

240

areas belonging to the empire were definitively lost. In the Balkans the Slavic peoples pressed closer. The empire was thereby shrunk to Byzantium as its center, to Greece and to Asia Minor: such was the extent of the Byzantine empire in the Middle Ages.

The internal organization of the empire was strengthened as the provinces were reorganized according to zones called *themata*, which were placed under the rule of the highest military authority. The army settled in and the military commander became the civil ruler. Imperial power centered in Byzantium was becoming more and more absolutistic.

The period from 711 to 843 is known as the age of iconoclasm. The Isaurian dynasty, which had a strong grip on political and social life and which held firm against the Bulgars in the north and the Arabs in the south, played a leading role in iconoclasm, in which dogmatic and political motives were woven together. The defenders of the icons were not only fighting to protect their own piety and the faith in the incarnation of the Word, but also resisting the interference of the emperor in matters that touched the faith and the church. These defenders were to be found among the monks and the people. Those who attacked the images—the emperor, his court, and the higher clergy—attacked the honor paid to images on the ground that it was contrary to the holiness of God and could lead to idol worship. They protested that they were trying to protect Orthodoxy from deformed growth among the people. At the same time they were also trying to check the great influence of the monks. The battle went on fiercely between irreconcilable parties. It so occupied the minds of people on both sides that it almost stopped theological creativity: more and more there was an appeal to the tradition of the Fathers. The position of the *iconoduli*, the defenders of the images, was affirmed by the seventh ecumenical council, Second Nicea (787), but this did not put an end to the struggle, which continued until 843. "Leaving aside those speculations, mostly pulled out of the air, about Greek inclination to images and Asian imagelessness, there still remains as a solid background the opposition between zealots and moderates. . . . There remains also the opposition between an enlightened religiosity and a more popular piety directed toward seeing and touching in order to make the content of faith tangible" (Beck, p. 89).

The Byzantine empire became even more completely "Greek" as a result of developments in the west: the Carolingians made the exarchate of Ravenna into a papal state and the pope crowned Charlemagne as emperor. This last event fell like a bomb in the east: at this time relationships with the west had never been more genuinely full of trust. This new event led to no good for the Byzantine empire. Internal problems were intensified by the crisis of trust in the relationship with Rome, but the tight organization of the empire and its juridical foundations forestalled serious threat.

The Byzantine empire reached its height under the Macedonian dynasty (867–1057). During this same period the schism between the churches in the east and west finally took place (under Photius, 867; definitively under Michael Cerularius, 1054). The end of this period was marked by the invasion of the Turks, who conquered Asia Minor, and by the Norsemen, who ended permanently imperial rule in southern Italy and Sicily. The glory of the Byzantines is still visible, however, in Palermo, Monreale, and Cefalù.

Emperor Basil I (867–886) spread the empire in the east as far as the Euphrates. His namesake, Basil II (976–1025), whose name is covered with glory in Byzantine history, established Byzantine power on the Danube, in Southern Italy, and in the east against Ottonians, Bulgars, Russians, and Arabs. His struggle was relentless, albeit only for a short time successful. The kingdom of the Bulgars was destroyed, thus securing the Byzantine sphere of influence in the Balkans. More important still was the cooperation with the princes of Kiev whereby "Russia" was converted to Byzantine Christendom (Prince Vladimir, 980–1015, married the daughter of Emperor Basil II).

Of great importance was the renewal of law, the revision of the *Codex Justiniani*, and the attention given to Greek culture. The *Basilika* of Leo VI were the most notable medieval rules of law for church and state; they were written in Greek and were a reworking of both Latin law and Greek common law. This new codification harked back to and depended upon tradition. It marked the endpoint of the development of the emperor's absolute power with his apparatus of officials and his highly centralized government, with its insistence on detail and its tight governmental structure.

The "medieval" period of the Byzantine empire was marked by decline and by attempts at revival. Under the Comneni (1081–1185) there was a kind of second blossoming during which the empire was able to maintain itself politically and protect its borders. There were, however, clear signs of disruption: the power of the nobility displacing the rigid governmental structure; the alliance with Venice had disastrous consequences for the treasury; the relations with the west, which had organized the crusades, remained unfriendly and tense. The nadir was reached with the fatal conquest of Byzantium by the

Venetians and the crusaders in 1204 and the establishment of the Latin empire. The old empire remained in power in Asia Minor, where resistance against the Latins was organized. The population of Byzantium supported this resistance, which succeeded in overthrowing the Latin power in Byzantium with the result that Michael VIII entered the city as emperor in 1261.

The Palaeologi ruled over the last centuries of the Byzantine empire, which had shrunk to the city of Byzantium itself. In 1350 there was no Byzantine influence left in the heartland of Asia Minor—the Turks ruled there. Even Thrace eventually had to be given up until the moment of total eclipse: the conquest of the city by the Turks in 1453.

Such is the history of an *Imperium* that built on a rich tradition and that took pride in that tradition, even in the darkest times. This tradition inspired renewal movements, creativity, dynamism, and especially strength against attack from outside. Finally this strength was so weakened that it could no longer resist. At last this centuries-old culture was denuded of its political power, but it continued to live in the Byzantine church, although now defensive and suspicious of old enemies, especially of those in the west.

B. THE BYZANTINE CHURCH

The Byzantine church became the bulwark of Orthodoxy and conquered the "east." That is to say, the old patriarchates were not able to resist Byzantine influence. If they wanted to call themselves Orthodox they had to be connected to *the* orthodox church, and this connection often led to the neglect of their own customs, theology, and liturgy. For some of these patriarchates, to support social or political independence it was necessary to separate from the emperor in Constantinople and the "melchites" (the followers of the emperor) as well as from Orthodoxy. As a result of such separations Monophysitism and Nestorianism arose. The separated national churches slowly shriveled up, but in widely scattered areas among small groups one can still find remnants of their old rites.

The Byzantine rite with its impressive ceremonial still flourishes. In the west it is usually what is meant by the term "eastern rite." There are indeed not a few unpublished sources of non-Byzantine rites that are more than worthy of study, but in fact the research will continue to focus especially on the Orthodox doctrine and worship of Byzantium. The influence of patriarchates such as those of Alexandria, Antioch, and Jerusalem, of Armenia and Ethiopia, constantly declined; they were no match for the new city on the Bosphorus and slowly disappeared. The Arab attacks on these centers sharpened their separation from Byzantium and hastened their eclipse; they became Islamic conclaves (Jerusalem) or only names (Antioch).

The patriarch of Constantinople began to call himself the "ecumenical patriarch," a title that indicates that the patriarch of the emperor's city shared in the authority of the emperor, with whom he maintained frequent contact. He had undisputed authority over the metropolitans who came under the authority of Byzantium, (Asia Minor, Thrace, Illyria). He (together with the emperor) convoked synods. The national synods especially had great authority. Since Byzantium was the "center of the world" (*oikumenē*) and the Byzantine empire understood itself to be a worldwide empire, these synods and councils had ecumenical significance. Initially most churches connected with Byzantium were represented at these synods. But after the Islamic conquests, "ecumenical" referred only to those churches that had survived under Byzantine rule, i.e., those remaining under the leadership of the patriarch and the emperor. Little was left, in practice, of *pentarchy*, leadership of the church by the five patriarchs (Rome, Constantinople, Alexandria, Antioch, Jerusalem). Byzantium assumed the leadership in the east (although it would later find a significant rival in Moscow). This ecumenical authority encountered the patriarch of the west, the pope of Rome. They were both so magisterial that there could be no question of dialogue, while there certainly was suspicion and ignorance of the other's deeper motives. The claims to primacy on the part of the pope of Rome were never recognized in Byzantium and came to be more and more clearly and definitively denied (867, 1054). Byzantium agreed that Rome might have ancient rights as an imperial and episcopal city, but it was impossible that they could be considered as exclusive: that would have seriously detracted from the honor of the ecumenical patriarch in the new Rome. On the other side, the patriarch in the west looked disparagingly upon the behavior of the patriarch of Byzantium and attempted as a counterstroke to exert his own claims to authority and power in a way that showed but slight sensitivity. As a result, relationships became strained and remained so for centuries, a situation that perhaps will continue. Every word spoken by both ecclesial centers had to be weighed on a scale and tested. The Byzantine church structure, with the bishops acting together under the leadership of the patriarch who has no claims to primacy such as those of the bishop of Rome, has a certain attractiveness. It is understandable that the east has defended this structure.

Despite the schism between the churches of the east and the west, which still has a sense of finality, there were remarkable parallels between the two, such as the unique positions enjoyed by the patriarchs of Rome and Byzantium. They were the accepted leaders of the churches: their word weighed heavily; their festal liturgy, which went with their position, was imitated by local churches; their regulation of church life by means of a well-oiled system of law was evident throughout the church. Just as the popes gradually worked out an all-embracing ecclesiastical law through competent canonists, so also did the patriarch of Byzantium, who was supported in this by the emperor and by the decrees of the synods and the councils. The canons of the councils were constantly consulted as the guide for the organization of church life, just as in the west. The authority of the councils was unsurpassed, as was that of the church Fathers: both formed the source for the constant emendation and refinement of church law, which was by definition traditional. This church law supported the pivotal position of the patriarch of Constantinople just as the civil law did that of the emperor.

The relationship between church and state in the Byzantine tradition differed from that in the Latin. Chapter 2 of this book has already touched upon this matter. The founder of the theory of the relationship between church and state was very likely Eusebius of Caesarea, who made no secret of his veneration for the Emperor Constantine. The emperor was the central figure, the God-sent Augustus! He represented not only the state but also the church. Together church and state formed Christendom: the link between the two was the emperor. The kingdom of the emperor was the epiphany of the kingdom of Christ; in this kingdom the *basileus*, the emperor, who is supreme, and the patriarch worked together as representatives of the *Kyrios*, the Lord, who was imaged in kingly manner in the apse of the basilicas or in the cupola of the churches. There was in principle no competition between state and church. There were certainly conflicts (especially because of the claims of the emperor), but these conflicts resulted in no "investiture controversy" as in the western church.

Nonetheless, there was a development in the relationship between church and state. "The empire had been and remained holy, but the source of this sacred character had previously been the ancient and absolute conception of the state as the reflection on earth of divine order. Now it became the recognition of the empire as a handmaiden of Christ. . . . The imperial power had finally ceased to be the one reflection in the world of divine power and was now itself subject to the truth preserved by the Church" (Schmemann, pp. 218–219). This change came about especially after iconoclasm when the orthodox faith, preserved by the church, came to precede the authority of the emperor. He was no longer an "absolute" prince but was subject to the Lord of the church and state. Theocracy was restored to its proper proportions. The pictures and statues of the emperor underwent a change at this time: he was no longer portrayed as a conqueror but as the servant of Christ. On the other hand, however, the patriarchs were bound to the emperor. This caused a narrowing of vision: the church of the Lord was the Byzantine church in the Byzantine state.

No wonder, then, that the liturgy over which the patriarch presided in the presence of the emperor and his court was alluring in its dazzling splendor. This rite became the model of eastern worship in the same way that the papal rite became the model for western worship. Still it must be said that the east always had a greater flexibility. Unity, not uniformity, was the principle and it came to expression in diversity. A parallel could be found in the important role that the common, or customary law, played in codifying social and ecclesiastical life. The customs of local churches were respected as were their local languages. The Byzantine liturgy thus became a genuinely ecumenical liturgy, a synthesis, an expression of a far-flung church deeply rooted in the lives of the people.

The shape of the Byzantine church was in a significant way determined by the monks, who, more than the higher clergy, maintained real contact with the people. The monastic tradition had been a lay movement anciently and even in later centuries was lay-oriented. The monks enjoyed the respect of the faithful and were consulted as the most experienced leaders, called upon in need and adversity. To the people, a church without monks was almost inconceivable. The monastic life was considered the highest attainable, a visible sign that the church was "not of this world." The monks were living warning signs against the secularization of the church, despite the fact that their warning was sometimes enfeebled by their own manner of life. The church and the emperors stimulated the monastic ideal and founded a great number of monasteries. At the beginning of iconoclasm, Byzantium counted thousands of monks, a large percentage of the total population. No wonder that the Isaurians, the iconoclasts, wanted to strike at the monks, for in their view the more men became monks, the fewer became soldiers; the more monks, the less taxes. It was also felt that the state lacked control because of the many privileges and exemptions granted to the monks. The monks were able to withstand the emperors, however, not only because of their numerical preponderance, which was already sufficient, but also because of their fanatical resistance.

Iconoclasm actually strengthened the position of the monks in the Byzantine tradition: the monk was a light for all who live in the darkness (so said the great abbot Theodore the Studite). The monastery was the heart of the church: Theodore proved this by making the Studios monastery the motherhouse of a family of reformed monasteries. Alongside the official theology the monks built up their own tradition of mystical theology: "the disclosure of the content of faith in the experience of life" (Schmemann, p. 232). In this theology the main concern was interior illumination through the contemplation of the mystery of God whereby one finally became a participant in the eternal light: such was the fault of the Alexandrian tradition (Origen), which through the Cappadocian monks had remained common property of Byzantine monasticism. This theology of mystical experience was brought to great heights by Symeon the New Theologian (945–1022); he was not able to avoid conflict with the official, "scholastic" theology, but nonetheless he made an indelible impression on Byzantine theology. The subsequent hesychasm of Gregory of Palamas proved this, and the monastic life of Mt. Athos carried on the mystical tradition.

C. THEOLOGY AND SPIRITUALITY

Literature

H.-G. Beck, *Kirche und theologische Literatur in byzantinischen Reich* (Munich, 1959).

J. Meyendorff, *Byzantine Theology* (New York, 1974).

The theology and spirituality of the Byzantine church cannot be summarized in a few lines. We will merely indicate some principal themes in these fields.

From what has just been said about the status of the monks, it can be deduced that two forms of doing theology have existed and still exist in the Byzantine tradition. The first form could be called "the official church theology," entirely based upon the tradition of the ecumenical councils and the doctrine of the "Fathers." This theology is defensive and more or less static, i.e., it endeavors to provide an undeviating interpretation of the tradition to guide the daily life of the church. New problems cannot be solved except by recourse to the traditional doctrine, for the truth has been determined once and for all. Theological thought has been brought to great heights in this

247

tradition, but this has not prevented it from surrounding its opera-
tions with an aura of alienation. There may be, perhaps, a new
orientation of Byzantine theology in the offing. Nonetheless, the
great themes of Byzantine theology remain: the trinity; the incarnation and glorification of the *Kyrios;* the *Theotokos;* the divinization of
the human person; the visualization of the mystery through signs
and symbols that point toward the coming kingdom of God. This
theology is sung about and meditated upon in the liturgy.

The other form of theology is mystical theology, or monastic
theology (or again *popular theology*), which, as has already been
remarked, is based upon the experience of God's eternal light,
through which the believer is able both to perceive and transcend
the ordinary course of life. This theology originates in contemplation,
which has also profoundly influenced both the spirituality and the
liturgy of the church. Wisdom is sought after more than either
doctrine or intellectual experience. This type of theology tends to
focus attention on piety, experience, and emotions; actually it is a
form of prayer and contemplation. Dogma is lived and not primarily
analyzed according to its significance or background; faith has primacy over theology. This theology is "empathetic."

The spirituality of the Byzantine church was the common patri-
mony of the clergy, the monks, and the faithful. No dichotomy took
place as in the western tradition between clergy and faithful. Most
likely it was the monks who were to be thanked for that. What is
more, this spirituality interpenetrated the liturgy: liturgy determined
spirituality and spirituality adapted liturgy to the needs of the congregation.

Even today, the faithful are familiar with the liturgy. That does
not mean that they know the ritual in detail or that they can follow
the texts. But they feel at home in the church with the icons, the
incense, the lights, and the colorful vestments, and they spiritedly
answer the diaconal calls to prayer with repeated acclamations
("Lord, have mercy"). The believer "experiences the holy services as
a series of ever new and meaningful moments, following one after
another, just as the services themselves follow each other, flowing
along from one to the other" (Bouman). This means that the people
are not only familiar with the celebration of the eucharist (the divine
liturgy), but equally so with the hours (morning and evening prayer
of Sunday) and other pious services of prayer (such as for the
Theotokos). All of this has the deepest roots in reverence for the holy,
for the signs in which the presence of the holy and the reality of
salvation among us is signified (thus the reverence for the altar, the

248

throne of the Lamb!). Familiarity and reverence are, in this spirituality, complementary components.

"In general, pious persons in the Christian east are convinced of the salvation that the redeemed human being has and they know at the same time that they are still 'on the way.' They are already in the sanctuary, but they still stand before the curtain behind which the light of glory, in which everything will finally be revealed, streams out from the Throne. The texture of the curtain is however such that without much difficulty they can make out the great contours of the rich pattern: signs which convert the reality of salvation to a human scale; the Holy Scripture and the Mysteries which are celebrated in the Church. These pious people do exactly what they ought to do. They bow deeply again and again. They do so out of reverence for the Holy, and in order to proclaim God's glory and goodness—and to ask that God might be merciful to poor sinners just as the Lord once forgave the thief and promised him the Kingdom" (C. A. Bouman, "Oosterse spiritualiteit," in *Chr. Costen en Hereniging* 13, 1961, 267–278; the quotation is from p. 278).

II. CULTURAL DATA

Literature

Byzance et la France médiévale. Paris exhibition in 1958.

Byzantine Art in the Collections of Soviet Museums (New York, 1978).

A. Grabar, *L'art byzantin au moyen âge* (Paris, 1963).

S. M. Pelakanidis, P. Christou, C. Tsioumis, & S. Kadas, *The Treasures of Mount Athos; Illuminated Manuscripts,* 2 vols. (Athens, 1974, 1975).

D. Talbot Rice, *Byzantine Art* (Harmondsworth, 1954).

In the discussion above it was noted that Byzantine culture was founded upon a blending of Greek, Latin, and "eastern" cultures. The greatness and the vitality of classical culture were preserved in Byzantium and developed: it was to this wealth that the Byzantine state always appealed, consciously or unconsciously, whenever there was a question of its playing the leading role in the world. On the other hand, this centuries-old culture so outshone the "barbarian" culture that the Byzantines found it hard to have much regard for it.

In this Byzantine culture the emperor became once again the central person. Since the emperor professed the Christian religion, the Christian world of thought was absorbed into the old culture, giving to it a new inspiration. Because of the interrelation of church and state, the church of Byzantium shared in the splendor and brilliance of the imperial court, which always had available the most gifted artists. The magnificence of the Byzantine churches was a consequence of the presence of the emperor. Christian and imperial motifs were interwoven: the future glory of the kingdom of the *Kyrios* was depicted in the imperial domed churches in a style that reflected the brilliance of the imperial court. Christ was the prototype of the emperor; the *Theotokos* was seen as the heavenly empress; the saints were their imperial household. The heavenly hierarchy was made visible in the hierarchic and hieratic structure of the Byzantine empire and church, all of which inspired the mosaics, miniatures, and paintings.

Various periods of Byzantine culture are to be distinguished by the different ways of artistic expression. The first period runs from the time of Justinian (527–565) to iconoclasm: characteristic of this art is the frontal view of a subject and hieratic composition. Iconoclasm brought all this to an abrupt end: for a long time religious art was forbidden. On the contrary, secular art was given every opportunity, with flower and animal motifs derived from the old classical art.

The second period (the golden age) shows the middle Byzantine style under the Macedonians, marked by a genuine renaissance of religious art. The style of this period lasted until the invasion of Byzantium by the crusaders (1204) and was widespread, especially in Sicily and the Balkans. Characteristic are the combination of classicism and realism, the coloring, the delicate technique, the golden background (e.g., Hosios Lukas, Daphni, Palermo, Monreale, Venice, Torcello).

The last period of Byzantine culture coincides with the Palaeologi (from 1261 on), once again a revival of art after the dark years of the dominion of the crusaders. It was a renewal that was again determined by tradition, now with a new lightness, a more human, elegant, approach, often against a background of landscape or buildings.

III. THE LITURGY:
ORDERS OF SERVICE AND TEXTS

Literature (see also chapter 2, literature list of section III, pp. 67–70):

GENERAL
I. H. Dalmais, *Les liturgies d'Orient* (Paris, 1959).

F. Heiler, *Die Ostkirchen* (Munich, 1971), see especially pp. 492–514 for bibliography.

A. Raes, *Introductio in liturgiam orientalem* (Rome, 1947).

I. Rahmani, *Les liturgies orientales et occidentales* (Beirut, 1929).

A. Schmemann, *Introduction to Liturgical Theology* (London & Portland, Me., 1966).

SOURCES

F. Brightman, *Liturgies Eastern and Western*, vol. 1, *Eastern Liturgies* (Oxford, 1896; repr. 1967).

H. Denzinger, *Ritus orientalium coptorum, syrorum, et armenorum in administrandis sacramentis* (Würzburg, 1863–1864, anast. repr.; Graz, 1961).

J. Goar, *Euchologion sive rituale Graecorum* (Venice, 1730; anast. repr., Graz, 1960).

E. Renaudet, *Liturgiarum orientalium collectio*, 2 vols. (Frankfurt, 1847; anast. repr., London, 1970).

BYZANTINE RITE

G. Bertonière, *The Historical Development of the Easter Vigil and Related Services in the Greek Church* (Rome, 1972).

J. Matéos, *La celebration de la Parole dans la liturgie byzantine* (Rome, 1971).

R. Taft, *The Great Entrance* (Rome, 1975).

E. Wellesz, *A History of Byzantine Music and Hymnography* (Oxford, 1949).

OTHER RITES

M. Hayek, *Liturgie maronite* (Mame, 1964).

Sarhad Y Hermiz Jamno, *La structure de la messe chaldéenne* (Rome, 1979).

J. Madey & G. Vavanikunnel, *Qurban; die Eucharistiefeier der Thomaschristen Indiens* (Paderborn, 1968).

———, *Taufe, Firmung und Busse in den Kirchen des Ostsyrischen Ritenkreises* (Einsiedeln, 1971).

J. Matéos, *Lelya-Sapra; essai d'interpretation de matines chaldéennes* (Rome, 1959).

G. Winkler, *Das armenische Initiationsrituale*, Orientalia Christiana Analecta 217 (Rome, 1982).

A. GENERAL DESCRIPTION

The history of Byzantine worship does not allow of such complete description as does that of the Roman rite in the west. For this several causes can be given. One gets the impression that the Byzantine rite, albeit rooted in the tradition, was celebrated in a flexible way. As a consequence tradition was conceived of as the action of handing on what had been received. Precisely because of this handing on, an appeal to the sources was not so pressing and necessary: the connection to the past was taken for granted. As a consequence there was no need for development and adaptation. Historical investigation of the liturgy thus only came about very recently, often in fact by researchers from the west. This meant again that the sources that one would like to have been able to consult still are not available to the extent needed for precise and detailed research. There is the further handicap that those who come from the western tradition are often unfamiliar with the practice and the ambience of the Byzantine rite. To offer some assistance in this matter, we give on pages 264–272 a list of technical terms and their historical background. Once again the general rule stands: those who wish to savor the richness of this liturgy must take the texts in hand and absorb the "genius" of the rite. Only then can a sort of conaturality arise. The same must be done if one is to appreciate the liturgy of the church, whether of the east or of the west.

In chapter 2, dealing with the liturgy of the fourth through sixth centuries, the available data on the development of worship in both east and west were studied and described. An extensive dossier of historical materials was available for that purpose. There is, however, a hiatus in our knowledge of the evolution of Byzantine worship from those earlier imperial roots. For the beginnings of that evolution *liturgical* documents are not available. We have the "hymns" of Romanos, who died about 555, and the mystagogy of Maximus the Confessor (580–662), but no liturgical sources.

We can only guess at the cause of this hiatus, which, in the case of the patriarchates outside of Constantinople, was perhaps due to the conquest by Islam and the practically complete isolation that followed. Only slowly did a revival come about in those areas, and then it was only a very limited one. As far as Constantinople was concerned, perhaps at that time it was under too much pressure from the attacks of Arabs, Persians, and barbarians to be able to produce new liturgical texts. Or perhaps a certain amount of "improvisation" and freedom in liturgical matters was still going on. It is understandable that no liturgical documentation exists from the time of iconoclasm. First, the church was simply torn apart by the fierce struggle. Second, there was a great deal of tension between secular clergy and the monks so that there scarcely could have been any liturgical development. And finally, many documents were almost certainly destroyed; the miniatures in the liturgical books also came under the ban against images.

The history of the Byzantine liturgy becomes clearer after the end of iconoclasm. It is the period in which the structure of the Byzantine rite took the form that it has kept until today. In this respect the origin and growth of the Byzantine synthesis is analogous to the development of the Roman rite in the Frankish-Germanic milieu (see chapter 3). The word "synthesis" is rightly used here: Greek and Syrian elements grew together, and secular and monastic traditions intermingled. These components of the Byzantine rite can be found without much difficulty in the present liturgical celebration: the intellectual Greek and the exuberant Syrian texts of responsories and hymns; the imperial aspect of the services, vestments, and furnishings of the church; and the popular nucleus of the ritual (in technical terms, *office cathédrale*) augmented by monastic additions.

1. THE TEXTS

The Greek or Syrian background of the liturgical texts cannot be described fully in this book. To do so the texts themselves would have to be exhaustively cited. For example, the structure and terminology of the anaphora of Basil, the great Cappadocian, would have to be compared with the antiphons and responsories or hymns of Christmas (cf. *The Festal Menaion*, M. Mary and K. Ware, trans., London, 1969, pp. 252–289). These are all profound, but very different, texts! In some a restrained mood dominates while in others the emotions are granted free rein. What is more, in the hymnic texts the poet meditates with his fellow monks in mind, while Basil's text gives more attention to the celebration in which the assembly of the faithful participates by prayer and acclamations. In the monastic communities the hymnic and meditative texts frequently took precedence over the responsorial psalmody. These texts are worthy of extensive study. The zenith of "hymnody" was reached in the *Kontakia* of Romanos the Melodist (published in *Sources chrétiennes* 99, 110, 114, 128, and translated by M. Carpenter, *Kontakia of Romanos, Byzantine Melodist*, 2 vols., Colombia, Mo., 1970, 1973).

2. THE IMPERIAL CHARACTER OF THE RITE

The imperial aspect of the Byzantine rite is obvious. The faithful participated visually in these liturgies. They saw the hierarchical church and the imperial court in their splendor as icons of the court of heaven. The heavenly worship was visualized in the earthly liturgy, especially when the heavenly *Kyrios* was represented by his earthly vicar. The simplicity and sobriety of the celebration of the meal of the Lord was replaced by a "sumptuous" cult, in which imaging and representation played an important part. The use of candles on elaborate candelabra, the burning of incense, the solemn processions, the reverence shown to the gospel book and the altar (symbols of the *Kyrios*), the use of the bow (from bowing the head to *metania*), the reverence for the sacred space surrounding the altar and for the president, who carries out the holy mystery with "silent" prayers, the festive choral of the liturgy, the intermediary role of the deacon between the president at the altar and the people in the nave: all of this breathes a holy atmosphere, a sense of the sacred.

Still the sacred character of the rite did not alienate the people, and their worship is still marked by an air of familiarity.

3. CATHEDRAL OFFICE AND MONASTIC OFFICE

The difference between *office cathédrale* (congregational worship, celebration for and with the congregation) and *office monastique* was already touched upon in chapter 2 (see pp. 94–98 and cf. Schmemann, *Introduction to Liturgical Theology*, pp. 116ff). The Byzantine synthesis consists in this, that the two forms intermingle after having gone through a development independent of each other in the preceding centuries.

The *office cathédrale* went through the following development: the oldest layer (see chapter 1) consisted of daily morning and evening prayer (lauds and vespers) with fixed psalms, hymns, and prayers. (The prayer was responsorial, involving the participation of everyone present.) Sunday was celebrated as the day of the resurrection and the expectation of the Lord's coming. Fasting was observed on Wednesdays and Fridays, and the annual celebration of Easter stood at the heart of the church's life.

The second layer coincided with the time of the peace of the church (see chapter 2). The congregational celebration continued, but now was changed because of the new status of the church. The church ruled time, christened society, and was marked by self-awareness. Liturgy became the cultic representation of the events of salvation history signalized in worship. Moreover, there was a strong interest in the precise formulation of the doctrines of the trinity and of Christ, an accentuation of the eminence of the hierarchy and a sacralizing of time and space. The sacral and solemn character of worship was enhanced by music; the *schola* was assigned its own role in the ceremony and the cantor became a special minister. And

254

along with the music, ceremonial also increased. Finally, there was an increase in devotion to the martyrs. In short, the character of worship altered because the church had altered after the peace of Constantine.

The *office monastique* had its own distinguishing traits. The most striking was the change in the psalmody: the whole psalter was prayed (recited). The continuous reading of the holy scripture came into use. The lengthiness of the services was a part of the asceticism of the monks and of their quest for heaven, in which the earthly had to be elevated as much as possible. Elements of contrition and penance were added (bowing, lying on the ground, fasting in order to acquire spiritual freedom). The eucharist belonged to the prayer rhythm of the monks and therefore was celebrated, if possible, every day. In short, worship was made essential to the ascetic ideal of the monks, who had turned away from the world in order to seek God's kingdom. For them, it was better to spend the greatest part of the day in prayer and thus to orient the spirit toward the things of God.

These two forms of liturgical practice existed side by side, sometimes in rivalry, soon giving rise to a polarization in which the two parties were the secular clergy on the one side and the monks on the other. The monastic element won out. The moral authority of the monks was so great that their manner of life and their manner of worship got the upper hand. The later Byzantine liturgical books show that the monastic tradition permeated the *office cathédrale*, augmented it, and more or less overwhelmed it: long psalmody, long scripture reading, extensive hymnic texts and meditations. The monastic tradition also provided for the multicolored spiritual profundity of the Byzantine rite. The cathedral liturgy nonetheless did not leave the monastic tradition untouched. If the monk strove to reach and to gaze upon the divine light, to be "as angels around the throne" (Pseudo-Dionysius, Maximus the Confessor), to live "undividedly" so as to reach God's dwelling, he discovered the same striving in the community's worship in the "divine liturgy," which was the reflection, the imaging of heavenly life. Thus, congregational liturgy deepened and stimulated contemplation. Here lay the root of the Byzantine synthesis, which was finally elaborated in Jerusalem (eleventh century) and accepted in Byzantium (thirteenth century).

We must be still more precise about this synthesis. There were two centers that were of great importance, namely Jerusalem and Constantinople, where the cathedral liturgy developed, each in its own way. In these two cities, moreover, there were two monasteries that in their turn codetermined the Byzantine rite: the Sabas monastery in the Kedron valley near Jerusalem and the Studios monastery in the western part of Constantinople.

4. JERUSALEM AND CONSTANTINOPLE

Jerusalem and Constantinople each had their own liturgies and both were widely disseminated. At Jerusalem the liturgy was celebrated at the historic places of Jesus' life, and the pericopes from the gospels appropriate to those places were read: there arose a historically textured liturgy enacting the salvation events commemorated during the year. This liturgy of Jerusalem spread rapidly throughout east and west, in Cappadocia and Armenia and thence to the imperial city on the Bosphorus. The emperor had made Jerusalem great; it was understandable that the customs of Jerusalem would be adopted as much as possible in the imperial city.

On the other hand there was also a movement back from Constantinople to Jerusalem, especially after it had been attacked by the Arabs. The imperial city had protected Jerusalem. Although we cannot give precise details, we know that in both cities the liturgies had grown in similarity.

The Sabas monastery near Jerusalem was founded in 478 or 483 and gave refuge to Syrian monks, among them Cosmas of Jerusalem, Andrew of Crete, and the brothers Theophanes and John of Damascus. From this monastery came a radical change in attitude toward hymnody: there the canon arose, a genre that replaced the *kontakion*. It is also assumed that it was in the Sabas monastery that the foundations were laid for the *typicon* (see pp. 259–260), which became an important book in the Byzantine rite. Although there is no documentary evidence for these developments, the tradition of that origin most likely contains a kernel of truth.

The monks of St. Sabas played a significant role in theological discussions, especially in the defense of Origen's theology. Since, on the other hand, they stayed closely bound to the orthodoxy of Constantinople, both their influence and their authority was great.

The Studios monastery wielded great authority in the revival after iconoclasm, an authority comparable with that of the monks of St. Sabas. The Studios, founded in 463, reached its apogee under the abbot Theodore (759–826) who renewed its rule (an important model for the later monasticism of Athos). One could compare the monks of the Studios with those of the monastery at Mainz, who in about 900 put together the great western compilation that we call the Pontifical; the monks of the Studios produced a similar work for the Byzantine rite. To them could be ascribed compilation of the *typicon*, the *octoechos,* the *parakletike,* the *triodion* and *pentecostarion.* It was Theodore who stimulated this work, into which he integrated the *typicon* tradition of St. Sabas in Jerusalem (see his *Hypotypose,* P.G. 99, 1704–1720).

To speak of the Byzantine synthesis is to denote the result of a centuries-long process of growth, a process still partly hidden, namely, the process of osmosis between cathedral and monastic liturgies. An analysis of sources makes possible a reconstruction of the various traditions (see Taft, Bertonière, in literature list on p. 251). In this process of growth, the monasteries of Jerusalem and Constantinople played a decisive role. The process of osmosis reached its peak in the thirteenth century, but Simeon of Thessalonica (bishop from 1410 to 1429) was still aware of the old distinction between the two traditions (cf. PG 155, 535–669). Those two traditions had intermingled while preserving the essential elements of each: worship is directed to God who calls humanity to the kingdom and gives the divine *kairos* in the signs of the liturgy. Worship is a faithful action of the congregation of the Lord, assembled in his Name: the Byzantine rite is essentially corporate, a celebration of the whole congregation and a rendering of the self-understanding of the church. In this regard the monks always remained connected to their church, and the local congregations were inspired by their example. The Byzantine rite was thus safeguarded from excessive clericalism.

B. SOURCES

The sources of the Byzantine rite are not yet completely available; of the sources of the other eastern rites we know still less. Thus, it is not yet possible to write a complete history of every liturgical book, because the necessary analyses have not been made. We will therefore give an overview of the books that are now in use and to that add a few summary historical remarks.

Besides the liturgical books themselves there are also liturgical commentaries—those of Patriarch Germanus, who was deposed during the time of iconoclasm, of Nicholas Cabasilas (died 1350), and of Simeon of Thessalonica (died 1429)—all of them carefully studied by R. Bornert, *Les commentaires byzantins de la divine Liturgie du VIIe au XVe siècle* (Paris, 1966).

1. A VARIETY OF BOOKS
In the Byzantine rite there is no book like the Roman missal or the Roman breviary—summary books that contain the *ordo* for eucharist

or the hours for every day of the year. There have indeed been attempts to compile an *anthologion* (a first attempt in 1587 in Venice) but this anthology has never been successful in the Byzantine church. This does not detract from the fact that for many people the new anthology published in Rome (*Anthologion tou holou eniautou,* 1967) with the *akolouthia* (order of service) for vespers, lauds, and the little hours and with the changeable parts from the *menaia* and the *parakletike,* can be of some practical value. In the Byzantine rite it is still the case, as it was in the early Middle Ages in the west (see chapter 3), that there are separate books for the various "officiants," the celebrant, the deacon, the reader, the cantor (the choir). It is a rule that every celebration is sung in the presence of the congregation. The various "officiants" then have their own books which contain the texts that they must use. This is so for the eucharist, for the hours (which are also celebrated communally) and (although here less clearly) for the other sacraments.

We should underscore yet again the fact that a celebration according to the Byzantine rite is communal by definition. A "silent" or privatized liturgy is not known. Song is an integral part of the liturgy and the cantor is important; he performs a major function that requires an arduous training. All this is true also of other eastern rites as well, e.g., in the Ethiopian church.

2. COLLECTIONS OF TEXTS

Two kinds of text collections are known, especially those containing hymnic material. First, there are collections according to the genre of the texts (*receuils génériques*), with all the existing texts that could be used in the liturgy. These collections are very extensive; the treasury of hymnody is inexhaustible and contains much more than is actually used in the liturgy. The publication of these collections of hymnic texts is taking place in the series *Monumenta musicae byzantinae.*

Second, there are the liturgical collections, prayers and hymns (and readings) arranged according to the *ordo* of the liturgy (of the eucharist or of the hours), i.e., liturgical books in the strict sense. In a certain way the liturgical books are anthologies, selections from the extensive material that exists and that is collected in the *receuils génériques.*

This distinction still plays a role in worship according to the Byzantine rite. The cantor uses books along the lines of the *receuils génériques* that contain the hymns. Such hymns as are needed for the

services he selects from books such as the *hirmologion*, the *kontakarion*, and the *sticherarion*. On the other hand, there are also books (e.g., the *menaia*, the *triodion*) that contain the text material as it must be used in the service. Which text must be used is precisely stated in the *typicon*. The liturgical collections, ordered according to the course of the church year, are of later date (thirteenth century).

The differences between these collections can be illustrated by considering the different ways holy scripture is used in the eastern and western rites. The complete Bible (i.e., both Old and New Testaments) might be described as a *receuil générique*, that is to say, those writings that have been determined in the tradition of the church as belonging to the canon are to be found in "the Bible." On the other hand, the *lectionaria* (the *epistolarium* and the *evangeliarium*) are typical liturgical books. One finds therein the pericopes arranged for reading in the liturgy. These pericopes taken together do not make up the whole scripture or Bible, for in the Sunday eucharist only certain appropriate readings (pericopes) are used. In the office, the scripture is more or less continuously read; the reader might therefore use the Bible. In the eucharist, only sections that have been collected in liturgical lectionaries are read. (The Byzantine rite, however, has preserved the gospels as a whole. The gospel book, sign of the presence of the Lord, contains all four gospels in their entirety; separate lists state which pericopes are to be used for the various Sundays.)

Thus, several technical terms have been used for the liturgical books (*kontakarion*, *typicon*), explanations of which can be found in the material that follows. In the description of the liturgical sources that now follows, we will consider only the *receuils liturgiques*, the liturgical books. For an overview of the existing sources and editions in the various eastern rites, one should consult A. Baumstark, *Comparative Liturgy* (London, 1958), pp. 214–235.

3. THE LITURGICAL BOOKS AND THEIR HISTORY

Typicon
This book contains the ordering of the liturgy of the hours and of the eucharist (*the* liturgy) throughout the church year, beginning with Easter. It states when the *octoechos* (see pp. 262–263) is used and which feasts are to be celebrated on a given date (calendar), and it gives rubrics for the prayers, readings, and hymns. For the analysis of the Byzantine rite it is an indispensible book.

Editions: A. Dimitrievsky, *Opisanie liturgicheskhikh rukopisey* (A De-

scription of Liturgical Manuscripts), vols. 1, 2 (Kiev, 1895; St. Petersburg, 1917); A. Papadopoulos-Kerameus, *Typikon tēs en Hierosolymois ekklēsias* (St. Petersburg, 1894), ms. Hagios Stauros, no. 43; J. Matéos, *Le Typicon de la grande Eglise* (ms. St. Croix no. 40, Xe siècle); vol. 1, *Le cycle des douze mois* (Rome, 1962); vol. 2, *Le cycle des fêtes mobiles* (Rome, 1963).

From early times there existed various liturgical books containing rules for the celebration of the hours and the divine liturgy. Lists of pericopes were included in the lectionaries. There were lists of feasts of saints and memorials in the book called *menologion*. These various rules were collected into one book, the *typicon*, of which the oldest exemplars go back to the ninth and tenth centuries and which were fully expanded in the twelfth century.

The oldest *typica* of the *office cathédrale* are the *Typicon* of the Great Church at Constantinople from the tenth century (Matéos) and of the *Anastasis* at Jerusalem from the twelfth century (Papadopoulos-Kerameus).

Monastic *typica* have also existed (*office monastique*) e.g., those of St. Sabas near Jerusalem and of the Studios in Constantinople. Old exemplars of these *typica* have not been preserved. The Sabas tradition can be found in the printed *typicon* from Venice in 1545. Legend says that this *typicon* was originally compiled at St. Sabas, was entirely reworked by John of Damascus, and was adopted by the Studios in Constantinople. There is a kernel of truth in the legend: the two monastic traditions did influence each other and together they adapted the patriarchal tradition.

The Greek *typicon* in current use was compiled at the beginning of the nineteenth century making use of the old *typicon* of Constantinople (Matéos) and that of Sabas (1545). In Russia the church relies entirely upon the Sabas *typicon* of 1545. At the local level the services are adapted according to need.

In the Greek church sections of the *typicon* are included in other liturgical books with the result that the liturgical texts came to be surrounded by rubrics as in the Roman books.

The history of the *typicon* illustrates the osmosis of the cathedral and monastic traditions, as well as the mutual bond between Jerusalem and Constantinople.

Euchologion

This book is comparable to the Roman *sacramentarium* (see chapter 3): it contains the priestly prayers for the hours, the divine liturgy, the sacraments, and the blessings. Added later were the diaconal litanies and several rubrics from the *typicon.* Actually the *euchologion* is a compilation from several *libelli,* little books of priestly prayers. The *ieraticon* (or *liturgicon*) is an abbreviated *euchologion:* it contains only the hours (vespers and lauds) and the divine liturgy. For the bishop there is the *archieraticon,* also an extract from the *euchologion.*

Edition: Apostolike Diakonia, Athens. Also Propaganda Fide, Rome (1873). *Source:* the oldest known manuscript of the Greek-Byzantine *euchologion* is the *Codex Barberini graecus 336* from the end of the eighth century. Published by J. Goar, *Euchologion sive rituale Graecorum* (Paris, 1647; 2nd ed., Venice, 1730). An anastatic reprint of this second edition is available (Graz, 1960). Cf. A. Stritmatter, "The *Barberinum S. Marci* of Jacques Goar," *Ephemerides Liturgicae* 47, 1933, pp. 329–397.

The history of the *euchologion* has not yet been written; for that a more exhaustive study of the sources is needed. Thus the central book of the Byzantine liturgy remains enveloped in mist. The *euchologion* is differentiated into three types: the cathedral type (as in the manuscript published by Goar); the monastic type (dating from the fourteenth century and influenced by the tradition of Palestine, exactly how is not known); and a blending of both these types.

The divine liturgy (of Basil and of John Chrysostom) included in the *euchologion* has been studied in minute detail (see chapter 2 and the bibliography in *Prex eucharistica,* pp. 223, 230).

The Lectionaries

The books are the *apostolos* with pericopes from Acts and the epistles, the *evangelion* (the gospels), and (though no longer in use) the *anagnosticon* with Old Testament pericopes. These last are at present included in the *triodion, pentecostarion,* and *menaia,* which will be described below.

The Psalter

This is used as a separate book. The psalms are divided into twenty *kathismata.* The Old and New Testament canticles are added to the psalter.

Horologion

The *horologion* is a book for the fourteen daily hours in which the unchangeable texts for the celebrant, the reader, and the choir, as well as the recurring psalms, are included. In addition, there are the variable *troparia* and *kontakia* for Sundays and feasts and for weekdays.

Current edition: Apostolike Diakonia, Athens. Most recent translation (in French): *La prière des heures* (Chevetogne, 1975); basic introduction by N. Egender, pp. 11–98.

Octoechos

This book contains the variable texts for the hours of the Sundays of the year. If the texts for the weekdays are also included then the book is called *parakletike.* The ordering of the variable Sunday texts follows a cycle of eight weeks, for every week a different tone (*echos, modus*).

Current edition: Apostolike Diakonia (Athens); also Propaganda Fide (1885). Most recent translation (in French): *Dimanche; office selon les huit tons* (Chevetogne, 1972).

The *ochotechos* is a hymnbook and one of the most important sources for the study of Byzantine hymnography. It contains a selection from the extensive hymnic material that the Byzantine rite possesses. It is attributed to John of Damascus, but this is certainly not true; most likely the final compilation of the book took place in the Studios monastery of Constantinople after iconoclasm. This does not mean, of course, that much material of poetic character did not come from outside of the Studios. We know the names of those to whom hymns are attributed: John of Damascus, Cosmas of Jerusalem, Andrew of Crete, Joseph the Hymnographer, Theodore the Studite. These names indicate a Jerusalem-Byzantium tradition as origin for the *octoechos.*

"The book of eight tones" is more recent by several centuries than the practice of singing according to the eight tones. (The difference is more or less that between the ninth and the twelfth centuries.) We cannot discuss here the musical aspect of the eight *echoi* (modes), but the number eight (the number of the mode is determined by the last tone) did dictate the structure for ordering the hymnic material. The recurring cycle of eight Sundays begins with the Sunday after Pentecost. It is possible, however, that the origin of this ordering goes back to the celebration of the Sundays in Easter, from Easter Sunday to and including Pentecost, the great fifty days. The number eight has always had an important symbolic value in Christian literature as referring to the completion of the resurrection of the Lord and to the perfect rest with God in the eschaton. Probably hymnic material was first arranged for these eight Sundays and then similar series were carried out for the other parts of the year.

The oldest layer of this hymnody is formed by the *stichera anastasima* (cf. *troparion* in the glossary of terms, p. 271) of vespers and lauds. Also very old (before the seventh century) are the *stichera anatolika;* their origin is disputed, but they are probably from Syria or Palestine; the author is unknown (although it is thought to be Anatolios of Constantinople). The third layer is formed by the *alphabetika* (hymns of which the strophes begin with the successive letters of the alphabet, *acrostichon*) and the *anabathmoi* (see p. 264). Further, one finds in the *octoechos* the rest of the variable material: *hypakoi, apolytikia, kathismata* (see p. 268) and especially the canon (see pp. 265–266) composed of several odes. The odes always contain a certain number of *troparia.* We will shortly return to all this material, which to an outsider must seem a practically impenetrable maze.

The oldest printed editions of the *octoechos* go back to 1521 (Greek) and 1492 (Cracow: Slavonic).

Triodion and Pentecostarion

These two books contain the variable parts of the hours for the Easter cycle (that is, for the ten weeks before Easter and for the fifty days of Easter, the Pentecost). The final redaction of these books was alloted to the Studios monastery of Constantinople, but the material is not only of Byzantium but also from Jerusalem. Manuscripts date from the tenth century.

Current edition: Apostolike Diakonia (Athens). *English translation of the Triodion:* M. Mary & K. Ware, *The Lenten Triodion* (London, 1980).

Menaia

These are liturgical books for every month of the year according to the festival calendar. They contain the proper texts for the feasts. The calendar begins on September 1, the traditional beginning of the civil year. On Sundays the texts from the *menaia* are combined with those from the *octoechos.* The book for each month also contains short descriptions of the lives of the saints (cf. the martyrology in the west). These short readings come from the monastic tradition and are read after the sixth ode of the canon; they are called *synaxaria* and are collected independently in the *synaxarion.* The manuscript tradition reaches back to the tenth century and the name Simeon Metaphrastes (ca. 960), the Byzantine hagiographer, must be mentioned here.

Current edition: Apostolike Diakonia (Athens). Also Propaganda Fide, 6 vols. (Rome, 1888–1901). *English translation* (for nine of the twelve great feasts): M. Mary & K. Ware, *The Festal Menaion* (London, 1969).

This description of the liturgical books is, to be sure, superficial. It is important to note once again that the actual contents of the books are most important for a knowledge of worship according to the Byzantine rite. The hymnic material especially makes this rite so rich and, for western tastes, at the same time so exuberant. In regard to this liturgical material, the difference is unbridgeable between the formulations of the Roman liturgy in their terseness, succinctness, and focus on essentials and those of the Byzantine rite in their exuberance. We have two styles grafted onto the one stem of the ecumenical confession of faith.

C. A GLOSSARY OF TERMS

Listed in this glossary are some of the terms that are important for a good understanding of the Byzantine rite. A few historical remarks are also provided along with the terms.

akolouthia: order of service, that is, the structure of variable and fixed texts for a given liturgical celebration. Both the rules for the service as well as the service itself are indicated by the term. In a more specific sense, *akolouthia* connotes the proper texts for a given feast such as the *troparia,* the *prokeimenon,* and the readings.

ambōn: a platform in the nave of the church from which the readings are proclaimed and the hymns are led. Anciently it was where the bishop and the presbytery took their place prior to the service of the altar. A reminder of this ambo is the *solea,* a semicircular extension in front of the middle doors of the *ikonostasis* where the deacon sings the litanies and the gospel. The Syriac *bema* was originally the *ambo,* but is now the term for the altar space.

amōmos: name for Psalm 119 in the *orthros* of Sunday.

anabathmoi: the so-called ascent or gradual psalms (119–133), pilgrims' songs. The term is also used to indicate the short *troparia* (strophes), composed on the themes of these psalms and joined together into groups (antiphons). They are sung on Sundays before the gospel in *orthros.* They are to be found in the *octoechos.* Perhaps originating from the Studios.

anagnosma: a reading. It can be noted that the reading of the Old Testament is reserved for the liturgy of the hours.

anatolikon: a series of strophes in the vespers and lauds of Sunday; Syrian, before the seventh century (Palestine?).

antiphonon: a short refrain, inserted between the verses of a given psalm. A single psalm can also have two antiphons, which implies an alternating performance by two choirs. *Antiphonon* can also mean a psalm or a group of psalms that is sung together with the antiphon (so, *pars pro toto*). A third meaning is a group of troparia called *anabathmoi.* Finally, *antiphonon* means a series of psalm verses together with a refrain and a *troparion* sung in the eucharist at the opening, i.e., the little entrance (*eisodos*). The antiphons were originally intended to be sung during the procession to the church. By the addition of the *prothesis* liturgy these antiphons have come into the liturgy itself. Cf. J. Matéos, *La célébration de la parole,* pp. 7–90.

apolytikion: a *troparion* at the end of vespers that is also repeated in the other hours. What is more, it is sung after the little entrance in the divine liturgy and therefore is called the "*troparion* of the day." Thus this *troparion* binds together all the services of the day.

aposticha: (or *apostichi troparia*) is a series of strophes sung at the end of vespers between the verses (*stichoi*) of a psalm (on Sunday Psalm 93, and in the week Psalm 123).

canon: a poetic genre in the Byzantine liturgy of Palestinian monastic origin. A canon is formed by poetic strophes inserted between the biblical canticles (each one of which is called an ode) that have a place in *orthros.* Originally the canon was made up of nine (or fourteen) biblical canticles (or odes) between which the strophes, the poetic texts, were added from the seventh century on. This poetry in the long run supplanted the biblical canticles. This means that the poetry still exists but the biblical songs of praise are no longer sung, with the exception of the song of Mary.

The now extant canon of nine odes is simply an example; many other canons are known—poetic texts without connection to the biblical canticles.

The origin of this poetic genre lies in the Syrian tradition, which was especially rich in hymnography (Bardesanes, Ephrem, Narsai). It appears that from early times poetic refrains (*troparia*) were inserted between psalm verses, so that it is not surprising that this also occurred in the case of the biblical canticles. The first canon poets known by name came from Syria (Andrew of Crete, John of Damascus, Cosmas of Jerusalem). The poetic genre of the canon, which they did not invent but did develop, was adopted by the Studios of Constantinople and placed definitively in the Byzantine rite by the monks of this monastery (the end of the eighth and the beginning of the ninth centuries).

Every strophe of a canon forms a complete whole. The strophes are joined together into series, one series for each canticle (and this series is now also called ode). The nine series of strophes belonging to the nine canticles, joined together into the canon, are performed according to the eight tones. The *hirmos* determines the melody and the rhythm of the following strophes in a series. The *hirmos* frequently contains references to the canticle to which the series of strophes was related but which has disappeared from use. The *hirmos* is repeated at the end of the series of strophes (the ode).

echos: mode (cf. "Octoechos," pp. 262–263); there are eight modes.

ectene: ectenes hikesia is the "litany of fervent supplication," a number of invocations made by the deacon and responded to by the people ("Lord, have mercy," "Grant it, O Lord"). Such communal prayer for all sorts of needs is very old. Justin mentions it (*Apol.* I, 67); the first letter of Clement (59–61) gives an example of it; the *Const. Ap.* VIII reports the litany form that still exists today; Egeria refers to the participation of the faithful in the prayer by means of the *kyrie eleison.* In other words, it is one of the constants in the Christian worship of east and west. The number of litanies increased in the course of time and thereby the sober structure of the service was affected. At present the Byzantine liturgy includes ten diaconal litanies! This means also that the role of the deacon became more and more important—a liaison between the faithful and the priest, between nave and altar.

Other names: *synapte,* consecutive supplications, connected to each other; *aitesis,* litany in the second half of vespers and lauds, and also at the offertory and the Lord's prayer in the divine liturgy (*para tou Kyriou aitesometha. . . . Paraschou, Kyrie*).

The litany is concluded with the *ecphonesis,* a sort of doxology that is sung aloud by the celebrant.

eisodos: entrance. The little entrance is a procession in which the deacon, carrying the gospel book and followed by the priest, enters the church from the altar space and then returns while the entrance song (*eisodion*) is being sung. The entrance with the gospel book is not the original form. Anciently the *eisodos* was the entrance of the patriarch and the *basileus* accompanied by the entrance song to begin the liturgy. The accompanying prayer still recalls the old meaning (". . . at our entrance make this to be an entrance of the holy angels also, to minister with us and with us to glorify your

266

goodness . . .". At present the little entrance is preceded by the *enarxis*, a psalmodic preface that precedes every service (liturgy and the hours).

The great entrance is the entrance with the gifts before the anaphora, an entrance accompanied by the singing of the cherubic hymn. It is the solemnization of an old rite already described by Justin, the deacons setting the gifts on the table after the intercessions. It is the act of cultically setting apart bread and wine that thereby take on a holy character, the holiness of the eucharist itself (see chapter 2). The East Syrian rite has preserved the simple entrance.

In the sources *eisodos* means the entrance of the patriarch and the entrance door of a church building.

heothinon: the gospel that is read on Sundays in *orthros* in the same way that the resurrection pericopes were read in Jerusalem in the morning service in the *Anastasis* (cf. Egeria). The reading consists of one of the eleven resurrection pericopes, which have been put together into a recurring series.

Heothinon can also mean the *troparion* that is known under the name *doxastikon*. There are eleven such strophes corresponding to the eleven resurrection pericopes, and one is sung after the psalms of praise, 148–150 (*ainoi*) in the Sunday *orthros*. They are supposed to have been written by Emperor Leo the Wise (886–912).

A final meaning for *heothinon* is to be found in the term *exapostilarion*. It is one of the strophes that correspond to the eleven resurrection pericopes and that are intended to be sung before lauds (the *ainoi*) in the Sunday *orthros*. They are attributed to Emperor Constantine VII (913–959).

The old morning psalms are thus both preceded and followed by strophes (*troparia*) that correspond to the resurrection pericopes of the Sunday (eleven in number in a series beginning on the first Sunday after Pentecost). See *Dimanche, office selon les huits tons*, pp. 138–148 and 151–158. The texts show that these hymns are designed to promote personal reflection arising from the gospel story.

hexapsalmos: the collection of psalms (3, 38, 63, 88, 103, 143) that is prayed at the beginning of *orthros*, that is, preceding both the variable psalms and the *ainoi*, the three morning psalms. Psalms 3 and 63 form the heart of this collection. The six psalms are divided into two groups of three, each group concluded with an Alleluia. During the singing of the second group, the priest in silence prays the twelve prayers of *orthros* (see *Dimanche*, pp. 102ff). The *hexapsalmos* belonged originally to the midnight office, preceding the psalmody of the night. Monastic influence is thus probable.

hirmos: the strophe (*troparion*) that determines the melody (and the meter) of the following strophes in an ode of a canon.

hypakoe: a Palestinian *troparion* (Jerusalem) that is found in the Sunday office after the third *stichologia* (see p. 271). It is probably a remnant of the old responsorial use of the psalms—the psalm reading was constantly interrupted by a refrain, e.g., Alleluia, that had no direct relationship to the psalm being read. The term comes from *hypakoein*, "to answer." Cf. *antiphonon* and *ephymnium*, q.v. under *kontakion*.

idiomelon: a *troparion* sung according to its own melody, in contrast to the *prosomoion*, a *troparion* sung according to a common melody (and rhythm).

kathisma: the psalter is divided into twenty sections or *kathismata*. The twenty *kathismata* are each further subdivided into three *stasis*, also called "antiphons." Precise directions are given as to which *kathisma* and *stasis* must be prayed in vespers or *orthros* (the so-called *cursus psalmodicus*). Of Palestinian origin. *Kathisma* also denotes the troparion that is sung in *orthros* after the little litany.

kontakion: a didactic piece of poetic genre; the term has been current since the ninth century but the genre is actually much older. The origin is the Syrian strophic homily (*madrasha*). Formally, it is a collection of many poetic strophes, each of an equal number of syllables and of the same rhythm, this being determined by the first, model strophe (*hirmos*). The first letters of the strophes are those of the alphabet or together make up a name (*acrostichon*). An introduction precedes the strophes (*prooimion* or *koukoulion*) and every strophe has a refrain (*ephymnium*) that was intended for acclamation by the people. The whole was performed to a certain melody.

The best-known *kontakia* poet is Romanos the Melodist who lived c. 500 in Constantinople, but who had come from Emesa (Homs) in Syria. He may well have learned this poetic genre in Syria since the origin of the *kontakia* is almost certainly to be sought there. The poetic homilies of Ephrem reflect the environment of their origin. Perhaps this Syrian poetic form goes even farther back in history, for example to metrical sermons (*prosa*) such as the paschal homily of Melito of Sardis. In any case it is clear that the *kontakion* could become so beloved because it depended on an old tradition of preaching, in which the faithful were involved by means of acclamations and which existed alongside of the "classical" sermon or homily.

The oldest *kontakia*, translated from Syriac into Greek and even into Latin, have not yet been sufficiently studied, although they have been widely used. A famous example is the *Akathistos hymnos*. By means of the *kontakia*, old Christian faith motifs have been preserved and passed on.

In the ninth century the *canon* pushed the *kontakion* into the background: the didactic poem had to give way to strophes, each of which forms a complete whole as regards subject matter (see *canon*).

At present the term *kontakion* is used for the strophe after the sixth ode of the *canon* and followed by the *oikos*. The *kontakion* of Christmas is the first strophe of an old *kontakion* of Romanos, one of the few remnants of the old *kontakia* in present use.

lite: a procession at the end of the vespers of feasts. The movement to the narthex of the church is accompanied by the singing of *troparia* (*stichera*); on arrival at the rear prayers are said for the needs of church and world (*lite* supplication).

luchnikon: signifies evening prayer or vespers, or a central portion of vespers, i.e., Psalms 141–142–130–117 together with the strophes (*stichera*), the *doxasticon*, the *theotokion*, the entrance with the light, and the hymn *phos hilaron* (see chapter 1).

Originally the *luchnikon* was the blessing of the light, an act of praise at the lighting of the light, symbol of the risen Lord, as for example in the *Apostolic Tradition* of Hippolytus, chap. 25; Basil, *De Spir. Sancto* 29 (PG 32, 205); *Const. Ap.* VIII, 35–37 (Funk 543–547); Egeria, *Pilgrimage* 24, 4; Prudentius, *Cathemerinon* V. Both the *phos hilaron* and the Latin Exsultet are hymns for welcoming the light. One can note both Jewish and late-classical practices in the background.

This light-blessing in the evening was then broadened. The term began to signify the evening service with its own evening psalms (*psalmi lucernares*), which meant that the light motif was to some extent pushed into the background. *Lucernarium* began to mean "evening sacrifice" or "evening prayer." These two traditions came together: one can still see this in Byzantine vespers (*hesperinos*).

orthros: morning prayer, beginning at the end of night and ending with the rising of the sun. In comparison with the Roman rite, *orthros* includes both night prayer and morning prayer (*matutinae laudes*). In *orthros* clearly two traditions have been joined, the "congregational" and the monastic, just as has been described above and will be discussed below under "the hours." What is sure is that the *ainoi* (Psalms 148–149–150) together with the hymn *Doxa* (*Gloria in Excelsis*) form the oldest core. The tradition of reading resurrection-pericopes in the morning comes from Jerusalem.

pannychis: a service that takes place throughout the whole night and the preceding evening; a vigil. In the Byzantine rite this means that vespers and lauds (*hesperinos* and *orthros*) are joined together (even though this does not take all night). In some monasteries, however, the whole psalter, with the accompanying *troparia,* and all odes are recited, making apparent the ascetic aspect of the *pannychis.* Such ascetic worship is also known in the monastic tradition of the west. The *pannychis* is used for Sundays and festivals.

paramone: this term signifies the eves of Christmas and Epiphany, i.e., December 24 and January 5. The term (*paramenein*) indicates that people remained originally in the church after vespers for the vigil (*pannychis*). Anciently a *paramone* occurred more frequently than just at Christmas and Epiphany.

The day of the vigil is marked by fasting, at least until noon, by the so-called Great Hours (i.e., prime, terce, sect, none in a solemn form and with proper texts), and by the celebration of the Divine Liturgy of Basil after vespers.

polyeleos: a name for Psalm 136 in which the word *eleos* recurs constantly ("for his *steadfast love* endures forever"). This psalm is found in the group 135–136–137 (and 45 on feasts of Mary). The whole group is thus called *polyeleos.* These psalms are sung with the refrain "Alleluia."

prokeimenon: a responsorial verse placed before a psalm and used as a refrain between the psalm verses. The psalm sung in responsorial manner (sung from the ambo by the *psaltes*) can also be denoted by the term.

The lector recites the first psalm verse, which is then repeated by the choir. Then the lector recites one or several verses, to each of which the choir responds by repeating the first verse. At the end the *psaltes* once again takes up the first verse, which is then repeated by the choir. A responsorial psalm, a *prokeimenon,* is found in the Divine Liturgy of Basil in the evening of Holy Saturday—Psalm 82 with the refrain: "Arise, O God, judge the earth, for to you belong all the nations" (*Triodion,* Athens, 1960, p. 442).

sticheron: poetic strophe between the verses of both the evening psalms and the morning psalms.

stichologia: verse-by-verse recitation of the psalms (one *kathisma* in vespers, three in lauds), which is a monastic use. The popular use is the response (*prokeimenon*). The manner of praying the psalms can vary—sung in choir or by the *psaltes*.

stichos: a verse of a psalm.

theotokion: a *troparion* (strophe) in honor of the Mother of God that concludes every series of songs (e.g., an ode in a canon). In the vespers of Saturday evening the vespers psalms 141–142–130–117 are concluded with a *theotokion* which, however, carries the name *dogmatikon.* There are eight of them, according to the eight tones, one used at every Saturday evening vespers (with which Sunday begins). The *dogmatikon* introduces the light procession. The term refers to the precise formulation of the dogma of the incarnation and of the role of the Mother of God therein.

On every Wednesday and Friday, on the days of Lent and Holy Week, and on other days of the year when the passion of the Lord is principally meditated upon, the *theotokion* is called a *staurotheotokion* and expresses the feelings of Mary under the cross (lament of the Mother of God, of Syrian origin).

By means of the *theotokion,* the Byzantine hours take on a pronounced marian character that is nonetheless always interwoven with the mystery of Christ (especially the incarnation). One should analyze the content of these *troparia* in order to trace Byzantine "mariology."

trisagion: this term does not mean the Thrice Holy in the anaphora (Sanctus) but the acclamation of the holy (*hagios*), strong (*ischuros*), and immortal (*athanatos*) God. It is a sort of ejaculatory prayer and was originally a refrain at the entrance procession. Its place before the first reading in the Divine Liturgy is a reminder of this fact.

troparion: a poetic genre in worship. A *troparion* is an extended response (or antiphon), but is simple in structure and in rhythm—a short metrical hymn of popular character. A *troparion* is often further indicated by specific names: *doxastikon, apolytikion, theotokion, exapostilarion.* The *eulogetaria* are *troparia* that surround a repetition of Psalm 119:12 in the *orthros* of Sunday. Especially famous are the *troparia* which begin with *semeron,* "today," whereby the mystery of the day is evoked.

SUMMARY OF THE TERMS

A study of the above list leads one to realize that these technical terms have much to do with the singing or reciting of hymnic and poetic texts in the liturgy. Hymnography is the core of Byzantine liturgy. The Christian mystery has been handed down by singing it. Therefore, these hymnic and poetic texts must not be read casually or unimaginatively: they are the hymn-texts of believers with their hearts on their tongues. It should also be apparent that the Divine Liturgy is not the only celebration; the liturgy of the hours is also at the heart of Byzantine worship, not least for the faithful. For this, information is to be found in the *Liturgisch Woordenboek, Supplement,* in J. Matéos, *Le Typicon de la grande Eglise,* vol. 2, pp. 279–329, in M. Mary and K. Ware, *The Festal Menaion,* pp. 544–562, and in *La prière des heures* (Chevetogne), pp. 501–519.

D. SUMMARIES OF THE LITURGICAL DATA

We will attempt in the following pages to give an overview of the principal celebrations according to the Byzantine rite, as a supplement to the information already given in chapter 2 (*passim,* esp. pp. 113–117).

1. THE HOURS

The hours in the Byzantine rite include: prayer in the middle of the night (*mesonykticon*), morning prayer (*orthros*), prime (*prote,* the first hour), terce (*trite*), sext (*hekte*), none (*enate*), vespers (*hesperinos*), and compline (*apodeipnon*). The prayer in the middle of night is one with morning prayer. It is a historical fact that in the monasteries, morning prayer was extended into the night (perpetual prayer). The oldest data on the little hours as well as morning and evening prayer are to be found in the Sabas-tradition of Jerusalem (*horologion* of the ninth century), while in the tenth century in Constantinople the little hours were not yet in general use, certainly not in the cathedral office. In other words, the little hours were of monastic origin, intended for psalm-prayer during the day at fixed times (just as in the west).

There may be perhaps an older layer of the liturgy of the hours in the East Syrian (Chaldean) rite, with only night, evening, and morning prayer (see Matéos, *Lelya-Sapra*).

Anciently the core of daily prayer consisted of prayers at morning and evening in which the local congregation took part as much as possible. This was so especially for Jerusalem, as described in chapter 2. There was a fixed series of refrain-psalms, hymns, and prayers. In

Jerusalem the appropriate reading came to be added. On the history of a morning office in some sense distinguished from the night office in cathedral and monastic traditions, see R. Taft, "Quaestiones Disputatae in the History of the Liturgy of the Hours," *Worship* 58, 1984, pp. 130–158, and see especially the bibliography found there.

Further discussion will be limited to description of the *orthros* and *hesperinos*.

Orthros of Sunday

The structure of *orthros*, in which a double tradition is visible, looks like this:

introductory acclamation, then the *hexapsalmos* (3, 38, 63, 88, 103, 143) together with the associated prayers of the priest (morning prayers). Psalms 3 and 63 are old morning psalms;

then follows the great litany (deacon), an antiphonal song made up of Psalm 118:26,27,29 and the *troparion* of the day (*apolytikion*);

psalmody: three *kathismata* (*stichologia*) according to the *cursus*. This monastic psalmody is abbreviated radically in the parish churches. After each *kathisma* there is a short litany (*ectene*) concluding with a *troparion* (also called a *kathisma*). In Sunday *orthros*, the third *kathisma* is Psalm 119 (praise of the Torah) or the *polyeleos* (see glossary of terms, p. 270) which is abbreviated in practice. This last *kathisma* is followed (only on Sundays) by the *eulogitaria*, which are *troparia* around Psalm 119:12 that sing the resurrection of the Lord (including the *troparion Myrophoroi gynaikes*, "Myrrh-bearing women");

then the *hypakoe* and the *anabathmoi* are sung. These were most likely old procession songs at the entering of the church from the narthex where all of the foregoing was prayed and sung (cf. Matéos, *Le typicon*, vol. 1, p. xxiii);

the gospel: in the Sunday office and after the lights have been lit, the appointed gospel account of the resurrection is then read from the gospel book that has been carried from the altar to the middle of the church. There are eleven resurrection pericopes. Earlier (before the tenth century), this reading took place after the morning psalms (*ainoi*) and the Gloria; now it is done before them. If it is a *pannychis* (that is, if the vespers of the evening before are joined to *orthros* as a vigil service) then a sort of intermission occurs here: every participant receives a piece of bread (originally perhaps a practical custom). At the same time the gospel book is presented to the faithful for reverencing (a kiss), which is also done even if there is no *artoklasia*, "breaking of bread";

during the reverencing of the gospel book, Psalm 51 is sung with a *troparion* and an extensive supplicatory prayer. This psalm is a fixed component of *orthros* in all rites. It is possible that in early times Psalm 51 concluded the night prayer and formed the transition to *orthros*;

the singing of the canon (the odes) was introduced at this point after the tenth century. In the *typicon* of the tenth century (ed. Matéos), the canon is not yet to be found. It is a monastic custom. The canon consists of biblical canticles that are surrounded by *troparia*. Actually this means that the biblical texts are no longer sung. This long section of the Sunday *orthros* has the following parts: the nine canticles (called odes—Ex 15:1–18; Dt 32:1–43; 1 Sm 1:1–10; Hb 3:1–19; Is 26:9–21; Jon 2:2–10; Dn 3:26–56; Dn 3:57–88; Lk 1:46–55 with 1:68–79), which are not sung except for the song of Mary; corresponding to each canticle are three canons (*anastasimos; stauroanastasimos; canon tes theotokou*)—these canons are also called odes. They always each contain the following texts—a *hirmos* (see above glossary, p. 268) and a group of *troparia* that are then concluded with a *theotokion*. After the third ode (corresponding to the third canticle), a *kathisma* is inserted; after the sixth ode come the *kontakion* of the day (see above glossary, pp. 268–269) and the *oikos*; after the ninth ode is sung the *exapostilarion* that corresponds to the resurrection pericope of the day (an *exapostilarion* is once again a *troparion* concluded by a *theotokion*). This complicated whole is called "the canon of the nine odes," that is, the ordering of *troparia* around the nine odes (biblical canticles). All of these hymnic texts were written in the monasteries and inserted into the cathedral *orthros*;

only now follows the heart of lauds, the *ainoi*, the morning psalms of praise (Psalms 148–149–150), alternating with refrains (strophes). These psalms are concluded with the *troparion heothinon* that corresponds to the one of the eleven resurrection pericopes that has been read (every *heothinon* is followed by a *theotikion*). Then follows the morning hymn: *Doxa* (*Gloria in Excelsis*);

orthros is concluded with supplicatory prayers (a very old use), blessing, and dismissal (*apolysis*).

From this description it should be clear how complicated, for outsiders, the structure of *orthros* is. The description cannot, of course, include the various texts. The purpose here is merely to sketch how strongly the monastic tradition has weighted down the old transparent morning prayer, which nonetheless still remains. Still, one ought to read the texts. (It is only since studying and praying those texts that I have begun to savor something of their piety.)

The old series of morning psalms must have included Psalms 63, 148, 149, 150, and perhaps 51. These were recited responsorially—by continual use they were known to all the faithful. This was also true of the morning hymn, *Doxa*. Probably also the song of the three young men (Daniel 3:57–88) belonged to the old popular core of morning prayer as a refrain-song. Moreover, the final litany and the dismissal surely go back to the earliest tradition. Inevitably one thinks of Egeria's description of the Jerusalem liturgy; even then psalmody, hymns (perhaps short strophes), and common supplicatory prayer made up morning prayer.

It is thus most probable that from the monastic tradition come the extensive psalmody, interwoven with poetic texts, and especially the great canon of nine odes. These were developed from the eighth century on, and after the tenth century came into the cathedral office.

There is uncertainty about the original place of the gospel. Is this reading of the resurrection pericope on Sunday morning a remnant from the old vigil of Sunday in Jerusalem? Or was the gospel reading an integral part of morning prayer after the lauds, that is the three psalms of praise, as in Constantinople (*typicon* of the tenth century)? Perhaps several traditions existed simultaneously.

Venerable elements are to be found in morning prayer, in both the Byzantine rite and the Roman. It is the morning praise of God, the creator of light, giver of the new light through the Risen One; the *berakah* to God the Lord; the Jewish substratum of Christian liturgy amplified by Christian meaning.

Vespers of Saturday Evening (Thus of Sunday; Hesperinos)
Parallel to morning prayer is the evening prayer of the congregation, which was also adopted by the monks into their rule. Vespers together with lauds and the Divine Liturgy make up the essence of the Christian eucharist, that is, of praise and thanksgiving to God. The structure is as follows:

after introductory prayers (including the Lord's prayer), the introductory Psalm 104 is prayed (sung). In the meanwhile the celebrant prays eight prayers (*euchas tou luchnikou*, lamp-lighting prayers) in silence. A great litany (*synapte*) concludes this opening. In the tenth century Psalm 86 was still used, sung responsively with the faithful. Psalms 93 and 68 are also mentioned in the sources. These three responsorial psalms were perhaps then concluded by a prayer of the priest; the sources mention sometimes three prayers;

psalmody: one *kathisma* (Psalms 1–8 on Saturday evening). The psalmody is omitted out of practical considerations in parish churches and replaced by several verses. The psalmody is monastic;

the heart of vespers: the evening Psalm 141 with a *troparion* or poetic verses. At the present, Psalms 142, 130, and 117 are also prayed and concluded with a *doxastikon* and a *theotokion;*

now the lights are lit (*lucernarium, luchnikon*) and during the singing of the old hymn *phos hilaron,* the priest and deacon enter with a smoking censer with which the church and the people present are incensed. Incense as an evening sacrifice is suggested by Psalm 141. Light and incense are the two intermingled motifs here. Bertonière (see literature list on p. 251) analyzes the evolution of this "grand rite" (pp. 29–58);

the *prokeimenon* follows as an introductory responsory to the reading from the Old Testament (which is often omitted);

the *ectene* follows;

on festivals the *lite* is inserted (see glossary, p. 269);

back in the church the *aposticha* are sung;

vespers are concluded with the song of Simeon (Luke 2:29–32) and the *trisagion,* the *troparion* of the day (*apolytikion*), and the *theotokion.* The blessing and dismissal conclude the service.

It is striking how well vespers has preserved the old elements and how much less they are flooded by the hymnic texts of monastic origin. It is also striking that in all eastern rites vespers has held the same structure and content: light ceremony and incense offering are mingled with each other. Vespers is the song of praise to the giver of light, the pure evening sacrifice of the congregation.

That lauds shows more monastic influence perhaps comes from the fact that lauds was preceded by night prayer, the prayer hour of the monks, that came to be coupled to morning prayer.

According to the ancient tradition, vespers signifies the beginning of the day. Just as the lighting of lights on Friday evening is the beginning of Sabbath, so the vespers of Saturday evening are the beginning of Sunday. On great festivals, vespers, which then begins later, is joined to the night office and lauds to form together the *pannychis*.

The Byzantine liturgical wealth lies especially in the offices of morning and evening prayer. They determine the image of Sunday or of the festival day, and by these hours time is sanctified and placed in the perspective of the coming kingdom of God. In spite of all the changes, the expectation of the "coming things" has stayed alive in the Byzantine rite. This rite has been too closely bound to Syrian spirituality to have lost the eschatological element.

2. FESTIVALS AND CELEBRATIONS THROUGHOUT THE YEAR

The heart of the celebration of the year in the Byzantine rite (and also in the other rites) is Sunday, which has maintained the character of the commemoration of the resurrection in all the texts (especially in the *heothina* that accompany the eleven resurrection pericopes in the Sunday *orthros*). Saturday is most usually closely connected to Sunday.

The church year of the Byzantine rite is divided into *three cycles* (the other eastern rites show many differences): the cycle of the *octoechos*, the paschal cycle, and the cycle of feasts on a fixed date.

The Cycle of the Octoechos

This cycle is made up of eight series (corresponding to the eight church tones) of seven offices for each day of a week, thus covering eight weeks, collected in the *parakletike* (also called the *octoechos*). The series of tones begins with the second Sunday of Easter, with a new tone for each of the following weeks, and begins anew after the eighth tone has been used in the eighth week, thus continuing until the next Lent.

The Paschal Cycle

This cycle is grouped around Easter Sunday, which falls on a variable date between March 22 and April 25 but is reckoned according to the Julian calendar. Easter Sunday is preceded by ten weeks of preparation (Great Lent) and followed by eight weeks of joy (Pentecost). The Great Week (Holy Week) presents a chain of celebrations just as in the fourth century in Jerusalem! The books that contain the texts are the *triodion* (for Great Lent) and the *pentecostarion* (for Easter and the eight weeks of Pentecost and the following Sunday).

The fasting of Lent is strict (cf. Islamic fasting): no meat, fish, milk

277

products, wine or oil; it is fully maintained in the monasteries. Cf. Alexander Schmemann, *Great Lent* (Crestwood, N.Y., 1974).

THE GREAT WEEK OR THE WEEK OF THE PASSION

Cf. *He hagia kai megalē Hebdomas*, Athens. On Monday, Tuesday, and Wednesday all four gospels are read in their entirety (divided into nine parts). On Wednesday there is in the monasteries a sort of service of penance.

GREAT AND HOLY THURSDAY

Vespers followed by the liturgy of Basil. The texts reflect on the significance of the footwashing, the betrayal of Judas, and the eucharist. After the Divine Liturgy there is a washing of the altar (very recent: 1873) and especially an enacting of the footwashing (a ritual of which the origin is unclear, perhaps having been influenced by the west). Every four or five years the *myron* (see pp. 285–288) is consecrated on this day by the bishop.

GREAT AND HOLY FRIDAY

The services begin at 2 A.M. The vigil consists of twelve readings from the passion of the Lord followed by an *antiphonon* (see the glossary of terms, p. 265) or a group of *troparia*, lyrical laments and meditations on the part of the faithful. "All of this office has something of the grandeur of a Greek tragedy" (Mercenier, p. 23). During the day the Royal Hours, the *Megalai Horai*, are sung: first, third, sixth, and ninth hours. In the afternoon after vespers follows the rite of the burial: the *epitaphion,* a cloth on which an image of the burial of the Lord is embroidered, is carried into the midst of the church, laid down, and covered with flowers.

GREAT AND HOLY SATURDAY

In the night (or later, in the evening) of Friday the *orthros* of Saturday is begun; it is marked especially by a protracted meditation on the paschal mystery: Jesus' descent into the underworld, into death, in order to restore life. This meditation is found in the *eulogia, troparia* that surround Psalm 119 (divided into three stanzas, *staseis*), one *troparion* corresponding to each verse of the psalm. The hope of the resurrection is stressed in the canon of nine odes which then follows. After the *ainoi* and the Gloria (Doxa) of *orthros,* there is once again a procession of the *epitaphion* together with the gospel book while the Trisagion is sung. Then the *epitaphion* is laid again at the same place while there is sung the *troparion,* "The noble Joseph, taking down your spotless body . . . ," which is a sort of *leitmotiv* of the whole service. Readings from Ezekiel 37:1–14; 1 Corinthians 5:6–8; Galatians 3:13–14; and Matthew 27:62–66 conclude the service.

The day of Saturday is then filled with the celebration of the night vigil, which since the fifth century has been steadily advanced from the night of Saturday–Sunday, to Saturday afternoon, and even to Saturday morning, as was formerly the case also in the west. The night vigil begins with the core of vespers: the singing of the evening psalms (with the *stichera*, see glossary, p. 271). During the singing of the evening hymn *Phos hilaron* the light is lit and carried in. Then follows the service of readings, fifteen in number, in which the themes of Easter and baptism are intertwined. The last reading (the song of the three young men in the fiery furnace) forms the transition to the celebration of the liturgy of Basil, in which the *trisagion* is replaced by the thrice-repeated text: "You who have been baptized into Christ, you have put on Christ." There follow Romans 6:3–12, Psalm 82 sung with a refrain (see *prokeimenon*, p. 270), and Matthew 28:1–20. All of this forms the core of the old vigil. Now a canon of nine odes is sung and in the middle of the night the Acts of the Apostles is read from beginning to end, at the conclusion of which the Easter Sunday service can begin.

THE GREAT SUNDAY OF PASCHA

This service begins with the bringing of the *epitaphion* into the altar space in a solemn procession where it is laid upon the altar. Everyone has received a candle, which is lit from the *trikirion*, a three-branched candelabra used for the blessing by the bishop. Everyone goes in a great light procession outside the church by way of the narthex. In the meanwhile all the lights in the church are lit. In front of the closed doors of the church the gospel is read in many languages: John 1 or Matthew 28 or Mark 16:1–8. The doors open! The people enter the church with joy. The great paschal canon attributed to John of Damascus is sung and this is concluded with the *ainoi* (lauds, Psalms 148–150) with *stichera*. With the cry "Christ is risen from the dead," everyone gives each other the kiss of peace. The Divine Liturgy is celebrated.

Vespers conclude the services of Sunday.

COMMENTARY

1. The course of the services, the ongoing celebration of the three days, is reminiscent of the celebration of Holy Week in Jerusalem as

described by Egeria, a continuous meditation and celebration, an unending procession, for the suffering Lord who has descended into death is risen. The high point is the *orthros* and Divine Liturgy of Easter Sunday: the light of the Risen One enlightens everyone present.

2. The form of the ancient vigil was gradually reduced to the structure of festal vespers. The celebration of baptism has all but disappeared from the vigil; some texts are still mindful of the old practice.

3. Of interest is the idea of the descent into death as a fixed component of the paschal celebration. This is an ancient Easter theme with Jewish-Christian roots.

4. The history of the Easter vigil has been written by Bertonière (see literature list, p. 251); the continuation of this work, which is to deal with the triduum, is eagerly awaited. The cathedral office in Constantinople in the tenth century was simpler than the present practice, as is apparent from the old *typicon* (ed. J. Matéos, *Le typicon de la Grande Eglise*, vol. 2, pp. 73–97; cf. Bertonière, pp. 99–153). The burial of the *epitaphion* in the services of Great Friday and Saturday are missing in this *typicon*. This *epitaphion* rite must then have been introduced later. Is it a monastic rite? Where does it come from? Have western practices been taken over in the east, or vice-versa? We do not know! The footwashing and the blessing of *myron* that we do find in the tenth-century liturgy of Thursday (Matéos, pp. 72–76) was a service carried out by the patriarch with his faithful. One gets the impression that the tenth-century *typicon* contains a simpler celebration of the three days. Since the tenth century various other rites must have been changed, probably "monasticized."

5. Brief selections from the texts based primarily on French and some available English translations follow:

the office of the sufferings of the Lord on Great Friday: E. Mercenier, *La prière des églises de rite byzantin*, II, 2, (Chevetogne, 1948), pp. 170–191;

the *kontakion* of Friday: "Come, let us all praise him who was crucified for our sakes; for him did Mary behold on the Tree, and she said, Even though thou hast endured crucifixion willingly thou art still my Son and my God (S. Nassar, *Divine Prayers and Services*, Brooklyn, 1961, p. 850; cf. this and the *oikos* in Mercenier, II, 2, p. 186);

the *eulogia* of Saturday: Mercenier, II, 2, pp. 218–244 (cf. Nassar, pp. 889–904);

the *kontakion* of Saturday: I. Hapgood, *Service Book*, Brooklyn, 1965, p. 222; cf. Mercenier, II, 2, p. 249.

the *stichera* of the *ainoi*: Mercenier, II, 2, p. 252.

the *hirmos* of the first ode of the *canon* of Sunday: "The Day of Resurrection! Let us be illumined, O ye people! The Passover, the Passover of the Lord! From death unto life, and from earth unto heaven hath Christ our God brought us over, singing a song of victory! Christ is risen from the dead!" (Hapgood, p. 227; cf. Mercenier, II, 2, p. 269).

the *kontakion* of Romanos for Easter Sunday: Mercenier, II, 2, p. 272. (Cf. the translation of the full text in M. Carpenter, *Kontakia of Romanos*, vol. 1, pp. 314–325.)

Easter Sunday begins the Pentecost, the fifty days of joy, in which the Sundays have a central position: the Sunday of Thomas, followed by the Sundays of the *Myrophoroi* (the myrrh-bearing women), of the paralytic, of the Samaritan woman, of the blind man, of the "fathers of the First Council of Nicea," and of the Trinity (Pentecost Sunday). Then there are also Ascension and All Saints (the Sunday after Pentecost). Worthy of especial notice are the Sundays with the great pericopes from John (chapters 4, 5, 9), which could be a remnant of the postbaptismal catecheses on the sacraments given to the neophytes. These Johannine pericopes are important types of Christian initiation in both east and west.

The Cycle of Feasts on a Fixed Date
This third cycle begins on September 1 and the textual material is to be found in the *menaia* (see pp. 263–264).
  The major feasts of fixed date are:

Genethlion tēs Theotokou, Nativity of the Theotokos, September 8;

Hypsōsis tou staurou, Exaltation of the Cross, September 14;

Eisodos tēs Theotokou, Presentation of the Theotokos, November 21;

Gennēsis tou Kyriou, Nativity of the Lord, December 25;

Theophaneia tou Kyriou, Theophany of the Lord, January 6;

Hypapantē tou Kyriou, Meeting of the Lord, February 2;

Evaggelismos tēs Theotokou, Annunciation of the Theotokos, March 25;

Metamorphōsis tou Kyriou, Transfiguration of the Lord, August 6;

Koimēsis tēs Theotokou, Dormition of the Theotokos, August 15.

Together with Palm Sunday, Ascension, and Pentecost Sunday, these are then the twelve major feasts.

The origin of the Christmas cycle is treated in chapter 2. Here follows only a sketch of how the feasts of Christmas and Theophany are presently celebrated, with a further mention of the Transfiguration.

CHRISTMAS

The picturesque background of the western Christmas is absent in the east. The texts of the Byzantine liturgy are poetic reflections about the Son of God who became human in order to deify humanity. The incarnation is the total change of humankind through the condescension of God. The theological wealth and poetic ecstasy of the texts are remarkable.

The celebration of Christmas includes: a *paramone* (vigil day) with the *megalai horai,* the great or royal hours, each with proper psalmody, lessons, and *troparia.* The feast begins with vespers in the evening: the evening psalms and their corresponding *stichera;* the entrance with the gospel book (and the light) while the evening hymn is sung. There follows an extended service of readings (the old vigil!), which is concluded with the liturgy of Basil. Great compline (also called "vigil") follows. In the early morning lauds begin (psalmody, gospel reading, canon of nine odes, etc.). Finally the Divine Liturgy of John Chrysostom is celebrated: it is then the morning of Christmas, December 25. All this makes up a complete *pannychis* that is preceded by a fast day with the royal hours—almost one continuous service (cf. Holy Week, pp. 278–279).

A selection from the texts:

stichera of the vesper psalms: M. Mary and K. Ware, *The Festal Menaion,* pp. 253–254;

the *troparia* for the readings of vespers: ibid., pp. 256, 259, 261;

aposticha: ibid., pp. 264–266;

apolytikion: "Your birth, O Christ our God, has filled all the earth with the light of knowledge! For by your birth those who adored the stars were taught by a star to worship you, the Sun of Justice, and to know you the Orient from on high, O Lord, glory to You!" (Monks of New Skete, *A Prayerbook,* Cambridge, N.Y., 1976, p. 607; cf. *The Festal Menaion,* p. 266);

the nine odes, especially the third ode (*The Festal Menaion*, pp. 270–271) and the sixth ode (ibid., pp. 276–277); with the famous *kontakion*:

"The Virgin today gives birth to the superessential One, and the earth proffers the cave to the unapproachable One. Angels with the shepherds sing songs of praise; the Magi, with the star to guide pursue their way. For there has been born, a newborn babe, the God before time. *Oikos:* Bethlehem opened Eden, come let us behold; we have found joy in this hidden place, come let us seize the pleasures of Paradise within the cave; there appeared an unwatered root which sprouted forgiveness; there was found an undug well from which David once yearned to drink; and there the Virgin brought forth an infant Who at once quenched their thirst, that of Adam and of David. Come, then, let us hasten to this place where there has been born a newborn babe, the God before time" (M. Carpenter, *Kontakia of Romanos*, vol. 1, p. 4; cf. *The Festal Menaion*, pp. 277–278).

One should note especially the word *semeron*, "today" (*hodie*): it expresses the actuality of God's grace in the celebration of the congregation. This is a lived conviction in both eastern and western liturgy.

THEOPHANY

Theophany is the older "Christmas feast" of the east, with roots into the third century, a celebration of light and water (baptism). The feast is unfolded from the gospel narrative of the appearance of the three-in-one God at the baptism of Jesus in the Jordan. Jesus, Lord and God, is the light of the world. The church celebrates the *heortē tōn phōtōn* (the feast of lights). The Lord enlightens the believers by the light of truth. Salvation comes to the believer through the mystery of water, which on this day is blessed by the invocation of God's name. This water is blessed not only for baptism, but for all the faithful who make use of it, as in the following text from the *stichera idiomela* of lauds:

διὰ λούτρου σωτηρία, Salvation comes through washing,

δι᾿ ὕδατος τὸ Πνεῦμα, and through water the Spirit:
διὰ καταδύσεως ἡ πρὸς Θεὸν ἡμῶν by descending into the water we
ἄνοδος γίνεται, ascend to God.

283

Θαυμάσια τὰ ἔργα σου, Κύριε.   Wonderful are Thy works, O Lord.

Text and translation: M. Mary & K. Ware, *The Festal Menāion,* p. 383.

The celebration of Theophany goes as follows: there is a *paramone* (vigil day, January 5) with the *megalai horai* in which are found proper psalmody, readings, and *troparia.* Vespers, the beginning of the feast, is a kind of vigil with the customary readings (after the evening psalms and the evening hymn), fifteen in number, in which the mystery of water is emphasized. After the readings the Divine Liturgy of Basil takes place, after which follows the great blessing of the waters (in which there are again five readings, an *ectene,* and a very long prayer of blessing). After the blessing, the building and all those present are sprinkled with water. The night vigil is continued with Great Compline after which pieces of bread are distributed (*artoklasia*). Directly following, lauds is prayed. In the morning the Divine Liturgy of Basil is celebrated. It is a *pannychis.* In the evening of January 6 there is a second vespers.

A selection from the texts:

the *troparia* of the royal hours: *The Festal Menaion,* pp. 314ff;

sticheron of vespers: ibid., pp. 338–339;

the ecstatic water blessing attributed to Sophronius, patriarch of Jerusalem: ibid., pp. 353–359;

the nine odes of the canon express the various themes of the feast: ibid., pp. 367–384.

TRANSFIGURATION

The important work is G. Habra, *La transfiguration selon les Pères grecs* (Paris, 1973). This feast meditates upon the transfiguration of the Lord and of humanity, which is given a mystical knowledge of the divinity of the Lord through his humanity. A text:

the nine odes: *The Festal Menaion,* pp. 482–495 (*exapostilarion,* p. 495: "Today on Tabor in the manifestation of Thy Light, O Word . . . we have seen the Father as Light and the Spirit as Light, guiding with light the whole creation").

MEMORIALS OF THE SAINTS

It is not possible to give a survey of the evolution of the calendar of the saints (see G. Dix, *The Shape of the Liturgy,* pp. 369–385).

However it could be useful to compare the Byzantine and Roman calendars of the tenth century (see J. Matéos, *Le typicon*, vol. 1, and P. Jounel, *Le culte des saints*, pp. 129–132). Such a comparison would show an increase, on the local level, of the number of memorials from the fourth to the tenth centuries. But it would also show some similarities that have to be traced back to an older stratum of the calendars (e.g., Nov. 30, St. Andrew; Dec. 29, Holy Innocents) or to an exchange of memorials (e.g., June 29, SS. Peter and Paul; August 15, Assumption/Dormition) or even to a common tradition (e.g. the memorials of John the Baptist, John the Evangelist, St. Michael, St. Stephen, SS. Philip and James).

Summary
The celebration of the church year in the Byzantine rite takes place according to the three cycles that have been described above. The great feasts—Sunday, the paschal cycle, the celebration of Christmas, and the feasts of the *Theotokos* and the apostles—all go back to a common tradition. This tradition probably has been preserved quite authentically in the East Syrian liturgy. This seems to be obvious from a reading of the East Syrian calendar (see J. Matéos, *Lelya-Sapra*, pp. 6–8).

3. THE CELEBRATION OF THE SACRAMENTS

Baptism and Anointing with Myron
The ordinary practice in the Byzantine rite is infant baptism. There are, however, still elements from adult baptism that have been preserved, just as in the Roman rite. The *typicon* of the tenth century presumes that baptism takes place in the paschal night (cf. Matéos, *Le typicon*, vol. 2, pp. 84–91), but this was not the only time it could be administered.

A differentiation between baptism with water and anointing with chrism, separating them into two celebrations (baptism and confirmation) is unknown in the eastern tradition. The priest anoints the child with *myron* after immersion in the water: baptism and anointing make up one whole. Also the eucharist is still in evidence: the baptized child receives the eucharistic wine. This means that Christian initiation in the Byzantine rite (and in the other eastern rites) continues to exist in its entirety.

Texts: J. Goar, *Euchologion*, pp. 261–309; *Mikron Euchologion* (Athens), *Apostolike Diakonia*; H. Denzinger, *Ritus orientalium* (Latin translation). *Commentary:* Raes, *Introductio*, pp. 115–154.

It is not only in initiation that the church is concerned with the newborn child. On the day of birth the priest visits mother and child and prays for them. On the eighth day, in the church, the child is named and signed with the cross. On the fortieth day after the birth, mother and child come to the church for the purification of the mother and the blessing of the child, keeping in mind Simeon who took the child Jesus in his arms. The purification rite originated after the eighth century, perhaps under influence from the west.

Baptism is administered at a time determined by the parents (sometimes a long time after the birth).

THE CATECHUMENATE

In the fourth century the catechumenate lasted into the weeks just before *pascha:* the catechumen became an *electus*, chosen for baptism and enlightenment (*phōtismos*). Of this tradition, especially that of the rite that was held on Saturday morning before the vigil, there is a remnant left: the practice of rejecting Satan and professing faith in Christ. In the *euchologion* (Goar, p. 274) this part of the rite is also intended to function exorcistically. The baptismal candidate is undressed and turned toward the east; the evil spirit is exsufflated and thrice the sign of the cross is made on the forehead (*sphragizein*). Hands are layed on, a prayer is said, and thrice an exorcism is pronounced by the priest. He says: "Expel from him (her) every evil and hidden impurity." The candidate is then turned to the west: three times the candidate, in answering the questions, rejects Satan, blowing and spitting him away. Then, turned to the east, the candidate cleaves to Christ (*suntassomai*) and promises to believe in him. The Symbol, the creed, is professed. All this is repeated three times! The candidate bows down to the Lord. One of the prayers is as follows:

"Open the eyes of his (her) understanding, that the light of the Gospel may shine brightly in him (her). Yoke unto his (her) life a radiant Angel, who shall deliver him (her) from every snare of the adversary. . . . And make him (her) a reason-endowed (*logike*) sheep in the holy flock of thy Christ, an honorable member of thy Church, a child and an heir of thy Kingdom . . ." (Goar, p. 277).

BAPTISM AND ANOINTING PROPER

The celebrant goes to the piscina (*kolumbēthra*). There is an incensing of the baptistery and an *ectene* (see list of terms). Then the blessing of the baptismal water takes place (together with exorcism and

286

making the sign of the cross). Then the prayer oil is blessed and mixed into the water while Alleluia is sung. The candidate is anointed on the forehead, the breast, the back, and the ears ("for the hearing of faith"). Then the whole body is anointed. Turned toward the east the candidate is now baptized by immersion: *Baptizetai ho doulos tou Theou, N., eis to onoma* . . . ("The servant of God, N., is baptized in the Name . . ."). The baptized is clothed and a prayer is spoken.

The blessing (*berakah*) over the water is a prayer to the Lord Jesus which acknowledges the sanctification of the water of the Jordan: by his baptism Jesus sanctified the water of the Jordan and filled it with the Holy Spirit. The prayer asks that by the same Spirit the baptismal water might be sanctified, might become a spring of life and forgiveness, that those baptized might, passing through the water, become new, made according to God's image in the Son, that they might share in the death and resurrection of that Son (see Goar, pp. 288–289).

A certain discrepancy also marks this ritual. We have already discovered it in the baptismal rite of the fourth and fifth centuries and that of the Roman ritual. That is to say, the *apotaxis* and the *syntaxis* (Saturday morning in fourth and fifth centuries) have been separated from the baptismal act (at the vigil in fourth and fifth centuries) and the blessing of the water has been interpolated between them. *Apotaxis, syntaxis* and confession of faith (two sides of the same thing) should have a place in the baptismal act itself as it is in the *Traditio Apostolica* of Hippolytus. Now there is a kind of duplication, while the two sides are separated.

A last remark concerns the prebaptismal anointing. In the Byzantine rite this anointing occurs with the oil of catechumens and is, in other words, a part of the exorcism just before baptism. In the old Syrian tradition (see chapter 1 above, pp. 52–53; cf. especially G. Winkler, *Das armenische Initiationrituale*), a prebaptismal anointing with chrism took place—a baptismal anointing as a gift of the Holy Spirit. This anointing is preserved in the East Syrian rite as the core element of baptism.

In the Byzantine rite, after the baptism with water comes the anointing with *myron* in the form of a cross (*sphragis*) with this accompanying text: "*Sphragis doreas pneumatos hagiou*," "The seal of the Holy Spirit which is given (to you)." This anointing forms a single whole with baptism, just as the Fathers had already declared (Cyril of Jerusalem, third mystagogical catechesis; *Synod of Laodicea*, ca. 350?, c. 48; see H. Riley, *Christian Initiation*, pp. 396–407).

Pseudo-Dionysius looked upon anointing with *myron* as *teleiosis*. *Myron* is a precious oil, prepared from balsam, olive oil, and various aromatic substances. Its consecration is reserved to the patriarch or the metropolitan (see Goar, *Euchologion*, pp. 501–517). The meaning of the *myron*, arising especially from its fragrance and its use in anointing, is that one is anointed by the Holy Spirit through whom one becomes "sweet-smelling."

"Let us . . . conclude our explanation by saying that the holy oil is mixed with fragrant substances and that in consequence it possesses a number of aromatic properties that bring fragrance to those who come in contact with it in the measure that the perfume has reached them. We learn from this that the transcendent fragrance of Jesus, our Lord, pours out its spiritual gifts on the powers of our souls filling them with delight. . . . We might add that when we are initiated into the sacrament by which we are born of God we receive the infusion of the Holy Spirit through anointing with the holy oil. This symbol seems to me to signify that he who for us, in his human form, received the consecration of the Holy Spirit, while preserving unchanged the essence of his divinity, himself provides for the infusion in us of the Holy Spirit" (Pseudo-Dionysius, *The Ecclesiastical Hierarchy*, IV, 3, quoted in D. Rutledge, *Cosmic Theology*, Staten Island, 1964, pp. 129–130, 136).

For the relation between the laying on of hands and anointing see L. Ligier, *La Confirmation* (Paris, 1973), pp. 51–236.

The song, "You who have been baptized into Christ, you have put on Christ," is the transition to the celebration of the eucharist in which Romans 6:3–11 and Matthew 28:16–20 are read. As is customary in all eastern rites, the newly baptized is given to drink from the eucharistic cup at communion.

The Divine Liturgy
Sources: F. Brightman, *Liturgies*, pp. 308–411; 527–552; J. Goar, *Euchologion*, pp. 47–158. Edition: *Apostolike Diakonia* (Athens).

A first description of the Divine Liturgy of the Byzantine rite has been given in chapter 2 where the structure of the ritual was sketched. Now we will attempt to describe its development to the present time.

The *akolouthia* (*ordo*) of the Divine Liturgy can be divided as follows:

1. the preparation (*proskomide*), *enarxis*, entrance;
2. the reading of the scripture, supplications (*ectenia*);
3. the procession (entrance) to the altar with the gifts together with the *pax* and the profession of faith;
4. the anaphora (the eucharistic prayer);
5. the Lord's prayer, the breaking of the bread, and communion;
6. finally, blessing and dismissal.

The greatest development lay in the first part, the preparation of the gifts, which took on its present shape only in the fifteenth century. If we compare the Byzantine rite with other rites, we discover both a fundamental correspondence and characteristic differences. The East Syrian rite, as we have noted, is of the greatest antiquity (see Sarhad Y Hermiz Jamno, *La structure de la messe chaldéenne*, Rome, 1979).

THE PROSKOMIDE

After the preparatory prayers before the *iconostasis*, the greeting of the altar, the vesting, and the hand-washing (all of these actions being accompanied by prayers), the celebrant and the deacon go to the *prothesis*, the preparation table. There they prepare the bread and chalice; a square of the bread (the *amnos*, the "lamb") is cut out as well as smaller pieces in commemoration of the Mother of God, the saints, the living, and the dead. Placed on the paten (*diskos*), these pieces are covered by the star-cover (*asteriskos*) and a cloth (*kalumna*). The gifts are censed together with the altar and the sanctuary.

Now follows the *enarxis*, the traditional preparation for the service (as is still the case in the East Syrian rite): the litany and the three antiphons (responsory psalms) are recited accompanying silent prayers by the celebrant. The hymn by Emperor Justinian, *ho monogenes huios*, is linked to the second antiphon. During the third antiphon the priest and deacon make their solemn entrance with the gospel book and burning candles, an entrance that is also accompanied by a silent prayer of the priest and the entrance song. After the entrance the *troparia* of the day and the saint and the *kontakion* are sung. The entrance is concluded with the Trisagion.

COMMENTARY

1. What seems to be the most original part of this section of the liturgy is the entrance of the celebrant, accompanied by a responsorial song (psalm), of which perhaps the Trisagion was the refrain.

The supplications after the antiphons are "extended" calls for prayer by the deacon. It is possible that this simple entrance developed into greater solemnity because of the imperial ambiance. Not only did the patriarch make his entrance, as did the emperor and his court, but so did Christ as represented by the gospel book: truly a "celestial" procession to the Divine Liturgy.

A fragment reminiscent of the original entrance may be found in the rubric, requiring that the celebrant take his place at the throne (the *cathedra*) just before the readings. The original entrance procession led to the *cathedra*.

2. The *enarxis* (beginning) was originally a service of prayer before the procession to the church took place, a kind of preparation of the assembly by means of common prayer.

3. The origin of the *proskomide* is not yet clear. It is not known why the gifts came to be prepared before the service. The *proskomide* (or *prothesis*) is a matter of record at the beginning of the ninth century; thus the origins of the rite can be traced back to the eighth century. The rite was finally fixed only in the fifteenth to sixteenth centuries (see R. Bornert, *Les commentaires byzantine*, pp. 148–150; 161–162; 227–229).

We only can guess why the *proskomide* was created. In reaction against iconoclasm? Due to allegorizing tendencies? Or has something been included in the liturgy that originally was not "liturgical," i.e., did the offering of the gifts to the clergy subsequently become ritualized?

4. The *amnos* (lamb)-rite of the *proskomide* focuses on the commemoration of the suffering of the Lord. As Nicolas Cabasilas, *Explication of the Divine Liturgy*, points out, the eucharist is a real sacrifice (*pragma*; see Bornert, pp. 229–233). The *prothesis* prayer asks for the blessing of the gifts and their acceptance on the heavenly altar (*thusiastèrion*).

It is striking that at the same time in the west the same tendency arises, i.e., the need to defend the reality (*veritas*) of the sacrament as a sacrifice.

5. The vesting prayers are the latest to become part of the rite. Cf. Simeon of Thessalonica (d. 1429; see R. Bornert, *Les commentaires byzantine*, pp. 245–263).

THE READING OF THE SCRIPTURES

The reading of the "apostle" is introduced by a *prokeimenon*, which was originally a responsorial song between the reading of the prophet (the Old Testament) and the apostle. The responsorial song is now only a torso. The gospel reading is introduced by the singing of Alleluia, as also by censing and silent prayer.

The Byzantine rite reads the apostle and the gospel. That means that the Old Testament reading has disappeared (seventh century). The East Syrian rite has preserved the old practice of reading from law and prophets, apostle and gospel (see G. Kunze, *Die gottesdienstliche Schriftlesung*, vol. 1, Göttingen, 1947, pp. 22–25, 75–103). For the readings in the tenth century *typicon* see J. Matéos, *Le Typicon de la grande Eglise*, vol. 2, pp. 214–231.

Actually there are many silent prayers by deacon and celebrant during the liturgy. These prayers must have become customary since the sixth century. They accentuate the holiness of the Mystery and the unworthiness of those who minister at the celebration of the Mystery. The analogy with western-Roman practice is striking (see Matéos, *Le Typicon*, pp. 296–300). See also the essay of Edmund Bishop, "Silent recitals in the mass of the faithful" (in R. Connolly, *The Liturgical Homilies of Narsai*, Cambridge, 1909, pp. 121–126).

The vicissitudes of the *ectene* (supplication) after the gospel reading and sometimes after the homily have been elucidated by J. Matéos (*La célébration de la parole dans la liturgie byzantine*, Rome, 1971, pp. 148–173). The first supplication (originally of penitential character) was introduced at this point in the seventh or eighth centuries; actually it is out of place, coming as it does before the prayer for catechumens. The original and genuine but now "blank" prayer of the faithful is found just before the great entrance.

THE CELEBRATION OF THE ALTAR

The famous Cherubic Hymn was, probably, once part of an antiphonal psalm; the *troparion* of that psalm was introduced into the Divine Liturgy at the Great Entrance in the second half of the sixth century. The central theme of this *troparion* is quite simple: "Let us lay aside all worldly care to receive the King of all," an anticipation of the *sursum corda* in the dialogue before the anaphora. The Cherubikon is the chant of the *oblatio*.

"The '*oblatio*' is not the 'offertory' in the modern sense of the term but the anaphora, as is obvious from the intended parallel *oblatio-oblatum* (in S. Augustine's *Retractationes* 2, 11). *Oblatum* can refer only to what happens during the anaphora, for what the people receive in communion are not merely offered but consecrated gifts.

"All this bears out what we have already shown . . . that the tendency to consider the Oriental pre-anaphoral rites, including the procession with the gifts and its accompanying chants, in terms of 'offertory,' 'offertory-procession,' 'offertory-chant,' is a prejudice based on later, largely Western, liturgical categories. Here again the Cherubicon betrays the primitiveness of the Byzantine Great-Entrance chants, a primitiveness that we shall see in other elements of the pre-anaphoral rites of CHR.

"Properly understood then, the Great-Entrance chant assumes a broader, more balanced liturgical role, tempering the exaggerated importance that has been assigned to the Great-Entrance procession in itself. For at the entrance we welcome the gifts, symbol of Christ, only with a view to their oblation and reception in communion . . ." (R. Taft, *The Great Entrance*, pp. 67–68).

The kiss of peace, in early times known as *signaculum, sphragis*, is a sign of mutual acceptance and confirmation of all that has gone before. It follows the transfer of gifts. But originally the kiss was given after the prayer of the faithful, just before the transfer of the gifts (cf. Justin's description of the rite in chapter 1 above). The reason for placing the kiss just before the anaphora lies in interpreting the text of Matthew 5:23–24 (Taft, pp. 375–383) at face value.

Timothy, patriarch of Constantinople (511–518), introduced the creed into the Divine Liturgy.

As far as the anaphora of the Divine Liturgy is concerned, we know already the anaphorae of St. Basil and of St. John Chrysostom (see chapter 2, pp. 127–128). The prayer of St. Basil is used in the liturgy of Christmas, Theophany, the Sundays of Lent (except Palm Sunday), and Thursday and Saturday of Holy Week; for the rest the prayer of St. John Chrysostom is used.

Both texts, in their own unique character, are examples of the height of Greek euchology. We need only mention the "grandeur" of the pre-Sanctus of the anaphora of St. Basil, the archaic character of the first stratum of the text of John Chrysostom. The notion, *prospheromen soi tēn logikēn tautēn latreian*, reaches back to early Christian euchology (see "Généalogie hypothétique de la prière eucharistique," *Questions liturgiques* 61, 1980, pp. 263–278, esp. p. 272). Finally there is the remarkable epiclesis of the anaphora of Chrysostom, with the phrase: "*metabolōn toi Pneumati sou tōi hagiōi*," the most explicit formula of transformation of the gifts in an epiclesis of the eastern tradition (see G. Wagner, *Der Ursprung der Chrysostomusliturgie*, p. 113).

COMMUNION

The central rites of this section are the Lord's Prayer, the "invitation" (*Ta hagia tois hagiois*), the breaking of the bread, and the communion of the celebrant and the faithful. These rites have been surrounded by secondary rites such as the *zeon* and silent prayers.

SUMMARY

We quote from the conclusion of Taft's study (*The Great Entrance*, pp. 426–427):

"Further developments in the 7th–10th centuries show signs of overburdening the rites with unnecessary elements. . . . The post-iconoclast changes in the disposition of the church led to the disappearance of the outside *skeuophylakion* and the consequent weakening of the Great Entrance as a truly functional procession. . . . Later medieval developments must be judged even more harshly. Most serious was the gradual loss of the true sense of the *accessus ad altare* and the notion that these rites in some way constitute an "offertory." In addition, the evolution of the diaconical transfer of gifts into a procession of the presbyters, the corruption of the text and scope of the *orate fratres* dialogue, the interruption of the chant with commemorations, the obscuring of the true scope and object of the first incensation by extending it to the icons, people, etc.—to say nothing of the addition of the *troparia* and other lesser formulae—are signs of a liturgy in decline. This means the victory of allegory over sober practicality and symbolism rooted in the true meaning of the sacramental rites."

One is forced to compare these facts in the evolution of the Byzantine rite with those we found in the western-Roman liturgy in the time of Amalarius of Metz, especially in the adaptation of the Roman mass in the Frankish realm (*Ordo Romanus* IV, V; see above, pp. 185ff.).

Two final remarks: not a few prayers of the Divine Liturgy are directed to the Lord Jesus or have a "vacillating" address (to the Father and to the Son). This may be due to a certain Monophysite influence in the Orthodox liturgy.

For the liturgy of the presanctified gifts (*he theia leitourgia tōn prohegiasmenōn*) we refer to Brightman, pp. 345–352. The earliest description is given in the *Chronicon paschale* (PG 92, 67–1028).

Penance

In the case of penance the diversity of practice, up to the present day, is great. Confession and absolution are not strictly regulated as in the western-Roman rite. The East Syrians have only the reconciliation; in other rites there is a general absolution of sins during the Divine Liturgy. In the Byzantine rite confession of sins (followed by *akoinonia*), penance, and forgiveness (absolution), are to be distinguished from each other. The individual confesses to the priest near the *iconostasis* but this individual's confession is situated within the common prayer of the priest with all the penitents. After the confession, a penance (*epitimie*) is imposed; reparation must first be made. The fixing of the penance is prescribed in a *Penitential* from the Byzantine Middle Ages attributed to John IV, patriarch of Constantinople (582–595). After the penance, absolution is given, the formulas for which are diverse and even left up to the priest. The Greek tradition provides prayers after the confession and a prayer after the *epitimie*. (See O. Wagner, "Bussdiziplin in der Tradition des Ostens," in *Liturgie et rémission des péchés*, Rome, 1975, pp. 251–264.)

Ordinations

Texts: Goar, *Euchologion*, pp. 194f., 203f. (reader, singer, and subdeacon); pp. 208ff. (deacon); pp. 242 (presbyter); and 249 (bishop); Denzinger, *Ritus orientalium*, II, pp. 1–363.

There is a distinction between "lower ordinations," called *cheirothesia* (reader, singer, subdeacon), and ordinations of deacon, presbyter, or bishop, called *cheirotonia*. It is noteworthy that all the eastern rites have maintained the early tradition that reception into the *ordo* is marked by the laying on of hands and prayer. The *traditio* of the *instrumenta* belonging to the office and the investiture with the liturgical garments, so important in the western ritual, is not known in the east, except among the Armenians (under influence of the west). The ritual of the Byzantine ordinations of deacon, priest, and bishop goes back to the *euchologion* of the eighth century, which has been taken over practically unchanged. One finds there the well-known call to prayer: *Hē theia charis* (see chapter 2, p. 139). This call to prayer at present generally accompanies the laying on of hands, which, however, ought to be seen as connected with the ordination prayer immediately following. The ordination prayers of the Byzantine rite are general in content and do not go back further than a document from the eighth century. In the ordination of a bishop, two long confessions of faith are made by the candidate, and the

294

opened gospel book is imposed on his head, a tradition that goes back to the fourth century.

The ordination rites of the other eastern traditions, especially those of the West Syrian tradition, are as a rule less sober than the Byzantine, but do have the traditional core (laying on of hands and prayer). For the texts see H. Denzinger, *Ritus orientalium.*

Marriage

Texts: Goar, *Euchologion,* pp. 310–325; Denzinger, *Ritus orientalium,* II, pp. 364–383. *Studies:* A. Raes, *Le marriage; sa célébration et sa spiritualité dans les églises d'Orient* (Chevetogne, 1958); K. Ritzer, *Formen, Riten* (LQF 38), pp. 101–150.

The marriage rite has two parts that were earlier also temporally separated from each other: the exchange of rings or the betrothal, and the crowning (*stephanoma*). The present texts go back to the *euchologion* of the eighth century with only small variants. The expressive power of the crowning is underscored by the three accompanying prayers, which are impressive in both length and content.

CONCLUSION

This survey of the Byzantine rite and its history is now finished. It remains incomplete: since the textual material could not be delved into sufficiently, there is the danger of superficiality; the history of the rite could be described only cursorily because the necessary data are lacking or because all the known data could not be examined in detail because of space limitations. Nonetheless, perhaps something of both the wealth and lavishness of the Byzantine synthesis has been portrayed, the synthesis that characteristically marked eastern Christendom. For a western believer it is good to read and to penetrate this experience of the Christian faith. To fully participate in it, however, will be difficult if not impossible. It is also not necessary. The announcement of salvation can be sung in many ways and can be celebrated in variegated garments and symbols! In the end, these all have to do with the same thing:

Ὠ φιλοθεάμονες τῶν ὑπὲρ νοῦν καὶ φιλήκοοι, μυστικῶς ἐποπτεύσωμεν Χριστὸν ἐξαστμάψαντα θεικαῖς ἀκτῖσι, καὶ ἐνηχθῶμεν τὴν τοῦ Γεννήτορος φωνὴν ἠγαπημένον

O come, let us who love to see and hear mysteries beyond human understanding, let us mystically gaze on Christ, shining in the brilliance of divine splen-

ἀνακηρύττουσαν Ἰιὸν τὸν
καταυγάσαντα τὴν ἀνθρωπίνην
ἀσθένειαν ἐν θαβὼρ, καὶ
πηγάσαντα φωτισμὸν ταῖς ψυχαῖς
ἡμῶν.

dour. Let us make the Father's
voice resound, telling all the
world that he is his beloved Son.
Let us rejoice, for on Mount Tabor he transforms the weakness
of humanity by his divine glory,
by flooding our souls with light.

Sticheron for little vespers of Transfiguration; translation by Monks of New
Skete, *A Prayerbook,* p. 680.

Chapter Six

Gain and Loss: Worship in the Writings
of the Reformers and the Counter-Reformation

The great reformers of the church in the west ordered worship
according to one important principle: the holy scripture, the word of
God, which they placed again at the heart of church life. They knew
but one criterion: is the church faithful to the word of God, in its life
and worship? They wanted to go back to the source. Unconsciously,
or sometimes consciously, they also took along in their baggage some
of the current practices that they condemned. As to worship, a man
like Luther was more medieval than we would suppose. The reformers achieved a gain in church life, but they nonetheless also be-
queathed a loss to their followers, that is, the loss of a clear view of
the tradition of the church as expressed in worship. Both gain
and loss.

The reaction of the Counter-Reformation was a glorification of the
true church that had braved all the centuries, a glorification that
swelled almost out of proportion. This sense of glorification was also
reflected in the liturgy of the Counter-Reformation.

I. HISTORICAL DATA

Literature

O. Chadwick, *The Reformation.* Pelican History of the Church, vol. 3
(Harmondsworth, 1968).

A. Mirgeler, *Geschichte Europas* (Freiburg, 1964).

G. Müller, *Die römische Kurie und die Reformation 1523–1534* (Gütersloh,
1969).

Oekumenische Kirchengeschichte, vol. 2 (Mainz, 1973), pp. 195–438.

A. THE HUMANISTS

"Everyone wanted reform, or professed to want reform. How to
reform and what to reform was not so clear. . . . For centuries men

blasphemed in their cups and bawdy songs, and improvised anti-clerical ditties for their drinking friends. Now these arguments were no longer confined to the tavern. They were becoming public property, the reading and the commonplace of honourable and educated men" (Chadwick, *The Reformation,* pp. 12, 18).

The waning Middle Ages had set the tone: people were deeply disappointed in both church and state. The call for reform was widespread, especially for reform of the church. In making such a call people looked to the past. The early church was the ideal from which the church had now strayed, so far that nothing seemed to remain from that early period. Holiness, purity, poverty, zealous faith had all disappeared, or so it was thought. The humanists with their growing historical insight had a distaste for what we now call "the Middle Ages." They saw it as a barbaric time of bad Latin and impossible metaphysics. Especially the clergy and the pope were responsible for all these ills. At the councils of Constance and Basel this dissatisfaction and a certain kind of antipapalism had already appeared, but now this tendency was becoming much more evident. Certain forms of anticlericalism were to be found not only in the scholarly circles but also among the faithful. Savonarola brought the city of Florence into revolt against the pope and "his clique," i.e., the Curia, which consisted mostly of the pope's relatives. The people began to criticize just like the learned. The development of printing brought books onto the market and many people learned to read them. Once people began to pore over the works of someone like Erasmus, it was not long before they too became reform-minded. The church, which had for many years looked upon learning and scholarship as its monopoly, now lost the claim and became the object of a bitter critique carried on by learning, once the church's handmaid.

Nascent humanism, especially that of the Italian Renaissance, had little concern for religion, but had instead a literary and philosophical bent. In the north, however, humanism inclined more toward interest in theology. For the humanists the church was a scandal, and the pope and his court, the bishops, and the friars had made it that way! Their knowledge was narrow, their ethical conduct below standard (concubinage, dishonesty, avarice), and teaching and preaching of the faith was at a low ebb. Erasmus, especially in *The Praise of Folly,* voiced the feelings of those days. The popes, the cardinals, the bishops, the theologians, the dreadfully stupid preachers, the religious, and the monks—all of them were scathingly dealt with in the book, which was printed and reprinted and read all over Europe.

B. PAPAL POWER

The power of the pope suffered setbacks. In Spain the state took control of the Inquisition; in England the church was controlled by the government; in France the pope made a concordat allowing the king to name the bishops (the Concordat of Bologna); in Germany the many princelings determined their own political course. The reformers, therefore, joined hands with the politically powerful, for there was not much that could be negotiated with Rome. Rapid decisions were possible only with the backing of the political authority. A bull from the pope could indeed be had for money, but in fact the power lay elsewhere.

"The old ideal of a unity in Christendom was collapsing before the rise of the national states. The Vatican still trumpeted forth the claims of an Innocent III or Boniface VIII to world dominion. . . . These vast pretensions corresponded to little enough in the cold reality of European politics. The Pope could sometimes secure what he wanted, but by diplomacy, no longer by decree. Bulls might thunder forth, and were still potent when they thundered, but behind the scenes there had been bargaining. To achieve anything important in France, Spain, Portugal, England, parts of Italy, parts of Germany, the Pope must secure the cooperation or the complaisance of the effective ruler" (Chadwick, *The Reformation*, p. 28).

C. SCHOLARSHIP

Scholarship went its own way and led to historical research and to discovery of the classics, of the world outside of Europe, and of the fact that the world was not the center of the universe. Theology lost its privileged place, and its pedestal was systematically undermined, for example, by the sharp pen of Erasmus (*Praise of Folly*, no. 53). Its underlying philosophy had become unusable since nominalism: the nominalists doubted all the pronouncements of metaphysics. They did indeed hold fast to the content of the faith, but they saw it only as a mystery concerning which reason could say nothing meaningful. The relationship between scholarship and faith thereby came to be entirely different. There was after all nothing that could be proved about things that you could not see.

"The rope of Nominalism was throttling the windpipe through which the philosophers had breathed. Soon after the beginning of the English Reformation, Oxford men were tearing the heavy folios of Duns Scotus and using them as wastepaper. *This symptom of an attitude to Duns Scotus was not a consequence of the Reformation, but a cause.* His majestic constructions looked like intellectual wastepaper" (Chadwick, *The Reformation*, p. 35, italics added).

D. ERASMUS' PEREGRINATIO RELIGIONIS

The humanists had great difficulty with popular piety. The veneration of the saints, the innumerable images and reliquaries, the devotions, the miracles of the sacred host, pilgrimages, indulgences: all of it scandalized the learned and the innovators, and especially Erasmus. His *Peregrinatio religionis* from the *Colloquia Familiaria* (*Opera omnia*, vol. 1, 1703, cols. 774–776; translation from Craig R. Thompson, *The Colloquies of Erasmus*, Chicago, 1965, pp. 288–291) is characteristic. In the passage that follows, the pilgrimage to Compostella is put under the magnifying glass in a conversation between a certain Menedemus and Ogygius:

Menedemus: Tell me, how is the excellent James?

Ogygius: Much colder than usual.

Menedemus: Why? Old age?

Ogygius: Joker! You know saints don't grow old. But this new-fangled notion that pervades the whole world results in his being greeted more seldom than usual. And if people do come, they merely greet him; they make no offering at all, or only a very slight one, declaring it would be better to contribute that money to the poor.

Menedemus: A wicked notion!

Ogygius: And thus so great an apostle, accustomed to shine from head to foot in gold and jewels, now stands a wooden figure with hardly a tallow candle to his name.

Then Ogygius says that there has come to light a letter from the Virgin Mary that she has written herself with the help of an angel. He reads the letter, the content of which speaks for itself:

"Mary, Mother of Jesus, to Glaucoplutus: greetings. Know that I am deeply grateful to you, a follower of Luther, for busily persuading people that the invocation of the saints is useless. Up to this time I was all but exhausted by the shameless entreaties of mortals. They demanded everything from me alone, as if my Son were always a baby (because he is carved and painted as such at my bosom), still needing his mother's consent and not daring to deny a person's prayer; fearful, that is, that if he did deny the petitioner something, I for my part would refuse him the breast when he was thirsty. And sometimes they ask of a Virgin what a modest youth would hardly dare ask of a bawd—things I'm ashamed to put into words. Sometimes a merchant, off for Spain to make a fortune, commits to me the chastity of his mistress. And a nun who has thrown off her veil and is preparing to run away entrusts me with her reputation for virtue—which she herself intends to sell. A profane soldier, hired to butcher people, cries upon me, 'Blessed Virgin, give me rich booty.' A gambler cries, 'Help me, blessed saint; I'll share my winnings with you!' And if they lose at dice they abuse me outrageously and curse me because I wouldn't favor their wickedness. A woman who abandons herself to a life of shame cries, 'Give me a fat income!' If I refuse anything, they protest at once, 'Then you're no mother of mercy.' Some people's prayers are not so irreverent as absurd. An unmarried girl cries, 'Mary, give me a rich and handsome bridegroom.' . . ."

More examples follow. And then:

"So am I alone, a woman and a virgin, to assist those who are sailing, fighting, trading, dicing, marrying, bearing children; to assist governors, kings and farmers? What I've described is very little in comparison with what I endure. But nowadays I'm troubled less by these matters. For this reason I would give you my heartiest thanks, did not this advantage bring a greater disadvantage along with it."

Here the true Erasmus comes out: he criticizes popular piety, but just as much he criticizes also the innovators who take no notice of Mary:

"I have more peace but less honor and wealth. Formerly I was hailed as 'Queen of Heaven, mistress of the world'; now I hear scarcely an 'Ave Maria' even from a few. . . . You're trying, they say, to remove from the churches whatever belongs to the saints. Now just consider what you're doing. . . . But me, however defenseless, you shall not eject unless at the same time you eject my

Son whom I hold in my arms. From him I will not be parted. Either you expel him along with me, or you leave us both here, unless you prefer to have a church without Christ. I wanted you to know this. Think carefully what to answer, for my mind is absolutely made up. From our stony house, on the Calends of August, in the year of my Son's passion 1524, I, the Virgin à Lapide, have signed this with my own hand."

II. CULTURAL DATA

Literature

L. Bouyer, *Autour d'Erasme* (Paris, 1955).

J. Burckhardt, *The Civilization of the Renaissance in Italy* (New York, 1950).

J. Huizinga, *The Waning of the Middle Ages* (Harmondsworth, 1965).

A. Lefranc, *La vie quotidienne au temps de la renaissance* (Paris, 1938).

F. van der Meer, *Atlas of Western Civilization* (London, 1960).

A. THE RENAISSANCE

The waning of the Middle Ages and the Italian Renaissance coincided to some extent. A new morning dawned in Florence and Venice, where one could find:

". . . the consciousness, not of a void left by the conclusion of an epoch, but of the passing of something absurd and the beginning of something better. There is a renewed zest for life. It was there that the new leading spirits broke with the traditional forms of thought which in their eyes had become meaningless. It was there that within a short time the world of wonderful new forms arose, and with them that new, that immediate and careful intuition of concrete reality . . . as we call it, the 'Early Renaissance' " (F. van der Meer, *Atlas,* p. 126).

The term "renaissance" means the rebirth of art and letters in Italy out of the barbarism of the Middle Ages. Attention was focused on the human being and on human ability. One was temperate, level-headed, individualistic, turning back to antiquity as a criterion. The Renaissance man was the first *homme clos* "who attempted to carry his world—a world as rich and manifold and active as possible—within himself and on the basis of that world to think, to work, to act, in good and in bad, with God or without God, in

302

the church or outside of the church" (A. L. Mayer, *Die Liturgie in der Europäischen Geistesgeschichte*, p. 71). Religious questions were viewed from a human standpoint and were turned over to leading minds of the time for evaluation. The Renaissance was characterized by a materialistic and rationalistic view of reality and by a far-reaching secularization. Where piety continued in existence, it was individualistic or highly active and disciplined.

"Like all advocates of a one-sidedly intellectual culture, Renaissance Man had created a world that was swept and garnished, but empty. He was unsocial, despised the masses, and lived his life with stoic inviolability. Some of the more forceful spirits fell for the attractions of the unbridled *Uebermensch*, and in almost all there was a weakening of the consciousness of sin and of the sense of the tragic in human life" (F. van der Meer, *Atlas*, p. 132).

B. THE BAROQUE PERIOD

The Renaissance broke up in 1527, most likely principally because of Michelangelo, who burst through the precarious compromise between faith and worldliness and brought movement into the static attitude of the Renaissance: thus the Baroque. The time of the Baroque was marked by a growing national consciousness in the west. Society disintegrated into national states with which the church was more or less bound. Each state insisted on its own rights, which were defended and imposed authoritatively. Baroque was the domi· nant style. Spain experienced the apex of its spiritual power and was characterized by an unequalled dynamism in all the facets of life (theater, its own architectural style, painting). France moved toward the *grand siècle*.

The person of the Baroque period wanted to see and hear with all the fibers of the body, to handle, to experience, to be in motion. The tranquility of the self-assured Renaissance was over; dynamic excess came to replace it. The Baroque period flourished in the midst of antitheses: the natural and the spiritual went together; intellect and sentiment; seriousness and play. All were involved with each other. Piety was subjective and exuberant.

"Strictly speaking of course, Baroque is a manner that achieves its powerfully moving effects by arbitrary and if need be senseless forms. It reduces all arts once more into an order, and by its dynamic harmonization of opposites marks a virtual return to mediaeval expressionism. It is, as it were, a new 'Gothic', in sensuous Italian forms" (F. van der Meer, *Atlas*, p. 176, translation emended).

C. THE REFORMATION

"The Reformation from a simple manifesto of a few fervent adherents . . . became a movement whose mysterious power developed into a veritable spiritual hurricane. It blew down humanist aestheticism like a house of cards. It sought out the people, and aroused in hundreds of thousands of consciences a new awareness of the problems of salvation and of the honour due to God. It first affected the Germans—rural and patrician even in their academics and politicians, and rough but by no means frivolous. From thence it spread to the people of other countries, and wherever the hurricane passed it left its indelible mark. The Reformation has irrevocably changed the spiritual climate in Northern Europe, in Catholic as well as non-Catholic lands—though in Spain least of all" (F. van der Meer, *Atlas*, p. 150).

For western Christendom the Reformation was to have irreparable consequences lasting for centuries, and even today the separation appears unbridgeable. The fissure went deep, even causing differences in types of human experience, and altering attitudes toward worship. In some areas the churches were emptied of images while the altar became an unremarkable, constantly less used table, with all attention focused on the pulpit. The liturgy became didactic. Symbolic action was impoverished. The medieval *veritas* was accepted but reinterpreted; the *figurae* largely disappeared. The Roman tradition (along with the Orthodox churches), on the contrary, sheltered the *figurae*.

III. THE LITURGY: ORDERS OF SERVICE AND TEXTS

Literature

R. Jasper and G. Cuming, *Prayers of the Eucharist, Early and Reformed,* 2nd ed. (New York, 1980).

B. Thompson, *Liturgies of the Western Church* (Cleveland, 1961).

Y. Brilioth, *Eucharistic Faith and Practice, Evangelical and Catholic* (London, 1965).

J. Fisher, *Christian Initiation; the Reformation Period* (London, 1970).

H. Goltzen, "Eucharistie, Entfaltung, Fehlentwicklung, Wiedergewinnung des eucharistischen Gebets im Mahle des Herrn," in Th. Sartory et al., *Die Eucharistie im Verständis der Konfessionen* (Recklinghausen, 1961), pp. 21–143.

L. Grönvik, *Die Taufe in der Theologie Martin Luthers* (Göttingen, 1968).

H. Hilgenfeld, *Mittelalterlich-traditionelle Elemente in Luthers Abendmahlschriften* (Zürich, 1971).

P. Jagger, *Christian Initiation 1552–1969* (London, 1970).

F. Mann, *Das Abendmahl beim jungen Luther* (Munich, 1971).

H. Meyer, *Luther und die Messe* (Paderborn, 1965).

F. Pratzner, *Messe und Kreuzesopfer* (Vienna, 1971).

L. Reed, *The Lutheran Liturgy* (Philadelphia, 1947).

V. Vajta, *Luther on Worship, An Interpretation* (Philadelphia, 1958).

J. Bergsma, *Die Reform der Messliturgie durch Johannes Bugenhagen (1485–1558)* (Kevelaer-Hildesheim, n.d.).

P. Brunner, "Wormser deutsche Messe," in *Kosmos und Ekklesia* (Festschrift W. Stählin) (Kassel, 1953), pp. 106–162.

S. Kjöllerström, *Missa Lincopensis* (Stockholm, 1941).

B. Klaus, "Die Nürnberger deutsche Messe (1524)," *Jahrbuch für Liturgik und Hymnologie*, 1, 1955, pp. 1–46.

I. Pahl, *Coena Domini,* vol. I (Freiburg, 1983).

J. Smend, *Die evangelischen deutschen Messen bis zu Luthers Deutscher Messe* (Göttingen, 1896; repr. 1967).

F. Hubert, *Die Strassburger liturgischen Ordungen im Zeitalter der Reformation* (Göttingen, 1900).

M. Jenny, *Die Einheit des Abendmahlsgottesdienstes bei den elsässischen und schweizerischen Reformatoren* (Zürich, 1968).

H. V. Old, *The Patristic Roots of Reformed Worship* (Zürich, 1975).

G. J. van der Poll, *Martin Bucer's Liturgical Ideas* (Assen, 1954).

J. Staedtke, *Die Theologie des jungen Bullinger* (Zürich, 1962).

G. W. Locher, *H. Zwingli in neuer Sicht* (Zürich, 1969).

J. Pollet, *H. Zwingli et la réforme en Suisse d'après les recherches récentes* (Paris, 1963).

F. Schmidt-Clausing, *Zwingli als Liturgiker* (Göttingen, 1952).

F. Schmidt-Clausing, *Zwinglis liturgische Formulare* (Frankfurt, 1970).

A. Ganoczy, *Le jeune Calvin* (Wiesbaden, 1966).

H. Grass, *Die Abendmahlslehre bei Luther und Calvin* (Gütersloh, 1954).

H. Janssen, "Die Abendmahlslehre Johannes Calvins," in Th. Sartory, et al., *Die Eucharistie im Verständnis der Konfessionen* (Recklinghausen, 1961), pp. 204–220 (the *confessio fidei de eucharistia*).

K. McDonnell, *John Calvin, the Church and the Eucharist* (Princeton, 1968).

H. Scholl, *Der Dienst des Gebetes nach Johannes Calvin* (Zürich, 1968).

W. Dankbaar, *Marten Micron; de christilicke ordinancien der nederlantscher ghemeinten te London (1554)* (The Hague, 1956).

A. Sprengel-Ruppenthal, *Mysterium und Riten nach der Londoner Kirchenordnung der Niederlände (c. 1550–1556)* (Cologne, 1967).

A. THE REFORMERS

When one studies the lives and work of the reformers, it becomes apparent that none of them began with a renewal of worship. They began with a critique of the church and with a new reflection on doctrine, which they wanted to bring back to its foundations, to the Old and New Testaments. The reform of the liturgy was a later result of that first critical impulse: the consequences of the critical stance were drawn in different ways and worship was correspondingly changed in different ways. Luther was led to propose modest liturgical revisions only because in his opinion his followers had tried to reform worship too quickly and too irresponsibly: his attitude was to become the heart of the "conservative reformation" (cf. J. Pelikan, *Obedient Rebels*, New York, 1964). Calvin was not interested primarily in the reform of worship. Perhaps Zwingli acted the most directly as a consistent liturgical reformer. For all of them preaching was at the heart of worship, and only baptism and the Lord's Supper could be coupled to preaching celebrations based in the scripture.

1. THE CONGREGATIONAL CELEBRATION OF BAPTISM

Luther

Luther wrote two orders for the celebration of baptism, and in both the most striking novelty was to make congregational participation possible by use of the vernacular:

. . . damit die paten und beystehende deste mehr zum glauben und ernstlicher andacht gereytzt werden, unnd die	. . . in order that the sponsors and others present may be stirred to greater faith and more earnest devotion, and that the

priester, so da teuffen, deste mehr vleysz um der zuhörer willen haben müssen.	priests who administer the baptism should show greater concern for the good of the hearers

Text: WA 12, 46. *Translation:* H. T. Lehman, ed., *Luther's Works,* vol. 53 (Philadelphia, 1965) p. 101.

In the rite itself, however, the traditional baptismal celebration is still easily recognizable. The *Taufbüchlein* of 1523 (WA 12, 42–48; see *Luther's Works,* vol. 53, pp. 96–101; cf. *Leiturgia,* vol. 5, Kassel, 1970, pp. 356–358) has the following order of service:

exorcism with exsufflation;

signing of the cross on forehead and breast with two traditional prayers;

gift of salt followed by prayer (the so-called Flood prayer);

three exorcisms (from the Latin tradition) with prayer;

the reading of the gospel (Mark 10:13–16) followed by the laying on of hands with the saying of the Lord's prayer by the priest and the sponsors, kneeling;

the so-called ephphatha rite (spittle applied to ears and nose and the words "Be opened");

the bringing of the child into the church, to the font;

the renunciation of the devil, the confession of faith in dialogue form, and the anointing with holy oil on breast and back;

there follows the baptism by dipping with the well-known formula (*"Ich taufe dich im Namen des Vaters . . ."*) and the anointing with oil on the head together with the *votum postbaptismale;*

greeting of peace, giving of the baptismal garment and the baptismal candle.

The ritual here described is not new. Luther essentially made a translation of the Roman ritual for baptism, abbreviating it and here and there adapting it.

The *Taufbüchlein* of 1526 (WA 19, 537–541; see *Luther's Works,* vol. 53, pp. 107–109; cf. *Leiturgia,* vol. 5, pp. 359–360) was composed to accommodate the opinions of those who found the 1523 order too marked by traditions, too unbiblical, and too external, as if ceremonies themselves could forgive sins. This book was a further abbreviation of the former order. The most striking change is that anointing was eliminated and thereby also the reference in sign to the Holy Spirit had disappeared. The laying on of hands was retained, as was exorcism, the signing with the cross, the renunciation of the devil, and the creed in question form.

What was really new in both baptismal orders was the *Sintflutgebet,* the "Flood prayer," which Luther most likely composed himself making use of older texts and themes but worded so that the theology of justification would be expressed:

Allmechtiger Ewiger Gott, der du hast durch die sindflutt, nach deynem gestrengen gericht die ungleubige welt verdampt, und den gleubigen Noe selbacht, nach deynen grossen barmhertzickeyt, erhalten. Unnd den verstockten Pharao mit allen seynen ym rotten meer ersewfft, und deyn volck Israel trockenn durch hyn gefuret, damit dis bad deyner heyligen tauffe zukunftig bezeychnet, und durch die tauffe deyns lieben kindes, unsers herren Jhesu Christi, den Jordan und alle wasser zur seyligen sindflutt und reychlicher abwasschung der sunden geheiliget und eingesetzt: wir bitten durch die selbe deyne grundlose barmherzickeit, du wolltist dieszen *N.* gnediglich ansehen und mit rechtem glawben ym geyst beseligen, das durch diesze heylsame sindflut an yhm ersauffe und unttergehe alles was yhm von Adam angepornn ist, und er selb datzugethan hat. Und er aus der ungleubigen zal gesondert, ynn der heyligen Arca der Christenheyt trocken und sicher behalten, allzeit brunstis ym geist, frolich ynn hoffnung,

Almighty eternal God, who according to thy righteous judgment didst condemn the unbelieving world through the flood and in thy great mercy didst preserve believing Noah and his family, and who didst drown hardhearted Pharoah with all his host in the Red Sea and didst lead thy people Israel through the same on dry ground, thereby prefiguring the bath of thy baptism, and who through the baptism of thy dear child, our Lord Jesus Christ, hast consecrated and set apart the Jordan and all water as a salutary flood and a rich and full washing away of sins: we pray through the same thy groundless mercy that thou wilt graciously behold this *N.* and bless *him* with true faith in the spirit so that by means of this saving flood all that has been born in *him* from Adam and which *he himself* has added thereto may be drowned in *him* and engulfed, and that *he* may be sundered from the number of the unbelieving, preserved dry and secure in the holy ark

| deynem namen diene, auff das er mit allen gleubigen deyner verheyssung ewigs leben zu erlangen wirdig werde, durch Jesum Christum unsern herrn. Amen. | of Christendom, serve thy name at all times fervent in spirit and joyful in hope, so that with all believers *he* may be made worthy to attain eternal life according to thy promise; through Jesus Christ our Lord. Amen. |

Text: WA 12, 43–44. *Translation: Luther's Works,* vol. 53, pp. 107–108.

From this prayer and indeed from the whole rite it is apparent that Luther saw more in the celebration of baptism than simply a reception into the Christian community, more even than a declaration of the forgiveness of sins. His conception of the sacrament was this: by the faithful celebration of the sacrament of water and its associated prayer, the child is forgiven the sin of Adam and bound to the risen Lord. "God makes the human person to be the temple of God, therefore, there is no place here for God's enemy. God places the presence of Christ into the life of the human person, and the person is thereby indissolubly bound with Christ; then the devil must give way. God gives the Spirit into the heart of the human person, therefore the evil spirit must be driven out. In the laying on of hands the person is received as the property of God" (Bruno Jordahn in *Leiturgia,* vol. 5, p. 424).

We will leave undiscussed here the *Kirchenordnungen,* liturgical orders for various area churches that for baptism were more or less dependent on one or the other of Luther's two formularies (but cf. *Leiturgia,* vol. 5, pp. 426ff.). We will mention, however, the *Strassburger Ordnungen,* which shows the influence of Martin Bucer. In his *Grund und Ursach* he wrote:

"Therefore our principal reformation is with baptism, since we by the Word teach that the exterior baptism is to be held as a sign of the proper baptism of Christ, that is, of the interior cleansing, rebirth and renewal . . . and that the washing away of sins and the renewal of the Spirit of all should only be attributed to Christ, who by his Spirit makes the elect pure, believing and blessed" (quoted in *Leiturgia,* vol. 5, p. 443).

So in Bucer the ritual is relativized—it is an external sign. The service is shifted into the realm of the inner life. The goal is to understand the word aright. Here we encounter the "naked" and didactic liturgy in which long exhortations and admonitions play a preponderant role. Of the ritual action only the pouring of water remains.

Zwingli

In 1525, Zwingli developed a baptismal ritual for the city of Zürich. The distribution of the rite between two spaces, at the door, or elsewhere, and at the font, has disappeared; the Flood prayer is changed; ritual action is for the most part excluded. Instead there is reading, preaching, and praying.

The order consists of

stating the name of the child;

the "Flood prayer";

the reading from Mark 10;

a question to the sponsor: "Do you wish this child to be baptized?";

the baptism with water and the gift of the white garment along with the greeting of peace.

Baptism is regarded as reception into the congregation, not so much as a celebration of God's grace for the child. This reception brings with it obligations which are mentioned repeatedly, but no allusion is made to rebirth through baptism. Since reception into the congregation is the principal purpose of the rite, exorcism (the combat against the devil) has become superfluous, for baptism is simply an affirmation of all that has been given to the child by surrounding the child with the congregation. Therefore it is not the child but the sponsors who are at the center of the baptismal ceremony. To them the exhortations and questions are addressed. One cannot really speak of celebration.

Calvin

In 1543 Calvin published a *forme d'administrer le batesme* (CR 34, 185–192), which he said was his alone and was not influenced by Bucer of Strassburg. Nonetheless, Bucer seems to have had some influence, for Calvin places the celebration of baptism in the context of a preaching service in the presence of the congregation "since Baptism is a solemn reception into the church which is done in the presence of the assembly" (CR 34, 185).

310

The service begins with the presentation of the child and a long exhortation which ends with a prayer and the Lord's prayer.

The sponsors promise to instruct the child in the doctrine of the faith as expressed in the creed, which is then recited. There is again an encouragement to live in the spirit of the gospel.

The child receives a name and is baptized, using the customary formula, with the congregation as witnesses. Thus, the baptismal formula is pronounced loudly.

The ritual ends with a long explanation as to why the traditional rites have been rejected ("since they were forged without God's word and in view of the fact that so many superstitions have sprung from them," CR 34, 191).

In Calvin's order of baptism reception into the congregation of Christians is prominent. The gifts of God (forgiveness, nonimputation of sins, the gift of the Spirit):

. . . nous sont conferées, quand il luy plaist nous incorporer en son Eglise par le Baptesme. Car en ce sacrement, il nous testifie la remission de noz péchéz, et pour ceste cause, il a ordonné le signe de l'eau, pour nous figurer que comme par cest element les ordures corporelles sont nettoyés ainsi il veult laver et purifier noz ames (CR 34, 187).	. . . are conferred upon us when it pleases God to incorporate us into the church by baptism. For in this sacrament God testifies to us the remission of our sins, and for this reason has ordained the sign of water in order to give us a figure how just as by this element corporal filth is cleaned away so God wishes to wash and purify our souls.

Note the external rite as testimony of what happens "internally": the purification of the soul.

2. THE PREACHING SERVICE AND THE CELEBRATION OF THE LORD'S SUPPER

What the reformers did to let the word of God resound in the congregation and to ground more firmly the faith of churchgoers was at the same time both new and traditional. They used a ritual framework that was already in existence: the preaching or pulpit service. They seized upon this practice precisely because it promised to achieve the renewal that they intended, a renewal not of rites but of people. What was new of course was the way they amplified this familiar ritual framework. For the reformers everything depended upon giving pride of place to the word of God in the holy scriptures: by recurrent public reading, by sound commentary and preaching, by the responding assent of the congregation in singing. Scripture services were held regularly, sometimes even daily. At them the Bible was read and interpreted. The readings and the preaching were surrounded by the congregational singing from the psalter, or from the new chorales, in the language of the people. This song affirmed what was preached and was moreover an expression of trust in God on the part of a sinful but justified people who felt themselves spiritually comforted. All this resulted in a new view of faith, a faith that could rely only on God's grace and could offer God nothing but a contrite heart. Further, these attitudes brought about new customs in worship. Some of the new customs seen especially in some Reformed areas included: changing the arrangement of the church, the east-west axis being broken by chairs gathered around the pulpit; instead of kneeling the congregation sitting quietly and listening; praying with one's eyes closed and listening to the words of the minister as he endeavored to express to God the sentiments of the congregation. All of this took place in churches that had been stripped of all ornamentation. How radical such practices must have seemed to a people who had just stepped out of the Middle Ages! Luther and his followers adhered most closely to the practices of the past. It was Calvin who converted his followers to an experience of faith that brought with it its own radically new image. Zwingli allowed an admixture of humanism. But all the reformers were at one in their passion for the scriptures and in their rejection of anything that they felt was not in accord with the scriptures, and which therefore must be reckoned as idolatry.

The Preaching Service in Medieval Practice
Since the ninth century the church in the west had made repeated attempts to increase the knowledge of the faith, and thus to put a damper on the more crass forms of devotional practice and superstition. Many writers criticized the popular piety of the time, accusing the preachers of the day of failing to give it sufficient foundation (Guibert of Nogent, Thomas Aquinas, Johannes Gerson; cf. J. Sumption, *Pilgrimage*, London, 1975).

The synods of the church instructed the clergy to preach on the content of the creed and the Lord's prayer (the doctrine of the faith) and on the ten commandments (ethics). These texts were to be repeatedly recited by the faithful so that everyone would know them by heart. In the meanwhile the *cathedra* had often disappeared from the apse and had given way to a pulpit that was set up closer to the faithful in the middle of the nave. The explanation of faith and morals based on the well-known texts recited by the faithful took place from this pulpit. During the period of high scholasticism this catechetical sermon developed into the thematic sermon, a discourse on the faith. The homily was given less attention.

The pulpit service was much loved. During the Middle Ages the official liturgy had become principally a clerical liturgy in which the faithful participated mainly by being present as observers, by seeing the rite. Latin was a great barrier to the faithful since only the clergy understood it. But the pulpit service took place in the vernacular; here was a direct contact between the preacher and the faithful. So the service was more informal and more popular, like the vernacular dramatic "plays" that had grown up around the official liturgy of the church. The consequence of preaching in the language of the people was that the sermon began to take an independent place within the official liturgy and developed into a service within the service.

After the reading of the Latin text of the pericopes, the scripture was then read in the vernacular from the pulpit, and the sermon followed. After the sermon came a series of announcements of various sorts. The preacher and the faithful together prayed the creed, the Lord's prayer, and the Ave Maria, and the decalogue was read. The service of preaching was concluded with a blessing. In later years there even came to be added a confession of sins and intercessions for the living and the dead. The old intercessions of ancient liturgy thus were to be found again in the medieval preaching service—now they appeared as the prayers of the pulpit liturgy (*prière du prône*). Hymns could be used as a setting for this service (for example, the *leise*, popular extensions of the prayer *Kyrie eleison*). Adding all these elements together one discovers a complete service at the pulpit that had fully developed by the end of the Middle Ages, especially in Germany and Switzerland. This pulpit liturgy was known to the reformers and adopted by them. An example of such a service could be found in the *Manuale* of the Basel pastor and professor Johann Ulrich Surgant from the year 1506 (cf. E. Weismann, "Der Predigtgottesdienst und die verwandten Formen," in *Leiturgia*, vol. 3, Kassel, 1956, pp. 1–98; for the order of Surgant see pp. 23–24; for the reformed order for a preaching service in Zurich and Basel see pp. 33–42; see also R. Zerfasz, *Die Streit um die Laienpredigt*, Freiburg, 1974, esp. pp. 85–190).

Renewal of Preaching

The central theme of the Reformation was the renewal of preaching. For the reformers a sermon meant the intepretation of the word of God that had been publicly read. Faithfulness to the word was the maxim; only the word had value for the congregation. In comparison, all the rest was not only *adiaphora*, i.e., things that do not matter, but for some of the reformers, even objectionable. The life of the church was to be judged and assessed according to scripture, the only source of faith, the only support for the congregation. Scripture determined discipline in the congregation. But at the deepest level, it was the reading and preaching of the scripture that signified the meeting between the faithful and the *bona gratia* of God, the comforter of the soul.

Ordenung Gottis Diensts, the ordering of public worship, was therefore above all concerned with the ordering of preaching. To the reformers services without preaching were pointless and everything had to be done with one goal in view: *"das das Wort ym Schwang gehe,"* "that the Word may go into full swing" (*WA* 12:37; cf. *Luther's Works*, vol. 53, p. 14). The service of preaching was prescribed by Luther, by Zwingli, and by the other reformers. For Luther in 1523 (with his characteristic tension between the old and the new), such preaching was an integral part of the daily office, of Sunday mass, and of Sunday vespers. For Zwingli in 1525, the resultant service was much more like the preaching service (*prône*) of the Middle Ages but now set free from the old liturgical context:

"The development of the preaching service as the principal Sunday service took place during the age of the reformation exclusively in southern German and Swiss territory where already in the late middle ages the pulpit liturgy had been the preferred custom. Middle and north Germany had their liturgical center in Wittenberg and adopted the purified mass" (Weismann, *Leiturgia*, vol. 3, p. 33).

In any case this meant that worship was to be determined and judged according to this principle: liturgy is preaching and mere "prattling and rattling" through forms is the same as unfaithfulness to the scripture. The public reading of scripture was closely connected to the sermon. In some Reformed areas or in the daily (not the Sunday) worship of Lutherans, the old traditional cycles of readings disappeared because now the readings were to be chosen *ad libitum*, preferably from a prescribed book, on a continuous, day-to-day basis. The feasts of the year also receded into the background—

or at least, among the Lutherans, most of the feasts of the saints. But the most important thing was that the congregation be made attentive to the word of God. Among the inheritors of the Swiss Reformation (and also among some Lutherans after the early balance had been lost) this meant that, no matter what the cost, all the images should disappear, the candles be snuffed, the icons be covered, in order to focus attention upon the preacher's exhortation, scriptural interpretaton, appeal, and reproof. The word of God was restored to honor, but the incarnate word had done more than merely use words! Alas, that was forgotten. Finally the pulpit became the *cathedra.*

The Lord's Supper, Not the Eucharist

One cannot close one's eyes to the crisis in sacramentality and to the abuses that had crept into the medieval practice of the faith. This is especially so of the celebration of the eucharist. Personal faith and the celebration of the rite had grown far apart from each other, and piety was directed more toward the peripheral than toward the essential. The almost exclusive attention paid to the real presence of Christ and to the effects of the sacrifice of the mass as bearing the sacrifice of the cross must be characterized as liturgical developments that can hardly be applauded. It is understandable that some aspects of the mass liturgy had become a thorn in the side of many people, including the reformers. Too great attention was paid to the periphery; there was too great an ease in appropriating the reality of salvation and cutting it up according to a human, calculating measure; there was too great a decline in the manner in which presiders presided. In short, it was not unjustified to point to the chasm between the liturgical celebration of the mass in the waning Middle Ages and that in the assemblies of the first Christians! If we add to this the general tendency toward change and improvement, then it becomes all the more understandable that the celebration of the eucharist especially was marked out for purification, a purification that at the same time would come to strike at the basic tradition.

What took place? The first attempts at a reform of the mass were gentle but certainly clear. The *Wormser deutsche Messe* (1524? see P. Brunner in literature list, p. 305) contains an adaptation of the Roman canon that is telling: in place of "our prayers and gifts," "your bread and wine," is said; where the old canon spoke of *sacrificium, munera, oblata,* at Worms the priest spoke of "prayer," "our prayer." What the congregation could offer was only a humble prayer, and that was all. While maintaining the mass otherwise

largely intact, *Luther* (in 1523 and 1526) left out the offertory prayers and avoided all sacrificial terminology. The canon or eucharistic prayer was shortened radically (1523) or exchanged for the institution narrative sung aloud and the "German Sanctus" inserted into the narrative as a congregational hymn, all of this preceded by a paraphrase of the Lord's prayer as an admonition and invitation to participation in communion (1526). Of the arrangement of the church Luther wrote:

"Here we retain the vestments, altar, and candles until they are used up or we are pleased to make a change. But we do not oppose anyone who would do otherwise. In the true mass, however, of real Christians, the altar should not remain where it is, and the priest should always face the people as Christ doubtlessly did in the Last Supper. But let that await its own time" (*Luther's Works*, vol. 53, p. 69).

In Basel, Zurich, Strassburg, and Geneva the reformers went more radically to work—the *ordo missae* was rejected; in its place there was developed a communion service or the Lord's Supper that was coupled to the pulpit service. The preaching service was the normal practice; the celebration of the Lord's Supper became the exception; according to Zwingli—but not Calvin!—it was to be held only four times a year and then it was shaped along the lines of exhortation and explanation. The didactic nature of the service was the result of a concern to let everyone participate in the grace of God with a believing and repentant heart. God alone was the giver; the congregation could offer nothing but prayer. In the reaction against former abuses the tendency was to underemphasize the sacrament as a celebration of the congregation or finally to let it disappear. In the Middle Ages the balance between word and sacrament had been lost, and in the long run the reformers did not succeed in restoring it. It is doubtful if such restoration was even possible, given the immediate liturgical prehistory, the lack of historical knowledge and resources, and the reformers' own inclinations. The reformers were preachers! Thus it was that for the Swiss the major part of the service of the Supper was to take place from the pulpit and only at the serving of communion would the table be used. The word of God was rediscovered but in many places the altar was torn down.

LUTHER

Texts and translations: Formula missae et communionis pro ecclesia wittenbergensi (1523), WA 12, 205–220 (Luther's Works, hereafter LW, vol. 53,

pp. 19–40); *Deutsche Messe und ordnung Gottis diensts* (1526), WA 19, 72–113 (*LW* 53, 61–90); *Von ordenung gottis diensts ynn der gemeyne* (1523), WA 12, 35–37 (*LW* 53, 11–14); *Ein sermon von dem hochwürdigen Sakrament des heiligen wahren Leichnams Christi und von der Bruderschaften* (1519), WA 2, 742–758 (*LW* 35, 45–73); *De captivitate babylonica* (1520), WA 6, 497–573 (*LW* 36, 3–126); *Ein sermon von dem neuen Testament* (1520), WA 6, 353–378 (*LW* 35, 75–111); *Vom Abendmahl Christi, Bekenntnis* (1528), WA 26, 261–509 (*LW* 37, 151–372).

The first thing needed for worship according to Luther was daily preaching; where there was no preaching, the Christian assembly was meaningless. Especially on Sundays preaching was necessary— at mass, he proposed, on the gospel, and at vespers on the epistle.

The *Formula Missae* (1523) was patterned clearly and recognizably on the Roman order of mass but with characteristic adaptations. The altar was retained but new prominence was given to the pulpit from which the sermon in the vernacular could either follow the creed or precede the whole mass, "since the Gospel is the voice crying in the wilderness and calling unbelievers to faith" (*LW* 53, 25). The mass itself and its variable texts remained in Latin. The offertory prayers were rejected and the canon so changed that every reminder of the sacrificial character of the mass disappeared. The canon was to be made up of the preface leading into the institution narrative (". . . through our Lord Jesus Christ who on the night in which he was betrayed . . .") and followed by the singing of the Sanctus. The "elevation" took place during the singing of "blessed is he who comes in the name of the Lord" and was retained "for the benefit of the weak in faith" (*LW* 53, 28). The *fractio* disappeared; the kiss of peace was interpreted as a formula for forgiveness before communion. The *Formula* is still formally Roman, but in substance it is widely separated from what the reformer called the "mercenary" mass.

The *German Mass* (1526) was an order of service that was put together by Luther under pressure to prepare a German-language service, and because he wanted to try to prevent complete chaos in worship due to the hasty reforms of the "*Schwärmer.*" It seems that Luther himself had difficulty with this formulary. The language was the vernacular for both prayers and hymns of which there was a growing repertory (cf. *LW* 53, 191ff.). The epistles and gospels of the church year were to be sung in German, and Luther had already begun to provide a *postille* (handbook) to help local pastors to preach on these texts. The canon was abolished and replaced by a paraphrase of the Lord' prayer, which could be spoken from the pulpit after the sermon or at the altar. The words of institution were intermingled with communion; the words over the bread were said just before the distribution of the bread; the words over the cup just before the sharing of the cup, with the "German Sanctus" and its corresponding "elevation" (which "signifies that Christ has commanded us to remember him") in between. The *German Mass* is the Lord's Supper, a communion service.

But the rite was not the important thing for Luther. He was principally interested in questions of content and he focused his attention on the theology of the eucharist. A strong strain of devotion to the real presence of Christ in the eucharist runs throughout Luther's theology, but without any attempt at philosophical definition. As early as 1519 he said:

"There are those who practice their arts and subtleties to such an extent that they ask where the bread remains when it is changed into Christ's flesh, and the wine when it is changed into His blood; also in what manner the whole Christ, His flesh and His blood, can be comprehended in so small a portion of bread and wine. What does it matter? It is enough to know that it is a divine sign, in which Christ's flesh and blood are truly present—how and where we leave to Him" (*Works of Martin Luther*, Philadelphia ed., vol. 2, 1915, p. 20).

The old Latin theological theme of the *commercium*, the exchange, important in the ancient liturgy, returns again but now with both a very new shape and a very old, Augustinian concept:

"Just as the bread is made out of many grains which have been ground and mixed together, and out of the many bodies of grain there comes the one body of the bread, in which each grain loses its form and body and acquires the common body of the bread, and as the drops of wine losing their own form become the body of one wine: so it should be with us, and is, indeed, if we use this sacrament aright. Christ with all His saints, by His love, takes upon Himself our form, fights with us against sin, death and all evil; this enkindles in us such love that we take His form, rely upon His righteousness, life and blessedness, and through the interchange of His blessings and our misfortunes are one loaf, one bread, one body, one drink, and have all things in common. This is a great sacrament, says Paul, that Christ and the Church are one flesh and bone. Again through this same love, we are to be changed and make the infirmities of all other Christians our own, take upon ourselves their form and their necessity and make theirs all the good that is within our power, that they may enjoy it. . . . See to it that you exercise and strengthen your faith, so that when you are sorrowful or your sins afflict you and you go to the sacrament or hear mass, you do so with a hearty desire for this sacrament and for what it means, and doubt not that you have what the sacrament signifies, that is, that you are certain Christ and all His saints come to you bringing all their virtues, sufferings and mercies, to live, work, suffer and die with you, and be wholly yours, to have all things in common with you. If you will exercise and strengthen this faith, you will experience what a rich and joyous wedding-supper and festival your God has prepared upon the altar for you" (*Works of Martin Luther*, pp. 17–18, 20).

The Lord's Supper, in Luther's developed theology, could have nothing to do with a sacrifice on the part of the church: it is the unique gift of God, the testament of the Lord for his people. God gives freely and if the human being accepts, in faith his or her sins are forgiven on the grounds of the sufferings of Christ. The sacrament is God's own declaration and witness that God is faithful, and that people can be assured of God's salvation. What is more, in the reading of the scripture and in preaching there is a similar grace-filled moment. This is why the grace of God, God's testament, God's faithfulness must be proclaimed to the congregation. Therefore, for Luther, the Roman canon had to be abolished: there can be no talk of sacrificial action by the church.

From the *German Mass* comes this characteristic text, a portion of the paraphrase of the Lord's prayer before communion:

Zum andern vermane ich euch ynn Christo, das yhr mit rechtem glauben des testaments Christi wahrnehmet und allermeist die wort, darynnen uns Christus sein leyb und blut zur vergebung schenkt, ym hertzen fest fasset, das yhr gedenckt und danckt der grundlosen Liebe, die er uns bewysen hat, da er uns durch sein blut von gots zorn, sund,

Secondly, I admonish you in Christ that you discern the Testament of Christ in true faith and, above all, take to heart the words wherein Christ imparts to us his body and his blood for the remission of our sins. That you remember and give thanks for his boundless love which he proved to us when he redeemed us from God's wrath, sin, death

todt und helle erloset hat, und darauff eusserlich das brod und weyn, das ist seynen leib und blut, zur sicherung und pfand zu euch nemet. Dem nach wollen wir ynn seynem namen und aus seynem befehl durch seyne eygene wort das testament also handeln und brauchen.

and hell by his own blood. And that in this faith you externally receive the bread and wine, i.e., his body and his blood, as the pledge and guarantee of this. In his name therefore, according to the command that he gave, let us use and receive the Testament.

Text: WA 19, 96. *Translation: Luther's Works,* vol. 53, pp. 79–80.

THE KIRCHENORDNUNGEN

Even before Luther's orders for mass had been proposed, the reform of the mass liturgy had become a reality. One of the earliest attempts, dated about 1522, was by Kaspar Kantz (Nördlingen), who inserted an admonition before the simplified canon (cf. J. Smend, *Die evangelischen deutschen Messen,* pp. 72–94). Especially interesting is the reworking of the canon in the *Wormser deutsche Messe* of 1524 or 1525, which should be compared with the *Nürnberger deutsche Messe* (see B. Klaus in the literature list, p. 305) and the *Missa Lincopensis* (see S. Kjöllerström in the literature list, p. 305).

In the Confession made at Augsburg in 1530 the Lutherans would say:

Falso accusantur ecclesiae nostrae quod missam aboleant. Retinetur enim missa apud nos et summa reverentia celebratur. Servantur et usitatae caerimoniae fere omnes, praeterquam quod latinis cantionibus admiscentur alicubi germanicae. . . .

Our churches are falsely accused of abolishing the Mass. Actually the Mass is retained among us and is celebrated with the greatest reverence. Almost all the customary ceremonies are also retained, except that German hymns are interspersed here and there among the parts sung in Latin. . . .

Text: Die Bekenntnisschriften der Evangelisch-Lutherischen Kirche, Göttingen, 1963, p. 91. *Translation: Augsburg Confession,* Article 24, 1–2; *The Book of Concord,* T. Tappert, ed., Philadelphia, 1978, p. 56.

And Philip Melanchthon would explain:

Initio hoc iterum praefandum

To begin with we must repeat the

est nos non abolere missam, sed religiose retinere ac defendere. Fiunt enim apud nos missae singulis dominicis et aliis festis, in quibus porrigitur sacramentum his, qui uti volunt, postquam sunt explorati atque absoluti. Et servantur usitate ceremoniae publicae, ordo lectionum, orationum, vestitus et alia similia.	prefatory statement that we do not abolish the Mass but religiously keep and defend it. In our churches Mass is celebrated every Sunday and on other festivals, when the sacrament is offered to those who wish for it after they have been examined and absolved. We keep traditional liturgical forms such as the order of the lessons, prayers, vestments, etc.

Text: Die Bekenntnisschriften. Translation: Apology of the Augsburg Confession, Article 24, 1; *The Book of Concord,* p. 249.

Thus after Luther's liturgical proposals there appeared in various places in Germany *Kirchenordnungen* in which the reorganization of church life, especially worship, was established. Extensive attention was given to the service of preaching and the Lord's Supper. Here we will mention a few examples and refer further to the analysis of L. Reed, *The Lutheran Liturgy,* pp. 86–109 and passim.

Important among these church orders was the *Braunschweiger Kirchenordnung* (Brunswick) prepared by J. Bugenhagen in 1528. The altar remains in use; the pulpit is intended only for the sermon. The Roman canon is omitted and instead the order is: exhortation, proper preface and Sanctus in Latin, Lord's prayer sung by the priest in German, words of institution over the bread and its distribution, words of institution over the cup and its distribution (the communion of everyone is presupposed). In other church orders the whole institution narrative is recited undivided and then the distribution takes place. Also important were the *Kirchenordnungen* of Nuremberg (1533) and of Cologne (1543). The name of A. Osiander is connected with the Nuremberg order, while Hermann von Wied, P. Melanchthon, and M. Bucer, put together the Cologne order making use of the work of Osiander. Both of these *Kirchenordnungen* were very likely known to Cranmer and used by him in the composition of the *Book of Common Prayer.*

Interesting examples of these *Ordnungen* are the *Ordnung* of Brunswick (*Coena Domini,* vol. 1, pp. 53–56) and the reworked Roman canon as it follows the preface and Sanctus in the early *Wormser deutsche Messe* (1524/1525?):

Darum aller güttigster vatter bitten und begeren wir undertheniglich durch Jesum Christum deinen sun unsern heren du wöllest disz dein brot und wein anschawen gesegnen und bene + deien.

Auch unser gebet so wir zu dem ersten für deine heylige Christliche kirche thun genediglichen annemen dieseibigen befriden behüten vereynigen und regieren durch den gantzen umkreysz der weltt mit keyser künig und allen unseren öbersten mit sampt allen deinen Christgläubigen.

O herr gedenck aller deiner diener und dienerin und aller umstender deren glauben und andacht dir wyssen ist für der selen und leibs heyl wir dich bitten uff das wir all durch hilff deines schirms bewaret werden durch Jesus Christum unseren Herren.

Darumb bitten wir. O herr wöllest dich unser und aller unser gebet genediglich annemen und alle unsere zeit noch deinem friden ordnen von ewiger verdamnisz erlösen und under die scharen deiner auszerwelten zelen durch Christum unseren Herren Amen.

O aller güttigster vatter barmherziger ewiger got hilff und schaff das dises brot und wein uns werd und sei der

Therefore all-good Father, we humbly pray and ask through Jesus Christ your Son our Lord that you would look upon, hallow and bless + this your bread and wine.

Also we ask you to graciously receive our prayer in the first place for your holy Christian church, to give it peace, to protect, unite and rule it throughout the whole wide world, with the emperor, the king and all our rulers, together with all your believers in Christ.

Remember, O Lord, all men and women who serve you and all those who are present here, whose faith and devotion are known to you, for the salvation of their soul and body; we ask you that we all might be preserved through the help of your protection through Jesus Christ our Lord.

Therefore we ask you, O Lord, that you will graciously receive our prayer and the prayer of us all and order all our time according to your peace, redeem us from eternal damnation and count us among the hosts of your elect, through Christ, our Lord. Amen.

O all-good Father, merciful eternal God, grant that your power may make this bread and wine become for us and be the true

warhafftig leib und das unschüldig blut deines aller liebstenn suns unsers herren Jesu Christi.

body and the innocent blood of your most beloved son, our Lord Jesus Christ.

There follows the institution narrative with the elevation. Then:

Deshalbenn herr wir deine diener betrachten des selbigen deines suns unsers herren Jesu Christi leiden und sterben aufferstentnusz von der hellenn und auch herliche auffart zu den hymmelen deiner götlichen maiestat da mit anbieten unser demutiges gebet daruff du mitt genedigem gütigen angesicht schawen und dir das gefallen lassest durch Jesum Christum unserne herren.

Therefore, Lord, we your servants look upon the suffering and death, of your self-same Son, Jesus Christ, his resurrection from hell and also his glorious ascension to the heaven of your divine majesty, and we offer therewith our humble prayer that you might look upon it with gracious favor and let it be pleasing to you through Jesus Christ our Lord.

Almechtiger got wir bitten dich demutiglichen schaff das unser gebet unnd begird uff den höchsten altar für das angesicht deiner götlichenn maiestat fürbracht werdt da mitt wir alle so von diesem allerheyligsten abentmol des leibs fleysch und blutes deines sunes entpfahen mitt allem götlichen segen und gnaden erfüllet werdenn. Durch den selben Jesum Christum unseren herren. Amen.

Almighty God, we ask you humbly to make our prayer and longing be brought to the highest altar before the face of your divine majesty that we all might so receive from this most holy supper of the body, flesh and blood of your Son that we might be filled with all divine blessing and grace. Through the same Jesus Christ our Lord. Amen.

Before communion there is this invitation (taken from the earlier mass of K. Kantz) while the priest lifts the bread and then the wine:

Secht aller liebsten das ist warlichen der heylig leychnam unsers herren Jesu Christi der für euch gelitten hat den biteren todt. Nemet hin und essen ien

Behold, all of you beloved, this is truly the holy body of our Lord Jesus who has suffered bitter death for you. Take and eat that he may feed, nourish and

das er euch speisznere und
bewar in das ewig leben. . . .
Last uns auch drincken den
kelch des heyls und anrufen den
namen des herren. Secht das ist
warlichen der thewer schatz des
kostbarlichen bluts unsers herren
Jesu Christi damit ir erkaufft
seindt. Nement hinn und
theylens mitt eynander zur
abweschung ewrer sündt. Amen.

preserve you to eternal life. . . .
Let us also drink the cup of salvation and call on the name of
the Lord. Behold this is truly the
costly treasure of the precious
blood of our Lord Jesus Christ
with which you have been
bought. Take and share it with
each other for the washing away
of your sin. Amen.

And here is the exhortation before communion from the *Kirchenord-nung* of Nuremberg (from J. Smend, *Die evangelischen deutschen Messen,* pp. 168–169; cf. *Coena Domini,* vol. 1, pp. 76–77):

Mein allerliebsten in Gott.
Dieweyl wir ytzo das abentessen
unsers lieben herren Jhesu
Christi wöllen bedenken und
halten, darin uns sein fleisch und
blut zur speys und zu einem
getrank, nicht des leybs, sunder
der seelen gegeben wirt: sollen
wir billich mit groszem fleysz ein
yglicher sich selbs brüfen, wie
Paulus sagt, und als dann von
disem brot essen und von dem
kelch drinken. Dann es sol nicht,
dann nur ein hungeriche seel,
die jre sünd erkennt, Gottes zorn
und den tod förcht, und nach
der gerechtigkeyt hungerich und
dürstig ist, dis heylig sacrament
empfahen. So wir aber uns selbs
brüfen, finden wir nichts in uns
dann sünd und tod, können
auch uns selbs in keynem weg
daraus helfen. Darumb hat unser
lieber herr Jhesus Christus sich
über erbarmet, ist umb unsernt

My most dearly beloved in God.
Since we intend to commemorate
and hold the supper of our dear
Lord Jesus Christ in which his
flesh and blood are given to us
as food and drink, not of the
body but of the soul, we ought
rightly each one with great care
make self-examination, as Paul
says, and then eat of this bread
and drink of the cup. For it
ought be no other than a hungry
soul, one which confesses its sin,
fears the wrath of God and
death, and is hungry and thirsty
for righteousness, which receives
this holy sacrament. When, however we examine ourselves, we
find nothing in us except sin and
death, and we also are in no
way able to help ourselves.
Therefore our Lord Jesus Christ
has had mercy on us, for our
sakes became human, that he
might fulfill the law for us and

willen mensch worden, das er
für uns das gesetz erfüllet und
lid, was wir mit unsern sünden
verschuldt hetten. Und das wir
das je festglich glauben und uns
frölich darauf verlassen möchten,
nam er nach dem abentessen das
brot, saget dank, brachs und
sprach: Nebmt hin und esset;
das ist mein leyb, der für euch
dargeben würt. Als wolt er
sagen: Das ich mensch bin
worden und alles das ich thue
und leyd, das ist alles ewer
eygen, für euch und euch zu gut
geschehen. Des zu worzeychen
gib ich euch myn leyb zur
speys. . . .

Des zu worzeychen gib ich
euch meyn blut zudrinken. Wer
nun also von disem brot iszt und
aus disem kelch drinkt, das ist:
wer disen worten, die er hört,
und disen zeychen, die er
empfecht, festiglich glaubt, der
bleybt in Christo, und Christus
in ym, und lebt ewiglich. Darbey
söllen wir nun seynes tods
gedenken und jm dank sagen,
ein jeglicher sein creusz auf sich
nehmen und dem herren
nachvolgen, und zuvor einer den
andern liebhaben, wie auch er
uns geliebt hat. Dann wir vil
sein ein brot und ein leyb, die
wir alle eynes brots teylhaftich
sein und aus eynem kelch
drinken. Das verleyhe uns Got
allen, das wirs wirdiglich
empfahen. Amen.

suffer what we had incurred.
And that we might firmly believe
that and joyfully trust it, after
supper he took bread, gave
thanks, broke it and said: Take
and eat; this is my body which is
given for you. As if he would
say: that I have become human
and everything that I do and suffer, all of it is yours, for you and
done for your good. To guarantee this I give you my body as
food. . . .

To guarantee this I give you
my blood to drink. Therefore
whoever now eats of this bread
and drinks from this cup, that is,
whoever firmly believes these
words which he hears and these
signs which he receives, abides
in Christ and Christ in him and
lives eternally. Therefore we
ought now to remember his
death and give him thanks, each
one take up his cross and follow
the Lord, and especially each
one love the others as he has
loved us. Then we will be one
bread and one body, since we all
are partakers of one bread and
drink from one cup. May God
grant us all that we worthily receive it. Amen.

Literature

Martin Bucer, *Grund und Ursach ausz gotlicher schrifft d'neuwerungen, an dem nachtmal des herren, so man die Mesz nennet, Tauf, Feyrtagen, bildern und gesang, in der gemein Christi, wann die zusammen kompt, durch und auff das wort gottes, zu Strasburg fürgenommen,* ed. R. Stupperich, in Bucer's *German Works,* vol. 1 (Gütersloh-Paris, 1960).

F. Hubert, *Die Strasburger liturgischen Ordnungen im Zeitalter der Reformation* (Göttingen, 1900), pp. 88–114.

I. Pahl, *Coena Domini,* vol. 1, pp. 299–337.

B. Thompson, *Liturgies of the Western Church,* pp. 159–181.

Martin Bucer is a central figure and his influence can be discerned in the writings of Calvin, Farel, Pollanus, Hermann von Wied, and Cranmer. In his theology the important topics of the Reformation are discussed with his own characteristic emphasis: the church and the priesthood of all believers (participation in worship); the assembly gathered around the preaching of the word; the action of the Holy Spirit in forming the true church; discipline in the congregation; the doctrine of the eucharist (faith itself is the eating of the gifts: Jesus is food for faith).

Bucer took over and completed the liturgical reformation begun in Strassburg by Theobald Schwarz. Starting in 1525 he introduced various revisions of the German mass first introduced in 1524 by Schwarz.

For Bucer the emphasis fell upon the preaching of the word, on exhortation, and on the participation of the faithful who were thus imbued with the Holy Spirit. In the order of service of 1534, Bucer had moderated his views: the reform had already established itself. The Strassburg orders of service showed the same traits we have already discussed in Reformed worship: use of a table instead of the altar; introduction of the vernacular; the pulpit as the central point of the service, where the reading, the sermon, and the exhortation take place; emphasis upon communion, which is received at the table and which is only meaningful after the proclamation of the scripture.

BASEL: OECOLAMPADIUS
Texts and translations: Das Testament Jesu Christi, das man bysher genent hat dye Mesz (1523), J. Smend, *Die evangelischen deutschen Messen,* pp. 49–71. *Form und Gestalt wie das Herren Nachtmal zu Basel gebraucht und gehalten*

werden (1525?), in J. Smend, op. cit., pp. 214–238. Translation in B. Thompson, *Liturgies of the Western Church*, pp. 211–215. *Ordnung des Herren Nachtmals* (1529, 1537), in M. Jenny, *Die Einheit des Abendmahlsgottesdienstes*, pp. 148–157. I. Pahl, *Coena Domini*, vol. 1, pp. 199–225.

The reform of the order of service was developed consistently by Oecolampadius: the preaching service was the main part of the celebration, with the entire communion rite, except for the actual distribution of the bread and wine, taking place at the pulpit. Thus there was a preaching service to which the supper might or might not be appended. This went further than the orders of service that have been described thus far and in which there was still a certain connection between scripture and table. Oecolampadius moved the service of the table into the pulpit—only distribution took place at the table. Further elements: latitude in preaching without reference to any prescribed series of pericopes; no definite schedule of feasts and seasons; self-examination and discipline so that the unworthy in the congregation might be excluded from the Lord's Supper; a strong accent upon the sufferings of Christ and the forgiveness of sins.

NEUCHÂTEL: FAREL

Text: La manière et façon (the oldest dated edition is from 1533) in M. Jenny, *Die Einheit des Abendmahlsgottesdienstes*, pp. 169–178 and *Coena Domini*, vol. 1, pp. 339–346. *Translation:* B. Thompson, *Liturgies of the Western Church*, pp. 216–224.

Farel must be mentioned since he very likely exercised an influence upon Calvin. He favored an independent scripture service led from the pulpit. Whenever the Lord's Supper was celebrated, it was preceded by this pulpit service, inherited from the old *prône*. The connection between the pulpit service and the supper was an instruction about the Lord's Supper with the imposition of excommunication or discipline and ending with a confession of sin, the Lord's prayer, the creed, and the declaration of pardon. Then the preacher would go to the table, say the words of institution, and distribute the gifts. Clearly, the sermon is the basic element to which the Lord's Supper can be appended. An independent order of service for the Lord's Supper no longer exists here.

ZÜRICH: ZWINGLI

Texts and translations: De canone missae epicheiresis, Corpus Reformatorum (hereafter *CR*) 89, 552–608. Translation in R. Jasper and G. Cuming, *Prayers of the Eucharist*, pp. 130–133. *Action oder Brauch des Nachtmals, Gedächtnis*

327

oder Danksagung Christi, wie sie auf Ostern zu Zürich angehebt im Jahr, als man zählt 1525, CR 91, 1–24. Translation in B. Thompson, *Liturgies of the Western Church*, pp. 149–156. I. Pahl, *Coena Domini*, vol. 1, pp. 181–198. *Züricher Kirchenordnung 1525*, CR 91, 687ff. *Züricher Kirchenordnung 1535*, CR 91, 704ff.

Zwingli's pulpit service was also the preaching service, the *prône*, described above. Zwingli probably intended to adhere consistently to the principle of the preaching service as the main service, also when the Lord's Supper was celebrated (which was to be only four times a year). One should note that when the supper was joined to the pulpit service and its sermon, he added to the celebration of the supper yet a second service of readings describing the institution and meaning of the eucharist in order to give the Lord's Supper an appropriate frame.

The earlier *Epicheireses* (1523), a series of canon prayers in Latin intended to replace the Roman canon, was completely in the spirit of Zwingli's theology. An invitation to the communion of the faithful is conjoined. The Roman outline of the mass is still basically intact.

Action oder Bruch ("Action or Use," 1525) is the new order of service: the communion, on the occasions when it is celebrated, connected to the preaching service. During the sermon the gifts are made ready on the table in the nave. After the preaching service the minister goes behind the table, facing the people. The service of the table, held only to provide communion for the faithful, is introduced by collect, epistle, Gloria, gospel, creed, and then by an exhortation, a communion prayer and the words of institution.

It seems that the word *Danksagung* as used by Zwingli and the other reformers had no real relationship to the early *eucharistia* or *berakah*, but must be understood as a thanksgiving for the *bona gratia* of God, received in the supper itself (similar to the *Danksagung* after communion, as in medieval piety and practice).

Whether Zwingli may be considered a creative liturgist (so Schmidt-Clausing) is doubtful. What he did do was put a personal stamp on the bond between scripture and table or between the table and the pulpit, thus most likely exercising a not insignificant influence upon others. But he understood very little about symbols: he felt that there is a gulf between God and humanity that could not be bridged. Even the word remained for him a human word by which God was not bound. Therefore worship, celebration and liturgy were terrains upon which, seemingly, it was difficult for Zwingli to be able to move.

Texts and translations: Institutio religionis christianae (first edition in 1536), book IV, chap. 17: *De coena domini.* Calvin's works in *CR,* I, cols. 118–140; a first sketch for an order of service is found in cols. 139–140. Translation in J. T. McNeill, ed., and F. L. Battles, trans., *Calvin: The Institutes of Christian Religion,* vol. 2 (Philadelphia, 1960), pp. 1359–1428. *Petit tracté de la saincte Cène de nostre Seigneur Iesus Christ* (1541), CR V, cols. 429–460. *La forme des prières et chantz ecclesiastiques avec la manière d'administrer les sacrements et consacrer le mariage selon la coutume de l'église ancienne* (1542), CR VI, cols. 161–208. English translation in B. Thompson, *Liturgies of the Western Church,* pp. 197–210. Probably Calvin had already composed a service when he was in Strassburg and thus before the 1542 service in Geneva, but the earlier text is not preserved (the so-called *pseudo-romana* of 1542 is not Calvin's). Through John Knox's *Forme of Prayers* (Geneva, 1556) the pattern set by Calvin was passed on to the English Protestants. I. Pahl, *Coena Domini,* vol. 1, pp. 347–367.

The Geneva order of service had a tight structure. The preaching service was an independent whole to which the Lord's Supper could be easily coupled. This communion service was to be announced on the preceding Sunday; it was Calvin's desire to have the Lord's Supper celebrated every week but he did not succeed in carrying this plan out. The celebration of the supper began with the communion prayer, which connected with the intercessions after the sermon. The creed followed, during which the bread and wine were prepared, and the words of institution after the creed. The participation in communion was introduced by a long exhortation, excommunication, instruction, and invitation. During the distribution of the bread and wine, psalms were sung or scripture was read to elucidate the significance of the supper. Here, too, as in other cases of the Reformed rite, the old order of mass had disappeared. The pulpit service stood at the heart of celebration, that is to say, "on occasion" communion could be added to preaching. The furnishings and decoration of the churches as well as the meaning of the liturgy had changed: altar and eucharist were rejected. The faithful participated mainly by listening to the preacher who fulfilled a central, even an "elevated" role, because he proclaimed the word of God as a faithful "dispenser." Here are several important texts:

CONFESSIO FIDEI DE EUCHARISTIA (1537)

Vitam spiritualem quam nobis Christus largitur, non in eo duntaxat sitam esse confitemur,	We confess that the spiritual life which Christ bestows upon us does not rest on the fact that he

quod spiritu suo nos vivificat, sed quod spiritus etiam sui sirtute carnis suae vivifacae nos facit participes qua participatione in vitam aeternam pascamur. Itaque quum de communione, quam cum Christo fideles habent, loquimur, non nimis carni et sanguini eius communicare ipsos intellegimus quam spiritui, ut ita totum Christum possideant. Siquidem quum aperte testetur scriptura, carnem Christi vere nobis esse cibum, et sanguinem eius vere potum: ipsis vero nos educari oportet constat, si vitam in Christo quaerimus. Iam nec exiguum quiddam aut vulgare docet apostolus, quum nos carnem de Christi carnem et ossa ex ossibus eius esse asserit: sed eximium nostrae cum ipsius corpore communionis mysterium ita designat, quod nullus verbis satis pro dignitate explicare queat. Caeterum istis nihil repugnat, quod Dominus noster in caelum sublatus localem corporis sui praesentiam nobis abstulit, quae hic minime exigitur. Nam utcunque nos in hac mortalitate peregrinantes in eodem loco cum ipso non includimur, aut continemur, nullis tamen finibus limitate est eius spiritus efficacia, quin vere copulare et in unum collegere possit, quae locorum spatiis sunt disiuncta. Ergo spiritum eius vinculum esse nostrae cum

vivifies us with his Spirit, but that his Spirit makes us participants in the virtue of his vivifying body, by which participation we are fed on eternal life. Hence when we speak of the communion which we have with Christ, we understand the faithful to communicate not less in his body and blood than in his Spirit, so that thus they possess the whole Christ. Now Scripture manifestly declares the body of Christ to be verily food for us and his blood verily drink. It thereby affirms that we ought to be truly nourished by them, if we seek life in Christ. It is no small or common thing that the apostle teaches, when he asserts that we are flesh of Christ's flesh and bone of his bone. Rather he points out the great mystery of our communion with his body, whose sublimity no one is able to explain adequately in words. For the rest it is no contradiction with this that our Lord is exalted in heaven, and so has withdrawn the local presence of his body from us, which is not here required. For though we as pilgrims in mortality are neither included nor contained in the same space with him, yet the efficacy of his Spirit is limited by no bounds, but is able really to unite and bring together into one things that are disjoined in local space. Hence we acknowledge that his Spirit is the bond of our participation in him, but in such manner that he really feeds us with the substance of the body

ipso participationis agnoscimus, sed ita ut nos ille carnis et sanguinis Domini substantiae vere ad immortalitatem pascat, et eorum participatione vivificet.

Hanc autem carnis et sanguinis sui communionem Christus sub panis et vini symbolis in sacrosancta sua coena offert, et exhibet omnibus qui eam rite celebrant juxta legitimum eius institutum.

and blood of the Lord to everlasting life, and vivifies us by participation in them.

This communion of his own body and blood Christ offers in his blessed Supper under the symbols of bread and wine, presenting them to all who rightly celebrate it according to his own proper institution.

Text: CR IX, col. 711. Translation: J. Reid, Calvin: Theological Treatises (Philadelphia, 1954), p. 168.

COMMUNION PRAYER FROM THE STRASSBURG SERVICE OF 1545

Père céleste plain de toute bonté et miséricorde, nous te prions que comme nostre Seigneur Jesus, non seullement a une fois offert en la croix son corps et son sang, pour la remission de noz pechez: mais aussi les nous veult communicquer, pour nourriture en vie eternelle: nous faire ceste grace, que de vraye sincerité de coeur, et d'un zele ardant, nous recevions de luy un si grand don et benefice: c'est que en certaine foy nous recevions son corps et son sang, voire luy tout entierement, comme luy estant vray Dieu et vray homme, est veritablement le sainct pain celeste, pour nous vivifier. Afin que nous ne vivions plus en nousmesmes et selon nostre nature, laquelle est toute corrumpue et vitieuse, mais que luy vive en nous, pour nous conduire à la vie saincte, bienheureuse et sempiternelle, par

Heavenly Father, full of all goodness and mercy, as our Lord Jesus Christ has not only offered His body and blood once on the Cross for the remission of our sins, but also desires to impart them to us as our nourishment unto everlasting life, we beseech thee to grant us this grace: that we may receive at His hands such a great gift and benefit with true sincerity of heart and with ardent zeal. In steadfast faith may we receive His body and blood, yea Christ Himself entire, who being true God and true man, is verily the holy bread of heaven which gives us life. So may we live no longer in ourselves, after our nature which is entirely corrupt and vicious, but may He live in us and lead us to the life that is holy, blessed and everlasting: whereby we may truly become

ainsi que nous soyons faitz vrayement participans du nouveau et eternel Testament asçavoir l'alliance de grace, estans certains et asseurez, que ton bon plaisir est de nous estre eternellement Père propice, ne nous imputant point noz fautes: et comme à tes enfants et heritiers bien aimez, de nous pourveoir de toutes choses necessaires, tant à l'ame comme au corps: afin que incessamment, nous te rendions gloire et action de grace, et magnifions ton Nom, par oeuvres et par parolles. Donne nous doncques en ceste maniere, Père celeste, de celebrer auiourd'huy la memoire et recordation bien-heureuse de ton cher Filz, nous exerciter en icelle, et annoncer le benefice de sa mort: afin que recevant nouvel accrois sement et fortiffication en Foy et tous biens, de tant plus grande fiance nous te renommions nostre Père, et nous glorifions en toy.

partakers of the new and eternal testament, the covenant of grace, assured that it is thy good pleasure to be our gracious Father forever, never reckoning our faults against us, and to provide for us, as thy well-beloved children and heirs, all our needs both of soul and body. Thus may we render praise and thanks unto thee without ceasing, and magnify thy name in word and deed. Grant us, therefore, O heavenly Father, so to celebrate this day the blessed memorial and remembrance of thy dear Son, to exercise ourselves in the same, and to proclaim the benefit of His death, that, receiving new growth and strength in faith and in all things good, we may with so much greater confidence proclaim thee our Father and glory in thee. . . .

Text: CR VI, col. 197. *Translation:* B. Thompson, *Liturgies of the Western Church,* pp. 204–205.

INSTRUCTION BEFORE COMMUNION FROM THE SERVICES OF GENEVA (1542) AND STRASSBURG (1545)

Premierement donques, croyons à ces promesses, que Jesus Christ, qui est la verité infallible, a prononcé de sa bouche; assavoir qu'il nous veult vrayement faire participans de son corps et de son sang: afin que nous le possedions entierement, en telle sorte, qu'il vive en nous, et nous en luy. Et

Above all, therefore, let us believe those promises which Jesus Christ, who is the unfailing truth, has spoken with His own lips: He is truly willing to make us partakers of His body and blood, in order that we may possess Him wholly and in such wise that He may live in

combien que nous ne voyons que du pain et du vin: toutesfois que nous ne doubtions point, qu'il accomplit spirituellement en noz ames, tout ce qu'il nous demonstre exterieurement, par ces signes visibles, c'est à dire qu'il est le pain celestiel, pour nous repaistre et nourrir à vie eternelle. Ainsi, que nous ne soyons point ingratz à la bonté infinie de nostre Sauveur lequel desploie toutes ses richesses et ses biens en ceste Table pour nous les distribuer. Car, en se donnant à nous, il nous rend tesmoignage que tout ce qu'ils a est nostre. Pourtant, recevons ce Sacrement comme un gage, que la vertu de sa mort et passion, nous est imputee à iustice, tout ainsi que si nous l'avions souffert en noz propres personnes. Que nous ne soyons point donques si pervers de nous reculer, où Jésus Christ nous convie si doulcement par sa parole. Mais en reputant la dignité de ce don precieulx, qu'il nous fait, presentons nous à luy d'un zele ardent: afin qu'il nous face capables de le recevoir.

Pour ce faire eslevons noz esprorz et noz coeurs en hault, ou est Jésus Christ en la gloire de son Père, et dont nous l'attendons en nostre redemption. Et ne nous amusons point à ces elemens terriens et corruptibles, que nous voyons à l'oeil, et touchons à la main pour le chercher là, comme s'il estoit encloz au pain ou au vin. Car lors noz ames seront

us and we in Him. And though we see but bread and wine, we must not doubt that He accomplishes spiritually in our souls all that He shows us outwardly by these visible signs, namely, that He is the bread of heaven to feed and nourish us unto eternal life. So, let us never be unmindful of the infinite goodness of our Saviour who spreads out all His riches and blessings on this Table, to impart them to us. For in giving Himself to us, He makes a testimony to us that all He has is ours. Therefore, let us receive this Sacrament as a pledge that the virtue of His death and passion is imputed to us for righteousness, even as though we had suffered in our own persons. May we never be so perverse as to draw away when Jesus Christ invites us so gently by His Word. But accounting the worthiness of this precious gift which He gives, let us present ourselves to Him with ardent zeal, that He may make us capable of receiving it.

To do so, let us lift our spirits and hearts on high where Jesus Christ is in the glory of his Father, whence we expect Him at our redemption. Let us not be fascinated by these earthly and corruptible elements which we see with our eyes and touch with our hands, seeking Him there as though He were enclosed in the bread or wine.

disposees à estre nourries et vivifices de sa substance, quand' elles seront ainsi eslevées, par dessus toutes choses terrestres, pour attaindre iusque ou Ciel et entrer au Royaulme de Dieu, où il habite. Contentons nous donques, d'avoir le pain et le vin pour signes et tesmoignages: cherchans spirituellement la verité, où la parolle de Dieu promet que nous la trouverons.

Then only shall our souls be disposed to be nourished and vivified by His substance when they are lifted up above all earthly things, attaining even to heaven, and entering the Kingdom of God where He dwells. Therefore let us be content to have the bread and wine as signs and witnesses, seeking the truth spiritually where the Word of God promises that we shall find it.

Text: CR V, cols. 199–200. *Translation:* B. Thompson, *Liturgies of the Western Church,* p. 207.

LONDON–EMDEN–THE PALATINATE: À LASCO AND MICRON

The liturgy of the Reformed congregations of the Netherlands goes back to orders of service that were composed in the Palatinate in Germany. Petrus Dathenus (1531–1588) had some connection with these orders of service, but the material they contain was taken mainly from the work of Johannes à Lasco (superintendent of the German- and French-speaking refugee congregations in London), which was probably reproduced in Dutch in abbreviated form by Marten Micron. With the emigration of refugees from London to north Germany (during the time of Mary Tudor) and the Palatinate, à Lasco's orders of service became important for the congregations in the Netherlands. It is also demonstrable that Zwingli, Calvin, and Bucer had an influence on the Dutch orders of service. See A. Sprengel-Ruppenthal, *Mysterium und Riten nach der Londoner Kirchenordnung der Niederlände (c. 1550–1556)* (Cologne, 1967), and *Coena Domini,* vol. 1, pp. 431–460; 525–535. Marten Micron's *Ordinancien* have been published by W. Dankbaar, *Marten Micron.* The *Liturgia Sacra* of Valérand Poullain (ed. A. Honders, Leiden, 1970; cf. *Coena Domini,* vol. 1, pp. 362–367) is also of importance for the study of the Dutch orders of service.

CONCLUSION

This schematic description of the Reformation preaching service and celebration of holy communion throws light on how some of the reforms took place. It is evident that the reformers did not simply

334

adapt the Roman liturgy of their day. They fundamentally altered the service, but in various ways. Among the Lutherans medieval material was maintained, but a new center was given to the whole in the accent on preaching and teaching. Later in Lutheran history, during the Enlightenment and the movements of Pietism, this center was to dominate even further, destroying much that was left of the old balance. Among the Reformed, not only was all external display rejected as in conflict with the holy scripture, but the old order of service itself was attacked at its very root. While it is true that the Swiss reformers relied upon the medieval preaching service, the use they made of it and the preeminent importance they attached to it—the preaching of the scripture as the only foundation for the church and its worship—resulted in a fundamental change. They restored the Word and proclaimed it in a new way, but at the cost of the celebration of the symbol, of the sacrament. Unfortunately neither the church of the waning Middle Ages nor that of the Reformation found the right equilibrium between word and sacrament.

The renewal of preaching in an understandable language was the great gain. The foundation of faith, a faith that alone justifies, was rediscovered. In the light of this faith every outward form of worship is actually of very relative significance. On the other hand, there was much in the church's tradition that is accessible to us of which the reformers were but imperfectly aware; otherwise they would have treated the essentials of the eucharistic celebration more carefully than they did. They would have rediscovered that the Christian eucharist consisted of such elements as memorial, praise, and the continuation of the Jewish *berakah*. They would have been able to express their sense of thanksgiving more fully. They would have understood more clearly what it means to say that the church celebrates the sacrifice of the Lord in the eucharist. They might have been guided by the formula *memores offerimus*, which unites so many church traditions. In all this what has been gained? What has been lost?

Then there is the question of the preaching service, especially in regard to the relation between the reading of the scriptures and the sermon. It seems that the sermon was the most important thing. Indicative of this was the abrogation in some Reformed circles of the prescribed series of pericopes, the emphasis being placed on the preacher's freedom of choice; the later custom of interpreting a scriptural text that had no clear connecton with the readings (as also in Roman Catholic liturgical practice, *mirabile dictu*); and most of all, the strongly didactic attitude of the reformers. If this is true, then it demonstrates once again how deep the reform had gone. In the best liturgical tradition, the reading of the scripture was actually a "sacrament," a reality, a story that was handed on, and of which the gospel book was a symbol. The reformation changed these concepts. The word of God was the preached word. Thus, it was easy for worship to become catechesis, and the church a lecture hall.

Finally: in Reformation worship there was faithful and believing prayer to God—in fixed formulas and in free improvisations—and an explosion of congregational song. The service of preaching and the celebration of the Lord's Supper were services of prayer and song! Dry analysis almost makes us forget this.

For daily prayer and the attempts at renewal of the office in early Reformation practice, see *Leiturgia*, vol. 3, pp. 187–214, and H. O. Old, "Daily Prayer in the Reformed Church of Strasbourg, 1525–1530," *Worship* 52, 1978, pp. 121–138.

B. THE ANGLICAN LITURGY

Literature

P. Bradshaw, *The Anglican Ordinal* (London, 1971).

F. Brightman, *The English Rite*, 2 vols. (London, 1921; repr. 1970).

G. Cuming, *A History of Anglican Liturgy* (London, 1960).

H. Davies, *Worship and Theology in England*, vols. 1–4 (Princeton, 1961–1975).

G. Dix, *The Shape of the Liturgy* (New York, 1981).

D. Harrison, ed., *The First and Second Prayer Books of King Edward the Sixth*, (London, 1972).

P. Jagger, *Christian Initiation 1552–1969* (London, 1970).

I. Pahl, *Coena Domini*, vol. 1, pp. 377–429.

H. B. Porter, *Jeremy Taylor, Liturgist* (London, 1979).

For the Methodist recension of the Anglican material see:

J. C. Bowmer, *The Lord's Supper in Methodism 1791–1960* (London, 1961).

W. Dunkle & J. Quillian, *Companion to the Book of Worship* (Nashville & New York, 1970).

J. White, *Introduction to Christian Worship* (Nashville, 1980).

The fascinating history of the liturgy of the Church of England in its early period can be discerned in the various editions of *The Book of Common Prayer and Administration of the Sacraments* and in the lives of the persons whose names are connected with that book.

The first edition of the *Book of Common Prayer,* the "First Prayer Book of Edward VI" of 1549, was principally the work of Thomas Cranmer, who made careful use of the "catholic" tradition, while also adapting it. The book contained Lutheran elements from Cologne and Nuremberg. The "Second Prayer Book of Edward VI" in 1552 was influenced more directly by the reformers, especially Bucer and Zwingli, as well as by Johannes à Lasco. The Reformed influence was especially noticeable in this edition, but this was to some extent reduced in later editions. The third edition, composed under Elizabeth and approved in 1559, was revised in 1662, although not fundamentally, and is still the official edition. (An improved, thoroughly revised edition was voted down in Parliament in 1928.) A new *Alternative Service Book* authorized for use "in conjunction with The Book of Common Prayer" was published in 1980. The American Episcopal Prayer Book–1789, 1892, 1928–was thoroughly revised and published in 1979.

The book begins with several general chapters and an overview of the scripture readings and psalms for the whole year; and a calendar. Then follow the actual orders of service:

morning prayer (matins and lauds joined together);

evening prayer (vespers and compline in one);

creed and litany (the first official liturgical prayer in English);

collects and lessons for all Sundays and feast days for the service of the word, which precedes the "Ministration of Holy Communion";

orders of service and other material for Holy Communion, both "public" and "private" baptism, baptism of adults, the catechism, confirmation, marriage, visitation and communion of the sick, burial, thanksgiving after childbirth, ordinations to the offices of bishop, priest, and deacon, and the anniversary of the coronation of the monarch;

finally several special prayers.

Many traditionally Catholic rites were preserved. Still for Cranmer and his advisors, the central concern was the renewal of holy communion and baptism and especially the proclamation of holy Scripture. In order to encourage good preaching, just as on the continent (in Luther's *postille,* for example), homilies in book form were published (1547) and made available to the clergy, who could use them as a source of inspiration for their sermons or even for reading from the pulpit.

It should be noted that the rubrics of the *Book of Common Prayer* were formulated with such a suppleness that they could be observed in a "reformed" way—i.e., without external display—or in a "catholic" way, i.e., directed toward a more developed ritual. The rubrics are directions and not laws: Cranmer had read Luther's works and knew his opinion of rites and ceremonies; he adopted this opinion and applied it, but with a feeling for style and a remarkable sensibility for the English language.

1. BAPTISM AND CONFIRMATION

Preferably, these sacraments were to be celebrated on Sunday for the sake of the congregation, since baptism was reception into the community. The faithful needed to witness that ceremony as a means of remembering their own baptism. Parents and sponsors had to be present with their child at the morning or the evening service.

The order of baptism was as follows: after an address there followed a prayer, the so-called Flood prayer of Luther and a prayer from the tradition. Mark 10:5–13 was read and the congregation addressed. The sponsors were apprised of their responsibility; they renounced Satan and confessed the faith in the name of the child. The child was then asked if it wanted to be baptized. Then followed the blessing of the baptismal water, the name-giving, and the baptism by immersion or pouring. The child was signed with the cross as a mark of reception into the community. A prayer, the Lord's prayer, and an allocution closed the baptismal service.

The text of the closing prayer follows:

"We yield thee hearty thanks, most merciful Father, that it hath pleased thee to regenerate this infant with thy Holy Spirit, to receive him for thine own Child by adoption, and to incorporate him into thy holy Church. And humbly we beseech thee to grant, that he, being dead unto sin, and living unto righteousness, and being buried with Christ in his death, may crucify the old man, and utterly abolish the whole body of sin; and that, as he is made partaker of the death of thy Son, he may also partake of his resurrection; so that finally with the residue of thy holy Church, he may be an inheritor of thine everlasting kingdom, through Christ our Lord. Amen."

Confirmation by the bishop was preserved in the Anglican tradition of the *Book of Common Prayer*, not by anointing but by laying on of hands (the early western tradition). There is little difference in content between confirmation in the Anglican tradition and that in the Roman Catholic tradition.

2. THE CELEBRATION OF THE LORD'S SUPPER

Cranmer, the main author and composer of the "The Supper of the Lord and the Holy Communion" (1549), "retained a deep religious impression from the old Latin service, which his controversial writings indeed might seem to belie, but which never allowed him to break altogether with the traditional forms of the Church's worship" (Brilioth, *Eucharistic Faith and Practice*, p. 95). Moreover he was too great an English stylist to express exclusively any one doctrinal position. He knew the orders of Osiander (Pfalz-Neuburg), of Bucer (Strasbourg), and of Hermann von Wied (Cologne, especially his Service of the Lord's Supper). He had seen what had been written by Zwingli (his Epicheiresis, for example). But he created his own masterpiece (Dix, *The Shape of the Liturgy*).

The structural patterns of Cranmer's Service of the Lord's Supper follow closely the medieval *Ordo Missae*, especially in the service of the word which contains the elements of the *Ordo*. Only one change comes to mind: the service opens with the Lord's prayer (by analogy with the office). After the service of the word there follows the service of the Lord's table with the eucharistic prayer, as a prelude to communion. As far as Cranmer's canon is concerned:

"Its most remarkable feature is its mere existence. The abolition of the Canon was an article of faith with all the continental Reformers. It is normally replaced by the Words of Institution, read as a lesson. Sometimes they are to be read facing the altar, as a prayer; and occasionally, as in the earliest Strasbourg rite or in Osiander's form for Pfalz-Neuburg, the place of the Canon is taken by a short collect. . . . Cranmer follows the subject-matter of the medieval Canon fairly closely, with enough literal translation to show that he took it as his starting-point; but he diverges freely from the actual language, and finally uses very little of it" (G. Cuming, *A History of Anglican Liturgy*, pp. 77–78).

The text is worthy of a detailed analysis, but we must limit ourselves by referring to Brightman, *The English Rite*, vol. 2, pp. 638–721, and to Cuming, *History*, pp. 78–80. A most striking point of Cranmer's canon, if our interpretation is correct, seems to be that a kind of anamnesis figures just before the institution, combined with an epicletic prayer:

"O God heauenly father, which of they tender mercie diddest geue thine only sonne Jesu Christ to suffre death upon the crosse for our redempcion, who made there (by his one oblacion once offered) a full, perfect, and sufficient sacrifyce, oblacion, and satysfaccyon, for the sinnes of the whole worlde, and did institute, and in his holy Gospell commaund us, to celebrate a perpetuall memory of that his precious death, untyll his comming again! Heare us (o merciful father) we besech thee; and with thy holy spirite and worde, vouchsafe to blesse and sanctifie these thy gyftes, and creatures of bread and wyne, that they maie be unto us the bodye and bloude of thy moste derely beloued sonne Jesus Christe" (1549 *Book of Common Prayer; Coena Domini,* vol. 1, pp. 399–400).

After the institution, but before the communion (in the 1552 and 1662 editions of the *Book of Common Prayer,* after communion) the canon continues as follows:

"O Lord . . . we thy humble servants [1549 *BCP* includes here a classic anamnesis] entirely desire thy fatherly goodness mercifully to accept this our sacrifice of praise and thanksgiving; most humbly beseeching thee to grant, that by the merits and death of the Son Jesus Christ, and through faith in his blood, we and all thy whole Church may obtain remission of our sins, and all other benefits of his passion. And here we offer and present unto thee, o Lord, ourselves, our souls and bodies, to be a reasonable, holy, and lively sacrifice unto thee, humbly beseeching thee, that all we, who are partakers of this holy Communion may be fulfilled with thy grace and heavenly benediction . . ." (1662 *Book of Common Prayer; Coena Domini,* vol. 1, p. 423).

Cranmer "hoped to satisfy the reforming zealots by suppressing all mention of oblation, to pacify the conservatives by keeping the time-hallowed frame-work, and to supply a positive, reformist-Catholic statement of what all had in common" (Cuming, *History,* p. 81). Comprehensiveness!

In conclusion we quote the judgment of Gregory Dix (*The Shape of the Liturgy,* p. 672):

"The true background of Cranmer's work is, as I have said, the contemporary post-mediaeval liturgical crisis and the *Kirchenord-*

nungen of the German and Swiss Reformation which sought to solve it. The rite of 1552 takes its natural place among these, and only when seen thus can its qualities and those of its creator be fully and fairly appreciated. Compared with the clumsy and formless rites which were evolved abroad, that of 1552 is the masterpiece . . . of literature, which no one could say of its companions; but he did more. As a piece of liturgical craftmanship it is in the first rank— once its intention is understood. It is not a disordered attempt at a catholic rite, but the only effective attempt ever made to give liturgical expression to the doctrine of 'justification by faith alone.' "

3. ORDINATIONS

The *Book of Common Prayer* contains orders of service for ordinations to the ministries of deacon, priest, and bishop. P. Bradshaw, whose work is mentioned in the literature list on p. 336, makes clear that the attempts of Cranmer to renew the ritual of ordination were partly successful. He simplified and clarified the rite. In place of the handing over of the *instrumenta* he restored the laying on of hands as the central sacramental action and fostered the participation of the faithful. But the ordination prayer, which anciently accompanied and expressed the laying on of hands, did not keep that function here. The laying on of hands was now accompanied by an induction formula.

At the ordination of a priest, presiding at the table was joined with proclamation: "And be thou a faithful dispenser of the Word of God, and of his holy sacraments." The priest was ordained as proclaimer of both God's word and sacrament: "Take thou Authority to preach the Word of God, and to minister the holy sacraments in the Congregation, where thou shalt be lawfully appointed thereunto." One should note the connection between word and sacrament and the expression "his [that is, God's] sacraments." In the ordination to priesthood as well as in other ordinations, the holy scriptures (or the New Testament) were handed over as a sign of induction into the office.

4. DAILY PRAYER

The *Book of Common Prayer* brought the traditional daily prayer as practiced in both east and west out of the clerical sphere and back into the congregation. Although it is true that the ideal was never achieved fully, it was nonetheless true that those who composed the *Book of Common Prayer* saw clearly that morning and evening prayer was a matter of congregational worship. Thus, morning prayer (matins) and evening prayer (evensong) became implanted in the English tradition. The structures of these prayer services were very simple: an introduction (*enarxis: votum*, confession of sin, Lord's prayer); psalmody (so arranged that the entire Psalter was completed in a month); scripture reading from Old and New Testaments (the Old Testament was completed once a year and the New Testament twice a year); a canticle or canticles; the creed; intercessions. In other words, this is the traditional structure.

C. THE HYMN

Literature

F. Blume, *Geschichte der evangelischen Kirchenmusik* (Kassel, 1965).

K.-M. Dierkes, *Anglikanische Frömmigkeit und Lehre im Kirchenlied* (Trier, 1969).

K. Fellerer, ed., *Geschichte der katholischen Kirchenmusik*, 2 vols. (Kassel, 1972, 1976).

O. J. Julian, *A Dictionary of Hymnology*, 3rd ed. 2 vols. (New York, 1957).

M. K. Stulken, *Hymnal Companion to the Lutheran Book of Worship* (Philadelphia, 1981).

Een compendium von achtergrondinformatie bij de 491 Gezangen uit het Liedboek voor de Kerken. G. van der Leeuw Stichting (Amsterdam, 1978).

The Reformation gave a strong impulse to the congregational hymn and to psalmody, to a strophic paraphrasing of the psalms. The hymn was considered not only as acclamation but also as preaching. According to Luther it was intended to let the word of God continue to sound in the hearts of the faithful and to keep it living there. Therefore it was not only the music, which stimulated the participation of the faithful, but also the text of the hymn that was important. The text reflects the church's teaching and its experience of faith. This means that for a good understanding of worship, a knowledge of Reformation hymnody and metrical psalmody is necessary—a knowledge that can come only from extensive reading and analysis. It is evident that this can be an arduous task: thousands of hymns exist in the Anglican tradition alone. The literature cited above, it is hoped, will be of help in finding a way through such a maze.

A careful study will show that Luther, unlike Calvin, encouraged his followers to develop the freely composed chorale as well as the setting of psalms and traditional texts. Due to Calvin's authority, however, for a long time (in the Netherlands, two centuries) singing in both the Anglican and the Reformed congregations consisted almost exclusively of psalms. Nonetheless in the long run Luther's way has been generally accepted, as can be ascertained from the plethora of hymnals that have been published by the different churches. The ecumenically designed Dutch hymnal of 1973, *Liedboek voor de Kerken*, or the American *Lutheran Book of Worship* of 1978 are recent examples.

D. THE COUNTER-REFORMATION

"The contrast between the Baroque spirit and that of the traditional liturgy was so great that they were two vastly different worlds. The new life-spirit which would wrap earth and heaven in one whirling tempest—how different from the quiet dignity of the old Roman orations. More than this: theological and religious thought, caught up in the swirl of the Counter-Reformation, was as different from the old Roman tradition as it is possible to be, granted the basis of the same Catholic faith. No one who learns to know the intellectual situation of the time will make it a matter of reproach that the period had found no closer tie to the liturgy.

"Through the controversy with the Reformers, the whole stress of thought on the Eucharist was directed to and bound down to the Real Presence, almost to the neglect of other aspects. . . . On the other hand, it is the heritage of the Middle Ages, purified and refined by the Tridentine reform, which really determines the religious picture of the Baroque period as well as the picture of its religious service. The great abuses have all disappeared. But still the Mass remains a service in which only the priest and his assistants have an active role. The faithful follow the divine action only from a distance" (J. Jungmann, *The Mass of the Roman Rite*, pp. 107–109).

The Baroque period in Roman Catholic worship created little of abiding value. A new spiritual *élan* could be felt in the church, a new vitality that was largely determined by the battle against the Reformation, an aggressive defense against those who denied both the truth and the one true church. This one true church was glorified and its worship celebrated in overpowering surroundings with grandiose paintings and polyphonic music. The liturgy was dazzling, but superficial; the heart of the liturgy was still concealed. Historical studies of worship were made but they were used to bolster the

Roman church's position against the Reformation. Apologetic thought was at an apex. The liturgy was celebrated with such an apologetic stance in mind: belief in the real presence of the Lord was expressed by elaborate processions, with adoration and exposition of the Blessed Sacrament. The church as bride of the glorious Lord, sharing in his glory, was celebrated and meditated upon. The sacramental mysticism was "optimistic": Christ lives on in the church through the sacraments; the divine is visible in the human. The teaching of the Council of Trent produced a great effusion of piety, especially toward the eucharist: the mass is the sacrifice of the church, which participates in the sacrifice of Christ in worship of the Father.

The participation of the faithful remained limited and indirect; now they could follow the mass by means of prayer books. These books were necessary because, since the Council of Trent, the worship of the Roman rite had been unified by the promulgation of valid liturgical books. These books contained the official liturgy of the church, in which nothing could be changed except by the central ecclesial authority. As a consequence, the separation between popular piety and church liturgy now became even greater. The ordained minister celebrated the worship of the church while the faithful had recourse to their own paraliturgical expressions of piety: private prayers, the rosary, meditation during the exposition of the sacrament, processions, the way of the cross. The faithful were *anwesend Abwesenden* ("present absent ones," Jungmann) in worship. Listening to music and looking at the artful decor of the church building was one form of Baroque participation in the liturgy. Once again we find a one-sidedness that had already been a problem in the Middle Ages and that was caused partly by the clericalization of the church. The faithful were excessively intent on gazing upon the "sacrament of the altar," the sacred host (cf. the *autos sacramentales* in Spain):

Nonetheless, during the Baroque period, under the influence of the Reformation and due to historical studies of liturgy predating the Middle Ages, the first renewal of worship began to take place. This renewal began cautiously. Little by little during the Latin celebration, hymns began to be sung in the vernacular (the birthplace of this practice was Germany!): a sermon-hymn, a hymn between the readings, at the offertory, and during communion. The *Mainzer Cantual* (1605) is eloquent testimony of this. Later attempts at liturgical renewal would be developed along these lines.

The real renewal would have to wait for a few centuries. For the Baroque period the mass was above all "consecration." The rest of the celebration was filled up, literally, by very long sermons that had little or nothing to do with the liturgy.

CONCLUSION

Gain and loss during the Reformation and Counter-Reformation have been sketched briefly. In spite of the brawling vitality and activity of the times, it must be concluded that for public worship the age did not produce any result that could serve as a foundation for future generations to build upon. Neither the Reformation nor the Counter-Reformation could provide such help because they were too much stuck in reaction, too concerned with apologetics in thought and life, too immersed in instruction and catechizing. The principle of *sola scriptura* was rigidly maintained; the appeal to the Middle Ages on the part of Trent and the Counter-Reformation was artificial. It is not surprising that from time to time renewal movements arose in various places, in the midst of what was otherwise loss. And the gain? Is not the discovery of the word of God and the biblical piety fostered a great gain? Did not the mystical piety of the time turn many eyes toward the kingdom of God? Was it not probably a gain that the uniformity of the Roman rite was strictly guarded for a while, and hence chaos prevented? It is simply that the guarding lasted too long.

Appendix

An Overview of Centuries: Attempts at Renewal

In this appendix we will make a great leap by bridging in a few pages several centuries: the seventeenth, eighteenth, nineteenth, and the first half of the twentieth, the period of stagnation (T. Klauser) in the liturgy of the churches. During these centuries there was little positive contribution to the growth of the Christian liturgy. This is true both for the east and the west. The Roman liturgy in the west was at a standstill because of adherence to the norms of the Council of Trent. Reformation worship showed no edifying traits; the tradition of the fathers of the Reformation was not continued and in a short time a decline set in. The Byzantine liturgy was seen exclusively in the context of what had been; evolution was rejected. We do not know sufficiently the causes of all this. But what could the *siècle des lumières*, what could cool "reason" mean for worship? *Belehrung* ("instruction") and *Erbauung* ("edification")? What could the liturgy expect from Romanticism? A taste for the infinite; an enthusiasm for mood and emotion?

Therefore we shall add to this history of Christian worship an appendix that is limited to those tendencies toward renewal that became especially visible in the twentieth century and developed up to recent times. We will describe this renewal and note briefly what preparation preceded it.

But there is another reason for calling this an appendix. When there is question of renewal in worship, the spotlight almost inevitably falls on the liturgy of the Roman patriarchate. This is not to say that there is no renewal elsewhere, but such renewal is verifiable only with greater difficulty; its extent is more limited and it is really too early to summarize all its parts. Nonetheless some of the aspects of present-day liturgical renewal in the churches of the Reformation will be considered here.

What was set in motion in the twentieth century by the liturgical movement in the Roman Catholic Church and crowned by the Second Vatican Council is unique in its comprehensiveness. The extensive application of this renewal is connected within the struc-

346

ture of the Roman Catholic Church in the west, of course, especially with its strong centralization of authority, but this does not detract from the fact that this is where the renewal is most clearly demonstrable. Renewal in the other western churches shows a close relationship to the Roman Catholic movement, along with a new perception of those churches' own liturgical sources. Once again: we are speaking here of *worship*, not of theology nor of philosophy.

1. THE BREVIARY OF CARDINAL QUIÑONES (1475–1540)

Quiñones made a serious attempt to set free the authentic spirit of the Christian tradition as it was found in the early church. At the same time he tried to introduce this spirit into the actual circumstances of church and social life. The liturgical ideas that inspired Quiñones were: a better distribution of the psalms of the hours during the week; the preeminence of the temporal cycle and consequently the diminishing of the memorials of the saints; great emphasis on the authentic and full reading of the scriptures; a simplification of the structure of the breviary. The success was remarkable: first edition in 1535; second revised edition in 1536 with 32 printings (in Venice, Paris, Antwerp, and Cologne).

2. THE NEO-GALLICAN LITURGY IN FRANCE

Literature: R. W. Franklin, "Guéranger and Variety in Unity," Worship 51, 1977, pp. 378–399.

The *grand siècle* of royal absolutism (Louis XIV) and the *siècle des lumières* that followed were characterized by an unequaled revival of intellectual life that in essence was antichurch and nonreligious. Reason was preeminent in this world, discovering in classical antiquity and in the Renaissance the ideal pattern of life. This movement exercised a substantial but indirect influence upon the church in France. The French church, supported by the "Sun King," began to show its independence, as is revealed in the intriguing history of gallicanism. This attitude had an effect on worship. The standardized and unified liturgy of the Council of Trent was accepted in France only with difficulty. There was rather a desire to proceed in a local, French manner in the composition of liturgical books, in the shaping of the liturgy, in the use of the tradition. In both liturgical Latin and in the composition of the books themselves, there was a desire to make improvements where they were felt to be necessary. And there was a desire to abbreviate and purify the liturgy of such elements as the legendary accounts of the saints. Very much against the wishes

347

of the Roman authorities, many French bishops favored this movement: toward the end of the eighteenth century many dioceses had
their own liturgy, formed on a neo-gallican, French basis, and they
maintained this form deep into the nineteenth century. The "French"
liturgical books were in general composed with care, using traditional
material that had been omitted from the Roman books.

Especially well-known are the *Missale* of Meaux (1709) and those
of Troyes (1736) and Paris (1736), the last of which was used as a
model. It had a great number of prefaces, new antiphons, prayers
over the gifts and after communion, and fewer feasts of saints. In
addition there were the Breviaries of Vienne (1671), Paris (1680),
and Paris (1736). These mark a trend in the development of a totally
new breviary with different scripture readings, a different division of
the psalter, and new hymns. Along with these new books there
arose the desire for the introduction of the vernacular into the
liturgy.

There is much to admire in this attempt at renewal, which was at
the time rejected by Rome but which since Vatican II has in fact
been followed on several points. It was founded on a considerable
historical knowledge that frequently yielded accuracy in the choice of
texts from the tradition. The structure of the liturgy was made more
apparent. A distinct effort was made toward understandability of the
liturgy, hence the interest in the vernacular. A central place was
accorded to scripture, and attempts were made to encourage the
participation of the faithful. On the other hand, this liturgy was
intellectual; in this age of the "Enlightenment," the structure of the
liturgy was of greater interest than the celebration of the mystery.
With all its efforts, this renewal remained somewhat cold and aloof,
rigorist and elitist. (See B. Plongeron, *Le procès de la fête à la fin de
l'ancien regime: le christianisme populaire*, Paris, 1976, pp. 171–198.
As far as the spirituality of the French school is concerned—Bérulle,
Condren, Olier—see L. Cognet, *La spiritualité moderne*, Paris, 1966,
pp. 310–410.)

3. THE ENLIGHTENMENT IN GERMANY

Literature

M. Probst, *Gottesdienst in Geist und Wahrheit* (Regensburg, 1976).

J. Steiner, *Liturgiereform in der Aufklärungszeit* (Freiburg, 1976).

The Enlightenment took place in Germany later than in France,
and in Germany it took an interest in religion. The *Aufklärung* was a

sort of exaltation of a land that had finally overcome the disastrous consequences of being divided into numerous small principalities and having suffered long and devastating wars. Germany rose out of lethargy and suddenly architecture blossomed: a late flourishing took place of the Rococo, the south-German Baroque.

Here we find the same attempts at a liturgical renewal, although now with a German accent. Reason and reasonableness were highly valued; the translations from the Latin are as thoroughly understandable as is the poetry. Among liturgical aims were: simplification of the services, a return to the essentials of the celebration and to the holy scripture, restoration of the participation of the faithful in worship, and therefore the introduction of the vernacular. Such were the points of the program of those who inaugurated a kind of liturgical movement. The movement was a reaction against the Baroque, but it did not go far enough or dig deeply enough.

Some of the German liturgical practices of those days continued. The most striking is the *Singmesse*, a celebration of the eucharist in which the priest followed the order of service and said the Latin texts according to the Tridentine rubrics and the faithful sang German songs (especially during the invariable parts of the mass, such as the Kyrie, Gloria, and Sanctus). Later this *Singmesse* became a *Betsingmesse:* German prayers for the faithful were also introduced into the Latin order of service, a practice obviously influenced by the *evangelische* liturgy. A German vespers, i.e., evening prayer for all the faithful, was introduced; baptism was celebrated in the vernacular and in some cases there began to be, over the protests of the Roman authorities, a complete *deutsche Messe*. Preaching was given some attention by improvements in the choice of pericopes.

It is worth noting that the *Aufklärung* (just as the Enlightenment in France) did not shun emotion and subjectivity in its striving for edification and the sentimental (cf. A. Mayer, *Die Liturgie in der europäischen Geistesgeschichte*, Darmstadt, 1971, pp. 185–245).

In the churches of the Reformation, puritanism, pietism, and the Enlightenment contributed little good to common worship. There was a sort of *Verödung der Gemeinden* ("depopulation of the congregations") because the basic principles of the fathers of the Reformation were forgotton. In Lutheran circles the frequency of celebration of the Lord's Supper was reduced radically. Freedom in worship was asserted, which meant that not much remained save for the sermon or the address, which sought to awaken the spiritual life of the listeners (cf. the *collegia pietatis* of P. Spener, 1635–1705). Little or no guidance was taken from the celebrations of the church year.

Perhaps this development was at its strongest in the Netherlands. Liturgical activity was directed toward producing "ease of mind" and a mood of excitement (see W. Nagel, *Geschichte des christlichen Gottesdienstes* (Berlin, 1962), pp. 138–164).

But there were two notable exceptions. The first was Nikolaus von Zinzendorf (1700–1760), whose name is connected with the Herrn-hutters. More than his contemporaries, he sensed the value of common worship, of language, of song, and of sign, and, what is more, he did not react against the tradition of the church but included it in his attempts at renewal of the life of prayer. He was certainly inspired by pietism, but a pietism that he applied in his own way. He was very critical of current preaching, especially the kind that was done in the rural areas, and paid much attention to communal song as a sign of the presence of the Spirit. In his *Liturgienbuch,* which appeared in 1744 and thereafter went through many reprintings, Zinzendorf remarked:

. . . einfach und unaffektiert, in der Kommunionsgelegenheiten sehr gemeinmäszig und herzlich, doch auch nicht schwärmerisch, sondern kirchenmäszig gehandelt werde.	. . . On the occasion of communion there should be an action which is simple and unaffected, very communal and from the heart, yet not in the manner of the enthusiasts but rather according to the spirit of the church.

The second exception was King Friedrich Wilhelm III of Prussia (1770–1840). He was most impressed by the Anglian liturgical tradition and he dealt with the liturgy on a solid historical basis. His influence was far-reaching despite the ideas of Schleiermacher (1768–1834), whose view that worship should be full of *Seligkeit* ("bliss") offered a weak foundation for the liturgy. Friedrich tried to reconcile Lutheran and Calvinist traditions with each other (and reaction against that contributed to a confessionalist Lutheran liturgical revival). What is more, the king wanted to check the current arbitrariness in the liturgy:

Alle Liturgien, welche in unserer Zeit erschienen, sind wie aus der Pistole geschossen . . . Wir müssen . . . auf Vater Luther recurrieren (1798).	All the liturgies which have appeared in our time are as if they had been shot from a pistol. . . . We must . . . go back to Father Luther.

His frequently reprinted and emended *Agenda für die evangelische Kirche in den königlich Preusischen Landen* became a model for later renewals.

4. THE CHURCH REFORM IN TUSCANY

Criticism of the centralization of authority in Rome could be heard in its own neighborhood, in Pistoia where Bishop Ricci together with Prince Leopold held a synod in 1786. The synod did not expect much from the central authority (the Congregation of Rites) and therefore it chose to go its own way—a way that led to no lasting success. It is interesting, however, to note that many of the Tuscan proposals for renewal were carried out in the whole church two centuries later by Vatican II. (See E. Cattaneo, *Introduzione alla storia della liturgia occidentale*, Rome, 1969, pp. 367–371.)

5. THE NINETEENTH CENTURY

Literature

R. W. Franklin, four articles on P. L. P. Guéranger and his times in *Worship* 49, 1975, pp. 318–328; 50, 1976, pp. 146–162; 51, 1977, pp. 378–399; 53, 1979, pp. 12–39.

L. Soltner, *Solesmes et Dom Guéranger 1805–1875* (Solesmes, 1974).

G. Cholvy, "Le catholicisme populaire en France au XIXe siècle," in *Le christianisme populaire* (Paris, 1976), pp. 171–198.

J. van Laarhoven in *De Kerk van 1770–1970* speaks about "the church and reaction" and "the church on the defensive," and such characterizations fit especially the years 1815 to 1880. Reaction and defense are not noted providing a good climate for renewal. What is more, the liberal bourgeois culture, and Romanticism with its irrational feelings, could contribute little to public worship.

There were, however, revival movements. First, there was a new inspiration in ecclesiology that came about through the works of J. A. Möhler (1796–1832).

But the liturgical renewal especially owed a great deal to the restored Benedictine tradition in France (Solesmes, Dom Guéranger) and in Germany (Beuron, Maria Laach, Dom Wolter).

Dom Guéranger, Abbot of Solesmes, had only one aim: to restore the old (i.e., medieval) and solemn Roman liturgy, and to once again reestablish it in his country. By his efforts the neogallican revival was in a short time uprooted. The Roman liturgy bore, in his opinion, no national traits. The one, holy, and apostolic liturgy of the pope carried with it a rich culture into the future; it was the celebration of the mystery and preserved the balance between reason and emotion, faith and experience; it was popular and not elitist. It alone was worship in spirit and truth, the true liturgy of the church. The writings of Dom Guéranger were read widely (e.g. *L'année liturgique*); his ideas were adopted.

Was Dom Guéranger the savior of the Roman liturgy, restorer of religious culture and style? Was his deepest intention not so much unification as a restored Roman-Gallican liturgy (Franklin, Soltner)? Or was he an ultramontane integralist with a *notion sentimentale* of the presence of Christ (Bouyer)? Was he thinking of parish liturgy in terms of the monastic ideal of the *opus divinum?* In any case, he was a son of a church on the defensive. In his opinion the best defense was the search for the traditional liturgy, for only there could the church find its lasting identity.

But it was not Dom Guéranger who uncovered the roots of Christian worship, but L. Duchesne, who in 1889 published his *Origines du culte chrétien,* laying the foundations for a movement that could no longer be stopped.

Among the Reformation churches we should mention the work of T. Kliefoth (1810–1895) and W. Löhe (1808–1872) in Germany. The reader may refer to H. Kressel, *Wilhelm Löhe als Liturg und Liturgiker* (Neuendettelsau, 1952), and Löhe's own tradition-conscious collection of orders of service, which was to be influential in Germany and also among Lutherans in America, *Agende für christliche Gemeinden des lutherischen Bekentnisses* (1844), published in Löhe's *Gesammelte Werke,* ed. K. Ganzert, vol. 7 (Neuendettelsau, 1953).

In England the Tractarians (Oxford Movement) focused the congregations again on the celebration (in word and sign) of the liturgy. Liturgical music flourished (translation of traditional hymns: J. M. Neale, 1818–1866; use of the Geneva psalter; the result: *Hymns Ancient and Modern,* 1861; rival edition: *The English Hymnal,* 1906); the choice of pericopes was improved; and the temporal cycle and the Order of Holy Communion were revised.

6. THE TWENTIETH CENTURY

Literature

B. Botte, *Le mouvement liturgique; témoignage et souvenirs* (Paris, 1973).

L. Bouyer, *Life and Liturgy* (London, 1956).

J. Hall, "The American Liturgical Movement; the Early Years," *Worship* 50, 1976, pp. 472–489.

E. Koenker, *The Liturgical Renaissance in the Roman Catholic Church* (Chicago, 1954).

O. Rousseau, *Histoire du mouvement liturgique* (Paris, 1945).

H. Schmidt, *Introductio in liturgiam occidentalem* (Rome, 1960), pp. 164–208 (with a bibliography).

J. Srawley, *The Liturgical Movement* (London, 1954).

The personal recollections of Dom Bernard Botte (died 1980), who himself experienced the beginning of the liturgical movement, are revealing. It is amazing that such a movement arose in an ecclesiastical atmosphere that did nothing to promote the movement. So far as liturgy was concerned, the Roman Catholic Church at the beginning of the twentieth century was no different than it had been at the end of the nineteenth. The education of the clergy was poor and consequently the preaching miserable. What was called exegesis scarcely deserved the name. Instruction in liturgy meant instruction in the rubrics, that is, in observing the Roman rules for public worship. This took place so consistently that the uniform Roman liturgy took on a worldwide character. The Roman church was one; the liturgy was one. This liturgical fortress had no weak spots, and it was unlikely that it could be overthrown. For that overthrow a sixty-year siege was necessary, and even still it has not been pulled down completely.

Nonetheless Dom Guéranger and his *L'année liturgique* did open people's eyes to the wealth of the liturgy; so did Cardinal I. Schuster of Milan in his *Liber sacramentorum*. The abbey of Beuron in Germany, later followed by Maria Laach, did important work in the translation of old Latin texts. And under all of this worked the vision of the Tübingen historian and theologian, J. A. Möhler (1796–1838), on the church and sacraments: new possibilities were discovered by looking farther back than the Middle Ages. When the renewal did come about in this century it rested on three pillars:

A. STUDY OF THE SOURCES

Step by step the history of the liturgy was mapped out as a result of studying the sources that were becoming constantly available in ever greater numbers. The various layers of the history of worship were discovered along with the actual principles operative in those layers. For example, it was discovered that what had long been famed as the Roman liturgy had become Roman in another sense, i.e., that the "curial" liturgy had become much different from the traditional *stadtrömische* liturgy, the communal worship of bishop and faithful in various churches of the city. This knowledge was to relativize significantly the Tridentine pattern of worship and provide a solid historical basis for various demands for renewal. Other liturgical traditions and the Jewish and Hellenistic roots of Christian liturgy were also discovered.

Since it is impossible to give here even half a survey of the marvelous erudition of so many pioneers of liturgical scholarship, the reader is referred to: P. Oppenheim, *Introductio historica in litteras liturgicas*, 2nd ed. (Torino, 1945); T. Vismans and L. Brinkhoff, *Critical Bibliography of Liturgical Literature* (Nijmegen, 1961); and O. Rousseau, *Histoire du mouvement liturgique* (Paris, 1945), pp. 45–55, 93–109, 111–130, 131–150, and passim.

B. THE THEOLOGY OF WORSHIP

The main works on this topic are listed in the selected bibliography in *The Study of Liturgy* (1978), pp. 3–4. For our purposes, the first author to mention is Dom Odo Casel (1886–1948). For his entire life he meditated on and studied the so-called *Mysterienlehre*. Casel's conviction was that the reality of the past saving events of the Lord is made present in the liturgy. In the liturgy of the church Christians meet Christ and his saving activity. Christian worship is the reactualization of the mystery of salvation. There is no question of a repetition of these saving events because Jesus' saving activity rests in God and has not been absorbed in the historical past.

Casel's contribution to the renewal of Christian cult was lasting, although his theology was controversial (see T. Filthaut, *La théologie des mystères; Exposé de la controverse*, Tournai, 1954).

Among other works of liturgical theology especially worthy of mention are: P. Brunner, *Worship in the Name of Jesus* (1968); E. Mascall, *Corpus Christi* (2nd ed., 1965); A. Schmemann, *Introduction to Liturgical Theology* (1966), respectively the significant Lutheran, Anglican, and Orthodox contributions to the discussion.

Under the influence of Dom Casel there developed a new and vital view of worship as memorial of the paschal mystery, of the death and resurrection of Christ, celebrated *in sacramento*. Growing attention was paid to the active presence of the Spirit in the church. The meaning of *ecclesia* was studied anew, leading from solid exegetical studies to the important concept of the theology of the local community and the participation of the assembly in worship. J.

354

Jungmann formulated the old principle of common worship: to the Father through Christ in the Spirit-assembled congregation, which is assisted by those who enact what is essentially a *ministerium*, a service. There was the discovery of the preeminent importance of the right balance between faith and sacrament and new studies of the evolution in sacramental rites, doctrine, and worship experience. And last but not least, the holy scriptures were at the center of this whole movement.

Worthy of special mention is Romano Guardini, whose *Vom Geist der Liturgie* (1918) stimulated liturgical renewal in his own thoroughly characteristic way. The conferences of Dom Columba Marmion (1858–1923), based both on the scripture (especially Paul) and on the liturgy, had a great impact (*Le Christ, vie de l'âme*, 1917).

C. THE PASTORAL-LITURGICAL RENEWAL

The foundations were laid: substantial historical knowledge; deepened theological insight. But the actual "fieldwork" still had to be done and that was both the most difficult and the most extensive of the labors. This fieldwork was started by Dom Lambert Beauduin (1873–1960), a priest associated with the *Société des Aumoniers du Travail* of the diocese of Liège and a Benedictine of Mont César, Louvain. From this abbey he made a beginning in the liturgical movement without being able to completely foresee its consequences. He appealed to the 1903 *motu proprio* of Pius X, entitled *Tra le sollecitudini*, in which the pope spoke about an "active participation in the most holy mysteries and in the public prayer of the church" (no. 7) by all the faithful. A new note after so many centuries! Beauduin, a pragmatic theologian with a good, sound feeling for the right moment for renewal, was especially struck by the words "active participation." He inaugurated his movement at a Congress in Mechelen (Malines) in 1905, at which he delivered a report on "The Prayer of the Church," at the request of Cardinal Mercier. His later book *La pieté de l'Église* is along the same lines: daring, to the point, putting his finger on the essentials. His famous saying—*Il foudrait démocratiser la liturgie* ("The liturgy must be democratized")—became the red thread of the renewal. But this renewal in fact had a rather tough time of it. In most parishes the liturgy remained as it had been.

Nonetheless, the fire was stirred up successively in Belgium (at Mont César, Afflighem); in the Netherlands (but very timidly and not supported by the episcopacy); in Germany (at Maria Laach, Beuron); in Austria (by Pius Parsch); in North America (by Virgil

Michel, Michael Mathis, Gerald Ellard, Godfrey Diekmann; at St. John's Abbey; by *Orate Fratres/Worship*); and finally also in France, which in the long run came to set the tone because there the *Nouvelle Théologie* emerged at the same time. The *Centre de Pastorale Liturgique* at Paris (founded partly by Beauduin) became a central exchange from which annual, and important, congresses were organized (Versailles and Vanves). These congresses, which were also organized in Belgium, Germany, and America (cf. the Liturgical Weeks—the *twenty-fifth* held at St. Louis in 1964) were effective: step by step a change in mentality was brought about and the call for an actual application of these new concepts in worship became louder. There were barriers to be surmounted but the insight and the ability to convince that marked the historians, the theologians, and the pastors were so strong that their collective wisdom was accepted more and more.

D. THE ECCLESIASTICAL AUTHORITIES

Renewal movements—at least in the Roman Catholic church—are often first watched with concern by the central authority, then accompanied with warnings, then tolerated for a long time and in the meanwhile considered, and finally with great prudence partly or entirely adopted. It is a long route, but also a fairly certain one, leading to results. A proof of this can be found in the Roman reaction to the liturgical movement. The concern, the prudence, the weighing and considering, and the adoption of the principles of this movement can be read between the lines of the decisions taken by the central authority. The movement had already been active for half a century before the Roman documents moved gradually toward its recognition. The remarkable thing, however, is that never before had Rome encountered a movement that led to such extensive results.

It has already been noted above that the pastoral attitude of Pope Pius X finally gave inspiration to the liturgical movement. His *motu proprio* (November 22, 1903) on church music, *Tra le sollecitudini*, contained in its introduction the essential words, *partecipazione attiva* ("active participation") of all the faithful. The same pope stimulated participation in the eucharist (frequent communion) in a decree, *Sacra Tridentina Synodus* (1905), followed by a *motu proprio* concerning the communion of children, *Quam singulari* (1910). Both decrees were of great importance for later developments, although the underlying practice of the second (i.e., communion without connection to eucharist) could be criticized. Finally, Pius X was planning a fundamental revision of the breviary to adapt it more to the circumstances of the time and to the needs of pastoral care. This revision got only as far as a rearrangement of the psalter, which was disposed throughout the week in a new way. The revision was not a minor one and was disputable on historical grounds (the old *laudes*, Psalms 148-149-150, disappeared as a set of three), but a clear advantage was that in the weekly cycle of psalms, Sunday again stood out as the most important day. All this work of Pius X might be judged after the fact as "piecework," but he nonetheless had made a beginning: honor to those to whom honor is due!

After Pius X there was a period of inactivity that in fact lasted until after World War II. In the meanwhile Rome resisted all the daring proposals from Germany and Austria, especially those concerning the introduction of the vernacular.

The encyclical letter *Mystici Corporis* (1943) of Pope Pius XII presented a new opening toward renewal: ecclesiology was carefully encouraged. His encyclical *Mediator Dei* (1947) went still further. A sound theology of worship was provided and the participation of the faithful in the liturgy was urged. Practical decisions now followed one upon the other: the possibility of the celebration of the eucharist in the evening (1947); the permission for the use of the vernacular for certain prayers from the *Rituale* (*e.g.* baptism, marriage, burial), especially in Germany and France. Profoundly important was the renewal of the celebration of the paschal vigil (1951, 1955). The "tyranny" of the "fast before communion" was abolished in 1953 and 1957, so that communion during the eucharistic celebration was stimulated. In 1955 the rubrics of the missal and the breviary were radically simplified. Rules were published in 1956 and 1958 for church music and its use in public worship.

In the Reformation churches the renewal has been less stormy, less imposing, and less comprehensive, but it certainly is there.

In the Anglican church the movement that called for changes in worship at first remained limited to a small group ("Parish and People"). Besides that, there was a long-lasting struggle between a more "catholicizing" side and those who wanted to appeal to the Reformation tradition. The result was a long-lasting time of frustration. But there has been much study dedicated to the orders of service in the *Book of Common Prayer* (the Alcuin Club publications), and to Christian worship in general (the Henry Bradshaw Society). *Alternative Services* (in England) and *Prayer Book Studies* (in America) were trial attempts at improving the orders of service. C. Buchanan, *Modern Anglican Liturgies 1958-1968* (London, 1968) and *Further Anglican Liturgies 1968-1975* (Nottingham, 1975), gives a survey of accomplishments outside of England. In 1979 the new American Episcopal *Book of Common Prayer* was published. The year 1980 saw the publication of the English *Alternative Service Book.*

The Lutheran church has also experienced a renewal movement: *Leiturgia,* vol. 1, pp. 74–80, gives a survey of this. There has been an attempt to conjoin the deepest insights of Lutheran liturgy with the early tradition of the church. One can say that in general the renewal has concentrated upon the reading of scripture, the eucharistic prayer (which has been rediscovered), church music, and the attempt to again reunite word and sacrament. Every generation has sought new ways to structure a living liturgy. The North American *Lutheran Book of Worship* published in 1978 is an example.

Reformation worship in the Netherlands owes a great deal to G. van der Leeuw, in spite of the controversies that his ideas have called forth. His name and ideals live on in the G. van der Leeuw Stichting, a society in which the renewers have been able to meet and work together. Of immense importance is the appearance of the new hymnal *Liedboek voor de Kerken* (1973), with its ecumenical hymn collection and its new metrical psalter.

In North America the liturgical work of the Consultation on Church Union and of the United Methodist church should be especially mentioned.

E. THE PROVISIONAL FINALE

We conclude this overview by referring to the Roman document that, as it were, received and summarized the movement of the first part of the century and that, as we hope, gives an ecumenical vision of Christian worship, the *Constitution on the Sacred Liturgy* of the Second Vatican Council, *Sacrosanctum Concilium* (December 1963). We quote a few parts of this document, which has led to such widespread ecumenical reform and which reflects a movement that is still not finished:

"2. For it is the liturgy through which, especially in the divine sacrifice of the Eucharist, 'the work of our redemption is accomplished,' and it is through the liturgy, especially, that the faithful are enabled to express in their lives and manifest to others the mystery of Christ and the real nature of the true Church. The Church is essentially both human and divine, visible but endowed with invisible realities, zealous in action and dedicated to contemplation, present in the world, but as a pilgrim, so constituted that in her the human is directed toward and subordinated to the divine, the visible to the invisible, action to contemplation, and this present world to that city yet to come, the object of our quest. The liturgy daily builds up those who are in the Church, making of them a holy temple of the Lord, a dwelling-place for God in the Spirit, to the mature measure of the fullness of Christ. At the same time it marvelously increases their power to preach Christ and thus show forth the Church, a sign lifted up among the nations, to those who are outside, a sign under which the scattered children of God may be gathered together until there is one fold and one shepherd.

"5. . . . The wonderful works of God among the people of the Old Testament were but a prelude to the work of Christ our Lord in redeeming mankind and giving perfect glory to God. He achieved his task principally by the paschal mystery of his blessed passion, resurrection from the dead, and glorious ascension, whereby 'dying, he destroyed our death, and rising, restored our life.' For it was from the side of Christ as he slept the sleep of death upon the cross that there came forth 'the wondrous sacrament of the whole Church.'

"7. To accomplish so great a work [the celebration of the paschal mystery in the eucharist] Christ is always present in his Church, especially in her liturgical celebrations. He is present in the Sacrifice of the Mass not only in the person of his minister . . . but especially in the eucharistic species. By his power he is present in the sacraments so that when anybody baptizes it is really Christ himself who baptizes. He is present in his word since it is he himself who speaks when the holy scriptures are read in the Church. Lastly, he is present when the Church prays and sings, for he has promised 'where two or three are gathered together in my name there am I in the midst of them' (Mt 18:20). . . .

"8. In the earthly liturgy we take part in a foretaste of that heavenly liturgy which is celebrated in the Holy City of Jerusalem toward which we journey as pilgrims, where Christ is sitting at the right hand of God, Minister of the holies and of the true tabernacle. With all the warriors of the heavenly army we sing a hymn of glory to the Lord; venerating the memory of the saints, we hope for some part and fellowship with them; we eagerly await the Saviour, Our Lord Jesus Christ, until he our life shall appear and we too will appear with him in glory.

"10. Nevertheless the liturgy is the summit toward which the activity of the Church is directed; it is also the fount from which all her power flows."

Afterword

The Christian churches, no matter how divided, are agreed in this, that their confession of faith is not based upon a "myth of eternal return" (Eliade), but upon a history that occurred, upon a tradition that even still is handed on. It is not that the history is the goal; what *was* is not glorified, but God's name is praised, because God *now* causes salvation and grace to occur. There is a history of God's salvation, but this history is told in order to establish the congregation in the faith that through God's grace salvation occurs.

It is good to write down here this early Christian truth, shared with the Jews. History becomes less history to the extent one approaches one's own time. But this does not mean that nothing more occurs, that there are no further historical events. This outline of the history of worship comes to an end, but the community of the faithful continues to come together at the call of the Lord for the celebration of the great reconciliation and for the breaking of the bread.

Expanded Contents

Index of Persons

General Index

375

Chrisma (Chrism), 174, 182, 285
Le Christ, vie de l'âme, Columba
    Marmion, 354
Christian initiation, 77, 80f., 102. See
    also Baptism
Christian Initiation, S. Fisher, 177
Christian Prayer through the
    Centuries, J.A. Jungmann, 94,
    223–225
Christian Rite and Christian Drama in
    the Middle Ages, O. Hardison,
    177
Christianity as state religion, 54f.
Christliche Passafeier und Abendmahl,
    R. Fenneberg, 40
Christmas, 103–105, 176, 196, 282–
    283
Church architecture, 94
Church, construction of, 187ff.
Church of England. See Anglican
    liturgy
Church order, Protestant, 320ff.
The Church at Prayer, ed. B. Botte
    and A.E. Martimort, 9
Church and state, relations between,
    245f., 250
Circumstantes, 229
Civil law, Roman, 2
Clement of Rome, letter of, 2, 14–
    17, 22, 41, 61, 117
Clerical office, 172
Clericalization of liturgy, 218, 344
Codex Justinianus, 60, 242
Coena Domini, I. Pahl, 328
Collecta (collects), 195
Collectarium, 172
Comes of Alcuin, 158
Commentaries, liturgical, 257
Communio sanctorum, 225
Communion, 32, 113, 118, 119, 123,
    186, 189, 215, 289, 293, 316,
    318, 319, 323–324, 337
    of children, 356
    fast before, 357
    frequent, 356

in the hand, 42
on the tongue, 230
Communis oratio, 184
Communis oratio, C. Bouman, 22
Community, Christian, vi, 2, 4, 47,
    200. See also Congregation
Comparative Liturgy, A. Baumstark,
    vii, 259
Competentes, 34, 108, 226
Compline, 96, 272, 275–277, 337
Confession of sins, 47–48, 93, 196–
    201, 215, 233–234, 342. See also
    Penance, Reconciliation
Confessors, feasts of, 105–107
Confirmatio, 182–183
Confirmation, 34ff., 107–109, 227–
    229, 337
    in Anglican rite, 338–339
    in Byzantine rite, 294
Confiteor, 184
Congregation, 8f., 11, 13, 17, 21, 32,
    35, 47, 48f., 90, 96, 97, 108,
    111, 113, 116, 119, 123, 126,
    131–132, 137, 200, 201, 202,
    254, 257, 315, 341, 342, 343,
    349
Congregational participation, 306ff.,
    310, 312
Congregations, primitive, 32, 48f.
Consecratio (consecration), 184–186,
    230, 344–345
Constantinople, vii, 1, 55, 57, 58, 59,
    78, 85, 86, 90–91, 104, 113,
    239ff., 251ff., 256f.
Constitution on the Sacred Liturgy, i,
    358–360
Constitutiones Apostolorum, ed.
    F. Funk, 76, 96, 138
Contestatio, 118, 182
Conventual mass, 193
Copts, 58, 88, 251
Corpus Troparum, ed. R. Jonsson, 177
Cosmos, 6
Councils
    of Basel, 298

381

384